RELIGION, SPIRITUALITY AND THE NEAR-DEATH EXPERIENCE

Whether resuscitated in the Emergency Room, struck by lightning or rescued at sea, people snatched from the jaws of death frequently report uncanny or otherworldly phenomena. Survivors of these mystifying voyages repeat the same familiar stories – testimonies of tunnels and paradisal gardens, encounters with an all-loving light, and heavenly (or sometimes hellish) visions. Where do people go during these encounters? What do they see? Why are their remarkable stories so often correlative? Are they persuasive evidence of life after physical death?

Religion, Spirituality and the Near-Death Experience is a dramatic and sustained response to decades of research into near-death experiences (NDEs) and the first to credibly bridge the gap between the competing factions of science and spirituality. Drawing on the latest scientific and psychological research within a framework of theological and philosophical argument, it asks what NDEs can and cannot tell us about God, the afterlife and the meaning of human existence. Is the NDE a genuine glimpse of the afterlife or simply a chemically induced hallucination? Can it offer realistic hope of immortality? What should we make of the fantastical claims of some near-death returnees, such as the congenitally blind who report having found themselves able to see? Can science adequately refute theological interpretations of NDEs in the absence of convincing medical explanations, and are religion and science necessarily in conflict?

Drawing on the unpublished testimonies of almost 100 NDE survivors gathered over thirty years, and including a full overview of new theories and controversies, this scrupulously researched book is the only complete and up-to-date introduction to a subject that defies conventional understanding. Neither a religious argument touting NDEs as hard evidence of God nor a scientific rebuke to spiritual interpretations, its balanced investigation of these much-reported yet baffling phenomena brings fresh urgency to the study of our hopes for a life beyond.

Mark Fox lectures in philosophy and religious studies at Joseph Chamberlain College in B̶ ̶ ̶ ̶ ̶ ̶ ̶ ̶ ̶ ̶mmittee of the Religiou̶ ̶ ̶ ̶ ̶ ̶ ̶ ̶ ̶;, Lampeter.

RELIGION, SPIRITUALITY AND THE NEAR-DEATH EXPERIENCE

Mark Fox

Routledge
Taylor & Francis Group

LONDON AND NEW YORK

First published 2003
by Routledge
11 New Fetter Lane, London EC4P 4EE

Simultaneously published in the USA and Canada
by Routledge
29 West 35th Street, New York, NY 10001

Routledge is an imprint of the Taylor & Francis Group

© 2003 Mark Fox

Typeset in Sabon by
Keystroke, Jacaranda Lodge, Wolverhampton
Printed and bound in Great Britain by
St Edmundsbury Press, Bury St Edmunds, Suffolk

British Library Cataloguing in Publication Data
A catalogue record for this book is available from the British Library

Library of Congress Cataloging in Publication Data
Fox, Mark, 1962–
Through the valley of the shadow of death : religion, spirituality, and
the near-death experience / Mark Fox.
p. cm.
Includes bibliographical references and index.
1. Near-death experiences–Religious aspects. I. Title.

BL55 .F69 2002
133.9′01′3–dc21

ISBN 0–415–28830–4 (hbk)
ISBN 0–415–28831–2 (pbk)

FOR TRACEY AND MY PARENTS,
WITH LOVE

CONTENTS

ACKNOWLEDGEMENTS

I should like to acknowledge my debt to a number of persons who helped to make this book possible.

I was given important advice, information and kind help throughout by Lisa Burke, Val Camroux, Patrick Faulkner, Paul Ford, Diana Hasting, Allan Kellehear, Tracey Kesterton, Peggy Morgan, Lynne Morris, Michael Perry, Kenneth Ring, Karl Smardon, Andy Smithson, Edward Vaughan, Andrew Wadsworth, Hayden Wells and by my students at Joseph Chamberlain College, Birmingham.

Iram Shabana provided helpful ideas, artwork and suggestions for the cover.

I should also like to acknowledge the help of the Religious Experience Research Centre at the University of Wales, Lampeter. The kind permission given by Director Peggy Morgan to access and use their archival material made much of this book possible.

INTRODUCTION
Searching for a theology of the near-death experience

The mysterious near-death experience

Whilst giving birth to her youngest child in February 1962, a mother from Warrenton, Missouri, suddenly experienced a massive haemorrhage. Hovering on the brink of death during emergency surgery, she suddenly lost consciousness and found herself sucked into a great whirling void 'in which sound was not sound but a tremendous vibrating hum'. At the point at which she felt she could stand no more of this deafening sound, her speed through the void slowed, and she found herself surrounded by a brilliant light. Alone, save for the felt presence of a seemingly invisible guide, she was led onwards, feeling overwhelming sensations of love and warmth. Caught up in her experience, she wanted nothing more than to move closer to 'an even greater light [which] seemed to be radiating from somewhere just ahead', all thoughts of her stricken medical condition now forgotten. Finally, she felt an overwhelming sense of desolation as she heard the firm instruction to 'return to your family, there will be another time for you here'. Afterwards, reflecting on the experience, she remarks how it has changed her life completely, infusing her with a sense of overwhelming love and well being, and helping her lose all fear of death.[1]

Recovering in hospital from wounds sustained in a tank explosion in Forli, Italy, in the closing years of the Second World War, a 28-year-old soldier suddenly found himself 'pulling out of my own body' before experiencing the unusual sensation of looking down on himself lying in the hospital bed from a viewpoint just below the ceiling. Thinking, 'That's strange!' he then

1

passed *through* the ceiling and found himself moving through a tunnel towards 'the sort of light you will get on a late spring, early summer morning just after sunrise when there's a certain amount of mist around'. Suddenly surrounded by the light, he found a pale, sandy surface beneath him and a vast crowd of people in the distance. Later on he will learn that he has died, and that a reception committee and subsequent judgement awaits him. Finally he awakes in his bed, amazed at the recollection of his experience, which seemed much more real than any dream.[2]

An 85-year-old Zambian grandmother of six interviewed by a medical doctor in Lusaka in the 1990s – whose reading about such 'near-death experiences' had aroused him to an interest in the subject – reported an experience she had undergone following a near-fatal stroke. Using imagery with which she was daily familiar, she described an experience of being 'put into a big calabash' – the hollow shell of a gourd – with a large opening at the end. Trying to escape from her confinement, she almost despaired, until a voice said, 'Be brave. Take my hand and come out. It is not yet your time to go.' Finally the stricken grandmother managed to escape from the dark and frightening shell on her own. Assessing the meaning of the experience in conversation with the doctor later, she was to conclude that 'someone was trying to bewitch me, but found that I was an innocent soul' (Morse and Perry 1992: 122–3).

A 22-year-old nightclub singer was being driven from the club where she worked late one night in 1973 when her vehicle was involved in a serious accident, resulting in serious injuries to her neck, back and leg. Although she had no sensations of any kind until reaching the hospital for emergency surgery, she was suddenly shocked to find that she could see every feature of the operation being conducted on her as if she were above it looking down. 'I knew it was me,' she would later tell researchers. 'I thought, "Well, that's kind of weird. What am I doing up here? . . . Am I dead?"' Reflecting on her experience years after the event, she finds it extraordinary. For not only was she unconscious at the time of her experience, she was also able to see for the first time in her life. Neither before her out-of-body episode nor after it has she been able to distinguish even light from dark. Blind from birth, she finds herself marvelling at the seemingly impossible fact that she was able to see for the first and only time in her life during her extraordinary experience (Ring and Cooper 1997: 110).

To heaven and back?

What are we to make of experiences such as these and other experiences reported from persons at or near the point of death? Are they simply hallucinations caused by drugs and the administration of anaesthetics? If so, how do we account for subjects' repeated claims that their experiences were of a different quality to 'mere' dreams, or for experiences which occurred where no drugs or anaesthetics were administered at all? Is the sense of leaving the body and viewing it from outside simply to be dismissed as a retrospective reconstruction of an event using memory and imagination? If so, how do we explain allegedly accurate claims that subjects have been able to witness distant events whilst 'apart' from their bodies – such as resuscitation attempts or persons in different rooms within hospital buildings – which could not have been seen unless these subjects were, in a real sense, temporarily elsewhere and thus able to actually see them? More controversially still, how might we account for a small but growing number of claims that perception is temporarily *improved* during such out-of-body states, even to the extent of affording blind persons the fleeting gift of sight? Might such accounts be finally providing us with proof that human beings possess both a physical vehicle and a non-physical 'something else': an immortal soul, perhaps, which at the point of death is able to leave the body in order to depart for 'other realms'?

And what of the repeated descriptions of recurrent motifs within such experiences: travelling through an area of darkness towards a comforting 'being of light', encountering dead relatives and friends and experiencing judgement in which one's deeds – good and bad – are finally revealed for external, objective, scrutiny? Might these apparently consistent characteristics of a great many claims provide a further nail in the coffin for the argument that near-death experiences (NDEs), as these experiences have come to be known, are simply very vivid dreams brought about by the onset of death? To be sure, many features of such NDEs appear to be described in terms of subjects' differing cultural expectations and familiarities; perhaps this explains why a Zambian woman would describe as a calabash what a Western man would describe as a tunnel. But, underneath such differences of description and interpretation, might we be able to detect a common experience which in some sense everybody has? And if we *can*, then beneath the differing social, cultural and religious descriptions of the comforting light at the end of such a tunnel (or calabash), might we be able to detect an underlying transcendent being that is somehow 'Lord of All': regardless of race, creed or colour?

Then there is the question surrounding our current understanding of how our brains work to create that which we call our 'selves'. Might we be able to extend current neuroscientific 'models' of consciousness in order to account for the distinctive NDE features of tunnels, lights and so on? Might such experiences even serve to extend our knowledge of brain processes such that we emerge from a study of them with our knowledge of consciousness enhanced? Or might the NDE itself emerge from such studies unexplained; even, perhaps, unexplainable, and therefore offering fresh hope to those who believe that selves are in essence immortal and hence indestructible?

Finally, there is the question of presenting a theological response to such experiences, and it is with this task that the current study will be partly concerned. For surely the claim that persons at or beyond the point of clinical death are able to have experiences seemingly suggestive of the soul's separation from the body might be expected to provoke some sort of theological response. Indeed, even the *possibility* that in such experiences we are being given a privileged glimpse into an underlying encounter with a divine reality, and revelation which is not dependent on faith or adherence to a particular creed or religious tradition, might also be expected to provoke an immediate and sustained debate within theology: together, perhaps, with related subdisciplines such as the philosophy and psychology of religion.

The need for a theological response to the NDE

As this book will shortly make clear, however, such vigorous and sustained debate has not been forthcoming. The result has been an incredible lack of knowledge within theology of research surrounding the NDE, particularly as regards the fashioning of a suitable response to it. The only major existing study, that of Carol Zaleski published in 1987, whilst outstanding in scope and execution, has now been overtaken by a mass of fresh data – such as the claim that the blind can temporarily see during NDEs – which may turn out to have crucial implications across a wide range of theological concerns: not least those to do with theology's understanding of personhood, death and dying (Zaleski 1987). These are big areas, yet many of the claims that near-death experiencers (NDErs) have made in the last quarter-century are such that they may well be said to *demand* a response which goes to the very heart of the West's understanding of what it is to be human, and what it is for human beings to die.

Phillip Wiebe, in a study of historical and contemporary Christic visions and apparitions, has drawn attention to the fact that any claims which appear to border on the 'psychic' or 'paranormal' have received a consistently impervious response from academics in recent years. Indeed, the optimism for the rigorous academic investigation of alleged phenomena such as telepathy and precognition shown by many of the early members of the Society for Psychical Research in the late nineteenth and early twentieth centuries – including figures outstanding in their respective fields such as William James, William Barrett and Henry Sidgwick – now resembles a historical curiosity rather than a trend which was to continue unbroken through subsequent decades. In fact, as Wiebe notes, many fields of academic enquiry, including theology and philosophy, have shown no interest in such phenomena (Wiebe 1997: 103). Perhaps this reticence to engage with what are clearly viewed as 'fringe' subjects may explain the 'deafening silence', as the respected *Christian Parapsychologist* journal's editor Canon Michael Perry describes it, on the part of theology and the philosophy of religion as regards their *response* to the questions posed by NDEs.[3] Certainly this silence has been unfortunate, for the current study will show that they have much to contribute. Also unfortunate is the fact that such a deafening silence has led to an almost total ignorance on the part of theologians and philosophers regarding the mass of research into NDEs that the last thirty years have produced. For the growing field of 'near-death studies', as it is called, has become an academic

5

subdiscipline that has produced a significant, diverse and growing body of research in its own right.

Overviewing existing theological responses

Three major concerns, arising out of the above recognitions, have therefore prompted me to produce this study. One is the concern simply to present an informed overview of some of the most important research to have arisen out of and around the field of near-death studies in its almost thirty-year history and to present it to a theologically and philosophically oriented audience for whom, I suspect, some of it will appear as an almost total surprise. To this end, chapter 1 presents a brief history of some of the major trends to have dominated this research, including the early work of 'pioneer' researchers in the field and the general contours of subsequent research and investigation, whilst chapter 2 presents and critically evaluates the few sustained theological responses to the phenomenon which the last quarter-century has seen. In an important sense, however, the *whole* study functions as such a history and needs to be seen thus. For such has been the extent of the research conducted within certain fields with a vested interest in 'explaining' the NDE that they have been given attention in their own right elsewhere in the study. To this end, for example, chapter 4 considers the large number of attempts that have been made from within neuroscience to respond to the NDE, presenting these within the context of their possessing an evolving history in their own right.

Responding to the NDE

A second major concern of this book is to go *beyond* a simple overview, however: for a great many questions posed by the NDE demand answers which theologians and philosophers have not yet provided, although they are in a good position to do so. Thus, for example, the contention that beneath various cultural and linguistic wrappings presented in NDE testimony lies a pure, uninterpreted, common core experience which, when correctly discerned and described, reveals a universal experience of the Divine or Ultimate Reality is one which theology and philosophy have yet to fully to engage with. This is unfortunate, given that the possibility that a common core may underlie the range of reported types of mystical and other 'varieties' of religious experience has long been an area of sustained reflection, discussion and controversy in both of these academic contexts. Chapter 3 will draw on this rich vein of existing insight and debate in order to test the hypothesis that a common core experience *can* be uncovered within differing and sometimes cross-cultural NDE testimonies. In order to do this, it will focus on one of the most fascinating and intriguing elements of many such testimonies: the 'being of light' which is claimed by many NDErs and near-death researchers alike to manifest a Divine or in some sense Ultimate presence, a presence usually identified in accordance with experients' own differing cultural and religious backgrounds. Thus, for example, the assertion is frequently made that whilst a Christian may identify the light as Jesus, a Jewish person may identify it as an angel, whilst a person of no particular religious persuasion may simply describe it in allegedly culturally neutral and religiously non-partisan terms as a 'being of light' or some other similar phrase. Chapter 3 will seek to test the philosophical and phenomenological adequacy of the claim that underlying this diversity of descriptions a common, cross-cultural core presence can be detected and described, drawing on the insights of a variety of scholars who in different ways have contributed much to similar attempts to detect underlying commonality within other reported types of religious experience during the last quarter-century. Throughout the analysis, the chapter will seek to show that the transfer of existing insights from one area of investigation of religious experience – in this case sophisticated theological, philosophical and specifically epistemological analyses of mysticism and other types of religious experience – to the somewhat different context of the NDE represents an example of how theology and philosophy might engage with the NDE in future studies; representing, as it does, just one of a large number of tools and methodologies which the theologian and/or philosopher might deploy in search of greater and deeper understandings of near-death testimony.

However, the existence and nature of the Divine is not the only issue in which theology and philosophy might be expected to have a keen, vested, interest. The claims made by a number of NDE researchers in recent years to have investigated and documented instances of temporary restoration of sight – including veridical observations of actual physical surroundings – to blind NDErs during their NDEs is currently an area of great controversy within near-death studies. In addition to being of great interest in themselves, such cases might be expected to have particular significance for theologians and philosophers. For if true, such claims would appear to provide powerful and compelling support for some form of body–soul *dualism*: the notion that human beings cannot simply be viewed as constituting a psychosomatic unity but as comprising a physical body and a non-physical, perhaps spiritual, soul or essence. Chapter 5 explores these potentially hugely significant claims of temporary sight on the part of blind NDErs in great detail. It assesses the strength of the claims themselves, exploring a number of currently celebrated case histories in depth in search of a better understanding of their actual strength, importance and significance.

A multidisciplinary perspective

As will become clear, the complexity of the questions surrounding the NDE demands an attempt at the construction of a framework that combines the maximum possible number of approaches to the phenomenon. Indeed, throughout the writing of this study I have been both reminded of and inspired by a vivid image used by Lewis Rambo in a recent study of conversion: an image which I have enjoyed and which I share as I reflect on the various disciplines which have something to contribute to the study of NDEs and which are represented in this book. Regarding existing conversion studies prior to his, Rambo has written that:

> As I read the literature, spoke with acknowledged experts, attended conferences and seminars, and shared reflections with numerous people, I began to believe that the published material on conversion resembled a metropolitan train yard crowded with separate tracks that ran parallel to each other, where each individual train had its own assigned track and never crossed over to another. I

began to suspect that only a few scholars of conversion were aware that the subject was traversed by more than one track, and that there could even be more than one train on each track.

(Rambo 1993: xiv)

As this book will make clear, this is a good image as regards the contemporary situation that exists amongst the range of disciplines that make up the diverse field of near-death studies. Thus, as we shall see, one track is currently occupied by neuroscientists such as Susan Blackmore and Ronald Siegel who have sought to approach NDEs in terms of shared neural structures giving consistency to a range of accounts which otherwise might be as diverse as 'mere' dreams. Theologians and Religious Studies experts such as Carol Zaleski, Paul Badham and I.P. Couliano occupy another track, attempting as they have in various ways to locate the NDE within the wider context of historical 'otherworld journey' narration across a range of religious cultures: Eastern, Western, ancient and modern. A third track is occupied by social scientists, who have in various ways attempted to bring insights from their own discipline to bear on the NDE, whether comparing Japanese and Buddhist near-death texts, extending the discussion across a sample of cross-cultural contemporary reports, considering them within the wider context of status passage, attempting to locate their popularity within a discussion of religious 'trends' in the post-1960s West, or using sophisticated quantitative analyses of near-death data in order to map NDEs' transformative effects. Finally, and perhaps most importantly, another track is occupied by the near-death researchers themselves, including pioneers within the field such as Raymond Moody, Kenneth Ring and Michael Sabom, who have attempted comparisons across a range of collected first-hand accounts and have been responsible for the various models which have driven and continue to drive research into such things as the possibility of a common core to a truly universal experience. And, as we shall have abundant cause to note, there are many other tracks, containing a great many other trains.

At some point, somebody is going to have to try and bring all of these data together, not simply in the form of a 'reader', but in the form of a *dialogue*: a junction at which all of the disciplines involved in the investigation and exploration of the NDE can meet and intersect. The current book is thus offered in part *as* such a junction, with its conclusion attempting to suggest further and future directions in which tracks might be laid.

The RERC study

In chapter 6, I present the results of another concern of this study: an attempt at a wholly new examination and analysis of NDE testimonies which I have dubbed the 'RERC study' – an original investigation of a total of over a hundred NDEs and NDE-like experiences conducted at first hand over a number of months in the spring and summer of 2000. Virtually all of the cases which make up the study are published here for the first time and have consequently never been examined or presented before, with some dating back over a quarter of a century and thus even pre-dating the coining of the term 'near-death experience' itself. The RERC study represents in one important sense the climax of this book, affording, as it does, the opportunity to present and to analyse a large amount of original NDE material as a means of testing conclusions drawn in earlier chapters and of proposing avenues for future research.

That such a large-scale investigation of hitherto unseen NDE testimonies was possible at all is wholly thanks to the archives of the Religious Experience Research Centre, founded by Sir Alister Hardy at Manchester College in Oxford in 1969 and now housed at the University of Wales, Lampeter.[4] The Centre currently holds over 6000 accounts of a range of religious experiences, a large proportion of them in the form of letters sent to Hardy and subsequent Directors of the Centre, mostly as a result of public requests for such material. Whilst the Centre has provided a valuable database of religious experiences for a wide range of studies, its substantial number of testimonies specifically featuring NDEs and similar experiences has never before been employed in a major study. There are, for example, a large number of out-of-body experiences in the archives, representing a rich resource for the examination of this particular NDE-related phenomenon. One keenly hoped-for spin-off from the present study is that scholars may be prompted, having read the current work, to access the Centre's archives for their own future studies of other, related or unrelated, varieties of religious experience.

Theoretical considerations

No theological response exists in a vacuum, and every book presupposes a particular audience. As will become clear, I operate from within a broadly philosophical theology, but am inevitably drawn into other areas as my subject dictates. And whilst chapter 2 in particular draws on a number of specifically Christian responses to NDEs, this study is not written for an exclusively Christian audience. Indeed, it is hoped that members of other faith traditions may take something away with them that will inspire their own reflection and response. There is certainly ample scope for such. As far as I am aware, for example, no single sustained response to the NDE exists within Islam: an incredible fact, given both its size and history of engagement with a rich range of types of religious experience. Even within Christianity, however, the NDE has seemingly been overlooked by a large number of denominations and traditions. Roman Catholic responses to the NDE over the last thirty years or so have been minimal, and no official Roman Catholic position currently exists on what is an incredibly widespread phenomenon in many Christian countries, both Catholic and non-Catholic. Again, it is hoped that this book will provoke debate where there is currently silence, for further, deeper and more sustained reflection and reaction to the NDE is clearly needed from many theological and religious quarters. This book attempts to stimulate and to produce a springboard for such reflection and reaction, in the hope that further and fruitful debate may ensue. More than that, it seeks to build bridges: for as will become clear, there is much about the near-death experience that remains fascinating and mysterious, and which demands more discussion and reflection than it has hitherto received.

Mark Fox
February 2002

PO Box 10618, Birmingham B8 2ZY
mark.fox@blueyonder.co.uk

1

A BRIEF HISTORY OF NDEs

Discovering the NDE

What happens as we die? And what, if anything, might follow our deaths? Commencing in the last quarter of the twentieth century and continuing into the twenty-first, new research based on the testimonies of persons who had 'died' before being resuscitated convinced many that these questions could finally be answered. For these people often made remarkable claims that they had journeyed to other worlds, meeting deceased friends and relatives and glimpsing heavenly fields and streams, before receiving a gentle but forgiving judgement by a loving, divine, 'being of light'. Their stories were deeply moving, apparently consistent, and seemed to baffle doctors and scientists. Indeed, many of these remarkable claims were themselves investigated and published by those self-same doctors and scientists. Could it really be true? Had twentieth-century medical science finally unlocked the mystery of death? And had it revealed that the human soul was, after all, capable of surviving the demise of the body?

These experiences were quickly given a name: 'near-death experiences' or 'NDEs'. Yet it is now widely agreed that this remarkable new era of research into the possibility of the soul's surviving death might not have happened at all had it not been for the pioneering work of one philosophically educated American physician: Dr Raymond Moody Junior. His first book, *Life After Life*, appeared in 1975 and has in the ensuing years sold approximately fourteen million copies. In the meantime, its author has become widely and publicly credited as the founding father of what has now come to be known as 'near-death studies'. He has, for example, been variously described as the 'pioneer of the whole NDE movement' (Blackmore 1993: 6), as 'the grandfather of the twentieth-century study of near-death experiences' (Bailey and Yates 1996: 25) and as the one who 'lifted the dark veil of something heretofore as unspeakable as the [near-] death experience' (Ebon 1977: 25). Indeed, regarding his place in the field of near-death research, one commentator has gone so far as to assert that what can be said of Moody is 'what was once said of the formidable Immanuel Kant: you can think with him, or you can think against him, but you cannot think without him' (Zaleski 1987: 103). Since the first appearance of *Life After Life*, persons from a wide range of Western and non-Western religions and cultures have come forward either to claim experiences similar to those popularized in his book or to offer studies of their own which appear to confirm many of his original findings. Two years after the appearance of *Life After Life*, an international body, the International Association for Near-Death Studies (IANDS), was founded to promote interest in and research into NDEs. Currently, in addition to publishing the *Journal of Near-Death Studies*, IANDS organizes conferences, local support groups for near-death experiencers (NDErs) and a number of other activities worldwide. Further academic research into the NDE has arisen within a wide variety of areas: primarily neuroscience, but also other areas of psychology as well as from within disciplines such as sociology and religious studies. Again: none of this existed before 1975. It seems clear in the light of all of this that any attempt to chart the contours of a short history of the NDE, as this chapter will seek to do, must begin with an examination of Moody's own work. Who was he? And to what extent is it accurate to view him as the one who first discovered 'actual case histories that reveal there is life after death', as his original publishers were to claim?

By his own account, Raymond Moody first developed an interest in such experiences in the late 1960s and early 1970s.[1] By the time of his first book's publication, he had assembled a case collection of approximately 150 such accounts from acquaintances and students that would provide the data upon which the book's most sensational findings were to be based. Indeed, *Life*

After Life is dedicated, cryptically, 'To George Ritchie M.D. and, through him, to the One whom he suggested': a reference to an NDEr whose wartime NDE profoundly impressed Moody at this time and would later find extended publication in its own right. Prior to the beginning of his fascination with return-from-death claims, however, Moody had received his undergraduate degree in philosophy from the University of Virginia, subsequently obtaining an MA and a PhD at the same university. In 1969, he became Assistant Professor of Philosophy at the university, where amongst other subjects he was to teach Plato's *Phaedo*, including its discussions of the nature of the soul and its immortality. According to Moody, it was at this point that a number of students began to approach him with claims to have undergone experiences that had convinced them that the soul is indeed immortal; most of these had occurred when they had been pronounced clinically dead, usually as a result of accidents. His interest piqued, Moody began to collect such cases and continued to do so when he entered the Medical College of Georgia in 1972, where he received his MD before taking up a residency in Psychiatry at the University of Virginia Medical Centre. By 1972, Moody had collected, by his own estimate, only 'about a dozen cases', but he began to lecture publicly on them in 1973 and finished *Life After Life* in 1974, by which time his case collection had grown to approximately 150 cases. These cases were to provide the majority of the testimonies that were to constitute the most sensational chapter of his landmark study, published the following year.

Life After Life

Constituting the bulk of *Life After Life*, in terms of both length and centrality to the work's overall thesis, was its second chapter 'The Experience of Dying'. Here, Moody presented much of the case collection upon which the book rests in the form of extracts from that collection, arranged and presented under a number of headings. He derived these, in turn, from an examination of what he perceived to be a number of common features that remained consistent across a large number of reports from his case collection. At the time of the writing of *Life After Life*, these headings numbered fifteen:

1 Ineffability
2 Hearing the news
3 Feelings of peace and quiet
4 The noise
5 The dark tunnel
6 Out of the body
7 Meeting others
8 The being of light
9 The review
10 The border or limit
11 Coming back
12 Telling others
13 Effects on lives
14 New views of death
15 Corroboration.

Crucially, Moody's central claim in *Life After Life* was that his respondents had reported to him an experience which possessed the consistency of shared, 'real', experience, rather than the randomness and confusion of 'mere' dreams. He attempted to support this by presenting a sizeable number of testimony-extracts within his book's longest section and an examination of some of these goes some way towards accounting for the popularity of his work, suffusing it, as they do, with a vivid, narrative appeal. Of his out-of-body experience following an accident, for example, one respondent's testimony reproduced by Moody described how he

> was sort of floating about five feet above the street, about five yards away from the car, I'd say, and I heard the echo of the crash dying away. I saw people come running up and crowding around the car, and I saw my friend get out of the car, obviously in shock. I could see my own body in the wreckage among all those people, and could see them trying to get it out. My legs were all twisted and there was blood all over the place.
>
> (Moody 1975: 37)

A respondent's journey through 'The dark tunnel' in which he heard what Moody described as 'The noise' was similarly dramatic:

One afternoon I became very sick, and they rushed me to the nearest hospital. When I arrived they decided they were going to have to put me to sleep, but why I don't know, because I was too young. Back in those days they used ether. They gave it to me by putting a cloth over my nose, and when they did, I was told afterwards, my heart stopped beating. I didn't know at that time that that was exactly what happened to me, but anyway when this happened I had an experience. Well, the first thing that happened – now I am going to describe it just the way I felt – was that I had this ringing noise brrrrrnnnnng-brrrrrnnnnng-brrrrrnnnnng, very rhythmic. Then I was moving through this – you're going to think this is weird – through this long dark place. It seemed like a sewer or something. I just can't describe it to you. I was moving, beating all the time with this noise, this ringing noise.

(Moody 1975: 31)

Dramatic also was the feature that was to dominate much later discussion: that of 'The being of light' which appeared to contain a gentle, loving, presence:

I became very weak, and I fell down. I began to feel a sort of drifting, a movement of my real being in and out of my body, and to hear beautiful music. I floated on down the hall and out the door onto the screened-in porch. There, it almost seemed that clouds, a pink mist really, began to gather around me, and then I floated right straight on through the screen, just as though it weren't there, and up into this pure crystal clear light, an illuminating white light. It was so beautiful and so bright, so radiant, but it didn't hurt my eyes. It's not any kind of light you can describe on earth. I didn't actually see a person in this light, and yet it has a special identity, it definitely does. It is a light of perfect understanding and perfect love.

(Moody 1975: 62–3)

Indeed, the vividness and the consistency of the experience he presented was further reinforced by being taken up and delivered by Moody as a '"model", a composite of the common elements found in very many stories' presented at the opening of the seminal second chapter. It is reproduced here, in full:

A man is dying and, as he reaches the point of greatest physical distress, he hears himself pronounced dead by his doctor. He begins to hear an uncomfortable noise, a loud ringing or buzzing, and at the same time feels himself moving very rapidly through a long, dark tunnel. After this, he suddenly finds himself outside of his own physical body, but still in the immediate physical environment, and he sees his own body from a distance, as though he is a spectator. He watches the resuscitation attempt from this unusual vantage point and is in a state of emotional upheaval.

After a while he collects himself and becomes more accustomed to his odd condition. He notices that he still has a 'body', but one of a very different nature and with very different powers from the physical body he has left behind. Soon other things begin to happen. Others come to meet and to help him. He glimpses the spirits of relatives and friends who have already died, and a loving, warm spirit of a kind he has never encountered before – a being of light – appears before him. This being asks him a question, nonverbally, to make him evaluate his life and helps him along by showing him a panoramic, instan-taneous playback of the major events of his life. At some point he finds himself approaching some sort of barrier or border, apparently representing the limit between earthly life and the next life. Yet, he finds that he must go back to the earth, that the time for his death has not yet come. At this point he resists, for by now he is taken up with his experiences in the afterlife and does not want to return. He is overwhelmed by intense feelings of joy, love, and peace. Despite his attitude, though, he somehow reunites with his physical body and lives.

Later he tries to tell others, but he has trouble doing so. In the first place, he can find no human words adequate to describe these unearthly episodes. He also finds that others scoff, so he stops telling other people. Still, the experience affects his life profoundly, especially his views about death and its relationship to life.

(Moody 1975: 21–3)

Here, what is clearly evident is that Moody had taken his fifteen allegedly recurring elements and linked them together with a plot in order to provide a *narrative* model of a 'typical' NDE as opposed to a simple list of common elements. Indeed, it is difficult to underestimate the importance of this model, for it became, essentially, the definition of 'near-death experience' that became accepted by many and hence guaranteed both the popularity and priority of Moody's original work. As we shall see, even where future studies were to deviate from his own, it was often clear that they began either as attempts to replicate the model from different collections of case studies or as attempts to refute it. Indeed, as we shall also see, it became for at least some researchers the typical experience which *neuroscience* was to be called upon to replicate and to explain, for the strong and vivid suggestion it gave of a shared, structured, consistency to NDErs' reports raised the intriguing possibility that the experience was neither dream, nor hallucination, nor delusion, but something far more *real*. As Moody himself was to remark in *Life After Life*:

It is my opinion that anyone looking into near-death experiences in an organized way is likely also to uncover such strange apparent corroboration. At least, I believe he will find enough to make him wonder whether near-death experiences, far from being dreams, might not belong in a very different category indeed.

(Moody 1975: 176–7)

Despite the appearance of a number of future studies which claimed to confirm many of Moody's initial conclusions, it is worth considering at the outset a few of the questionable aspects of his handling of the material which was to underlie his model. In the first chapter of *Life After Life*, for example, he admitted that of his 150 accounts, 'no two . . . are precisely identical' (Moody 1975: 23). He also declared that 'I have found no one person who reports every single component of the composite experience' (Moody 1975: 23). In addition, it was again clear from his comments upon the model that no single account matched it exactly, and that only just over half of its features (eight) were reported by 'very many' of his respondents, with 'few' reporting up to twelve. Again, Moody conceded that no one element of the composite experience was reported to him by every member of his study group, that elements which only occurred in single accounts were not included in the abstract, and, further, that the *order* in which elements were experienced by his group of NDErs in fact contained at least some variation. Thus, on the one hand he was forced to conclude:

> The order in which a dying person goes through the various stages ... may vary from that given in my 'theoretical model'. To give one example, various persons have reported seeing the 'being of light' before, or at the same time, they left their physical bodies, and not as in the 'model', some time afterward.
>
> (Moody 1975: 24)

He added to this, however, that 'the order in which the stages occur in the model is a very typical order, and wide variations are unusual' (Moody 1975: 24).

Future chapters of *this* study will seek to explore in considerably more detail the extent to which NDErs' experiences really *do* share a significant number of common elements. However, even this brief acknowledgement of the potential weaknesses of Moody's handling of his material *en route* to his model might lead at least some to wonder whether it *reflects* an underlying consistency within reports or *imposes* a false consistency on what are in fact a very diverse collection of accounts. It is also instructive to consider how a *single* element such as 'The dark tunnel' was arrived at in the list of common features. In his narrative model, as we have seen, Moody noted this aspect of a typical NDEr's experience as one in which he 'feels himself moving very rapidly through a long dark tunnel'. An examination of the presented extracts from the case collection as revealed in *Life After Life*, however, reveals that the darkness is not invariably described as tunnel-shaped. To be sure, the designation 'tunnel' is sometimes used, for example by an NDEr who stated that 'I felt like I was riding on a roller coaster train at an amusement park, going through this tunnel at a tremendous speed' (Moody 1975: 32).

Elsewhere, however, Moody's respondents revealed a variety of ways of describing this apparently consistent feature of their experiences. One talked of 'just floating and tumbling through space'; another claimed that 'I had the feeling that I was moving through a deep, very dark valley'; another talked of entering 'head first into a narrow and very, very dark passageway'; whilst another explained that he was:

> in an utterly black, dark void. It is very difficult to explain, but I felt as if I were moving in a vacuum, just through blackness. Yet, I was quite conscious. It was like being in a cylinder which had no air in it. It was a feeling of limbo, of being half-way here, and half-way somewhere else.
>
> (Moody 1975: 32)

Another of Moody's respondents felt the need to resort to incorrect use of Biblical metaphor in order to do justice to her experience, writing:

> Suddenly, I was in a very dark, very deep valley. It was as though there was a pathway, almost a road, through the valley, and I was going down the path . . . Later, after I was well, the thought came to me, 'Well, now I know what the Bible means by "the valley of the shadow of death", because I've been there'.
>
> (Moody 1975: 33–4)

Given the diversity of descriptors being used in order to express the experience, it is difficult to see why 'tunnel' should be so favoured, or even how an identical experience is being variously described. As Moody again was to admit:

> Many different words are used to describe this space. I have heard [it] described as a cave, a well, a trough, an enclosure, a tunnel, a funnel, a vacuum, a void, a sewer,

a valley, and a cylinder. *Although people use different terminology here, it is clear that they are all trying to express some one idea.*

(Moody 1975: 30–1; emphasis mine)

This cluster of questions concerning the adequacy of Moody's methodology – and the doubts which it raises concerning the repeated claim made in his book for the presence of significant consistency within near-death reports – is in one important sense puzzling. For if such flaws existed in his treatment of his original data, how did it come to be that his book was so well received, and how was it that it became so very popular and influential? Given such weaknesses, what might explain the strength of popularity of *Life After Life*, amongst early near-death researchers and laypersons alike?

This is a complex cluster of questions. To begin with, it is clear that Moody's work was not aimed at an academic audience, and this may itself give clues as to its broad, popular appeal. Indeed, *Life After Life* is non-technical and accessible to the point of warmth and friendliness. Writer Martin Ebon paints a pen picture of Moody the man which dovetails well with his assessment of *Life After Life* when he writes of its author that 'In his writing, as well as in his public and private appearances, Dr. Moody encourages an easy confidence, a candor that prompts men and women to confide in him as they have not confided in anyone else in their lives' (Ebon 1977: 25). Indeed, a casual reading of *Life After Life* reveals a relaxed, easy style, well summed up again by Ebon when he describes it as 'folksy . . . but sophisticated folksy' (Ebon 1977: 26). From the outset, Moody appeared neutral and unbiased about the presuppositions, content and result of his study, creating an effect both disarming and attractive to the non-specialist and technical reader alike. At the beginning of *Life After Life*, for example, he wrote that 'This book, written as it is by a human being, naturally reflects the background, opinions and prejudices of its author' (Moody 1975: 3). Later he was to reveal a religious upbringing 'not as a set of fixed doctrines, but rather as a concern with spiritual and religious doctrines, teachings and questions', ensuring an appeal to a large number of Westerners for whom religious dogmatism had become increasingly impossible during the 1960s and 1970s (Moody 1975: 4). In addition, the strong implication carried throughout *Life After Life* that no single, currently existing scientific explanation of the NDE was sufficient to explain each of its component elements added to its appeal by suggesting that something was occurring that science was seemingly powerless to explain. That this admission was being made by a scientist – indeed, by a physician – seemed to add to the impression that something was being offered that scientifically educated Westerners could accept with confidence. Indeed, by presenting such an intriguing enigma to science, Moody the scientist was also virtually guaranteeing that other, more detailed, scientific explorations of NDEs could not be far away. And, as we shall see, it was not long before they arrived.

Astral projection and out-of-body experiences

In spite of Moody's disavowal of any knowledge of parapsychological literature generally, it is clear that *Life After Life* fitted chronologically and developmentally into an ongoing, widely shared, and increasingly popular twentieth-century concern to detect empirical evidence of both the existence of the human soul as distinct from the body and that soul's ability to survive the body's death. Some writers, for example, have cited the late nineteenth- and early twentieth- century preoccupation with spiritualism as reminiscent of the contemporary popular fascination with NDEs. In both contexts, it is alleged, dogma is replaced in a climate of religious uncertainty by attempts to provide actual evidential proof of life after death, with NDEs updating, where necessary, outmoded components of spiritualism such as the 'silver cord' joining body and soul (Zaleski 1987: 117–19). Other historical parallels might plausibly be added to this, including theosophy with its complex descriptions of the transcendent realms to which the liberated soul may travel and the late nineteenth and early twentieth centuries' interest in astral projection and out-of-body experiences (OBEs) as found in the popular testimony-driven works of astral projectors such as Oliver Fox (Fox 1962). Later twentieth-century experimenters with astral projection included Robert Monroe, an American businessman living in Virginia who, like Fox, discovered an apparently latent ability to project spontaneously whilst at rest. His first experiences took place in the 1950s and, again in common with Fox, he later learned to project at will, visiting a range of different realms or locales varying widely in their similarity to the physical Earth (Monroe 1971). In the 1960s, Robert Crookall began a significant series of studies of OBEs and attempted a classification of them in accordance with whether or not the subject was well, exhausted or near death at the time (Crookall 1961), but probably the most complex twentieth-century attempt at classification of 'types' of OBEs was made by Celia Green and published by Oxford's then Institute of Psychophysical Research in 1961. In the work, Green was to present a number of testimonies that clearly resembled some of the NDEs presented by Moody and others just a few years later, of which the following is a good example:

> I was in hospital having had an operation for peritonitis; I developed pneumonia and was very ill. The ward was L shaped; so that anyone in bed at one part of the ward could not see round the corner.
>
> One morning I felt myself floating upwards, and found I was looking down on the rest of the patients. I could see myself; propped up against pillows, very white and ill. I saw the sister and nurse rush to my bed with oxygen. Then everything went blank. The next I remember; was opening my eyes to see the sister bending over me.
>
> (Green 1968: 121)

Interestingly, the account also bears significant parallels with many contemporary NDE claims, particularly in the subject's concern to present information as confirmatory proof that the experience was no mere hallucination:

> I told [the sister] what had happened; but at first she thought I was rambling. Then I said, 'There is a big woman sitting up in bed with her head wrapped in bandages; and she is knitting something with blue wool. She has a very red face.' This certainly shook her; as apparently the lady concerned had a mastoid operation and was just as I described.

She was not allowed out of bed; and of course I hadn't been up at all. After several other details; such as the time by the clock on the wall (which had broken down) I convinced her that at least something strange had happened to me.

(Green 1968: 121)

Deathbed Visions and *At the Hour of Death*

The closest antecedents to Moody's work appeared at two distinct points within the twentieth century, separated by some fifty years. The first of these, *Deathbed Visions: The Psychical Experiences of the Dying*, appeared in 1926 and is still widely regarded as a classic. Barrett, a founding member of the Society for Psychical Research (SPR) in 1882, was interested throughout his life in a range of what would now be described as paranormal phenomena, including telepathy, hallucinations, the claims of spiritualism, and the sometimes unusual experiences of the dying. This latter interest was to lead to *Deathbed Visions*, in which Barrett (together with his wife) set out to collect and to classify a range of unusual experiences reported by the dying or those attendant upon them during their final hours. Comparable in length to *Life After Life*, *Deathbed Visions* contained a number of testimonies collected by the Barretts and grouped under a number of distinct categories. These included:

1   Visions seen by the dying of persons unknown by them to be dead
2   Visions seen by the dying of persons known by them to be dead, and death-bed visions seen by others
3   Visions seen by the dying of living persons at a distance – in some cases reciprocal
4   Music heard at the time of death by the dying or by persons present at a death-bed
5   Visions of the spirit of a dying person leaving the body.

As with *Life After Life*, these classificatory elements and features were derived from testimonies, and liberally illustrated with extracts *from* those testimonies. Thus, for example, under the second category Barrett reproduced the following extract, penned by one Rev. W.G. Horder:

> A friend of mine, of a mind naturally indisposed to faith, and at the time quite sceptical about a future life, tells me of the following incident, which made a deep impression upon him, and even wakened belief in immortality:
>
> His brother, a young man of about 25 years of age, had been seized with brain fever, which at last rendered him quite unconscious for about 24 hours, but just before death he raised himself in his bed, resting himself upon his hand and said, 'Who is that at the bottom of my bed?' His mother, who was sitting by his bedside, said, 'There is no one there, my dear.' He said, 'Don't you see Emma' (a departed sister) 'standing at the foot of the bed?' She said, 'No, there is no one there, my dear.' 'Yes, there is,' he said, 'It is Emma. I am coming, I am ready'; and fell back and died.
>
> (Barrett 1986: 48)

Similarly, under the category of 'Music heard at the time of death by the dying or by persons present at a death-bed', Barrett reproduced a case from the SPR's own journal:

> We found Jack lying on his back with his eyes fixed on the ceiling, and his face lighted up with the brightest of smiles. After a little while Jack awoke and used the words 'Heaven' and 'beautiful' as well as he could by means of his lips and facial expression. As he became more conscious he also told us in the same manner that his brother Tom and his sister Harriet were coming to see him. This we considered very unlikely as they lived some distance off, but shortly afterwards a cab drove up from which they alighted. They had sent no intimation of their coming, nor had anyone else. After Jack's partial recovery, when he was able to write or converse upon his fingers, he told us that he had been allowed to see into Heaven and to hear most beautiful music.
>
> (Barrett 1986: 100)

Barrett's work foreshadowed Moody's in a number of ways. First, both researchers plainly showed themselves to be interested in similar subject matter, concerning themselves with experiences taking place at the limits of this life, which, for them, hinted at the possibility of worlds other than this one. In addition, each presented a broadly sympathetic approach to the material they presented whilst anticipating the possibility that others might be less well disposed to it. Barrett – anticipating the critical reception from within the scientific community which his book might be expected to receive – even quoted Goethe at one point:

> in the sciences . . . if anyone advances anything new . . . people resist with all their might; they speak of the new view with contempt, as if it were not worth the trouble of even so much as an investigation or a regard; and thus a new truth may wait a long time before it can win its way.
> (Barrett 1986: 9)

In similar vein, Moody was to show himself well prepared for critical reaction to many of the claims made in *Life After Life*, closing its introduction by acknowledging that many 'will find the claims made in this book incredible and [their] first reaction will be to dismiss them out of hand' and empathizing from his own initial experience: this had been his first reaction upon encountering NDEs. However, by the end of *Life After Life*, it was difficult to avoid the conclusion that Moody, like Barrett, thought that something of major scientific import was occurring in the testimonies he had uncovered, despite the anticipated adverse institutional reaction.

One other significant twentieth-century study of death and dying may help us to locate *Life After Life* even more firmly within this contemporary Western, scientific context, despite appearing a few years *after* Moody's book's first publication. In 1977, researchers Karlis Osis and Erlendur Haraldsson published *At the Hour of Death*, a study of approximately 1000 cases of deathbed visions collected from the United States and India. Like Barrett's work (which the authors acknowledged as inspiration for their own study), *At the Hour of Death* dealt directly with experiences of the dying which included apparently paranormal visions and apprehensions of transcendent realms and figures, including visions of dead relatives, heavenly 'planes', religious figures, and apparently paranormal episodes observed by those *around* the deathbed. Indeed, the claim of Osis and Haraldsson to have begun serious research on their project in the 1960s serves to date their study significantly earlier than Moody's, for, as we have seen, during this time he was only just encountering the cases that were to pique his interest and to lead into the serious research for *Life After Life*.

Interestingly, whilst in the 1977 first edition of their book Osis and Haraldsson readily asserted that their findings were in agreement with Moody's, in the *second* edition they went on to highlight some interesting differences. Thus, for example, in the first edition they admitted that the 'life review' element of Moody's model appeared infrequently in their own collection of accounts. In the introduction to the second edition, they added to this the fact that the 'being of light' was also absent from their data. Intriguingly, they suggested at this point in their investigations: 'Maybe Moody created a new myth, or provided a newer, more attractive vocabulary for describing religious figures in this space age of ours' (Osis and Haraldsson 1997: xv). Indeed, a closer inspection of *At the Hour of Death* reveals that it owes far more to Barrett for inspiration than it does to Moody, although in several key respects it resembles the work of both. No attempt is made, for example, at the construction of a model into which the experiences of all dying and/or clinically dead patients can be said to fit. Two chapters of the study have the reports of resuscitated patients as their overall theme, but the bulk of the study is taken up with deathbed visions of the dying, rather than the clinically – and hence temporarily – dead. Like both Moody and Barrett, however, Osis and Haraldsson once again presented a pre-eminently testimony-driven study in which the possibility of transcendent realms was asserted via a detailed and generally sympathetic investigation of the claims of those who had apparently seen them or visited them. Like *Life After Life* and *Deathbed Visions*, *At the Hour of Death* was generously peppered with the testimonies upon which its assertions were based, whilst its authors, like Barrett and Moody, seemed quite willing to embrace the notion that research such as theirs appeared to support the possibility of life after death.

Life after *Life After Life*

During its preparation, Moody could have had little idea of the controversy that *Life After Life* was to trigger. Whilst he had anticipated reaction to his book from a variety of sources, writing in its opening pages that his research must surely have implications for a number of fields, including psychology, psychiatry, medicine, philosophy, theology and religion, it could scarcely be imagined in the mid-1970s that his work would also be foundational for the entirely new academic subdiscipline of near-death studies, together with a global research organization devoted to the exploration of the phenomenon he had done so much to unearth.

However, within two years of the initial appearance of *Life After Life*, the International Association for Near Death Studies (IANDS) had been formed with the express purpose of fostering further research into NDEs amongst interested physicians. Many of these, including Kenneth Ring, Bruce Greyson and Michael Sabom, would go on to produce studies of NDEs of their own in which they were to show themselves to be equal to Moody in their ability to collect and to classify NDE data and generally better than he at producing fully scientific and quantitative analyses of it. Indeed, by this time, Moody himself had already penned a sequel to his first book entitled *Reflections on Life After Life* in which he presented some new discoveries including a handful of further prototypical elements reported by NDErs such as 'visions of knowledge' (forgotten upon resuscitation), visits to celestial 'cities of light', encounters with a realm of 'bewildered spirits', and a variety of dramatic and seemingly miraculous supernatural rescues of persons on the brink of death. In *Reflections*, Moody also began to speculate in more detail on a number of issues which *Life After Life* had only begun to raise, including the nature of the judgement undergone by NDErs, some implications for (and initial reactions from) the ministry, the nature of NDEs in attempted suicide cases, some further historical antecedents to the NDE, and a closing question-and-answer session in which he attempted to answer some of the questions which *Life After Life* had created. In an appendix entitled 'Methodological considerations', Moody also began to discuss in greater detail his criteria for defining and classifying NDEs and, most interestingly of all, his interviewing techniques: techniques to which we will need to return for a fuller examination in future chapters.

Testing the Moody model

By the late-1970s, however, a key concern of the early IANDS researchers was to test Moody's discovery of a common core to NDEs by producing independent studies of their own. Kenneth Ring was one of the first to attempt this in detail and at length. By his own admission, his initial interest in NDEs was triggered by his reading of *Life After Life*, an interest which was to lead to a series of studies exploring a number of aspects of near-death experiences, beginning in 1980 with his first work *Life at Death: A Scientific Investigation of Near Death Experiences*. Here, Ring credited Moody's work as a redirecting influence upon his own life, writing in his introduction that reading *Life After Life* was responsible for lifting him out of a phase of feeling 'spiritually adrift' and setting his life on an entirely different path. Subsequently he was to go on to found the Near Death Hotel, a place where NDErs could meet, share their experiences, learn from one another, and find opportunities to aid the progress of research into their own apparent encounters with death's 'other side'. In much later research Ring would diversify still further, becoming arguably the most influential researcher into NDEs during the 1980s and 1990s. In addition to some startling claims concerning the perceptual abilities of blind and visually-impaired people during NDEs, he would also go on to suggest that near-death testimonies might be fruitfully used in a range of therapeutic and potentially life-saving contexts: perhaps reflecting his own early experience of the solace and existentially redirecting power to be had from reading the near-death accounts of others in Moody's original work.

In 1980, however, Ring was chiefly concerned to produce a more systematic study of NDEs than Moody had presented in *Life After Life*. Impressed by the seemingly common pattern discerned by Moody within near-death reports, Ring presented in *Life at Death* a study of the testimonies of fifty-four NDErs in which he confirmed that such a pattern did indeed exist, made up of the following sequential stages:

1   Peace and a sense of well-being
2   Separation from the body
3   Entering the darkness
4   Seeing the light
5   Entering the light.

From these elements or stages, Ring attempted to derive a model which turned out to be both similar and dissimilar to Moody's own. Thus, for example, whilst including in his model elements such as the noise, the tunnel, the life review, and the light, other elements such as the 'border' or 'limit' – Moody's tenth 'element' – were not present. Overall, however, in his five-stage core experience Ring had at the very least replicated the contours of Moody's own core NDE: a significant achievement indicating that Moody had been right to argue for at least a degree of commonality across accounts (Ring 1980). Subsequent researchers would be inclined to accept Ring's more cautious stage model over Moody's complex narrative in future studies of their own.

Arguably, however, the most significant early testing and development of Moody's initial findings was to appear shortly after Ring's work. Entitled *Recollections of Death* and appearing in 1982, it was written by another physician, Michael Sabom, who, together with colleague Sarah Kreutziger, based extensive research on a survey of the experiences of 100 respondents. In the first chapter of this work Sabom began by telling the story of how he became involved in the study of NDEs. Attending a Methodist church in 1976 during his first year of cardiology at the University of Florida, he had been intrigued by a Sunday School presentation of Moody's *Life After Life*. Sceptical at first, Sabom later came to conduct his own preliminary investigation into NDEs in order to present Moody's findings to another church audience along with Kreutziger. For the presentation, Sabom decided to interview some survivors of clinical death. The third patient he interviewed turned out to have had an NDE. As he was to note: 'At the conclusion of the interview, I had the distinct feeling that what this woman had shared with me that night was a deeply personal glimpse into an aspect of medicine of which I knew nothing' (Sabom 1982: 17). So began Sabom's involvement in the research that was to culminate in *Recollections of Death*.

Several things, however, bothered Sabom at the outset of the investigation. For one, he was concerned that Moody's presentation had been a self-admittedly 'non-scientific' one. Like Ring, therefore, Sabom wanted to know more. In particular, he was curious to know exactly what percentage of NDErs' experiences fitted Moody's model NDE. Would a more strictly controlled quantitative study of NDErs' experiences such as the one he envisaged confirm the Moody model or undermine it? In addition, Sabom was curious as to the *backgrounds* of persons reporting NDEs. What, for example, of their social, educational, professional and – above all – *religious* backgrounds? Might these have any bearing on the occurrence and/or detail of their experiences? Finally, Sabom was interested in the medical circumstances surrounding NDEs. Several questions concerned him here. In particular, he was interested to know whether or not certain medical conditions were more conducive to the occurrence of NDEs than others. He was also interested to know, particularly in cases where detailed notes were kept of the procedures used on patients, whether or not their allegedly out-of-body observations could be checked against records made of those procedures. If, as a result of such comparisons, NDErs' out-of-body observations turned out to be substantially correct, what might this imply regarding the conventional neuroscientific view of sensory awareness as physical and wholly brain-dependent? Clearly, with such questions setting the agenda, the fledgling discipline of near-death studies might now expect a detailed, controlled, empirical and, above all, scientifically respectable investigation which was concerned to ask the very questions concerning the existence of the soul and the possibilities for human immortality which the existence of NDEs was beginning to suggest.

By the end of the study, it was clear that subjects' religious background had little or no bearing on the possibility of their having an NDE. As its careful statistical analysis clearly showed, Christians, persons of other religions, agnostics and atheists all tended to report NDEs containing core features such as encounters with light, episodes of darkness and encounters with otherworldly figures. What was striking, however, was the fact that persons tended only to report encountering specific figures that corresponded to their general background and expectations, although they might register surprise at the fact of the encounter itself.

The study also concluded that as a result of an NDEr's experience 'no change in the basic type of religious belief occurred – that is, no agnostic became a believer, no Protestant a Catholic, no Catholic a Jew' (Sabom 1982: 179). Thus whilst a deepening of religious commitment might occur as a result of an NDE, there were no reports of conversions. Of course, such a study, conducted via interviews of persons within one area of the United States in the late 1970s and early 1980s, could not claim to be fully cross-cultural. Persons interested in near-death research still had a long wait for a comprehensively cross-cultural study (and in many respects are still waiting). However, the study *had* found that religious background neither caused nor seemingly prevented a subject's NDE, although it did seem to have a significant bearing on *whom* NDErs might expect to encounter on the other side of death.

As regards the checking of the accuracy of Moody's model, Sabom and Kreutziger's findings appeared somewhat ambiguous. 'Our goal', they argued, 'was to gather enough information about each experience so that it could later be evaluated on the basis of ten separate elements which had been derived from Moody's description of the experience in *Life After Life*' (Sabom 1982: 25). Notable here is the fact that Moody's model was pared down from fifteen to ten elements for checking. 'The noise', for example, was removed, and the resultant checked characteristics became: subjective sense of being dead, predominant emotional content, sense of bodily separation, observation of physical objects and events (for example resuscitation procedures), dark region or void, life review, a light, entering a transcendent dimension, encountering others, and return. To what extent, then, was this *smaller* model confirmed? Whilst some of its features were clearly encountered, others seemed to occur with little or no frequency in the study. Only 3 per cent of the studies' respondents reported the life review, for example (Sabom 1982: 74). Further, there seemed a large degree of diversity of detail in the topographies and populations of the otherworldly realms visited by respondents. Whilst an impressive total of 54 per cent of respondents reported a visit to a 'transcendental environment', this environment upon closer inspection seemed to include a wide array of figures and elements (Sabom 1982: 67–80). Thus, in addition to the commonly reported friends, relatives and religious figures, subjects also reported rather more bizarre encounters, including an encounter with two khaki-clad military figures who tried to dissuade an NDEr from returning to life and a 'verbal inter-rogation by nurses about possible subversive activities' (Sabom 1982: 73).

What, by common consent, constituted the most impressive aspect of the 1982 study was its presentation of a small but detailed number of accounts in which observations made by NDErs whilst apparently out-of-body were cross-checked with surgical records of the actual medical emergency – including surgical procedures used – and comparisons made. As a result of this, one patient's description of how 'my head was covered and the rest of my body was draped with more than one sheet, separate sheets laid in layers' was correlated with the surgeon's description that the body was 'draped in the customary sterile fashion' (Sabom 1982: 97–8). Whilst it could be argued that the patient knew this either as a result of being aware of how his body was draped before he was anaesthetized or as a result of some kind of residual tactile awareness whilst unconscious, less easy to explain are the patient's apparently accurate descriptions of how his own heart looked when removed by the surgeon, and how it was subsequently held and manipulated during the operation. Thus, regarding the actual colour of his heart, the subject reported that 'One general area to the right or left was darker than the rest instead of all being the same color.' For Sabom, this corresponded significantly to the surgeon's description that 'the ventricular aneurysm was dissected free . . . The aneurysm was seen to be very large' (Sabom 1982: 98). Again, the subject described how 'He [the surgeon] cut pieces of my heart off. He raised it and twisted it this way and that way and took quite a bit of time examining it and looking at different things.' This, again, was compared with the surgeon's report that 'An incision was made over the most prominent portion of the aneurysm after the heart had been turned upside down in the pericardial wall . . . The entire aneurysm was reselected' (Sabom 1982: 98). Once again, such a correlation – together with other descriptions of procedures by other patients, including accurate accounts of details such as the movement and specific positions of needles on technical instruments – seemed to indicate that patients may actually have been able to observe details of their own operations and resuscitations from vantage points apart from their bodies during the out-of-body 'phases' of their NDEs.

The obvious objection to these clearly staggering contentions was that these subjects were creating imaginative accounts of surgical procedures powered by existing knowledge of what their operations might be expected to be like. For it might have been possible for patients to obtain information about crucial medical procedures from other sources, such as reading, casual conversation, or even imagination and fantasy. In order to answer this criticism, a control experiment was carried out in which a group of non-NDErs were asked to *imagine* the details of their operations and their subsequent accounts then checked with the actual descriptions of their operations given by NDErs who had apparently 'viewed' them. In the event the depictions given by non-NDErs differed from those of the NDErs in that they all tended to include mistakes in their accounts. Common errors included the supposition that mouth-to-mouth resuscitation would be applied to patients to clear airways and even wrong descriptions of the heights to which patients might be expected to 'jump' from their beds during attempts to restart the heart during CPR procedures (Sabom 1982: 157–61).

Overall, the weight of evidence amassed during this phase of the investigation appeared to suggest that no existing conventional medical or neuroscientific theory or theories could explain what was occurring: a conclusion echoing the prior contentions of Moody and Ring. This, together with the careful presentation of such data in *Recollections of Death*, ensured that it provided arguably the most compelling evidence to date for the existence of some sort of out-of-body perception gained by certain persons during NDEs. Whether such NDE 'observations' are genuinely veridical is still, over twenty years on, a matter of some debate. As we will see, experiments have been subsequently undertaken to put such contentions on a surer footing. In 1982, however, it appeared that the issue was being settled very much in favour of some form of body–soul dualism being demonstrated in the checked claims of NDErs: yet another apparent confirmation of the initial claims made by Moody.

Transformed by the light

Beginning in the mid-1980s, however, a number of studies began to appear which signalled a shift in researchers' attentions away from the testing of the work of pioneers such as Moody and towards an examination of other aspects of the NDE. In particular, a large number of studies began to concentrate solely on the *after-effects* allegedly produced by the NDE. Indeed, this new focus would continue to draw wide attention in the closing years of the twentieth century and on into the beginning of the twenty-first to such an extent that it is legitimate to see this aspect of the study of the NDE as constituting a separate phase of investigation. To be sure, attention had been paid to the consequences of having an NDE from the beginning of research into the phenomenon. Moody had noted in *Life After Life* that a number of NDErs had related how 'they felt that their lives were broadened and deepened by their experience' and consequently had become 'more reflective and more concerned with ultimate philosophical issues' (Moody 1975: 89). Similar conclusions were drawn by Sabom and Kreutziger who found that NDErs often reported dramatically new attitudes towards their own death in the years following their NDEs, a deepening of conventional religious faith and a renewed interest in loving and caring elements within human relationships (Sabom 1982: 172–81). However, it was Kenneth Ring, in his 1984 study *Heading Toward Omega*, who was to be the first researcher to explore such transformations systematically and in detail. At the beginning of his study, Ring drew attention to the fact that it was not simply the case that NDEs had the power to transform the way the West viewed death and dying; rather, thanks to the changes in outlook and lifestyle reported by NDErs and apparently occasioned by the fact of having an NDE, they also possessed the power to change views of living and of the meaning of life. In the years since the publication of *Life At Death*, Ring had begun to strike up often deep friendships with a large and growing number of NDErs at the Near Death Hotel, a counselling centre and meeting-place for NDErs centred upon Ring's own home in Connecticut, where, by his own estimate, 'more NDEs have been recounted after dinner than at any other single location in the world' (Ring 1984: 25). Through such meetings and discussions,

Ring began to learn more about NDEs, concluding that to understand their true significance it was necessary to look beyond the fact
of their occurrence to their *after-effects*: the ways – often profound
and quantifiable – in which they had changed the lives of NDErs.
For Ring, herein lay the real meaning of the NDE, and it was this
realization that was to prompt *Heading Toward Omega* and which
was to constitute its primary focus.

What was becoming central for Ring as a result of his
developing understanding of the NDE was the recognition that it
was merely a 'seed experience' (Ring 1984: 27). In fact, for him,
the NDE's true nature, meaning and significance could only
become apparent – for experiencer and researcher alike – after
it had, in effect, matured and ripened within the lives of NDErs
themselves. Thus he was to write that:

> As NDErs 'mature' following their experience, the nature
> of that seed experience – its meaning, if you like – becomes
> increasingly manifest. And as more and more of these
> NDErs begin to mature, there seems to be a significance
> also in their sheer numbers and not merely in their form.
>
> (Ring 1984: 27–8)

Indeed, for Ring, this conclusion appears to have constituted a
turning-point in much the same way that his first discovery of *Life
After Life* proved to be: with the difference that, this time, his
discovery contained implications for the entire *future* understanding of the NDE. For in making the transition to examining
the fruit rather than the seed, Ring was claiming to have produced
a corrective to much early near-death research. The passage of
almost a decade of near-death studies had only lately allowed such
a perspective, Ring noted, and that was why

> all of us early researchers necessarily missed the full
> meaning of the phenomenon with which we were dealing.
> We were observing the garden, as it were, just after
> seeding. But now enough time has elapsed and we can see
> more clearly just what has been sown. We begin to
> understand that we have seen only a small fraction of the
> beauty before us.

Ring's self-confessed aim in *Heading Toward Omega* was to 'describe something of that greater beauty' (Ring 1984: 28).

There were, however, other contrasts between *Life at Death* and its sequel. For one thing, Ring's conversations at the Near Death Hotel had produced fruit of their own in the form of a much larger body of data than had been available to him during the writing of his first book. For *Heading Toward Omega*, he was able to draw upon 42 direct interviews, 174 questionnaires and 62 (out of a total of 150) letters from NDErs who reported life-changes subsequent to their initial experiences. Despite the relative strength of the sample size, however, there were numerous problems in presenting such a study as a properly controlled one, admitted by Ring from the outset. On the one hand, his sample was not randomly selected and he provided no control study. In addition, many of his interviews were informal – 'It is hard to interview a friend as strictly as one might a stranger, especially at the Near-Death Hotel' – and Ring was forced to concede that his study contained 'major shortcomings' (Ring 1984: 29–30). Nevertheless, he was able early on to frame and test his 'spiritual catalyst hypothesis', which provided a succinct summation of many of his second study's overall conclusions whilst summarizing his own understanding of the NDE at this time. Thus, he was to write, the NDE:

> is essentially a spiritual experience that serves as a catalyst for spiritual awakening and development. Moreover, the spiritual development that unfolds following an NDE tends to take a particular form. Finally, as a by-product of this spiritual development, NDErs tend to manifest a variety of psychic abilities afterward that are an inherent part of their transformation.
>
> (Ring 1984: 51)

The testing and consequent illustration and reinforcement of such a position were to occupy Ring throughout the study's remaining pages.

One thing that was notable about *Heading Toward Omega* was its liberal use of testimonies. More than any researcher before him, Ring was showing himself willing to let NDErs speak by and large for themselves and at length. His conclusions, however, were succinct, based around various self-constructed survey question-naires that provided him with some startling results. Overall, he concluded that having an NDE was a consistently life-enhancing experience, leaving marked effects which improved NDErs' lives both spiritually and psychically, and creating lasting, beneficial, effects on their personalities. His 'Life Changes Questionnaire', for example, measuring aspects of NDErs' personalities both before and after their NDEs, revealed that they typically as a result of their experiences had high feelings of self-esteem, increased concern with spiritual (as opposed to conventionally religious) matters, a strong sense of purpose in life, an increased tendency to pray, an elevated belief in life after death, and a strong sense of the need for social justice. From this admittedly retrospective comparison of NDErs' personalities both before and after their experiences Ring was to conclude that the NDE 'not only changes an individual's life but often completely and radically transforms it' (Ring 1984: 120). Indeed, this transformation appeared to touch every area of NDErs' lives, leading to an enhanced appreciation for life, a genuine concern for the well being of others, a decreased desire to be seen to impress others, and a general disregard for material possessions. An enhanced quest for meaning in life was also typically reported subsequent to an NDE, well illustrated by one NDEr who told Ring that:

> My purpose and my outlook on life became from that point on a searching . . . Books became my friends . . . I found myself on a college campus, which was somewhere I had always wanted to be when I was younger, but I never got to do . . . I went back to school. . . .
>
> (Ring 1984: 137)

One conclusion stressed by Ring concerned the nature of the spiritual quest fired by the NDE, for whilst in some respects NDErs became more conventionally religious, their searchings mainly took place *outside* established religion and within a more unconventional spiritual sphere. By adding another self-devised scale of measurement, the 'Religious Belief Inventory', to his 'Life Changes Questionnaire', together with another scale of religious measurement devised by then IANDS director Bruce Greyson, Ring was able to conclude that NDErs' enhanced spirituality subsequent to their NDEs often took personal, nonconventional, unorthodox forms. This led him to conclude that after their experiences 'NDErs are likely to shift towards a universalistically spiritual orientation . . . very clearly in accord with a general spiritual – rather than religious – orientation toward life' (Ring 1984: 145). This conclusion is well illustrated by the testimony of a respondent who told Ring:

> I was brought up in the Bible Belt and when I was a child
> I was very religious . . . I mean I was taught certain things
> and I believed them as a child and adhered to them . . . just
> out of rote. But *after* this [her NDE], it made me *less*
> religious formally but probably more religious inwardly
> . . . I don't think I was in church one time since [my NDE],
> but I think I'm spiritually stronger than I ever was before.
> (Ring 1984: 154, emphases in the original)

A second questionnaire, the 'Psychic Experience Inventory', was devised to test for yet another post-NDE development: the allegedly increased occurrence of psychic abilities following a near-death experience. These were duly found, with many respondents reporting increased telepathic, precognitive and synchronous experiences in the years after their NDEs, whilst others reported greater use of intuition and increased episodes of déjà vu.

As if these findings were not already controversial, towards the end of his study Ring was to make even more startling claims. For in addition to claiming to have seen episodes from their own future lives during NDEs – a phenomenon that Ring was to dub the 'Personal Flashforward' (PF) – many of Ring's respondents also reported wider, more collective visions of humanity's future, which he was to label as 'Prophetic Visions' (PVs). These included geophysical changes, earthquakes, increased volcanic activity, landmass changes, meteorological changes, supply and economic breakdowns, the possibility of nuclear war and a final, more positive vision of a new era of peace and human unity. From an analysis and comparison of these claims, Ring concluded that the future of humanity would not extend far beyond the beginning of the twenty-first century and would be characterized by massive upheavals beginning in the 1980s followed by 'a new era in human history marked by human brotherhood, universal love, and world peace' (Ring 1984: 197).

It is clear that Ring's *Heading Toward Omega* was a radical departure from what had preceded it in the field of near-death studies, and that he was at this point making bold, controversial – even fantastic – claims. Given the radical conclusions he had ultimately drawn, it was somewhat ironic therefore that he would claim in the closing chapters of his book to have found a *biological* basis for NDErs' experiences. Crucial here was Ring's increasing realization that it was not necessary to come close to death to have an NDE but, rather, that NDEs belonged to a much wider family of experiences which shared NDE-like features including out-of-body experiences, feelings of bliss, and lights. These experiences, Ring noted, were reported by persons in a wide variety of contexts and circumstances including meditation, childbirth without apparent complications, and church worship. In searching for a known phenomenon that underlay all such experiences and circumstances, Ring hit upon the effects of radically altered breathing patterns, which might be expected if a person was suddenly to suffer a major trauma such as a traffic accident or cardiac arrest but which might also be expected as a result of adopting certain meditative and prayerful practices which also called for modifications to breathing, particularly those carried out by practitioners of disciplines such as *kundalini* yoga (Ring 1984: 220–51).

All of these combined insights were to lead Ring to one final conclusion. For now it seemed to him that the NDE was not simply a seed experience but that NDErs and other spiritually awakened persons were themselves seeds: of a whole new human order which would be called forth as a result of the drastic changes that were to convulse the planet in the closing years of the twentieth century. In all of this, however, the hand of evolution was at work, together with cause for hope, for as the end of the old order was at hand, nature was calling forth a new one to take its place: one in which spirituality, the rebirth of human virtue, and higher knowledge were to be distinguishing features. Thus it was that *Heading Toward Omega*, despite its dire warnings for the future, ended on a note of optimism, with Ring claiming that NDErs represented nothing less than 'the next stage of human evolution' in its ascent towards eventual 'conscious reunion with the Divine' (Ring 1984: 269).

Return from Death

As may have become clear, by the mid-1980s, near-death studies had already undergone a number of unexpected developments. Indeed, for many outside the field, these developments were, and largely remain, entirely unknown. But yet another unexpected development was to occur within a few months of the publication of Ring's second book, when, in 1985, British researcher Margot Grey published a study which appeared to duplicate, and hence reinforce, many of Ring's already controversial conclusions: with one notable exception.

Grey's interest in NDEs was sparked by her own experience, which occurred in India in 1976. Seriously ill with an undiagnosed illness, her temperature soared to a dangerous 105 degrees and her condition began to be accompanied by a series of strange experiences, including an out-of-body experience, entry into a black void, movement along a dark tunnel, and an entry into a brilliant and comforting light. The feelings of love, joy and rapture which Grey felt whilst in the light were described vividly in her book's preface, as were the after-effects which the entire episode left with her, leading to a new-found determination once she had fully recovered to 'study the phenomena that I had experienced in order to try to discover what other people experienced when apparently on the threshold of imminent death' (Grey 1985: xiv).

Grey's researches took her to the University of Connecticut in 1981 and it was at this time that she first met Kenneth Ring. Later, on a visit to London in 1984, Ring was to renew the friendship that had blossomed three years before, and it was at this time that he 'exchanged books' with her: a copy of *Heading Toward Omega* for a copy of *Return from Death*. As Ring took up the story in his Foreword to Grey's study: 'I betook myself up to her study to begin reading her manuscript. It was there that I gradually became extremely agitated, even shocked, by what I read' (Grey 1985: x). What surprised Ring so was that Grey had managed to duplicate many of his findings as presented in *Heading Toward Omega*. Indeed, a reading of *Return from Death* reveals that this was at least partly intentional, for one of Grey's main concerns in her own study was to gather a number of testimonies from near-death survivors in order to test whether or not Ring's five-stage model of NDEs could be replicated on the basis of a study of British, rather than American, NDErs. Her conclusion in one crucial sense was that it *could* be replicated, for on the basis of an eventual examination of the experiences of thirty-two English and nine American NDErs, Grey was forced to conclude that:

> I found that the respondents' testimonies clearly showed that in most cases there was evidence of the common basic features noted by Dr. Ring, and that the consistent pattern of the 'core experience' is, moreover, inclined to be revealed in a particular sequence regardless of nationality.
> (Grey 1985: 31–2)

However, Grey was to replicate Ring's findings in some other important senses also. Her study of the after-effects created by undergoing NDEs also drew conclusions comparable to Ring's, and Grey was to conclude that subsequent to their experiences (and apparently caused by them) NDErs reported heightened senses of love for humanity, increased desires for knowledge, development of new gifts and talents such as healing, increased belief in life after death, increased conviction of God's existence, and changes in religious attitudes away from conventional beliefs and practices towards more diverse, unorthodox spiritualities. She was even to discover apparent confirmation of some of Ring's more controversial assertions, including the development of paranormal abilities such as telepathy and precognition, and the presence during some NDErs' experiences of visions of their own futures and the future of humanity at large. As regards the latter, Grey was to confirm Ring's future scenario of a planet convulsed by earthquakes, volcanoes, food shortages, social unrest, disease, climate changes and nuclear war, all followed by, as one of her respondents was to describe, 'a Golden Age in which people would live in love and harmony with each other and all of nature' (Grey 1985: 133). Once again, the 1980s were declared to be particularly

43

significant. In addition to all of these striking parallels to Ring's work, Grey was even to suggest a similar mechanism for explaining why so many non-NDErs could undergo experiences strikingly similar to NDEs, and *Return from Death* included a chapter tracing the possible influence of practices such as *kundalini* yoga in creating NDE-like 'enlightenments', including feelings of bliss and peace, tunnels, lights and life transformations.

Grey's study did, however, differ from Ring's in one crucial respect. For whereas neither *Life at Death* nor *Heading Toward Omega* was to present any NDEs which were anything other than positive or pleasant, Grey was to present in *Return from Death* a number of testimonies which bore witness to experiences that were decidedly negative and unpleasant. To be sure, Grey was not the first researcher to draw attention to cases such as these. In 1978 American researcher and committed Christian Maurice Rawlings had created considerable controversy with the publication of *Beyond Death's Door*, the first study to suggest that not all NDEs might be pleasant or life-enhancing. Here, Rawlings was to use such cases as an apologetic tool as support for the truth of the Christian gospel, a position he was to consistently maintain in a number of subsequent studies, as chapter 2 of this study will show in more detail. Whilst not sharing Rawlings's conclusions in this regard, in *Return from Death* Grey nonetheless introduced a crucial modification to Ring's five-stage model in order to accommodate those few cases (five out of her total database of forty-one NDEs) that were negative or unpleasant in nature. In these, she detected a five-stage pattern in which subjects underwent episodes including fear and a sense of panic, out-of-body experiences, entry into a black void, the sensing of an evil force, and entry into a hell-like environment. Certainly, a small number of Grey's respondents reported intense feelings of fear throughout their experiences, one remarking that 'I don't even like to think about it now because I can feel the terror again' (Grey 1985: 64), and another commenting: 'There are a lot of other things that may have happened that I don't remember. Maybe I'm afraid to remember' (Grey 1985: 69). More dramatic, however, were the descriptions of the hellish realms and their occupants that appeared in Grey's book. In this respect, for example, one man who had a cardiac arrest found himself going down, deep down into the earth. There was anger and I felt this horrible fear. Everything was grey. The noise was fearsome, with snarling and crashing like maddened wild animals, gnashing their teeth. I knew where I was without having to ask. I was in hell. There was this terrible feeling of being lost. It wasn't all fire and brimstone like we were taught. I remember this feeling of coldness. There were other things there whirling about. And there were two beings of some kind near me. I believe one was evil, maybe the Devil. He was the force that was tugging me deeper and deeper down into that awful place. I felt enveloped by dark, black evil. I remember frantically trying to put this two-piece puzzle together. I had to get it done or suffer some terrible, nameless punishment. You don't hear any words, you sense it all. Well, there was no way this puzzle would fit and I remember being in a panic. The other being I'm sure now was Jesus. I remember somehow knowing that He could save me. I tried to shout His name but I couldn't, there was this screaming in my head. Then I felt I was rushing through that black void again. I opened my eyes and my wife and the doctors were leaning over me, telling me everything was going to be alright.

(Grey 1985: 70)

Overall, with the appearance of *Return from Death*, Grey had done more than simply reaffirm many of Ring's key contentions. In one crucial respect, she had lent public support to the view of a tiny handful of researchers such as Maurice Rawlings that existing studies of NDEs had painted a false picture of an experience in which it was always blissful and uplifting to die. Although she had only unearthed a small number of negative NDEs, these were of an intensity and vividness sufficient to warrant further study. Indeed, the controversy surrounding the existence of such experiences was to be extended in future years by researchers who either continued to dispute their existence or significance or who drew attention to crucial questions surrounding their correct interpretation. To date no single study devoted to the detailed exploration of entirely negative NDEs has emerged: reflecting, perhaps, a deeper need to believe that only reward awaits the departed soul after death.

The 1990s

In the late 1980s and early 1990s, however, a large number of studies continued to appear which were devoted exclusively to the consistently positive nature of NDEs themselves and particularly to their benign transformative effects. Of these, one of the most detailed would be by Australian researcher and IANDS member Cherie Sutherland, whose study *Reborn in the Light* appeared in 1992. As with Grey's study, Sutherland's research was inspired by her own NDE that occurred during the birth of her son in 1971. Kenneth Ring, who by this time was gaining recognition as the world's foremost researcher into NDEs, once again supplied the foreword to a study that ultimately shared the conclusions of the 'transformation' studies that had gone before. More than any study before it, however, Sutherland's book was to make extensive use of detailed and sophisticated quantitative statistical analysis – her background was in sociology – and the result was to be a substantial body of research that added rich confirmation to the growing consensus that the effects of NDEs were almost wholly beneficial.

In keeping with existing studies such as those of Ring and Grey, Sutherland's *Reborn in the Light* concluded, on the basis of interviews with fifty Australian subjects, that NDErs typically become more spiritual and correspondingly less conventionally religious as a result of their experiences. In this respect, she was to be more precise in her definition of 'spiritual' than either Ring or Grey had been, drawing attention to NDErs' behaviour patterns subsequent to their experiences which began to include increased attention to private prayer, meditation, quest for spiritual values and supernatural guidance. Many of Sutherland's respondents were forthright in their condemnation of organized religions such as Christianity, with one subject venting feelings 'of anger and rage at the indoctrination of organized religion', whilst another expressed the view that 'church and religion are totally divorced from spirituality' (Sutherland 1992: 104–5).

Again in common with Ring and Grey, Sutherland reported a range of other life-changes across a broad band of areas. Her NDErs, she claimed, tended to have an increased belief in life after death subsequent to their experiences, reported higher levels of psychic abilities (such as telepathy, clairvoyance, precognition and intuition) and claimed a shift in values away from materialistic and this-worldly concerns towards a greater desire for higher things, including solitude, spiritual advancement and involvement in altruistic activities. Unlike Ring and Grey, however, and very possibly because the crucial decade of the 1980s had by this time passed off without incident, Sutherland's respondents reported no prophetic visions for the future of the planet which included drastic upheavals followed by a new age. Interestingly, however, her book *did* contain a departure in a new direction that was to be followed by others – even Ring – within the field. For here, and for the first time, a major study was to suggest that the NDE and its after-effects might be of value for *everyone*, providing the promise of transformation for those who had never been near death or had never undergone an NDE-like experience at all. In this vein, and at the very end of her study, Sutherland was to write of her interviewees that:

> Almost all of them are changed by the experience and through their interactions with others these changes move beyond the personal, beyond the lives of individual experiencers into the social realm, presaging a profound transformation of great benefit to society as a whole.
>
> (Sutherland 1992: 243)

What Sutherland appeared to be suggesting at the very climax of her research was that the experiences of NDErs might, if disseminated widely enough, become a potent force for a wider, even global transformation of values, in keeping with the value changes professed by a small number of privileged NDErs: value changes which studies such as her own had done so much to uncover and present to a wider reading public. The notion that the NDE might become such a powerful force for change in this way, spreading its message particularly through spiritually impoverished, death-denying and conventionally irreligious societies such as those of the developed world, was one which was to gain support from a number of key researchers in the 1990s, notably Ring himself. That the NDE might be democratized in this way carried an obvious appeal; for now, thanks to the experiences of others passed on via a kind of spiritual osmosis of research and the written word, everyone could potentially pass through death and back into a fuller, richer life without putting themselves in any physical danger at all.

Further developments

Whilst attention was turning to the effects on NDErs of their experiences, other studies which set out to explore other aspects of the NDE were beginning to appear in the early 1990s, triggering several key areas of major debate for which the *Journal of Near-Death Studies* became a leading forum. Many of these areas, in turn, developed their own histories, with a variety of dissenting views arising within a range of academic contexts. As will become clear, future chapters will take up and examine many of these in considerable detail; consequently we will only briefly list them here before returning later for a more detailed examination of how they too fit in to the NDE's evolving history.

By the late 1980s and early 1990s, despite the consistent assertions of many researchers that no existing conventional neuroscientific explanation was capable of accounting for every aspect of the NDE, a number of other researchers continued to demur, leading to a growing number of studies of the phenomenon from psychologists, surgeons and neuroscientists throughout the world. The overall objectives of these were often to show that neuroscience was capable after all of accounting for every element of the NDE, usually by breaking down each component part of the experience – such as the light, the tunnel and so on – and positing a different set of neurological processes to explain each one. Other studies from within roughly the same contexts sought to demonstrate the opposite: that no existing understanding of neuroscience could possibly account for every feature of NDErs' experiences. Chapter 4 will devote detailed attention to the complexities of this debate which is still ongoing and, as we will see, continues to divide specialist opinion.

The question of the accuracy of observations made by persons during their NDEs continues. To settle this matter for good, a number of attempts were made in the years following 1975 to obtain confirmation of NDErs' claims to have made accurate observations whilst they were apparently apart from their bodies in order to confirm findings such as those made in the early 1980s by Sabom and Kreutziger. By the late 1990s, a significant body of research existed claiming to show that many NDErs actually enjoy significant perceptual *enhancement* during their NDEs. By the late 1990s it was even being claimed that congenitally blind persons have on documented occasions been able to see during their NDEs for the first and only time in their lives: an obviously remarkable claim. Apparently serious and sustained pieces of research which seem to demonstrate empirically and effectively that observations made by NDErs during their out-of-body experiences may turn out to be both measurable and veridical, together with claims that during their NDEs the blind can see, pose a wide range of questions to many areas of human understanding, not least to areas such as philosophy, psychology and theology. Central to many of these is the issue of *dualism*: the notion that human beings cannot simply be reduced to a psycho-somatic unity but may instead possess a soul or spirit in addition to a body. Moreover, any thoroughly documented claim that this additional component of the self can apparently survive the death of the body leads to questions in which religion, in particular, may be expected to express a key interest, raising, as it does, issues pertaining to the possibility and nature of an afterlife. Such is the obvious importance of this research to the current study that further discussion of its history will again be reserved for a future chapter.

The 1990s also began to see a small but significant number of studies that sought to explore the possible occurrence of NDEs in children. Foremost amongst these was *Closer to the Light*, an investigation of the experiences of twelve child NDErs which was co-researched by paediatrician Melvin Morse, anaesthetics expert Don Tyler, Director of Child Neurology at the University of Washington Dr Jerrold Milstein, and editor of the *Journal of Near-Death Studies* (*JN-DS*) Dr Bruce Greyson. The study, headed by Morse, sought to determine whether children as well as adults underwent NDEs, and if they did, whether these compared with the experiences of adults. Children's experiences, argued Morse, might be expected to be particularly interesting, given that they would not have had time to acquire the cultural baggage of adults and therefore might be expected to narrate correspondingly pure experiences of the NDE's core, perhaps permitting researchers to glimpse the NDE in its 'essence'.

Questionable as this final assertion of Morse's was, his overall conclusions were relatively uncontroversial, at least within the context of near-death research by the final decade of the twentieth century. As a result of an examination of the NDEs of twelve child subjects, Morse and the team concluded that the children in their study group certainly had experiences that conformed in essence and outline with those of adults (including comparable transformative effects) and that their experiences could not be explained by recourse to conventional neuroscientific knowledge. Concluding that 'The near-death experience remains a mystery', Morse was to go on throughout the 1990s to produce a number of other studies of NDEs and NDE-related episodes, including his own report into the transformative effects of NDEs upon NDErs which was to present a range of positive fruits comparable to those described in detail by Ring, Grey and Sutherland (Morse and Perry 1991: 226). Sutherland herself was to go on to produce a study of NDEs in children in her native Australia, *Children of the Light*; finding, like Morse, that children there report such experiences too (Sutherland 1995).

Whilst neuroscience emerged early on as offering potentially key insights into the nature of the NDE, other areas of psychology would also claim to usefully explore and explain them as years went by, not least those of analytical (Jungian) psychology. One early attempt in this regard was that of Catholic theologian John J. Heaney, whose study of theology and parapsychology, *The Sacred and the Psychic*, was to claim in the early 1980s that NDEs are, in fact, 'archetypal, symbolical experiences' (Heaney 1984: 143). Whilst conceding the point that the question of life after death is not principally solved by the study of NDEs, Heaney here suggested that the NDE may still provide a salvific function as an *archetype*: providing for NDErs a sense of peace and joy, a markedly spiritual reorientation, and an enhanced sense of charity and growth. Such an assertion, coming as it did before much attention was being paid to the transformative effects of NDEs, seems in retrospect remarkably prescient, and others in more recent years – most notably philosopher and Jungian analyst Michael Grosso – have added more detail to the assertion that the NDE may, in some sense, be seen as explicable in terms of analytical psychology's complex theory of archetypes. This has led, in turn, to discussion of the question of whether the NDE might be seen in terms of mythology: perhaps even constituting a 'modern myth of death'. We will explore this contention in more detail in chapter 7.

Present and future concerns

It is clear that by the closing years of the twentieth century the NDE had generated massive and complex debate. What, then, of its alleged discoverer? Where had the research of the founding father of near-death studies taken him by this time? Raymond Moody's contibutions to the field continued sporadically through the 1980s and into the 1990s. A third study of NDEs, *The Light Beyond*, produced with researcher and co-author Paul Perry in 1988, added little to the substance and content of his first two by now best-selling books. A temporary departure from the NDE in 1990 saw the publication of *Life Before Life*, also written with Paul Perry and exploring the possibility and therapeutic value of the exploration of alleged past lives via hypnotic regression. Its arguably most controversial aspect – apart from the possibility of whether or not regressive hypnosis *does* provide access to alleged past lives – was Moody's own description of the previous incarnations which he himself claimed to have lived through and unearthed thanks to the methods described in his book. Outlined in a chapter entitled 'The nine other lives of Raymond Moody', these included a 'proto-human' ('Definitely an arboreal creature, I lived high in the trees in the comfort of branches and leaves. I was surprisingly man-like, but not an ape'), a twelve-year-old African boy, an old but muscular boat-builder, an animal-skin-clad hunter of mammoths, a worker on a public works project 'near the dawn of civilization', a man about to be thrown into a lion's pit in ancient Rome, a nobleman from around the same place and era, and both a Middle Eastern artist and a later, female, artist (Moody and Perry 1990: 13–32).

Eyebrow-raising as this might have appeared for many who were impressed by the restrained, even understated tone of Moody's previous books, it was as nothing compared to his next book, *Reunions*, written with Paul Perry and published in 1993. Central to the book was the presentation of the results gained by Moody as a result of experiments with mirror-gazing, inspired by his own extended reading on subjects such as visions, dream incubation, hypnagogia and claims throughout history that apparitions might be conjured up by staring for long periods into mirrors. As a result of this reading and research, Moody constructed a psychomanteum at his home in Alabama: a darkened room containing only dim illumination with one wall consisting solely of a large mirror. As a result of studying the experiences of visitors to the psychomanteum (who were invited to spend long periods staring into the mirror), Moody claimed in *Reunions* to have been successful in finding a way of facilitating apparitions, effectively allowing subjects to see or even converse with deceased friends and relations whilst not needing to come near death in order to do so. Indeed, many of Moody's subjects in these experiments allegedly reported extremely vivid encounters with their departed loved ones, claiming on occasion even tactile sensations of holding, hugging and kissing.

As with *Life After Life* and its sequels, much of *Reunions* was given over to the presentation of subjects' testimonies, and the book included a number of extracts that described moving encounters with deceased loved ones as a result of the Alabama experiments. One of these, as described by a man who was apparently reunited with his mother, states:

> There is no doubt that the person I saw in the mirror was my mother! I don't know where she came from, but I am convinced that what I saw was the real person. She was looking out at me from the mirror. I couldn't tell what clothing she was wearing, but I could tell that she was in her later seventies, about the same age as she was when she died. However, she looked healthier and happier than she had at the end of her life.

Her lips didn't move, but she spoke to me, and I clearly heard what she had to say. She said, 'I'm fine,' and smiled happily.

I stayed as relaxed as I could and just looked at her. My hands were tingling, and I could feel my heart-beat pick up speed. Then I decided to talk to her. I said, 'It's good to see you again.' 'It's good to see you too,' she replied. That was it. She simply disappeared.

(Moody and Perry 1993: 89)

Another testimony-extract described an experience in which a woman's grandfather apparently *stepped out of* the mirror:

I was so happy to see him that I began to cry. Through the tears I could still see him in the mirror. Then he seemed to get closer and he must have come out of the mirror because the next thing I knew he was holding me and hugging me. It felt like he said something like, 'It's okay, don't cry.'

Before I knew it, he was gone. I can still feel his touch. I also feel warm, like someone has been hugging me.

It was great to see him again. He was happy and that's good. Even though I miss him, it's nice to know that he's happy where he is.

(Moody and Perry 1993: 93)

Moody's odyssey had by now taken him in some unusual and clearly controversial directions, and the reaction that *Reunions* provoked is not difficult to imagine. Michael Sabom, for example, reflecting on the psychomanteum experiments and his past acquaintance with the founder of near-death studies, was later to write in deeply critical tones of the directions in which Moody's research was taking him (Sabom 1998: 143–6). Indeed, by the end of the twentieth century, as future chapters will show, it would become clear that many of the 'pioneers' of what had now come to be called the 'NDE movement' had developed deep differences between themselves tinged with a degree of personal enmity, not least because of the differing conclusions they had drawn concerning the meaning of the NDE within the context of religion.

Regardless of any attempt to impose any rigorous theological interpretation upon the phenomenon, it is clear that by the first quarter-century of its history the NDE had already raised many questions that academic theologians might have been expected to have eagerly attempted to grapple with. At the very least, it might have been expected that the major religions themselves, particularly in the West, would have followed the developments outlined in this chapter keenly and with great interest. Surprisingly, in fact, this turned out not to be the case.

2

A DEAFENING SILENCE
Theology and the NDE

To Die is Gain

In 1975, at approximately the same time as Raymond Moody's *Life After Life* first saw publication, German Lutheran minister Johann Christophe Hampe was working on a similar study of his own that appeared, in English, in 1979 under the title *To Die is Gain*. Hampe's book remains little known by near-death researchers and theologians alike, yet it is interesting for a number of reasons. Appearing independently of Moody's early work, for example, it is unlike other early studies of NDEs in being clearly uninfluenced by *Life After Life*. Additionally, Hampe's study is largely based around experiences that had already been published by the time of *To Die is Gain*, many of them in psychic and paranormal publications and including experiences of victims of mountain climbing accidents and the proceedings of the *Society for Psychical Research*. Overall, however – and most importantly for the purposes of the current chapter – Hampe's study represents the very first attempt from within the context of theology to investigate the phenomenon that only later became known as the 'near-death experience'.

Introducing his book as the 'testimony of an encounter', and having been confronted by a large number of reports of dying people, Hampe at the outset declares himself 'surprised and bewildered' by their testimonies (Hampe 1979: xiii). In the preface, for example, he remarks that the accounts 'forced me to think afresh about what awaits us in the act of dying', and that as a consequence 'I was forced to surrender the notions I already had about dying – which I had thought were incontestable – in order to acquire new, clear, finer ones' (Hampe 1979: xiii). In fact, these discoveries appear to have carried deep implications for Hampe, prompting a 'conversion' comparable to Ring's experience of reading *Life After Life*. One of his final recommendations is that the 'discovery' of such experiences might be applied within the pastoral field: for the conclusions derived from studying such experiences have, he writes, deep implications for our understanding of death, and for our dealings with both the dying and the bereaved.

What, then, does Hampe present in this work that convinced him during its writing that dying is quite different from what he had previously thought it to be? Taking them very much at face value, Hampe claims to have discerned a commonality to his respondents' reports which suggests to him that something more real than a dream or hallucination is occurring and from which he concludes that such reports permit a view of death as seen 'from within'. Indeed, central to this work is Hampe's presentation *of* that commonality, with the delineation of a number of key, common elements being described in its longest chapter, 'Dying seen from within'. Overall, Hampe discerns three characteristics to the unfolding experience of dying in *To Die is Gain*: the 'escape of the "self"' (akin to an out-of-body experience), a 'life panorama' (akin to what later became known within near-death studies as the 'life review') and an 'expansion of the self' in dying which includes a form of enhanced consciousness: not at all, Hampe muses, the sort of thing we would expect as life is extinguished in the act of dying.

The *escape of the self* he describes as an awakening and intensification of consciousness in which the 'I' locates within the head and then departs the body. Throughout, he remarks, there is a calmness and an extreme state of mental lucidity, and having left the body the 'self' may even hover around it for a while before departing. Refraining from speculating upon possible psychological explanations for this out-of-body stage of dying, Hampe interprets what he is describing along *dualistic* lines. Indeed, for him, a form of body–soul dualism is very much suggested by such experiences, and this is a point that he will return to in later chapters in order to consider its possibility, its theological appropriateness and its implications.

Having left the body, he continues, the dying then move on to what he describes as a *panorama*; a form of judgement consisting of a 'remarkable review and selection' of important things which occurred during their lives (Hampe 1979: 50). That this experience is not a mere dream is discounted by a number of things. First, there is the all-important commonality underlying the reports. Second, there is the fact that something seems to be happening apart from the body – to which the observer appears to relate as a fascinated spectator. And third, there is the incredible vividness of the events being experienced: 'a closeness to reality which dreams never attain' (Hampe 1979: 51). In addition, there appears to be a sense in which the self engages in a form of *self-judgement* as the panorama unfolds. It also contains a 'liberating and redeeming character' enabling dying persons to 'work with it, and with the self that is realized in it', as the following extract illustrates:

> I saw all the scenes, not only as protagonist but as observer at the same time. It was . . . as if I had experienced the whole simultaneously from above and below, or from the side, or alternately from every side. I hovered above myself. I observed myself from every side and listened to what I was saying. My whole soul was a sensitive instrument, my conscience immediately weighed up my actions and judged me and what I did.
>
> (Hampe 1979: 60)

Throughout the experience, Hampe notes, there is a persistent *expansion of the Self* that may include unusual perceptions such as vivid colours, lights, music and communication with unseen presences. Sometimes tunnels are reported, and a kind of border frequently separates this world from the next. Again, Hampe illustrates this phase of the experience with a rich range of testimony-extracts, of which the following is typical:

> I was moving at high speed towards a net of great luminosity. The strands and knots where the luminous lines intersected were vibrating with tremendous cold energy. The grid appeared as a barrier that I did not want to move through, and for a brief moment my speed

appeared to slow down. Then I was in the grid. The instant I made contact with it, the vibrant luminosity increased to a blinding intensity which drained, absorbed and transformed me at the same time. There was no pain. The sensation was neither pleasant nor unpleasant but completely consuming. . . .

(Hampe 1979: 65)

Throughout, the author shows himself aware of historical parallels to the events he is describing. As regards the escape of the self from the body, for example, he cites the concept of translation as found within certain medieval writings, and he quotes at length from the experience of the Irish abbot Furseus who fell ill, was taken to be dead, and was nearly buried before reviving with a tale of a journey to another realm complete with angels and menacing demons. As regards the 'light', Hampe cites the *Tibetan Book of the Dead* for comparison. The closest parallel, however, he discerns in the experiences of Christian mystics. Thus, he writes:

The very loss of what we call in everyday life 'complete consciousness' seems to make possible the experience of escape or 'exit', the panorama, and the expansion. That corresponds to the experiences of all the mystics: the superconsciousness of the unity of the spirit that hovers protectively round us and receives us can only begin when the soul, in the words of John of the Cross, no longer 'clings to created things' or relies on its own strength out of habit and inclination.

(Hampe 1979: 83)

In view of all of this, he concludes that dying may indeed be quite different from what we had supposed it to be, but not so different that we cannot discover interesting and comparable historical and cross-cultural parallels to it.

In common with other researchers, Hampe notes that the experience ends with a return to the body and hence a return to life. What is unusual here, however, is Hampe's description of how the return occurs. For unlike virtually anybody else who has uncovered such testimonies, Hampe maintains that the dying 'return' to their bodies via a *reversal* of the process by which they left: for example, if they journeyed to the 'superconscious' realm through a tunnel, they return back through it. Thus, of one respondent he writes: 'once more he experiences night, the black tunnel, and then what we call waking up' (Hampe 1979: 90). Further, and anticipating later research, Hampe draws attention to the transformative effects of such experiences and the possible therapeutic application of his discoveries, devoting a chapter to ways in which exposure to such experiences may have beneficial results in the fields of medicine, pastoral counselling, and for the clergy generally. For the discovery that death may not be the end leads logically, for him, to the conclusion that it is no longer to be anticipated with fear and dread but actually as a form of *gain*. In this vein, he writes:

> If dying is not oppression, my knowledge that I am going to die will no longer oppress me. Instead of making me feel melancholy it will expand and deepen me . . . My loneliness is broken because these experiences strengthen my belief in the continuance of an indestructible core in me and my fellow men.
>
> (Hampe 1979: 134–5)

Talk of an 'indestructible core' raises the question of dualism and its theological and philosophical possibility and implications. Hampe, as a philosopher and theologian, is well aware of this, and of what is at stake in affirming that experiences such as those he has presented actually reinforce arguments for it. He does not struggle, however, to concede that such experiences support the argument for distinguishing mortal flesh from eternal soul. Thus, he writes, 'dying can be equated with entry into the kingdom in which we can suffer no pain, because the organ through which the soul can experience pain has remained behind' (Hampe 1979: 99–100). In dying, therefore, 'the self leaves the body, [and] sees the body lying beneath it like an empty shell or a discarded dress' (Hampe 1979: 102). How might this be reconciled with the Christian notion that life after death comes by way of a final *bodily* resurrection on the last day? Hampe appears to see resolution of this issue as relatively unproblematic, for life itself is possible, he argues, only because the body and the soul coexist, like an organ and an organist who are both needed to operate together if music is to be played. Whilst, he asserts, we must be careful not to create dogmas out of our discovery of what the dying experience, at the same time such experiences may be instrumental in correcting some unhelpful or even incorrect notions about what dying actually consists of: including the notion that at death the self simply ceases to exist. Indeed, the idea of death as extinction – even temporary extinction – he describes as something which both paralyses faith and stands 'in contradiction to observations I have made and convictions I have gained in other fields' (Hampe 1979: 110). Although he does not specify what these observations made in other fields might be, it would be reasonable to surmise that his encounters with the testimonies of the dying loom large. Crucially, however, Hampe also argues that the hypothesis 'cannot be harmonised with important New Testament statements either' (Hampe 1979: 110). Indeed, for him, the New Testament teaches continued fellowship with God after death, a contention reinforced by the reports he has discovered from the dying and the nearly dead.

Hampe's book constitutes the first of a very small number of specific studies to have emerged from the theological world dedicated as a specific response to the unusual claims of those such as NDErs. It is perhaps surprising, therefore, that it should be so infrequently encountered in existing literature on the NDE. For it is clear that it contains a number of virtues which might be expected to be of interest to anybody concerned to take such experiences seriously, especially theologians and philosophers. Proceeding from a very different set of testimonies, working independently of the early American near-death researchers and writing from within a very different context for a very different audience, Hampe manages in *To Die is Gain* to replicate many of the findings of Moody and others: particularly as regards his discovery of a degree of commonality across reports, the characteristics of a possible core experience, and the fact that such experiences appear to be transformative. To be sure, he does *not* detect certain features of the model NDEs produced by his American counterparts: there are no reports of Moody's buzzing, ringing noise, for example, and few of Hampe's respondents appear to encounter deceased relatives. Nonetheless, many if not most of the characteristics of the American researchers' early models *are* present: including the sensation of being out of body, the subjective realness of the experience as compared with mere dreams or imagination, the expansion of consciousness, the tunnel, light, the life review and the ensuing transformation in lifestyle subsequent to the experience.

However, its usefulness as a form of early control study is not the only merit of Hampe's unjustly neglected work; it is also clear that he was concerned at the outset of the modern era of interest in various aspects of the NDE to explore the theological implications of the experiences reported by those near death. Hampe was the first, therefore, to consider the implications of such experiences for our evaluation of dualism, the first to consider such experiences in detail in the light of Biblical teaching, the first to suggest that such experiences may be used therapeutically with the dying and the bereaved, and the first to posit the possibility that such experiences may have enormous implications for theologians more generally grappling with the problem of the meaning of death. Given all of these key insights into the significance of 'dying seen from within' for those working within the fields of theology and religious studies, it might reasonably have been expected that Hampe's early study would be quickly followed by others. This, however, would not turn out to be the case.

A deafening silence?

It is tempting to speculate as to why. Perhaps theologians early on simply took it as read that such experiences were to be expected at or near the point of death and therefore busied themselves with other things. Conversely, it may be that such lack of interest actually masks a deeper distrust on the part of most or all academics towards what are seen to be paranormal claims. Carol Zaleski has written that theologians in fact feel *safer* when treating claims of journeys to other worlds as metaphors or literary motifs rather than as actual journeys and that as a consequence they 'attenuate the visionary virus until it is so weak that it produces immunity instead of contagion' (Zaleski 1987: 184). In fact, theology and religious studies are in an unusual position as regards this whole area, given that there is considerable overlap between many religious claims and those made by parapsychologists. Indeed, sometimes it is difficult to decide where, exactly, a particular phenomenon should be located. Does the examination of claims to miraculous healing, for example, belong to the domain of theology or parapsychology? Is an NDE to be properly defined as a *religious* experience or as a paranormal one? And what are the implications of the decisions made over such issues for the ways in which such claims are approached?

Up to a point, the caution shown by academics regarding the acceptance and exploration of paranormal claims *might* be justified by the fact that controversy rages amongst scholars as to the existence of replicable and reliable experimental proof for a wide range of claimed phenomena such as ESP, telekinesis, and the ability to 'channel' information from beyond the grave.[1] And as this study will later demonstrate, even seemingly hard cases which promise to prove the existence of phenomena such as extrasensory perception at or near the point of death are in many ways flawed, requiring careful examination and qualification rather than simple and straightforward acceptance. Yet, this being said, it is by no means certain that *all* such claims may turn out to be found wanting after investigation. In fact, theology's silence becomes all the more puzzling when we consider the possibility of intriguing relationships between a wide range of phenomena such as pre-cognition and prophecy, poltergeist manifestations and demon possession, and the study of apparitions and any discussion of the resurrection of Jesus.

In the event, Hampe's early study of NDE-like claims was not followed by a succession of further theological studies of the phenomenon. In fact, the one acknowledged theologian on the editorial board of the *Journal of Near-Death Studies*, Canon Michael Perry, has recently remarked that there has been a 'deafening silence' from within theology regarding the interpretation, meaning and significance of the NDE.[2] One consequence of this has been that whilst in the previous chapter it was possible to present the NDE's history as an evolving history, with later work building on earlier research and clusters of different research areas developing and taking near-death studies through various phases, no such comparable history can be written in *this* chapter concerning theology's engagement with the NDE. Neither theologians nor philosophers have engaged at any length in discussion with each other over the phenomenon, and there are only a very few theologians who have evolved theories designed to explore the NDE in the light of recent discoveries about its nature and significance: possibly because very few theologians have shown any awareness of these discoveries. In fact, as we shall see, far from constituting any systematic or dynamic engagement with NDEs, theology's few responses to them often stand alone, like a series of isolated islands showing little or no evidence of pattern, development or, indeed, history.

Hans Kung: *Eternal Life?*

In 1982, for example, renowned German scholar Hans Kung attempted a theological response to what had by now come to be known as the NDE. Unlike Hampe, Kung did not devote an entire book to the subject, but sought instead to locate it within the context of a much wider theological study of the fact, history and meaning of death. The study, *Ewiges Leben? – Eternal Life? –* attempts, in fact, to combine a study of NDEs with a study of other aspects of death and dying including existential and psycho-analytical approaches to death, models of death and the afterlife within the world's religions, the meaning of resurrection, difficulties in understanding the resurrection of Jesus, and issues to do with euthanasia and eschatology.

Kung begins his chapter-long treatment of the NDE in *Eternal Life?* by providing his readers with a brief overview of the research to which he is responding. By 1982, a handful of studies into the NDE already existed, and Kung shows himself familiar with the work of Moody in the United States, together with that of his own compatriot Hampe. What Kung seeks in the light of such research is a critical evaluation of the claims being made, but he stresses at the outset that such an evaluation will limit itself to the 'decisive question' of whether or not the NDE genuinely qualifies as proof for and evidence of life after death. It is unclear why Kung limits himself to this one issue to the exclusion of all others that may be of interest to theology generally. After all, later in his book, he will move beyond his core concern of the possibility of life after death to embrace issues at the heart of medical ethics and elsewhere. Nonetheless, it is with the *strength* of NDE claims as evidence that NDErs have had 'a view of the other side' that Kung is primarily and solely concerned.

To begin with, he quickly establishes that NDEs provide better potential empirical evidence for life after death than do parapsychological research in general and the evidence from spiritualism in particular. Indeed, it is apparent early on that Kung is a theologian who has reservations about paranormal claims. Thus, whilst he writes that parapsychological research 'should not be dismissed *a priori* as nonsense', he quickly adds that 'The frontiers . . . between serious science and charlatanry are fluid, particularly in the field of parapsychology' (Kung 1984: 26). In the case of spiritualism, he adds, caution is particularly advised, for

> understandable as is the desire to provide psychological or at least parapsychological support for a belief in life after death, the attempt to base this belief on such an insecure, unverified and perhaps unverifiable empirical foundation produces at best a false security instead of a serious certainty.
>
> (Kung 1984: 27)

Thus we are thrown back on the evidence from NDEs. Kung finds it plainly undeniable that such experiences take place. What is crucial for him, however, is how such experiences should be correctly *interpreted*. First, he notes that phenomena apparently similar to NDEs occur in other 'peculiar' mental states which are not connected with any kind of death or near-death episode; they occur in the midst of life and are themselves never presented as evidence for any kind of immortality. Of these, he writes, 'If the phenomena associated with drugs, narcosis, suggestion, brain-operations, etc, cannot be understood as evidence of a "hereafter", why can the phenomena connected with experiences of resuscitated people be so understood?' (Kung 1984: 28). Then, he notes, there is the possibility that medical science will one day explain phenomena such as NDEs, further weakening the claim that they 'prove' life after death. However, the argument upon which Kung's analysis chiefly rests is that NDEs cannot be said to provide proof of immortality because no resuscitated NDEr was ever genuinely dead. In this context, he draws a careful distinction between *clinical death* (the absence of any vital signs associated with life such as breathing and heartbeat) and *biological death* (the irrevocable and permanent loss of brain function). Even Raymond Moody, he argues, is forced to concede that none of his respondents were really dead in the biological sense, quoting Moody's admission that 'Obviously, by this definition, none of my cases would qualify [as instances of biological death] since they all involved resuscitation' (Moody 1975: 150). Indeed, the necessity not to blur the distinction between clinical and biological death is for Kung the 'crucial factor'. In this vein, he writes:

> The persons once dangerously ill, examined by Moody and now by many others, perhaps experienced *dying*, but certainly not *death*. Consequently, dying and death must be clearly distinguished. Dying means the physico-psychological events immediately preceding death, which are irrevocably halted with the advent of death. Dying then is the way, death the 'destination'. And none of these investigated had reached this 'destination'.
> (Kung 1984: 33; emphasis in the original)

This recognition, in turn, leads to the central focus of Kung's response, which is that far from being evidence of what awaits us on the other side of the grave, the experiences collected by Moody and his co-researchers were 'experiences of people very close to real death, who mistakenly thought they were dying, but eventually did not die'. As a result, he argues, 'Close as they were to the threshold of death, they never passed over it' (Kung 1984: 33). All of this, of course, has implications for the theologian engaged in any quest to answer the question as to whether or not NDEs qualify as proof of life after death. Kung raises the question, and answers it emphatically:

> What then do these experiences of dying imply for life after death? To put it briefly, nothing! For I regard it as a duty of theological truthfulness to answer clearly that experiences of this kind prove nothing about a possible

life after death: it is a question here of the last five minutes *before* death and not of an eternal life *after* death.

(Kung 1984: 33–4; emphasis in the original)

It follows from this recognition, therefore, that:

> These passing minutes do not settle the question of where the dying person goes: into non-being or into new being . . . Moody and numerous like-minded people deserve respect when, as Christians, they advocate belief in an eternal life. But, considered more closely, their arguments are *ad rem*, they are inadequate and refer only to the present time and not to eternity. They assume what they hope, if not strictly to prove, at least to suggest. But all the phenomena of light, however striking, do not amount to a proof or even to an indication of an entry into a bright eternal light. . . .

(Kung 1984: 34)

Thus, it would appear that Kung might see fit to dismiss the whole area of near-death study as a waste of time. This is not, however, exactly the case, for he still sees the NDE debate as opening up the question of the possibility of eternal life beyond the confines of religion and theology and into the arena of the medical profession. Furthermore, these experiences of dying still hold out the promise that the very last stages of our lives may not be as fearful as we might have thought. To this extent, therefore, near-death research has proved both informative and useful. Overall, however, Kung stresses that 'the theologian in particular must be careful not to indulge in wishful thinking, must avoid a hasty appropriation of medical conclusions for theological purposes and must judge the phenomena described with the utmost caution and solicitude' (Kung 1984: 25). Such an 'objective analysis', for Kung, yields no evidence that in the NDE we find data that theology must recognize as proof of life after death.

These conclusions are forceful and stand in stark contrast to those of Hampe in several obvious respects. It is somewhat disappointing, however, that Kung's study confines itself to one question, that of the possibility of the NDE as evidence for belief in eternal life, when so many other questions and issues remain unexamined. Thus, for example, Kung attempts no cross-cultural or historical comparison of similar reports across religions. Neither does he attempt to explore some of the epistemological complexities involved in assessing the claims of NDErs that their reports were real. Neither does he attempt to discuss what the broad popular interest in NDEs – even in 1982 – might be said to *mean*. Similarly ignored is the existence of the apparent common core to such reports, and the implications of such for any attempt to interpret the overall meaning of the phenomenon. Overall, in fact, Kung's analysis reveals a superficiality and a reluctance to ask questions at the very point at which many of the really interesting questions *start*.

Nonetheless, in the same way that Hampe's study began to raise questions that theology and philosophy might need to consider in order to address the NDE, Kung's study clearly succeeds in addressing the important questions of what death is, where it begins and ends, and whether in NDErs' testimonies we are being afforded glimpses of what happens after death or merely whilst we die. All of these are obviously crucial considerations within any serious theological response to the phenomenon. And of the interesting and pertinent questions neglected by Kung, some at least were to be taken up by theologians in other more comprehensive and less reductive responses.

Paul Badham: *Immortality or Extinction?*

At approximately the same time as Kung's *Eternal Life* entered its original German publication, British theologians Paul and Linda Badham published *Immortality or Extinction?*, a detailed examination of the arguments both for and against human immortality, containing a theological appraisal of NDEs. In this work, they raise a number of theological and philosophical issues proceeding from their engagement with the NDE, some of which we have already encountered. Echoing Kung, for example, they contend that whilst the occurrence of such experiences is not really in doubt, their correct *interpretation* is a crucial, central, issue, and whilst they contend that there is no *absolutely* unambiguous evidence that NDErs were really dead, nonetheless they conclude that:

> Near-Death Experiences are . . . of the utmost importance
> to research in life after death, for the evidential features
> in the reports made by resuscitated persons about their
> supposed observations provide some of the strongest
> grounds for supposing that the separation of the self from
> the body is possible.
>
> (Badham and Badham 1982: 78)

Clearly, therefore, the Badhams in this work detect in the evidence
from NDEs at least *possible* grounds for belief in some form
of body–soul dualism. Indeed, elsewhere in *Immortality or
Extinction?* this interpretation is clear and unambiguous, leading
the authors to the conclusion that during an NDE 'what appears
to happen is that the soul leaves the body and begins to move
on to another mode of existence' (Badham and Badham 1982:
89). Indeed, as we shall shortly see, in recent years Paul Badham
has made an appeal for a large-scale research project that would
put such a far-reaching contention beyond reasonable doubt.

Elsewhere in their study the authors raise other important issues
with which we are by now familiar. Of these, one crucial and
central area of particular interest concerns the possibility that a
cross-cultural common core may underlie the varieties of reported
NDEs. In this context, the study addresses the interesting puzzle
of why, if such a core should exist, the otherworldly figures
encountered by NDErs should correspond so closely with their
cultural and religious expectations and traditions: Christians
see Christ, for example, but never figures from other religious
traditions. In attempting to account for this, the authors begin by
drawing on a form of projection theory, asserting that:

> Some element of projection must . . . be present, for the
> percipients often claim to see not only departed relatives
> and friends, but also religious figures from their own
> particular traditions. Evangelicals often 'see' Jesus,
> Catholics 'see' Mary, saints or angels, whilst Hindus 'see'
> Yama, the god of death or other Hindu deities and atheists
> simply talk of a 'being of light'.
>
> (Badham and Badham 1982: 86)

Nonetheless, they recognize that this observation needs to be consistent with the fact that a number of common stages or features *do* seem to exist within NDEs, despite the obviously culture-specific features that occur in all testimonies, and they solve this problem in much the same way as we have seen Moody and the other near-death researchers do: by positing a common core which appears to be consistent yet culturally coloured and shaped when it appears in testimony. Thus, in an important conclusion, they assert that

> whatever 'entity' is seen it appears to fulfil a similar role and is evidently an important part of many near-death experiences. If there is any sense in talking of 'the religious experience of mankind' one might perhaps expect that any manifestation of the Divine presence would be interpreted within the religious and cultural tradition of the percipient.
>
> (Badham and Badham 1982: 86)

Clearly, this set of conclusions broadly matches Moody's observation in *Life After Life* that the 'being of light' remains a constant 'core' figure throughout NDEs, and that

> whilst the . . . description of the being of light is utterly invariable, the identification of the being varies from individual to individual and seems to be largely a function of the religious background, training, or beliefs of the person involved.
>
> (Moody 1975: 59)

What might serve to test this hypothesis would be a thoroughly cross-cultural comparison of NDE accounts: both geographical and historical. Once again, it might be expected that theology and religious studies would play a crucial part in the production of this sort of study, heir, as they are, to a wealth of 'otherworldly journey' narratives from within a rich range of religious traditions. Only to a limited extent has this been the case, although in a recent and important paper Paul Badham (1997) has himself attempted to locate and evaluate the NDE within the context of a range of comparable historical, Christian and non-Christian accounts, ranging from St Paul and St John of the Cross to Tibetan and Japanese Buddhism. He then poses the question as to whether such experiences – the NDE included – provide a substantial experiential basis for life after death. As with his position in *Immortality or Extinction?* Badham answers this question with an affirmative.

In the paper, he is at pains to contrast the clarity and profundity of NDErs' reports with the apparently diffuse and vague accounts of religious experience which exist elsewhere, leading him to the conclusion that the NDE 'shares many of the characteristics of the deepest religious experiences known to humanity, and yet through modern resuscitation techniques has become available to hundreds and thousands of ordinary people' (Badham 1997: 5). Thus, for Badham, modern techniques of bringing persons back from the dead have essentially democratized experiences that once happened only to a privileged few. In fact, he suggests that no fewer than 25,000 such accounts, which involve a 'series of religious experiences of a mystical type including "encounters" with a bright light sometimes perceived in personal terms and identified with a figure from the percipients' own religious traditions' have now been reported all over the world. Echoing contentions already reached in *Immortality or Extinction?*, he concludes that 'The pattern of experiencing appears to be common across religious traditions, cultures and world-views though naturally the terminology used in the religious descriptions is culture specific' (Badham 1997: 5).

In support of this final contention, he compares contemporary NDE reports with a range of comparable, cross-cultural reports, citing studies of shamanism, cross-cultural research into out-of-body experiences in primitive cultures, St Paul's boast in 2 Corinthians 12:1–5 of 'A Christian man who . . . was caught up into paradise, and heard words so secret that human lips may not repeat them', and many claims of otherworldly journeys from within Pure Land Buddhism and the *Tibetan Book of the Dead*. In cases like these, he notes, some kind of common core is either being asserted or can be detected. Of the *Tibetan Book of the Dead*, for example, Badham notes the contention, clearly supportive of his own epistemological position, that 'The Dharmakaya (The Divine Being) of clear light will appear [to the newly-dead] in what ever shape will benefit all beings' and he quotes the commentary of Lama Kazi Dawa-Samdup on this verse which, discussing the *identity* of the light, states that:

> To appeal to a Shaivite devotee, the form of Shiva is assumed; to a Buddhist the form of the Buddha Shakya Muni; to a Christian, the form of Jesus; to a Muslim the form of the Prophet; and so for other religious devotees, and for all manner and conditions of mankind a form appropriate to the occasion.
> (Evans-Wentz 1957: 98, quoted in Badham 1997: 11)

Having introduced these interesting historical and cross-cultural narratives, Badham then turns to some contemporary studies of NDEs – some of which we have already noted – which again appear to support the hypothesis that within NDEs 'the Reality glimpsed was of more universal significance than simply to one's inherited tradition' (Fenwick and Fenwick 1995: 11). Once again, therefore, the existence of some sort of common cross-cultural religious or spiritual core experience disclosed in NDEs is stressed.

Overall, Badham views the recent upsurge of reports of NDEs as important to a revitalizing of both belief in God and the hope for a future life. In this respect, it is timely that our increased abilities to revive those who have experienced both should come at a time and within a context where, as he admits, 'religious experiencing in its classic form does not appear to be anything like as prevalent as it once was'. Into such a context of spiritual aridity, Badham suggests that 'the experiential foundation for belief in a future life' may derive 'both from religious experience of a relationship with God, and from the reports of people who, near the frontier of death, believe they have caught a glimpse of a life beyond' (Badham 1997: 12). From his paper overall, it is clear that he believes that the latter set of claimed experiences have a particular and fundamental role to play in reviving such belief.

Yet there are problems with this position, and Badham fully acknowledges these. For example, he acknowledges that experiences such as NDEs do not necessarily have an impact which is 'epistemically coercive', even for experiencers. In this regard, he cites a highly unusual NDE undergone by philosopher A.J. Ayer, which, vivid though it was, failed to draw from him any response greater than the observation that 'my recent experiences have slightly weakened my conviction that my genuine death . . . will be the end of me, though I continue to hope that it will' (Badham 1997: 13) In addition, Badham admits that the NDE possesses the same weakness as any other claimed variety of religious experience as regards its ability to provide actual *proof* of the reality of some sort of transcendence, for, as with 'all religious experiences, what convinces the percipient does not necessarily influence the thinking of one who is merely told of another's experience' (Badham 1997: 12). Indeed, as he freely admits, all we possess are 'subjective reports' (Badham 1997: 13). These, however, we *do* have in abundance. Thus it is that at the end of his paper Badham makes some recommendations as to the directions which *future* research might take, in order to put the hope for belief in a future life disclosed by NDEs onto a more epistemologically persuasive footing. First, he appeals for a worldwide comparison of the many thousands of NDE reports currently on file.

> There is certainly value in such a project . . . if it could be totally established that thousands of people from totally disparate cultures, world-views and backgrounds have all reported a common set of experiences near the point of death . . . this does at least provide some grounds for supposing that this might be what happens at that point.
> (Badham 1997: 13)

However, this being said, Badham also shows himself aware of the problematical nature of what is at stake in taking NDEs at face value as proof that the soul survives the death of the body. Indeed, he sees standing in opposition to this position that 'mass of evidence that human consciousness cannot possibly subsist except within a functioning physical brain' (Badham 1997: 13). In order to decide this one way or the other, therefore, Badham proposes that some kind of test might be devised in order to assess the accuracy of perceptions claimed as evidence that during NDEs 'something' leaves the body. Thus, he suggests, a 'prospective survey could be done in hospital contexts where it could be established on a non-anecdotal basis whether or not correct observation actually took place that could not be accounted for by any "natural" means' (Badham 1997: 14). To this end, he proposes the 'placing of objects in cardiac wards and casualty units which could only be seen and described by an agent actually looking down from the ceiling'. In this way, 'if a number of cases of correct "seeing" could be proven beyond dispute, the principle that consciousness can exist outside the body would have been established, and one roadblock across the path of belief in immortality would be removed' (Badham 1997: 13). To date, no such study has definitively established what Badham seeks to establish in the way he seeks to establish it: even with subjects who, whilst not near death, claim the ability to detach part of themselves and to 'remote view' targets placed at a distance from them.[3] However, his is clearly a sensible and eminently possible experiment, given the existence of a sufficient number of NDEs within a set period at a given, chosen, location, and certainly Badham's conclusions and suggestions for future research are far-reaching. We are reminded yet again of the ongoing quest to find a common core to NDE reports, and the production of a range of cross-cultural parallels to the NDE clearly moves this quest in fresh and fruitful directions. In his desire to see in historical and cross-cultural studies of otherworldly journeys evidence of such a common core, however, he fails to fully consider the complexity of processes such as intertextuality and cultural dissemination: processes which might at least offer plausible explanations of how reports of such 'journeys' may contain common themes which extend across cultural and historical boundaries. It might be expected that such hypotheses would be deserving of detailed discussion within any study which seeks to account for common features across a range of testimony-driven experiential claims, NDEs amongst them.

Also lacking in Badham's discussion of the evidence for such a core is a full acknowledgement of a host of *philosophical* questions surrounding its existence or even its very possibility. Positing a common core to any kind of religious experience requires an epistemological caution and, at least, a recognition of the many objections to it which have been voiced in recent years from within philosophy and the philosophy of religion. Such recognitions loom large in some of the theological responses to the NDE which remain for us to consider in this chapter, however, and examination of these may enable us to create a fuller theological response to the phenomenon than has so far emerged. To these therefore we now turn.

I.P. Couliano: *Out of this World?*

One outstanding attempt made within the recent era of near-death studies to locate the NDE within the context of otherworld journey narratives globally and historically has been that produced by the late and acclaimed historian of religious thought, I.P. Couliano of the University of Chicago. His detailed history of such tales, *Out of this World: Otherworldly Journeys from Gilgamesh to Albert Einstein*, compares the NDE with a range of ecstatic visionary experiences. His expressed aim is to provide a cross-cultural historical survey of journeys to other realms reported throughout the world's religions and philosophies (including 'journeys' to heaven, hell and other planets) and to encompass claims from out-of-body and near-death experiences. The result is a rich descriptive and phenomenological presentation, which, whilst not designed chiefly as a comparative survey, nonetheless draws conclusions regarding possible parallels between such travellers' tales and concludes with some possible reasons for these (Couliano 1991).

Couliano acknowledges that there has been a recent upsurge of interest in such reports, manifesting itself in a widespread popular interest in NDEs. Discussing the reasons for this, he suggests that developments in science, including recent discoveries in physics and mathematics, have opened up the possibility for many that 'this visible universe is only a convention based on our perception' and have therefore opened the door to a renewed interest in mystical ways of gaining knowledge, including knowledge of other worlds (Couliano 1991: 12). Most of his study is made up of a descriptive analysis of the other worlds portrayed within otherworldly journey narration across a very broad range of cultural traditions and shows convincingly that the upsurge of contemporary interest in such reports is simply part of a vast and complex matrix of existing narratives and traditions. The result is a recognition that otherworldly journeys are reported in virtually every variety of human cultural, religious and philosophical tradition known to us: from palaeolithic times through to the present day. No overview of Couliano's survey is adequate to do justice to this contention – which is soundly supported throughout – but we may nonetheless take time here to examine some of the most detailed and interesting accounts which suggest analogues to certain modern NDE reports.

Couliano lists in detail all of the historical narratives with which, as we have already seen, Badham has sought to compare the NDE. In *Out of this World*, however, he broadens the range of the investigation considerably. Thus, for example, he shows an especial interest in shamanism, and particularly in the experiences of shamanic initiates, who undergo 'a powerful depression and a shocking near-death experience' before obtaining their powers (Couliano 1991: 41). He traces the experiences of ecstatics in ancient Iran and later Persian traditions, including that of one Viraz, who died in 276, and whose experiences are related in *The Book of Arda Viraz*. In this extended narrative, the righteous Viraz is urged to drink a potion to release his soul from his body in order to test the veracity of Zoroastrianism. At first he does not want to, but upon the urging of the priests he does so, having made a will and having settled all of his affairs to the satisfaction of his sister-wives. Finally performing the rites of the dead and drinking the potion, Viraz promptly dies for seven days before returning to life with a remarkably complex tale of a journey both to a heavenly and to a hellish realm, and bringing greetings from a range of figures which he had encountered there, including Ohrmazd, the archangels and Zarathustra. After the manner of one of Moody's respondents relating a tale from a hospital bed, Viraz quickly relates his journey to a scribe, including its onset, wherein, having 'died', he stays by his body for a while, 'rejoicing in its liberation and singing Avestan hymns of praise to Ohrmazd'. Finally moving on, Viraz faces a form of judgement, going from thence to a tour of the four levels of heaven and the four levels of hell, in the former ascending as high as the highest heaven and encountering 'the endless light, where the paradise of Ohrmazd is located'. Finally, he meets Ohrmazd, who commands the gods Srosh and Adur to show him the blissful rewards of the good and the dreadful punishments of the wicked in the lowest hell (Couliano 1991: 107–13).

Moving on, Couliano turns his attention to a very different context and set of cultural narratives: those of a number of celebrated Greek philosophers and medicine men. Plato's myth of Er, recounted in Book Ten of the *Republic* (and recognized, albeit briefly, as a possible parallel to the NDE in *Life After Life*), is given detailed attention, but it is a number of lesser-known parallels from within this context which are especially interesting, including the experience of Aridaeus of Soli, as related by Plutarch. According to Plutarch, as recorded in his *De sera numinis vindicta*, Aridaeus

> fell from a certain height upon the nape of his neck and died . . . The third day he was carried away to be buried when he came back to himself and rapidly recovered, after which he underwent a complete change in his lifestyle. The Cicilians cannot recall anyone more correct in his promises, more pious toward the gods, more terrible for his enemies and more reliable for his friends.
>
> (Couliano 1991: 149)

Indeed, so changed by the experience in his habits and behaviour is Aridaeus that he quickly acquires a new name, and is henceforth known as Thespesius, meaning 'divine' or 'wonderful'.

What, then, was the nature of the experience that changed Aridaeus into Thespesius? Having 'died', Aridaeus's soul apparently exits his body through his head. After an initial bout of shock in finding himself still alive but transformed, Aridaeus begins to enjoy his new state, in which sight and hearing are regained, along with other powers which appear to represent an improvement on those which he possessed whilst in his physical body. Thus, for example, he can now see around him on all sides seemingly effortlessly. His soul is 'Open like a single eye'; it can now 'see around in all directions at once' and can even 'move in all directions easily and quickly' (Couliano 1991: 150). In his new state, Aridaeus can also see the souls of the newly dead rising from the earth, some easily and directly but others – mostly frightened – following a more disordered course. At this point, he sees the soul of a deceased relative who had died young, and who calls him by his new name. He then undergoes a complex sequence of experiences in which he learns of the punishment of the wicked and the mechanism by which souls are reborn to live again. At the end of his experience, Aridaeus rejoins his body, revives and lives again.

Probably because his main objective is a phenomenological study of otherworldly journey narratives rather than a comparative one, Couliano does not draw attention to the remarkable features that this episode has in common with modern NDE testimonies. Like Aridaeus's account, however, many contemporary NDE narratives contain features in which NDErs claim enhancement of perceptual skills, and the ability to move freely in any direction they please. Indeed, as we will see in a later chapter, Kenneth Ring has recently made much of such reports in his attempts to claim that NDEs actually represent *new ways* of seeing and knowing, which bypass the conventional senses and which existing scientific and biological paradigms are inadequate to explain. Again like many contemporary NDErs, Aridaeus encounters and communicates with deceased relatives: one of a very small number of pre-modern accounts presented by Couliano that includes such a contemporary motif. Indeed, it is virtually the only one in his book containing this feature. Like many contemporary reports, Plutarch puts emphasis on Aridaeus's transformation as a result of his experience, echoing, as we have already seen, the second wave of NDE studies that has drawn considerable and consistent attention to this motif. Indeed, it is arguably in this extended account in Plutarch that we encounter one of the most striking historical parallels to the modern NDE.

There are, however, further accounts of otherworldly journey narration to which Couliano draws detailed attention. He notes the dualism expressed in Gnosticism, with its accounts of the soul's journeyings through the spheres to other planets. He also notes the large volume of otherworldly journey narratives that exist from the Early Middle Ages, which he dubs 'The apogee of otherworldly journeys'. One particularly interesting text cited from this period is that of Gregory the Great, entitled *Dialogues About the Lives and Miracles of the Italian Fathers* (Couliano 1991: 215). This contains no fewer than three NDE-like reports, with two apparently interwoven. Here, an unnamed soldier at the point of death undergoes a vision of the unfortunate state of one Stephen, who had himself been granted a vision of hell some three years prior but had not repented. The soldier witnesses a bridge over a smoky, smelly river, which leads to 'pleasant green meadows full of sweet flowers'. Whilst the bridge widens to let the righteous pass, it narrows when the wicked try to cross. Indeed, in this context it is notable that, unlike, say, the tunnel or passageway in modern NDE accounts, the bridge here functions not as a simple mode of access to the 'other side' but as a form of judgement which actually determines fitness for admittance into it. The soldier witnesses Stephen on the bridge. His sins nearly condemn him, and he nearly falls off, but at the last minute good angels see him and rescue him (Couliano 1991: 215–16). Couliano also records the chronicles of Bede of Tours (672–735), who himself features a number of near-death-like experiences in his writings (Couliano 1991: 216). Such accounts loom large – and are given concentrated treatment – in the work of theologian Carol Zaleski, about whom we shall shortly have something to say. We thus reserve further discussion of medieval otherworldly journey narratives for later in the chapter.

It will have become apparent, even from this small summary of his study, that Couliano does much to contribute to any attempt at a large-scale cross-cultural and historical survey of NDE literature of the sort proposed by Paul Badham. As his study is primarily descriptive, Couliano freely admits that he draws no particular overall conclusions. One exception to this, however, is his outline attempt at discerning some sort of commonality beneath the rich range of reported features contained within his accounts. One constantly recurring motif, for example, appears to be the belief in the existence and ability of a 'free soul' to survive the death of the body as some sort of ghost. It is also clearly the case that virtually all such reports assert that, under certain conditions, this soul or ghost can separate from the body and visit another world. Quite what these conditions are, however, throws us back on the sheer cultural variety of such reports (Couliano 1991: 232). For otherworld travellers depart for other realms in a variety of ways. Indeed, Couliano notes that 'Swooning, dreaming, experiencing near death, being in states of consciousness altered by means of hallucinogens, and undergoing sensory deprivation or its opposite ... are some of the situations in which separation can occur.'

In Jewish accounts, drug-induced journeys or those encountered near death are not reported; indeed, a state of depression seems to suffice to prompt the episode. But the Greek traditions favour near-death triggers, and the Iranian accounts, such as that of the righteous Viraz, feature journeys caused chiefly by the taking of hallucinogens (Couliano 1991: 232–4).

A further common and notable feature, for Couliano, concerns the relationship between the complexity of the experience and the complexity of the tradition in which it is embedded. In short, he observes, the more complex the tradition, the more complex the experience, and complex traditions tend to produce complex *interpretations* of experience. As an example, he notes the sophistication of the Tibetan Buddhist appreciation of the world of the otherworld traveller as in some sense mind-dependent: 'inner' rather than 'outer'. What is undeniable overall, he argues, is that otherworldly journey narratives constitute a *genre* and can thus be 'envisioned as a literary genre' (Couliano 1991: 7). Does this necessarily relegate them to the realm of mere fiction, therefore? Couliano asserts that this is not necessarily the case, although he leaves aside any attempt at really detailed discussion of whether any kind of common experiential core may underlie the varieties of reported experience in favour of an explanation of how the genre's relative consistency, longevity and apparent universality may be explained in terms of *intertextuality*, rather than by explanations which appeal to 'genetic transmission or the unhelpfully vague affirmation that some collective unconscious lies behind our individual psyches' (Couliano 1991: 9).

Couliano's treatment of intertextuality deserves some comment here, as it appears to be important to his understanding of how otherworld journey narration revolves around a small number of fixed themes and thus may be said to contain a set of common motifs or plots. The *word* intertextuality suggests the influence of one text, or narrative, upon another, in such a way that certain details of plot or characterization in one may be accounted for by the influence of the plot and characterization of another. As regards otherworldly journey narration, however, Couliano favours a much simpler and more basic explanation of how the process operates, defining intertextuality in a broader sense as 'a widespread phenomenon that can be in part explained by our mental tendency to cast every new experience in old expressive moulds' (Couliano 1991: 7). As regards the experiences of otherworld visionaries, Couliano suggests that what a visionary actually experiences is shaped by expectations arising out of his or her previously existing cultural and linguistic tradition, or becomes so after the event. In this way, he asserts, 'intertextuality can, mostly unconsciously, interfere with the original version to the point that the visionary is convinced that his or her experience falls into an ancient and venerable pattern illustrated by many other visionaries', citing the 'vast mystical literature' from within Judaism, Christianity and Islam 'in which there are only a few variations on a basic theme' (Couliano 1991: 7). Couliano does not state what he means by 'original version' here, and it is not clear from the context what is meant by the phrase. Is he suggesting some sort of pre-interpretative core that is shaped by an experient's cultural and linguistic heritage, in ways analogous to Badham's common core hypothesis?

A possible clue comes from the assertion that follows, in which he writes that 'This by no means implies that at least some of the visions are not authentic; it simply shows to what extent inter-textuality operates' (Couliano 1991: 7–8). It is not clear here what 'authentic' means either, but what *is* clear is that Couliano believes that intertextuality may operate unconsciously and that he does not believe that a whole narrative or text is necessary to ensure the shaping and transmission of the otherworldly narrative genre within – and possibly across – traditions. Instead, he writes, intertextuality is 'a mental phenomenon, and concerns "texts" sometimes written but usually unwritten' (Couliano 1991: 8). Thus, cultural transmission of ideas and motifs is 'complex . . . [but] . . . not dependent on complete transmission of sets of ideas' (Couliano 1991: 9). Indeed, he goes so far as to call this recog-nition the 'cognitive assumption' of his whole study, writing that 'the cognitive assumption of this book is that a simple set of rules would generate similar results in the minds of human beings for a virtually infinite period of time' (Couliano 1991: 9). In the case of otherworldly journey narration, these rules 'could be, for example: "There is another world; the other world is located in heaven; there is body and soul; the body dies, and the soul goes to the other world"'. Overall, Couliano views the 'individual traditions shown in detail' in his own study to be 'based on such sets of rules' (Couliano 1991: 9).

By enabling us to view otherworldly journey narration in this way, Couliano presents us with a whole new way of accounting for a common core within testimonies to experiences such as NDEs. Indeed, in the light of what he has contended regarding the cultural forces that shape testimonies, two options might be considered concerning its existence. The first is that a common core exists which becomes shaped in accordance with cultural and linguistic expectations and interpretations (that is, a simple set of rules suffices to shape it into a recognizable narrative). The second is that no such core exists and instead an inherited set of rules, motifs and conventions is passed along traditions – and perhaps between traditions – which gives rise to consistently encountered motifs that can be located firmly within a genre. As we have already seen, it is difficult to know quite which option Couliano favours. At the very least, however, we are now in a position to appreciate more fully the forces that shape testimonies into recognizable types, and thus 'fix' them within certain genres, and to appreciate more fully the context within which the NDE can be located and examined. For far from making a discovery as a result of advances in medical technology, it would appear that the modern era of near-death studies has merely *rediscovered* a type of narrative that has been recorded since the dawn of human civilization. Paradoxically, then, it appears that in addition to simply pointing *forward* to what may lie in wait for us beyond the grave, the NDE also points *backward* to the history of human beings as storytelling creatures with a perennial need to describe other worlds.

NDEs and mysticism

Suggestions that NDEs might resemble other, recognizable types of religious experience invites a further comparison between the NDE and another variety of religious experience not yet considered: that of mysticism. This attempt at comparison, however, is not without considerable difficulties, for the literature on mysticism is vast and universal and there remains lively debate as to what, exactly, constitutes a 'mystical' experience. This being acknowledged, the comparison of the experiences of mystics (however much their experiences may be said to differ one from another) with those of NDErs might still yield useful insights into the NDE, particularly when it is considered that like NDEs, mystical experiences have been reported not just *historically* within the world's religions, but are reported *presently* within them also. In holding up mystical experience alongside the NDE for analysis, therefore, researchers may be able more readily to compare like with like, particularly if mystical and NDE reports from identical or similar cultural contexts are considered. At this point, it may simply become useful to ask whether or not such comparisons have in fact been carried out, and, if so, to attempt to ascertain and evaluate whether they have yielded findings of any significance.

It is notable yet again that the student of NDEs has little literature with which to work. One study, however, is deserving of some attention. In *The Near Death Experience: Mysticism or Madness*, theologian and spiritual counsellor Judith Cressy compares both historical and contemporary reports of mystical experience to the NDE, in a work arising out of her clinical work with both modern-day mystics and NDErs. Drawing on insights gained in this way, Cressy concludes that NDEs are but 'one of a broader group of experiences called mystical or spiritual', for there are various contexts within which mystical experiences might occur, she writes, death being one of them (Cressy 1994: 64). However, they may occur within other contexts also, including 'childbirth, personal crisis, attending the death of another, or simply spontaneously' (Cressy 1994: 64). Certainly, she notes, the NDE has received a certain contemporary prominence as a particular subcategory of mystical experience, largely due to the fact that so many people have had NDEs. Yet these are but a proportion of those who have had other comparable transcendent experiences. In fact, she asserts, NDEs may help shed light on mystical experiences:

> I believe that the introduction of the NDE into the larger category of mystical experience can serve to clarify the meaning of 'mystical' to the public, the individual mystic, and the seeker. If one has had an experience similar to

an NDE, with attendant light, love, information and
especially transformation, then one has had a mystical
experience.

(Cressy 1994: 64–5)

Certainly, Cressy perceives in various details popularly
recounted by NDErs clear parallels with mystical experience.
First, she draws attention to some of the insights gained by NDErs
during their NDEs. Of these, she highlights the realization of
the interconnectedness of all things, writing: 'The vision of the
interconnectedness of all knowledge and all life that characterizes
many NDEs is a reflection of the high mystical state of unity
consciousness. NDErs have experienced the essential oneness of
being' (Cressy 1994: 74). She also notes other parallels, drawing
attention to the transformative effects produced in the lives of
both mystics and NDErs as a result of their experiences. Here,
she notes, changes in the sense and meaning of the self reported
by NDErs and mystics are similar, including increased feelings
of self-worth and enhanced feelings of love for humankind.
She sees here a clear parallel between the experiences of
modern mystics, NDErs and celebrated mystics throughout
history, including St John of the Cross, who as a result of
his experience developed the concept of 'spiritual friendship for
all'. Additionally, Cressy views both NDErs and mystics as
existing either on the margins of or outside established religious
traditions, but united in a common appreciation of a universal
spirituality which transcends doctrinal difference and division.
In language echoing that of near-death researchers Kenneth
Ring and Margot Grey, she notes how 'Mystics are united in a
common experience, like the NDEr. They are more like each other
than the ordinary worshipper in any of the world's religious
traditions. They, too, tend to be experiential, spiritual, universal
and pluralistic' (Cressy 1994: 72). Furthermore, she perceives
that the NDE, like mystical experience, unfolds in stages,
each revealing a correspondingly deeper experience, with few
mystics or NDErs reaching the most profound levels possible. In
fact, she asserts, NDErs who fail to attain the deeper, more
complex NDE stages, such as the experience of heavenly realms,
are likely to return as 'psychics rather than mystics'. Whatever

they might return as, however, they require help to integrate their experiences into the flow of ongoing, 'normal' life. Within this context, she warns, we must be careful not to complicate matters by putting NDErs on any kind of pedestal, for whilst they may have glimpsed things not revealed to everyone, they 'are not yet perfected saints' (Cressy 1994: 72). Instead, we should recognize the *opportunities* afforded by NDEs to both NDErs and mystics alike, for by making the reality of mystical experience widely known, 'the reality of the NDE' may actually 'modify the present tendency of Christian spiritual directors to reduce mysticism to ordinary reality, and [thus] revitalize the supernatural ecstasy of St John [of the Cross] and St Theresa [of Avila]' (Cressy 1994: 72).

Cressy sees interesting parallels between the experiences of celebrated mystics throughout history and the reports of modern-day NDErs, quoting Elizabeth Petroff's observation in this regard that:

> A surprising number of biographies and autobiographies tell of an apparent dying, often when a teenager, of being taken for dead and perhaps even put in a coffin but then miraculously coming back to life, often with an explicit visionary message for the world. This happened to Christina Mirabilis, Catherine of Siena, Magdalena Beuthler, St Theresa of Avila and Julian of Norwich.
>
> (Cressy 1994: 65)

Selecting Theresa of Avila from this celebrated list, Cressy quotes her experience at length:

> I thought I was being carried up to Heaven: the first persons I saw there were my mother and father, and such great things happened in so short a time . . . I wish I could give a description of at least the smallest part of what I learned, but when I try to discover a way of doing so, I find it impossible, for while the light we see here and that other light are both light, there is no comparison between the two and the brightness of the sun seems quite dull if compared with the other. [Afterwards] I was . . . left with

very little fear of death, of which previously I had been very much afraid.

(Cressy 1994: 63)

Carol Zaleski: from *Otherworld Journeys* to *The Life of the World to Come*

Cressy's perception of historical parallels with the NDE in the reports of mystics, like Couliano's historical and cross-cultural survey of otherworld journey narratives, suggests that this is a fruitful area for theologians, in particular, to explore. A very sophisticated study which merits detailed attention here is that of Carol Zaleski, whose *Otherworld Journeys: Accounts of Near-Death Experience in Medieval and Modern Times* appeared in 1987 and remains unsurpassed as a thoroughgoing attempt to bring the tools of theology – specifically the study of religions – to bear upon a variety of claimed journeys to transcendent realms, modern NDEs amongst them. More recently, Zaleski has produced a generally *Christian* response to NDEs, *The Life of the World to Come: Near-Death Experience and Christian Hope* (1996), based around her 1993 Albert Cardinal Meyer lectures at the University of St Mary of the Lake/Mundelein Seminary. As will become clear, many of the themes which have been emerging during this chapter as deserving of consideration also appear in Zaleski's studies, together with some fresh approaches that promise to move the discussion onto higher and potentially more fruitful levels.

Dominating *Otherworld Journeys* is Zaleski's recognition of the power and importance of the *religious imagination* as the originator of vivid and compelling testimonies to religious experience, including otherworldly journeys. It is in terms of this perennial power, she asserts, that we should seek to view the NDE. In fact, for her it is the vivid imaginative detail and narrative structure of NDE testimonies that account for the current popularity of books about them, and not simply the frequency with which such experiences are reported. Overall, therefore, Zaleski suggests a 'Copernican revolution' in our thinking. Instead of viewing NDEs as actual journeys to other worlds, she writes, we need to begin to view them instead as an 'imaginative form' which assumes its structure and content via a complex process involving conscious and unconscious interaction with and within a specific cultural context. Seen in this way, the NDE becomes 'through and through a work of the socially conditioned religious imagination . . . formed in conversation with society' (Zaleski 1987: 190).

From this assertion, a number of others arise. First, in common with Couliano, Zaleski views the NDE as a contemporary manifestation of a much more basic and historically ongoing human endeavour to picture and describe other worlds, one which has in earlier ages manifested itself in a rich range of otherworldly journey tales. In demonstration of this, Zaleski chooses to focus her own study in large part upon a comparison of modern NDE accounts with comparable stories contained within medieval vision literature. She finds contrasts in detail attributable to the fact that such narratives tend to be composed in accordance with rules derived from the specific culture or society of their author. A number of vivid examples suffice to demonstrate this. Thus, for example, Zaleski considers the identity of the psychopomp in modern NDE reports: the figure who typically 'comes for' the NDEr in order to escort him or her to the other side. In modern – particularly Western – accounts, this is typically a deceased friend or relative. In medieval vision literature, by contrast, we encounter as psychopomp a saint of a particular order, a fact explained when we recognize that the 'feudal compact of the soul with the patron saint . . . has [today] been replaced by more democratic, less hierarchical forms of solidarity and protection, such as that afforded by family members and friends' (Zaleski 1987: 54–5). In similar fashion, tunnels have replaced bridges as the mode of access to the other side, due to the contemporary Western familiarity with them as a means of transition from one place to another: hence their absence from medieval otherworld journey narratives and their presence in modern Western ones (Zaleski 1987: 57–60). These and other comparable contrasts indicate, for Zaleski, that the rules for composition of the otherworldly journey narrative have changed in accordance with wider historical and societal changes within the cultures concerned.

However, the process by which otherworldly journey narratives are composed is more complex than has so far been suggested. For it is never simply the case that an otherworldly vision is composed *solely* by the visionary. We also have to consider the role of *those to whom the story is told*, who themselves contribute to the overall shaping and composition of the final, fixed, narrative. In this regard, in a telling quote worth citing in full, Zaleski asserts of the medieval accounts that:

> we cannot simply peel away the literary wrapper and put our hands on an unembellished event. Even when a vision actually did occur, it is likely to have been reworked many times before being recorded. The vision is a collaborative effort, produced by the interaction of the visionary with neighbors, counselors, the narrator, and other interested parties. One cannot point to the moment when the vision changed from a matter of personal confession into a public project; rather, it is built up in layers placed over one another like a series of trans-parencies. Though a bottom layer of actual experience may be present in some (but certainly not in all) vision stories, its contours are nearly indistinguishable from those of the superimposed images through which we discern it.
>
> (Zaleski 1987: 86)

What, then, of the 'bottom layer of actual experience'? Does it constitute a sort of primary transparency that remains common throughout all cultures? If so, can we ever peel away the layers of interpretation that sit on top of it in order to discern an original, uninterpreted, experience common to them all? For Zaleski, this is plainly not possible. Indeed, she writes, the 'benefits' of viewing the NDE as a product of the culturally conditioned religious imagination are only accessible 'if we are willing to renounce the notion that some original and essential religious experience can be discriminated from subsequent layers of cultural shaping' (Zaleski 1987: 195). Important for her conclusion in this regard is a contention from Gordon Kaufman that:

> Our 'religious experience', whatever this turns out to be, is never a raw, preconceptual, pre-linguistic experience,

the undialectical foundation on which theology can be
built. It (like all the rest of experience) is always a
construction or composite, heavily dependent for its form
and qualities on the learned terms and concepts which
give it particular flavor and shape.[4]

Commenting on this passage, Zaleski adds that it serves as a
timely reminder that we should 'not make the assumption that
the visionary who sees Christ or Krishna is only "labelling" an
underlying experience which can be described more accurately
and directly as encounter with a "being of light" or the "higher
self"' for 'such modern expressions may seem more palatable, but
they are no less culturally determined or mythically cultivated'
(Zaleski 1987: 195).

Such obvious epistemological caution throws fresh light on
attempts such as those to discern a culturally invariant 'being of
light' (Moody) or 'divine presence' (Badham) underlying the
varieties of reported interpretations made by NDErs in their
testimonies. For such attempts fail, in Zaleski's terms, to recognize
that labels such as 'being of light' are themselves interpretation-
rich and culture-specific. Furthermore, for Zaleski, such attempts
also fail to recognize that the notion of raw experience upon or
around which is wrapped a particular interpretative description
is inappropriate anyway. For both her and Kaufman, interpretation runs throughout any given experience. The possibility
of any 'raw, preconceptual, pre-linguistic experience' is therefore
ruled out a priori. In short, there is no common core to religious
experience – the NDE included – because there *can be* no common
core.

Kaufman and Zaleski have not been alone in holding to such a
view of religious experience in recent years. This position – that
religious experience is '"nothing but" interpretation', to use
Caroline Davis's useful phrase – has been held in various different
forms by many theologians, philosophers and philosophers of
religion, including Anthony Flew, Steven Katz, George Lindbeck,
and Don Cupitt.[5] If correct, it would certainly preclude any
further discussion of the possibility of a common core to NDEs,
and would render superfluous suggestions such as Badham's that
a massive, computer-assisted cross-cultural study be undertaken

to look for one. The question arises, of course, as to whether it *is* correct. Couliano, as we have seen, has been ambivalent with regard to the possibility of a common core within NDEs. Even Zaleski, in recent years, appears to have modified her position somewhat, writing in the *The Life of the World to Come* that 'similarities suggest that there are some enduring – perhaps even universal – features of near-death experience', whilst continuing to assert that: 'The differences make it clear, however, that near-death experiences, and the literature that describes them, are profoundly shaped by cultural expectations' (Zaleski 1996: 33). Clearly, the question of whether a common core does exist at the centre of the varieties of reported near-death experiences has been emerging throughout this chapter as an important area for theological and philosophical focus. We shall therefore have much more to say about it in the following chapter.

Also emerging throughout this chapter as needful of much more detailed treatment in its own right has been the subject of dualism within the context of the NDE. Once again, it is a subject upon which Carol Zaleski has interesting things to say. To begin with, she notes that the apparent dualism implied by many NDE reports may be problematical for some Christian theologians, for the NDE, taken at face value, appears to portray death 'as a pleasant gentle transition': a far cry from the view that it represents a sharp and decisive rupture in human being which can only be repaired by an omnipotent Deity who raises the dead on the last day (Zaleski 1996: 54–8). This being acknowledged, however, what of the plainly dualistic implications of the claims made by some NDErs to have viewed their bodies at a distance or to have made other observations whilst apparently unconscious? Once again, Zaleski's preferred solution is to turn to the role of the imagination in the shaping and construction of near-death testimony. Thus, she writes in *The Life of the World to Come* that, 'The people who testify to near-death experience are neither Platonists nor Cartesians, yet they find it natural to speak of leaving their bodies in this way. *There simply is no other way for the imagination to dramatize the experience of death*: the soul quits the body and yet continues to have a form' (Zaleski 1996: 62–3; emphasis mine). Indeed, there is a certain inevitability that we will find death portrayed in this way in near-death testimony, she writes, for 'dualism and somatomorphism are inescapable laws governing the imaginative construction of the sense of self' (Zaleski 1996: 63). Thus, in Zaleski's final reckoning, not simply the apparently heavenly realms visited by the immortal self, with their culture-specific detail, guides and population, but also the very representation of that self in testimony, are accounted for by an appeal to the seemingly endless powers of the human imagination.

We are clearly a long way at this point from viewing NDEs in the way that some near-death researchers and theologians have done: as empirical proof of the immortal soul's survival of bodily death. However, even if such should *not* turn out to be the case, this, for Zaleski, does not strip NDEs of all value, for whilst such experiences 'may prove nothing about human propects for continued existence after death . . . they do provide, at the least, a narrative pledge that our animating values have an enduring reality which is not going to be taken away by death' (Zaleski 1996: 76). It is difficult to determine quite what Zaleski means by 'narrative pledge' in this context, although a hint may be provided where she speaks further of the NDE as containing a 'vesperal quality', and therefore affording us a 'first sighting of death rather than a direct experience of it . . . a visionary anticipation, mediated by the images of death and beyond that are engraved on one's psyche and embedded in one's culture' (Zaleski 1996: 23). Seen in this way, she writes, whilst 'near-death testimony does not provide objective evidence for an afterlife, yet I will contend that it is something more than a mere grab bag of subjective experiences irrelevant to Christian hope' (Zaleski 1996: 23). In sum and overall therefore, the value of near-death testimony may reside in what it is telling us about *ourselves*, as culture-, symbol- and image-bound beings, and in what it reveals to us about our ongoing beliefs and hopes regarding what may await us after death, rather than in its provision of proof positive that we will, indeed, one day be able to make the transition from death to life.

In fact, Zaleski's 'Copernican revolution', when explained as straightforwardly as this, may seem to many to be a somewhat reductionist one. In *Otherworld Journeys*, however, she shows herself to be well aware of the possibility of this charge, and her response lies in part in a careful consideration of the role of *theology itself* in evaluating phenomena such as NDEs and particularly the images and symbols they contain. We certainly continue to have a need for such symbols, she writes, for 'Such understanding as we do receive of the transcendent comes to us through symbols, and it is through symbols that we communicate this understanding to one another' (Zaleski 1987: 191). For Zaleski, however, such symbols of transcendence 'can lose potency with time', and can hence fall into a state of weakness – even disrepair – in which they fail to communicate transcendence to us, failing in the process to enable us to communicate it effectively to each other. At such a time, she asserts, 'the laws of religious imagination no longer bind us' but instead 'call on us to register the changes that a new situation demands' (Zaleski 1987: 194). Theology's role is to monitor this process, and to participate in the 'the art of detecting and serving these changing needs of religious symbol systems', with theologians being prepared as necessary to participate 'in a rhythm of creation and destruction rather than a progressive conquest of truth' (Zaleski 1987: 194). Thus, theology becomes a *therapeutic* rather than a *theoretical* discipline and, viewed in this way, will not seek to evaluate NDErs' claims by attempting to measure them against a fixed and timeless template in order to evaluate their truth or falsity. Indeed, it is hard to see where such a template would reside or where it could be found. Instead, theology's task becomes to assess the health of our symbols, including those found within near-death testimonies. Pragmatic considerations, including an analysis of the fruits for life which such experiences bring, combined with a sensitivity to the changing needs of culture and society, are offered by Zaleski as possible criteria by which this may be achieved. In this way, we can stop attempting, as some theologians have done, to evaluate the NDE by attempting to measure it against some timeless level of orthodoxy or by attempting to measure its success or failure as a proof of life after death. For such things seem always destined to evade our fumbling grasp and our symbols can only ever be healthy; but never perfect. Theology, on Zaleski's reckoning, thus becomes a vital discipline in which the power of symbolic truth – including the potency of its expression – can be monitored, assessed and even, on occasion, revitalized.

This is a subtle position indeed, and one that we have not yet encountered within our current overview of theological responses to the NDE. Vigorous and original as it is, however, it is vulnerable to criticism at a number of key points. Whilst we shall need to return to these in the chapters that follow, two may be singled out for immediate attention here. First, it is clear that Zaleski seems very confident in her knowledge of what the 'laws of the religious imagination' are and are not capable of. In fact, there is a sense in which, with her constant stress upon the role of these laws in the construction of near-death reports, Zaleski may simply not be listening sharply enough to what NDErs are saying in their testimonies. For it will have become clear by now that few, if any, NDErs would agree with her that their experience was an imaginative construct. For them, the NDE has a vividness and reality that sets it qualitatively apart from any attempt to define it in terms of imagination or unconscious inventiveness. A further, second, criticism may be levelled at Zaleski's understanding of the nature of theology itself. As we have already noted, she appears to incline towards a position of theological non-realism in her understanding of what theology is – and, by extension, what religions may be said to be. Not everybody, of course, would subscribe to such a view. For others, one key task of theology is indeed to sort Truth from error, usually by attempting to measure the correctness or truthfulness of a claim being made against criteria – including scripture, tradition and established practice – that exist for just such a purpose. As we have already had cause to note, Hampe at least acknowledges the necessity to do this in *To Die is Gain*. For those occupying such a position, there is of course a 'Truth once revealed', against which all claims – including those of NDErs – must be measured.

A truth once revealed

The notion of a revealed and hence universal and binding scriptural template against which the NDE should be measured has been encountered in a number of different places throughout the brief history of near-death studies. One cluster of religious responses to the NDE has come from those who have sought to show that the NDE is, essentially, demonic in nature and who appeal to a conservative Christian reading of scripture to support this view. This has in particular been the position of a wide number of evangelical Christian scholars such as John Weldon, Zola Levitt and Florence Bulle, who have argued that the 'being of light' in particular has a malevolent purpose in deceiving unwary NDErs into thinking that death is, for everyone, a pleasant experience with the promise of reward to follow. In fact, argues Bulle, citing scriptural texts such as 2 Corinthians 11:14 ('for Satan himself masquerades as an angel of light'), the opposite is the case, and the light is in fact Satan, who can appear as 'a bright shining creature or as some semblance of illumination', in order to deceive the unsaved (Bulle 1983: 195). Indeed, it is notable that NDE researchers such as Maurice Rawlings and Michael Sabom occupy positions that are broadly similar to these. Their assertion has been that *some* NDEs are possibly demonic and deceptive in origin, particularly those of non-Christians, and this argument has in recent years aroused fierce discussion in the pages of the *Journal of Near-Death Studies* and elsewhere. Indeed, so harsh has the controversy become over this issue that we shall need to return and consider it again in chapter 7. It is worth noting at this point, however, that a similar position has been espoused from a very different Christian context – that of Eastern Orthodoxy – by theologian Fr Seraphim Rose, whose study *The Soul After Death: Contemporary 'After-Death' Experiences in the Light of the Orthodox Teaching on the Afterlife* (1980) appeared in the very early years of near-death studies. Here, Rose appeals to the teaching of Eastern Orthodox saints and teachers in order to evaluate the claims of NDErs, concluding that their experiences occur in a normally invisible part of this world rather than any genuine heavenly realm. In fact, he argues, NDEs take place in a realm about which Eastern Orthodoxy has much to say: that of the 'aerial tollhouses'. These abodes of fallen spirits are set along the soul's journey to heaven and contain our accusers who lie in wait to present the newly deceased with an account of their earthly sins. Like many Western (Evangelical) Christians, therefore – although for very different reasons – Rose cautions against taking NDErs' own interpretations of their experiences at face value, for they are in actuality victims of deceiving spirits. Even the light is not to be trusted, he writes, for

Orthodox ascetic literature is filled with warnings against trusting any kind of 'light' that might appear to one; and when one begins to interpret such a light as an 'angel' or even 'Christ', it is clear that one has already fallen into deception, weaving a 'reality' out of one's own imagination even before the fallen spirits have begun their own work of deception.

(Rose 1980: 117)

As a counter to the danger of being deceived by the claims of NDErs, Rose advises immersion in Eastern Orthodox teaching and its contention that spiritual experience must be tested against a 'truth once revealed'. 'Only with the idea', he writes, 'that there is a revealed truth that is above all experience, can this occult realm be enlightened, its true nature recognized and a discernment made between this lower realm and the higher realm of heaven' (Rose 1980: 119).

Indeed, the need for discernment as to the true nature and location of the realm visited by NDErs is urged from within a very different theological context to that of Eastern Orthodoxy: that of Tibetan Buddhism. As far back as the writing of *Life After Life*, Raymond Moody noted that *The Tibetan Book of the Dead* contained accounts of experiences similar to those undergone by NDErs and this contention has been reinforced in recent years by Sogyal Rinpoche, whose work has often been concerned to bring the *Book* to the attention of Westerners. In *The Tibetan Book of Living and Dying* (1992), Rinpoche devotes considerable attention to the NDE, writing that it should be correctly perceived as occurring within the various *bardo* states encountered after death, as set out in *The Tibetan Book of the Dead*, a manual designed to be read in the presence of the dying who are about to encounter realities to which they need to awaken.

According to this eighth-century text, writes Rinpoche, consciousness at the point of death is said to pass through a series of *bardo* states, with each of these offering the possibility of awakening and illumination. It is in the detail of these *bardo* states as set out in *The Tibetan Book of the Dead* that Rinpoche notes some striking parallels with the experiences of present-day NDErs.

In the *bardo* of dying, for example, the 'Ground luminosity' or 'Clear light' dawns, a phenomenon which he compares to the 'Being of light' described so frequently within NDErs' testimonies. Persons might, in addition, be granted particular supernatural powers, including the ability to see their own bodies or to know of occurrences far away. In the 'luminous *bardo* of dharmata' various deities may appear, producing a complex phantasmagoria of lights, patterns and sounds. Interestingly, Rinpoche stresses that whilst the appearance of the deities is 'a universal and fundamental experience', their identity 'can take on forms we are most familiar with in our lives. For example, for Christian practitioners, the deities might take the form of Christ or the Virgin Mary'. Underlying each culturally specific identification, however, 'it is important to recognize that there is definitely no difference whatsoever in [the deities'] fundamental nature'. And whatever form the deities take, their purpose is the same: to help us (Rinpoche 1992: 284). Indeed, throughout the various *bardo* states, help is at hand and the opportunities for enlightenment are ever-present. However, enlightenment can only come when the self realizes that the *bardos* themselves are only mental states, and hence (powerful) illusions. This returns us to a reconsideration of the location of the experiences undergone by NDErs. For whilst much contemporary near-death literature, as we have seen, tends to favour a dualistic interpretation of NDErs' experiences, *The Tibetan Book of the Dead* alerts us to the fact that the experience takes place in *mental* space and is indeed a product of experiencers' various mental states. Indeed, Couliano makes this point as well, noting that

> the logic of [*The Tibetan Book of the Dead*] is not to displace popular representations of the world of the dead, but to reinterpret them as sheer mental states that create powerful illusions. It is ultimately you who write the script for your own death, and it depends on you whether you turn it into an endless horror show, a divine comedy, or nothing at all. This realization brings recognition of the *bardo* state, and its recognition brings immediate liberation.
>
> (Couliano 1991: 97)

There is much more in Rinpoche's fascinating comparison of the experiences of NDErs and the descriptions given of the dying process in *The Tibetan Book of the Dead* that might be highlighted here, but one further phenomenon to which he draws attention is worthy of particular note. This is the recognition by Tibetans of the existence of the delok: a word derived from the Tibetan *de lok*, meaning 'returned from death'. This description, he writes, is traditionally given to those who 'die' and find themselves travelling in the *bardo* realm before returning to their normal lives again. Their experiences may include visits to heavenly and hellish states, encounters with protective deities, and they frequently find it difficult afterwards to get anybody to believe their stories. As an illustration of a delok's experience, Rinpoche cites the celebrated sixteenth-century Tibetan Ligza Chokyi, who, having died, saw her own body (mistaking it for a clothed pig), attempted to communicate with her still-living relatives, heard the voice of her deceased father, and followed him to the *bardo* realm 'which appeared to her like a country' (Rinpoche 1992: 330). Eventually she was told that an error had been made concerning her name and she returned to life again. Rinpoche notes that the phenomenon of the delok is not simply a historical curiosity in Tibet, but was reported until recent times and continues in Tibetan Himalayan regions in the present day. Although little known in the West, he argues, it is clear that the experiences of deloks and NDErs contain significant parallels. Intriguing historical experiences such as that undergone by Ligza Chokyi would seem to reinforce this contention.

Patterns and agendas

Isolated islands though they may have been, the responses to the NDE that this chapter has explored have nonetheless revealed a chain of issues that have emerged as needful of deeper exploration than they have so far received. One of these, as we have consistently noted, is the issue of dualism. Another is the issue of whether or not the NDE is best seen as a 'variant' or 'subcategory' of other, already documented types of religious experiences such as those claimed historically and cross-culturally by mystics. This possibility, in turn, raises the issue of a common core to NDEs:

whether such can be discerned beneath layers of cultural shaping or whether the whole experience is itself a product of such forces. This issue raises the related question of what any common core might consist of, what it might mean, and whether or not it bears any resemblance to the elaborate NDE narratives and models constructed by near-death researchers and explored in detail in chapter 1. This issue, finally, invites us to consider whether or not our early twenty-first-century understanding of neuroscience might contribute significantly to the study of NDEs, what its place should be in any such study, and whether it may yet carry the final word. In an important sense, therefore, the questions and problems uncovered in the opening chapters of this study have set the agenda for what must follow. That this agenda carries implications for theology and philosophy is clear. Whether or not these disciplines can, in turn, contribute in any constructive sense to our ongoing quest to explore the mysteries still contained within the phenomenon of near-death experiences will be for future chapters to reveal.

3

DEFINING THE LIGHT

Language, epistemology and the NDE

In search of common features

What sets NDEs apart from simple dreams? One possible answer to this may lie in their *consistency*, for descriptions of episodes of darkness, encounters with light, and overwhelming sensations of peace and joy appear within NDErs' testimonies over and over again. Even if we baulk at accepting the elaborate NDE models that emerged early on within the field of near-death research, we are surely justified when confronted repeatedly by such motifs in asserting some sort of common core to NDE reports – a core that is not necessarily explained away by well-known processes such as intertextuality.

This, at least, has been the conclusion of a sizeable number of near-death researchers and other interested scholars who in recent years have been concerned to discern and explain an underlying commonality to near-death testimonies but do not want to embrace the existence of a complex model such as Moody's. Researcher James McClenon, for example, has advanced two possible ways of accounting for common features within a range of what he dubs 'wondrous event' narratives, including NDEs. Comparing otherworldly journey stories within medieval Chinese and Japanese 'anomalous event literature' (which he perceives as comparable to contemporary NDEs), McClenon concludes that underlying clearly culturally specific features encountered within each narrative group are '*universal* features that are intrinsic to NDEs' (McClenon 1994: 168; emphasis in the original). Rejecting the notion of cultural diffusion as an explanation for this (a position he dubs the 'cultural source' hypothesis), McClenon advances what he dubs the 'experiential source' hypothesis: the contention that such features are simply intrinsic to this particular type of experience. In similar vein, in her study of the transformative effects of NDEs, *Reborn in the Light*, Australian NDE researcher Cherie Sutherland draws a distinction between 'deep structures' which seem to recur throughout many NDEs universally and historically and 'surface structures' which may be unique to certain cases, arguing that:

> The fact that [NDErs] have been to another realm could be said to form part of the deep structure of the experience, whereas their description or interpretation of what they encountered could be seen to form part of the surface structure. I would argue that it is in terms of these surface structures that cultural conditioning *could* have an influence.
>
> (Sutherland 1992: 30; emphasis in the original)

It is important to be clear as to what, exactly, is being asserted here. Sutherland is suggesting that there is a core experience – for her, the actual detail of some other realm to which NDErs travel – which in testimony is overlaid or mixed with the 'surface structure' of experients' own culturally conditioned attempts to articulate or interpret the experience of visiting that realm. This she offers as a possible explanation as to why, for example, the darkness is variously interpreted as 'a tunnel, a valley, a culvert or a void' and why even the geography of the transcendent realm appears to differ from experient to experient (Sutherland 1992: 30).

It is useful to compare these contentions with some very similar ones that have surfaced repeatedly in studies of NDEs in recent years. Writing in *The Truth in the Light*, for example, Peter and Elizabeth Fenwick, whilst examining their collection of British NDE reports in search of 'consistency . . . rather than difference', conclude that 'they all contain features of a more "typical" NDE. *It's as though the same underlying pattern is indeed there, but it is being interpreted in a different way to show a different world*' (Fenwick and Fenwick 1995: 158; emphasis mine). In broadly similar vein, near-death researchers Bruce Greyson and Nancy

Evans Bush have asserted that 'Cross-cultural studies as well as Western case collections [of NDEs] reveal a recognizable pattern irrespective of background belief system or specific content of a set of experiences' (Bailey and Yates 1996: 226), while, as a result of a number of detailed studies of various aspects of NDEs, researcher Melvin Morse has consistently concluded that there is a recognizable 'core NDE' overlaid with 'secondary embellishments, descriptions of various details and figures that come from a person's personal and cultural background' (Morse and Perry 1992: 226).

This is by no means an exhaustive list of researchers who have argued in this way, but it is worth noting that even so-called sceptical writers have in recent years reached generally similar conclusions. Thus, for example, we find Susan Blackmore asserting in her study *Dying to Live* that 'we find not a complete duplication of an identical experience but rather similar features appearing in different forms across times and cultures', before concluding that some sort of common core must therefore exist which neuroscience must (and can) explain. This is an admittedly far cry from Sutherland's 'other realms' hypothesis, but, like Sutherland (although for different reasons), Blackmore is forced to conclude, starkly, that 'Consistency we have' (Blackmore 1993: 19–20).

In short, what many NDE researchers working within a number of differing academic disciplines are asserting is that an essential or core experience can be theoretically separated from the cultural and religious embellishments within which it eventually appears, disguised, in testimony. Such a position, if true, appears to offer a way of viewing NDEs neither as clear windows into transcendent realities nor as mere mirrors reflecting nothing more than a bundle of culturally derived fantasies and psychosocial expectations. In this way, we arrive at the apparently paradoxical consistency-and-diversity that has been seen by many to characterize both historical and contemporary cross-cultural claims to near-death experience.

Defining common features

One question that may have emerged with particular force in the light of this and previous chapters is that which seeks to ask what, precisely, *constitutes* the claimed core NDE. Certainly, over the years, there has been no shortage of attempts to *define* such a core. As we have already noted, researchers Kenneth Ring and Margot Grey, as a result of their own collections of NDE testimonies in America and the UK, have argued for a core consisting of peace and a sense of well-being, separation from the body, entering the darkness, seeing the light, and entering the light (Ring 1980, 1984; Grey 1985). Comparably, Peter and Elizabeth Fenwick have proposed a core containing 'the light which is seen, the feelings of peace or joy evoked, the ambivalence about dying – the knowledge that even though you may not want to go, if it is not your time, then you have to return' (Fenwick and Fenwick 1995: 159). Sutherland (1992: 30) proposes a 'deep structure' consisting of an experience in which people 'can leave their bodies, pass into an area of darkness, move toward a light, enter a world of preternatural beauty and encounter beings such as deceased loved ones or friends who communicate with them before they return', whilst McClenon asserts that both Chinese and Japanese medieval vision narratives contain comparable features including 'belief in life immediately after death, in guides who carry the experiencers through a transition area, in a deity who administers a life review, and in an otherworldly hierarchy' (McClenon 1994: 183). Finally, in addition to all of this, and in large part due to studies of NDEs in children together with a comparison of African and American near-death testimonies, researcher Melvin Morse has recently concluded that 'NDEs are essentially the same, exhibiting the same core elements of going up tunnels, seeing people dressed in white, and so forth'. In keeping with other researchers, he adds, 'They interpret them differently, because of their culture' (Morse and Perry 1992: 124).

Cross-cultural studies

Whilst it seems that there is no shortage of existing *Western* data, what is needed to further explore the possibility of a genuinely universal core is more detailed cross-cultural research examining both historical and contemporary NDEs. Possibly because of the short history of near-death studies, together with a relative paucity of contributions to the field from within the disciplines of anthropology, sociology and theology, such research has yet to be fully or even seriously undertaken. Karlis Osis and Erlendur Haraldsson's *At the Hour of Death* is an exception to this, where the authors have concluded on the basis of a comparison of American and Indian NDEs that 'The majority of Hindu patients saw visions essentially similar to those of American Christians', including psychopomps, feelings of serenity, peace and elation and generally paradisiacal transcendental realms (Osis and Haraldsson 1997: 154).

The sole substantial *sociological* study exclusively devoted to the investigation of NDEs, Allan Kellehear's *Experiences Near Death*, is promising within this context insofar as its author has also recently – albeit tentatively – advanced the possibility of some kind of cross-cultural core to NDE reports. Whilst acknowledging that the search for this core is problematical, Kellehear examines accounts from a diverse range of cultures including Melanesia, Micronesia, Native America, Aboriginal Australia and Maori before concluding that, whilst it is not as uniform as some existing Western studies have suggested, nonetheless the data *do* seem to suggest that it exists. Thus, for example, whilst disputing the notion that a tunnel is cross-cultural – and thus part of a larger cluster of common features – Kellehear suggests that a 'period of darkness' may be, as we have already seen. This, he asserts, may then itself be 'subject to culture-specific interpretations: a tunnel for Westerners, subterranean caverns for Melanesians, and so on' (Kellehear 1996: 35). Similarly, his research indicates that other features may be universal too, including encounters with 'other beings' and the arrival at an 'other world'. Whilst such a stripped-down core is once again a long way away from more complex models, it does at least have the benefit of some cross-cultural support. To be sure, there are certain – self-admitted – problems with Kellehear's research. His database, whilst wide in scope, is small, and the cases he cites are all reproduced second-hand. Kellehear also acknowledges that 'language translation is . . . a problem' (Kellehear 1996: 39); a problem, we may assume, that does not arise when concentrating on exclusively Western English-language accounts. Nevertheless, his study goes some way to answering the objection that Western lists of NDE common features are not universal in scope. So too does a further, less recent comparison of American and Indian NDE accounts undertaken by Satwant Pasricha and Ian Stevenson, which once again concluded that, whilst culture-specific features are discernible within both testimony-groups, a degree of commonality can be found also, including a life review, encounters with a 'being of light or religious figure' and meetings with deceased relatives (Pasricha and Stevenson 1986).

Theology and the common core

Even the possibility of the existence of a historical and cross-cultural common core to NDEs has a variety of potentially enormous implications, and it is no surprise therefore that it has attracted a great deal of interest from a number of quarters, including – as we noted in the previous chapter – theology. There, we saw that a number of theological responses to NDEs have isolated the possibility of such a core as of major significance to theology and religious studies, with some scholars going so far as to assert that the 'being of light' *may* even be viewed as part of the essential 'religious experience of mankind' (Badham and Badham 1982: 86). Indeed, discussion of the identity of such a being may be expected to be of great interest to theologians and near-death researchers alike, given that some sort of light event or presence *is* so often encountered within NDErs' testimonies. The additional fact that it is so often identified in religious terms, together with the fact that light is discerned as part of a core NDE by virtually *all* Western NDE researchers as well as in a number of cross-cultural studies (such as those of Pasricha and Stevenson and Osis and Haraldsson), makes this element of the NDE an excellent focus for any theological discussion of what may be fundamental to its cross-cultural or invariant essence.

What makes discussion of the light and its identity even *more* interesting, however, is the fact that even a casual reading of near-death testimonies reveals that it is identified in so many vivid and different ways by so many different respondents, both within and across cultures. Consider, for example, the following testimonies:

1   Fifteen years ago when I was fifty-nine I had a heart attack. An iron band around my chest was getting tighter

and tighter. The doctor came, and when he left to ring for an ambulance he warned me not to move on any account. Then everything became warm and bright and light and beautiful. The iron band was gone and I was travelling along a tunnel. It was light, light, light. I didn't move my feet, I just 'floated' I suppose. But it was calm and peaceful and just lovely. Gradually there was a brilliant light at the end – really brilliant – and I knew I was going right into the glowing heart of that light, but then I saw a group of people between me and the light. I knew them; my brother, who had died a few years before, was gesticulating delightedly as I approached. Their faces were so happy and welcoming. Then somehow my mother became detached from the group. She shook her head and waved her hand (rather like a windscreen wiper) and I stopped, and I heard the doctor say, 'She's coming round,' and I was in my bed and the doctor and my husband were there. My first words to the doctor were, 'Why did you bring me back?'

(Fenwick and Fenwick 1995: 59)

2   I got up and walked into the hall to go get a drink, and it was at that point, as they found out later, that my appendix ruptured. I became very weak, and I fell down. I began to feel a sort of drifting, a movement of my real being in and out of my body, and to hear beautiful music. I floated on down the hall and out the door onto the screened-in porch. There, it almost seemed that clouds, a pink mist really, began to gather around me, and then I floated right straight on through the screen, just as though it weren't there, and up into this pure crystal light, an illuminating white light. It was beautiful, and so bright, so radiant, but it didn't hurt my eyes. It's not any kind of light you can describe on earth. I didn't actually see a person in this light, and yet it has a special identity, it definitely does. It is a light of perfect understanding and perfect love.

(Moody 1975: 62)

3   I attempted to go through a doorway, but my brother was blocking my view and wouldn't let me see what was behind him . . . Then I saw what was behind him. It was a bright angel. An angel of light. I felt encompassed by this force of love from this angel that was searching and probing my deepest thoughts. I was being searched and then I seemed to be allowed to sense the presence of spirits of some other loved ones who had died previously. Then my whole body jumped upward from the electric jolt they gave me, and I knew I was back on earth again.

(Rawlings 1978: 87)

4   I think that I was surrounded by what I can only describe as a reception committee. Frank [a deceased Sunday School teacher known to the respondent in childhood] was one of these. Another was my saintly Roman Catholic doctor who had just previously died . . . They did have a physical shape; it's hard to describe, but it somehow combined the youth and vigour of twenty-one year-olds, with a sense of perfect maturity. As for Jesus, in that place of light, Jesus was the light itself. This does not mean that he was an abstraction, he was as much a 'person' as all the others. He was prophet, priest and king. I knew him by the nail holes in his hands and feet, and by the way he looked at me.

(Grey 1985: 53)

5   I was to come back, but there was no road for me to follow, so the voice said, 'Let him go down.' Then there was a beam of light and I walked along it. I walked down the steps, and when I turned to look there was nothing but forest. I stood there and thought, 'if they have started mourning for me, I won't go because the voice said "Stand there and listen. If there is no mourning and no dogs howling, you go back. But if there is mourning you come back."'

So I walked along the beam of light, through the forest and along a narrow path. I came back to my house and re-entered my body and was alive again.

(Rogo 1989: 148–9)

6   [I] saw the great white light, and it was brilliant. It was
    what we call Shunyata, or total emptiness. In this empti-
    ness – which is not a fearful thing, but a marvellous thing
    – there was peace, calm, a sense of being freed from the
    ego. I didn't achieve enlightenment, but I got a taste of
    what it might be like.

                                          (Berman 1996: 103)

At first sight, giving a definitive identity to the light appears
impossible because of the widely differing descriptions given by
the respondents. In the first testimony, for example, the light is
simply described *as* a light, with no personality or identity ascribed
to it. In the second, light is again described, but with the additional
assertion that it possesses personality: a 'special identity . . . of
perfect understanding and perfect love'. In the third account, the
light is clearly identified: 'It was a bright angel'. In the fourth
account, the identity is clearer still: the light is Jesus as prophet and
priest and king. In the fifth account the light seems to be a kind
of *path* that the NDEr follows in order to find and return to his
body. Finally, in the sixth account, a distinctively Buddhist
identification of the light reveals it to be Shunyata, an emptiness
which is understood by some Buddhists to be the ultimate goal of
Buddhism.

One possibility, of course, is that there is *more than one light*.
If we are to accept for a moment the contention that during NDEs
journeys to heavenly or other non-physical realms *are* being made,
perhaps persons who die and embark on these journeys encounter
either separate, distinct, heavenly beings, particular to their own
traditions and glowing brightly, or a variety of lights containing
no discernible personalities but which nonetheless appear to
perform a variety of functions, such as lighting the way to or from
the heavenly realms or providing the ultimate goal of enlightenment. So perhaps Jesus really *did* greet the fourth of the above
respondents, an angel the third, and so on, with the fifth respondent simply traversing a kind of highway of light and the sixth
approaching – but not entering – Shunyata. Indeed, according to
this possibility, there is no reason why *other* beings and features
may not lie in wait after death for NDErs belonging to other

traditions too: Krishna, Moses, other light paths, and so on. For atheists and/or agnostics with no particular religious affiliation, perhaps a religiously neutral light – with or without personality – awaits amongst all the others, perhaps busier than most but certainly with a surprise in store.

However, such a scenario sounds somewhat banal, and it is therefore no surprise that in the published literature dealing with NDEs it has seldom been advanced. Preferred is the second option, similar to Badham's position expressed above, that some sort of transcendent core being is encountered by everybody but interpreted by them in accordance with their respective cultural backgrounds. Indeed, Raymond Moody himself was perhaps the first to advance such a position with respect to NDEs, arguing in *Life After Life* that:

> Interestingly, while the . . . description of the being of light is utterly invariable, the identification of the being varies from individual to individual and seems to be largely a function of the religious background, training, or beliefs of the person involved. Thus, most of those who are Christians in training or belief identify the light as Christ and sometimes draw Biblical parallels in support of their interpretation. A Jewish man and woman identified the light as an 'angel'. It was clear, though, in both cases that the subjects did not mean to imply that the being had wings, played a harp, or even had a human shape or appearance. *There was only the light.*
>
> (Moody 1975: 59; emphasis mine)

Later, he concludes that: 'though the description of the being of light is invariable, the identity ascribed to it changes, apparently as a function of the religious background of the individual' (Moody 1975: 140).

Now, what might be said concerning *this* explanation as to the variability of the light-being's identity? On the surface, it certainly seems attractive. As we have already seen, Moody is not the only near-death researcher to discern elements of a common core –

including a light-being – underlying NDErs' testimonies which become taken up and interpreted in their narratives. Indeed, one possible reason for the current popularity of this explanation is its resonance with the West's contemporary pluralistic tendencies. Many of us almost instinctively feel comfortable with an afterlife in which, regardless of race, culture, or creed, we are met by the same 'being'. It seems to confirm our deeply held suspicion that all paths, somehow, lead to the same Truth and are equally valid as far as our salvation and/or well-being is concerned, in this life and the next.

Identifying the light: epistemological considerations

It is only when we look under the surface of this explanation of the light-being's true identity that problems begin to arise. To begin with, the contention that at the core of this encounter is a somehow religiously non-partisan and theologically neutral being of light seems rather arbitrary and raises all sorts of questions. First, it fails to do adequate justice to accounts where a light is reported, but no personality – no being – is claimed for it, such as in the first, fifth and sixth accounts considered above. Second, it may be questioned whether, whatever the identity imposed upon the light by a given respondent, it is, at root, simply the sort of being in itself that, say, Moody supposes it to be: that is, a 'being of light'. In particular, attention might be drawn to the seeming *arbitrariness* of this identification. Returning again to a consideration of the six accounts cited above, and setting aside for a moment the problems for the common core hypothesis which the first, fifth and sixth accounts might reasonably be said to raise, we might wish to ask why it could not equally be concluded that – the fifth account, perhaps, aside – five of the respondents were actually 'seeing' Jesus with only the fourth respondent identifying him correctly. Perhaps the other respondents were guilty of under- or misinterpretation. Or the fourth respondent was guilty of over- or misinterpreting what was, in fact, simply an angel. Or a light. Or Shunyata. We do not really know for sure, and neither, we may suppose, does Moody or any other researcher. Indeed, perhaps Moody is simply under- or misinterpreting an encounter with Jesus or an angel or Shunyata when he makes his contention that the being encountered is *really* a sort of culturally and religiously neutral 'being of light'. Indeed, as was noted in the last chapter, there is at least a possibility that *all* NDErs are wrong in their identification of the light in positive, heavenly terms, and that, as some writers have asserted, the being of light is none other than the devil in disguise, appearing in a garb designed to deceive and ultimately entrap the unwary. Although most near-death researchers would reject such a conclusion, we have no a priori grounds for ruling it out, save, perhaps, a wish that such should not turn out to be the case.

It is clear, then, that any attempt to claim the existence of some sort of invariant 'being of light' (Moody) or 'manifestation of the Divine presence' (Badham and Badham) underlying the varieties of reported encounters claimed by NDErs also raises a variety of questions and may even present insoluble problems. Given the diversity of ascribed interpretations of the light encountered in so many NDErs' testimonies, therefore, a third alternative may present itself at this point. This is *that there is no possibility of any underlying, culturally neutral, 'pure' core experience actually existing, and that all respondents are simply having different and internally generated 'projected' experiences.* What would make this position different from the first one considered (that is, that there is more than one heavenly light-being or event) is, first, that it would wish to assert that supernatural, transcendent realms do not exist (and hence genuinely otherworldly light-beings or events do not exist) and, second, that it would wish to ascribe a powerful role to the experients' cultural – possibly pre-eminently linguistic – background together with internal psychological processes in the creation and shaping of such realms. We may also theoretically posit a *weaker* form of this alternative, which would wish to agree that an experient's cultural and linguistic background may indeed play a crucial role in shaping any claimed experience from its inception and throughout its duration (and therefore not simply playing a more secondary role in interpreting the event after its occurrence) but which would also wish to keep open the possibility that some sort of external, possibly transcendent, trigger might be responsible for its occurrence in the first place. Indeed, this theoretical position may not particularly wish to concern itself with what that trigger might be, preferring instead to merely highlight the epistemological complexities involved in any attempt to isolate a pure, interpretation-free core event from its inevitable interpretive shaping. What both stronger and weaker forms of this position agree on, however, is that it is epistemologically naive to assert that experience and interpretation can be separated in such a simple way that it may be possible to penetrate the latter in order to arrive at a complete or adequate description of the former. Both variations of this position would wish to assert that no isolation or description of what the light motif encountered by NDErs in their experiences actually is in itself can ever be possible, either because it does not exist or because its potential existence can never be ascertained or described.

Mental models

As if all of this was not complex enough, yet another position must be allowed for in any discussion of the possible origin, nature and identity of the light. This is the position – again undergirded by naturalistic assumptions which it shares with the weaker form of the alternative considered above – *that there is a common core to NDErs' accounts and that the key elements of such a core are each explainable by appeal to different neurological causes which can be identified as occurring in a brain at or near the point of death*. This position would wish to assert, for example, that developing understandings in recent years of the modification of brain function brought about by the onset of the dying process have uncovered a series of wholly biological and neurological causes for every element of the core NDE – the light included – which may be expected to take place within that process. Perhaps the most well-known exponent of such a position is UK researcher Susan Blackmore, who has in recent years developed a highly sophisticated model of what might be expected to happen within a dying brain and which purports to account for many common features – including the sensation of moving towards light – reported by NDErs. On her reckoning, the fact that so many NDEs appear to contain common motifs is explained by the fact that we all share the same neural organization and are thus 'wired' for the same or similar experiences. Clearly, the possibility that a wholly neuroscientific explanation such as this may turn out to explain the NDE – including the possibility of commonality of detail – is of great importance to any overall study of the NDE such as this one. For this reason, we will reserve further discussion of this crucial aspect of our investigation for the following chapter.

What we are left with as the focus of *this* chapter will be to test whether it is possible, epistemologically and phenomenologically, to isolate the identity of the light encountered by many NDErs which allows us to describe it as it is in itself. A positive result here may open up the possibility that other aspects of any common core underlying NDErs' reports may be similarly identified. Indeed, the potential benefits and outcomes of such an analysis are staggering. If it should turn out, for example, to be possible to positively and definitively identify the light, then we may indeed, as Badham suggests, have finally penetrated deeply into the mystery of the Divine Presence which is central to the religious experience of humankind; this may perhaps even allow us in the process to adjudicate between the competing truth-claims of the world's great religions in accordance with their adequacy in explaining or predicting what *really* awaits us after death. Even if such should not turn out to be possible, however, some rather more modest areas of achievement might still be anticipated. For it may have become the case that theologians, having read thus far, are beginning to feel a sense of déjà vu concerning what we are discussing here within the context of NDEs. Those familiar with the literature surrounding the possibility of an identifiable common core to *mysticism*, for example, may even suspect that the philosophical and phenomenological arguments which have surrounded such a possibility are simply being rehashed here around yet another variety of religious experience. This, however, is not at all what is being proposed. To be sure, such arguments will shortly emerge as important to the present enquiry, and it will be interesting to see whether insights already attained within the very specific context of mysticism can be carried over to illuminate unresolved issues surrounding NDEs. More than this, however, it is hoped that conclusions derived from a detailed epistemological analysis of key claims of NDErs will actually serve as either reinforcement or corrective to conclusions drawn within the related but distinct field of mystical analysis, to the betterment of our understanding of religious experience overall. Even further, it might be expected that many of those involved in the collection and interpretation of NDE data within the field of near-death studies may be wholly unaware of the insights into such interpretation which theology and philosophy may be able to provide. For them, therefore, it is to be hoped that this chapter may introduce such insights for the first time, inviting them also, perhaps, to a deeper and richer investigation of *other* tools and resources which these disciplines may usefully contribute to the still-infant field of near-death studies, to the betterment of their – and consequently everybody's – understanding of the phenomenon overall. Moreover, it remains a key aim of this chapter, as of the current study in general, to underline once again for theologians and philosophers the rich resources which exist within theology and the philosophy of religion which may be applied, developed and refined within any ongoing attempt to respond coherently and constructively to the claims of NDErs. To these diverse but related tasks we now turn.

The Nature of Doctrine

The question of the precise nature of the relationship between what is experienced by those reporting a range of religious experiences and their subsequent interpretations of those experiences has long been of keen interest to philosophers and theologians. George Lindbeck, for example, in a study which has aroused considerable debate amongst both philosophers and theologians, uses such an analysis within the context of his own attempt to assess the possibility of a common core both to religions and – by extension – religious *experiences* (Lindbeck 1984). Whilst his discussion does not extend to an examination of specifically *near-death* experiences, the fact that the possibility of a common core to religious experiencing is of central importance to him makes his analysis of direct relevance to the current chapter, and will thus repay close scrutiny. Foremost amongst his contentions is the assertion that language plays a crucial part in the structuring of religious experience – including a variety of types of religious experiences – and he examines in detail the implications of this in his book *The Nature of Doctrine*.

He begins by questioning many of the assumptions that stand behind the notion that an ineffable core experience underlies the varieties of reported religious experiences, such as mysticism, dubbing such a position 'experiential-expressivism', and questioning its logical and empirical basis. His preferred option is a position he dubs the 'cultural-linguistic' alternative, and it is with the outworking of this position that the bulk of his analysis rests. For Lindbeck, any religion 'can be viewed as a kind of cultural and/or linguistic framework or medium that shapes the entirety of life and thought. It functions somewhat like a Kantian *a priori*, although in this case the *a priori* is a set of acquired skills that could be different' (Lindbeck 1984: 33). Thus, the experiential–expressive notion, that religious experience is primary and later becomes shaped and interpreted by experients, will not suffice for Lindbeck. To be sure, as he readily acknowledges, this is a long-standing position within the philosophy of religion and the study of religions, and it is encountered in a variety of places; typified, perhaps, by Otto's contention that the *numinous* is a primary datum of religious experience which, whilst it is incapable of being articulated, is taken up and variously interpreted when attempts are made to describe it.[1] For Lindbeck, however, the recognition of the crucial and ubiquitous role of language in structuring and shaping human experience – including religious experience – calls forth a need for a reversal of the 'inner' and the 'outer' as regards contentions of such a kind. Instead, he writes, we should more properly see religion as

> similar to an idiom that makes possible the description of realities, the formulation of beliefs, *and the expressing of inner attitudes, feelings, and sentiments*. Like a culture or language, it is a communal phenomenon that shapes the subjectivities of individuals rather than being primarily a manifestation of those subjectivities.
>
> (Lindbeck 1984: 33; emphasis mine)

In other words, language shapes and structures even those apparently pre-reflective inner experiences – such as the numinous – that were once thought to be prior to their articulation. *Instead, it is the means of articulation itself that makes possible the experience*. In a crucial passage in this regard, Lindbeck writes that: 'Instead of deriving external features of a religion from inner experience, it is the inner experiences which are viewed as derivative', adding that

> the linguistic-cultural model is part of an outlook that stresses the degree to which human experience is shaped, molded, and in a sense constituted by cultural and linguistic forms. There are numberless thoughts we cannot think, sentiments we cannot have, and realities we cannot perceive unless we learn to use the appropriate symbol systems.
>
> (Lindbeck 1984: 34)

At this point, it may be reasonable to enquire of Lindbeck as to the extent to which cultural and linguistic forms constitute human experience. Is there nothing outside language? In fact, he appears unclear as to whether or not language is *solely* constitutive of experience, or whether certain types of experiences are, essentially, pre-linguistic. Thus, for example, writing of the experiences of mystics, he writes that 'What these have in common can be easily understood quite naturalistically as consisting, for example, of the "oceanic feelings" of which Freud spoke', suggesting, first, that naturalistic assumptions regarding the possibility of a transcendent origin have informed at least this part of his analysis and second that some sort of supra-linguistic core to mysticism may, after all, exist. But he quickly adds the qualification that

> a cultural-linguistic outlook . . . would add (as Freud did not) that [the mystic's] feelings become ingredients in a wide variety of experiences of the world, of self, and – the believer would say – of God that depend on different perceptual categories . . . and forms of practice;

and therefore

> religion, including mysticism, need not be described as something universal arising from within the depths of

individuals and diversely and inadequately objectified in particular faiths; it can at least as plausibly be construed as a class name for a variegated set of cultural-linguistic systems that, at least in some cases, differentially shape and produce our most profound sentiments, attitudes, and awarenesses.

(Lindbeck 1984: 40)

Whilst many believers, including mystics, might wish to question the assertion that their experiences merely arose from within their own depths, the use of the word 'produce' here is significant, and suggests that Lindbeck does in *some* sense view language as the producer of experience. The important thing to grasp, however, is that for him experience and interpretation are inextricably linked, with experients' cultural and linguistic *repertoires* of concepts, expectations and practices standing as crucial shapers of what their – potentially diverse – experiences will be like. Thus, he writes: 'First come the objectivities of the religion, its language, doctrines, liturgies, and modes of action, and it is through these that passions are shaped into various kinds of what is called religious experience' (Lindbeck 1984: 39). Indeed, even those most vivid, solitary and, in some cases, life-changing religious experiences of individuals are interpreted by Lindbeck in the light of the fact that language precedes – and in some sense therefore causes – experience. Thus: 'Luther did not invent his doctrine of justification by faith because he had a tower experience, but rather the tower experience was made possible by his discovering (or thinking he had discovered) the doctrine in the Bible' (Lindbeck 1984: 39). As regards the possibility of the existence of a common core to various types of religious experience, the foregoing analysis leads Lindbeck to the inevitable conclusion that no such thing is possible. For if languages shape experience, and a variety of diverse languages exist, then the idea that some sort of inner or cross-cultural existence of God can be common to all religions must be replaced with the recognition that

there can be no experiential core, because, so the argument goes, the experiences that religions evoke and mold are as varied as the interpretive schemes they embody.

*Adherents of different religions do not diversely thema-
tize the same experience; rather, they have different
experiences.*

(Lindbeck 1984: 40; emphasis mine)

We are returned here to one of the central contentions that this
chapter is attempting to explore: what does Lindbeck offer in his
cultural-linguistic approach to the understanding of religious
experience which might enable us to assess more clearly the
possibility and nature of a common core to NDEs?

NDEs and cultural–linguistic analysis

To begin with, it will have become clear that if Lindbeck is correct
in his analysis of what is constitutive of religious experience, then
no such core is possible. Instead, on his reckoning, what we would
expect to find would be a diverse range of experients having a
diverse range of experiences, deriving their variety from their
differing linguistic–cultural backgrounds. By the same token,
those (potential) experients with no conception of an afterlife,
or with no fixed conception of things like tunnels leading to it
or lights (with or without identity and personality) encountered
within it, would be expected to report no such experiences at all.
At the very least, therefore, Lindbeck may be seen to provide
explanations of why there is a clear diversity of detail within many
NDErs' reports, together with an explanation of why not all
persons pronounced clinically dead report NDEs.

Indeed, upon further reflection, Lindbeck's analysis appears to
greatly enhance our understanding of a number of additional
aspects of NDEs reported by very many NDErs. It helps explain,
for example, why a researcher such as Michael Sabom has
uncovered no evidence that an NDEr has ever converted as a result
of having an NDE. For Lindbeck, this fact is easily explainable by
the fact that existing beliefs actually produce, shape and mould
NDErs' varied experiences. If such should be the case, it would
indeed follow that no NDEr could ever be confronted by an
experience that threatened to overthrow his or her world view, for
the world view itself would have actually been instrumental in
creating and defining the experience, ruling out in advance any

possibility that it might contain anomalous details sufficient to call the world view into question.

Upon closer inspection, however, the evidence derived from NDEs appears to provide considerable grounds for treating the cultural–linguistic alternative with caution. To begin with, for example, what might such an understanding of religious experience make of persons who clearly hold no prior belief in any form of life after death but who nonetheless report NDEs, such as the philosopher and celebrated atheist A.J. Ayer, whose NDE took place in May 1988 when he was in hospital recovering from pneumonia? It is hard in such an instance to see how an existing cultural–linguistic system such as Ayer's could have produced an experience which ran so counter to itself, considering that throughout his life Ayer held a carefully thought-out and passionately articulated set of beliefs which would appear to have ruled out for him any hope or expectation of life after death. Yet Ayer *did* have an NDE: one, moreover, that was extraordinary, detailed and vivid, containing an encounter with light and an attempt at communication with guardian beings responsible for the periodic inspection of time and space.[2]

In addition, and particularly in the cases where NDEs with classic features such as tunnels and lights are reported, we might wish to question where NDErs actually derive their cultural–linguistic NDE pattern from. Simply stated: where has the language come from which creates the possibility for the existence of NDEs containing such features? For it is clear that such experiences, complete with recurring motifs such as the traversing of a period of darkness towards a light, do not represent part of any of the religious traditions of the West, the culture which has seen the greatest incidence of NDE reports to date. Indeed, what is most marked about Western society is the scepticism about the possibility of life after death which prevailed when NDEs first began to be reported in significant numbers and which continues to prevail. Of course, Lindbeck might retort that in the years since Moody's *Life After Life*, the features of the NDE have become so familiar to so many – within the West and elsewhere – that the language of the NDE has become widely and popularly circulated and hence easily absorbed or learned. The problem with this contention, however, is the fact that it fails to account for NDEs that were reported *before* the modern onset of interest in such experiences that began with the publication of Moody's 1975 study. In fact, as chapter 6 of this study will demonstrate in some detail, there are a number of accounts of NDEs currently housed in the archives of the Religious Experience Research Centre (RERC) at the University of Wales, Lampeter – a Centre originally established at Manchester College in Oxford by biologist Sir Alister Hardy in 1969 for the express purpose of collecting and examining reports of religious experience – which pre-date Moody's work by some years. In advance of that chapter, for example, consider the following letter to the Centre, written in August 1971 and concerning an experience that had occurred some decades before:

> The ultimate proof to me of life after death and the love of God came just after the birth of my daughter.
>
> It had been a long and difficult birth and I was very exhausted. As nurse helped me to sit up, I remember saying 'I do feel funny'. Everything whirled and blackness formed a tunnel, a long, long tunnel with an opening at the other end which glowed with a bright light.
>
> Down, down into the whirling blackness. It seemed a long time before I reached the opening and found myself floating gently in a soft warm mist, all golden as with sunlight, soft music and a feeling of complete happiness, and such peace as passes all understanding was mine; faces came out of the mist, smiled and faded away.
>
> I seemed to be fully conscious and knowing that I had 'died' yet I lived. God's plan of good death had no sting. Then came the remembrance of the baby – who would look after her if I stayed?
>
> My next reaction was to pain: my face stung as the doctor slapped first one side, then the other – hard.
>
> As I opened my eyes he greeted me with 'You naughty girl, you've given me the biggest fright of my life.' He looked startled when I answered, 'Don't begrudge me that: it was absolutely wonderful.'
>
> I still feel *very* grateful and humble for this experience, certainly have no fear of death, knowing it is as simple as walking from one room to another.[3]

Even a cursory examination of this account reveals details of what has come to be known as the near-death experience, such as the tunnel and light motifs and feelings of bliss and peace, which were apparently being experienced *and reported* at a time when such things were nowhere near as widely discussed and familiar to people as they are now – and when even the term 'near-death experience' did not exist. Where, therefore, did this correspondent derive the language of the NDE that created the possibility and detail of her experience?

One further issue that may have loomed particularly large in the light of the above analysis of the cultural–linguistic understanding of the construction of religious experience is the question of where Lindbeck derives the *evidence* that language is such a powerful shaper/creator of such experience. Does such a contention possess any solid empirical grounding? Whilst the assertion that 'This is a complex thesis, and its full discussion lies beyond the scope of this essay' suggests that he is in possession or more data than he reveals, the data that he *does* reveal are open to criticism at various points (Lindbeck 1984: 37). He appeals, for example, to studies that have been carried out with tribes that do not have separate words for green and blue which have apparently shown that members of such tribes cannot therefore discriminate between the two colours. The accompanying rider, that this observation has been made 'erroneously, according to some observers', in fact fails to do justice to the fact that *most* interpretations of these particular data incline towards the view that the lack of language *does not* result in a lack of colour differentiation, but *does* hamper the attempts that tribal members make to *describe* the differences (which they do, in fact, perceive). Thus, for example, Caroline Davis suggests that whilst linguistic factors may have little effect on what is perceived, 'they do affect one's ability to codify percepts and thus to remember experiences, to communicate experiences to others, and to relate experiences to each other' (Davis 1989: 148). Further, even if we *were* to accept the thesis that language may in some sense create or shape experience, we are given no suggestion as to how this may occur. For whilst it may be one thing to assert that language is in some sense the creator/shaper of experience, it is another to describe sufficiently the mechanism by which this feat is actually achieved, and nowhere does Lindbeck attempt to grapple with the problem of how language is actually turned into experience: a crucial question, given the amount of creative power which language is said to possess in his overall analysis. As regards the potential composition of the NDE, therefore, even given the possibility that tighter data than that which he presents are available to him and lead him to the conclusion that language does powerfully shape – even create – experience, we are still left with the question as to how that process may be said to operate. As things stand, the question is simply left hanging.

There may also be said to be a further problem with his dismissal of the possibility of a common core to certain types of experience which, whilst claimed to exist, are said to be ineffable. Recall: for Lindbeck, unless the distinctive features of such a core can be specified, the assertion of its commonality 'becomes logically and empirically vacuous' (Lindbeck 1984: 32). Whilst the force of the charge must be admitted, it is clear that it fails to recognize that what is said to be most important by many religious experiencers – including, perhaps pre-eminently, mystics but also many NDErs – is in fact precisely that aspect of their experience which they *cannot* articulate. Perhaps in these instances something is occurring which transcends the limits of both language and logic. Certainly that is, and has been, the contention of many NDErs whose experiences appear to them to be ineffable precisely *because* they transcend the traditional categories of quantification, description and analysis. The following account, written by a a First World War soldier who 'died' in a mine explosion, illustrates this point well:

> Words are so limiting. How can they describe this burning confrontation which is as vivid today as it was fifty-odd years ago? I try to make little comparisons with worldly joys, but these are so trivial. Relaxing in a warm bath after a hard game; swimming at night in a phosphorescent tropic sea; finding the trail again after being lost in the jungle; seeing light at the end of long research; waking pain-free after an operation; being helped in my gardening by a friendly blackbird; listening to the Sahara as it settled for the night after a day's searing heat – such glimpses

of the underlying peace which accompanies Love's release
from fear or stress can come to all of us. They bring
assurance to those who think. They wake joy, but are only
faint echoes of my out-of-time communion with the heart
of joy Itself in ecstasy of becoming, the new birth.[4]

'Language, Epistemology, Mysticism'

There are clearly a number of significant weaknesses with the
cultural–linguistic understanding of religious experience which our
concentration on the data from NDE testimonies has done much
to reveal. However, even given the existence of such shortcomings,
it might still be argued that Lindbeck's analysis retains useful
insights of clear relevance to the current discussion in its insistence
that there are very real *complexities* involved in trying to separate
experiences as they occur, somehow, 'in themselves' from their
interpretation and subsequent articulation. Such complexities
are suggested still more strongly in a study which, whilst pre-
dating Lindbeck's work, nonetheless shares many of its operating
assumptions and has in recent years triggered considerable and
ongoing debate. The study, a paper by Steven Katz entitled
'Language, Epistemology and Mysticism' which appeared in a
symposium devoted to the philosophical analysis of mystical
claims, *Mysticism and Philosophical Analysis*, has attained classic
status since it first appeared in 1978, and, whilst almost a quarter-
century old, continues to draw significant debate and discussion.
In his own recent postmodern critique of mysticism, for example,
Don Cupitt denoted the appearance of Katz's paper as a watershed
in the study of religious experience, asserting – contentiously, as
we shall see – that it marked the death of the prevailing view
of religious experiences as standing somehow prior to their
expression in language, and arguing that '[a]fter the publication
of Steven Katz' symposium, people quickly acknowledged
that religious experiences are everywhere couched in the locally
available symbolic vocabulary' (Cupitt 1998: 21). In fact, *contra*
Cupitt, an entire symposium, the proceedings of which were edited
by Robert K. C. Forman, *The Problem of Pure Consciousness*, was
recently devoted to an analysis and *refutation* of the position
occupied by Katz in his original paper (Forman 1990). More

recently still, Matthew Bagger has responded forcefully to Forman's edited critique of Katz, and in the process has produced a spirited defence of a variety of aspects of the original 1978 study (Bagger 1999: 90–108ff.). Clearly, Katz's study has generated wide-ranging and ongoing debate and at this point we may usefully pose a threefold question in relation to it, once again within the context of the study of NDEs, by asking: (a) what was and is its overall position? (b) how may the current chapter contribute to the discussion it provoked? and (c) how may Katz's insights allow us to decide whether the light encountered by many NDErs ever can or will be definitively identified?

Broadly speaking, throughout 'Language, Epistemology and Mysticism', Katz is concerned to outline in detail the episte-mological complexities involved in any attempt to understand mystics' reports of their experiences: complexities which assume even greater significance when any attempt is made to discern and outline a universally shared common core to their claims. From the outset, therefore, it promises to add much to our overall enquiry. Katz begins by examining three possible positions regarding what may be said to be common to all mystical expe-riences, and sets them out as follows:

I   All mystical experiences are the same; even their descriptions reflect an underlying similarity which transcends cultural or religious diversity.

The second, more sophisticated, form can be presented as arguing:

II   All mystical experiences are the same but the mystics' *reports about* their experiences are culturally bound. Thus they use the available symbols of their cultural–religious milieu to describe their experience.

The third and most sophisticated form can be presented as arguing:

III   All mystical experience can be divided into a small class of 'types' which cut across cultural boundaries. Though the language used by mystics to describe their experience is culturally bound, their experience is not (Katz 1978: 23–4).

Ultimately, Katz will reject all three of these positions on various grounds: even the third and most sophisticated form which, as he admits, has been occupied by some of the most apparently rigorous analysts of mystical experience, including R.C. Zaehner, W.T. Stace and Ninian Smart. In their place, Katz will substitute a view of mystics' experiences as differing often quite markedly across religions and cultures, with the differences being conditioned and caused by the differing cultural and religious sensibilities – and hence *expectations* – of the mystics and mystical groups concerned. Thus, he asserts, far from sharing a common cross-cultural essence, mystical experiences are formed and shaped throughout and from the outset by the religious training, background and beliefs of the mystics involved. It is not the case, therefore, that a common experience is subject to post-experiential shaping by mystical subjects. Indeed, at the beginning of his paper, Katz declares that 'forcing multifarious and extremely variegated forms of mystical experience into improper interpretive categories' as options 1, 2 and 3 essentially do, gives a misleading impression of commonality-in-diversity but is, in fact, a result of the 'reductive and inflexible' typologies adopted by theorists such as Zaehner and Stace. In place of their positions, Katz presents his study as a corrective and a 'plea for the recognition of differences' (Katz 1978: 25).

At the outset, Katz sets out the foundational – and widely quoted – claim that will run throughout his essay:

> *There are NO pure (i.e unmediated) experiences.* Neither mystical experience nor more ordinary forms of experience give any indication, or any grounds for believing, that they are unmediated. That is to say, *all* experience is processed through, organized by, and makes itself available to us in extremely complex epistemological ways. The notion of unmediated experience seems, if not self-contradictory, at best empty.
>
> (Katz 1978: 26; emphasis in the original)

In similar vein he continues:

> This 'mediated' aspect of all our experience seems
> an inescapable feature of any epistemological inquiry,
> including the inquiry into mysticism, which has to be
> properly acknowledged if our investigation of experience,
> including mystical experience, is to get very far. Yet this
> feature of experience has somehow been overlooked or
> underplayed by every major investigator of mystical
> experience whose work is known to me. *A proper evalu-*
> *ation of this fact leads to the recognition that in order to*
> *understand mysticism it is not just a question of studying*
> *the reports of the mystic after the experiential event but*
> *of acknowledging that the experience itself as well as the*
> *form in which it is reported is shaped by concepts which*
> *the mystic brings to, and which shape, his experience.*
>
> (Katz 1978: 26; emphasis mine)

Once again it is important to be clear as to what, precisely, is being
argued here and throughout. As with Lindbeck, Katz wants to
assert the ubiquity of interpretation in the shaping and mediating
of experience. Thus, we cannot simply peel away post-experiential
interpretation by any given mystic in order to arrive at what
his or her foundational experience was and is, somehow, in
itself. Rather, we must be prepared to accept the fact that all
experience, including religious experience, is shaped throughout
by concepts which we bring to, and which shape and make
possible, our experience. In other words, concepts, including
linguistic concepts, shape mystical experiences in advance and
throughout and therefore no intelligible mystical experience of
any kind may be said to be possible in the absence of such
ubiquitous conceptual shaping. In this regard, consider the
assertion of Caroline Franks Davis:

> Perception of any type is never a purely physical activity;
> it involves the whole person. We are not passive recipients
> of ready-made representations of our environment; rather,
> stimuli from that environment must be processed by
> various interpretive mechanisms before they can have any

significance for us, and constitute a perceptual experience (as opposed to mere sensation). Such an experience is thus the product of complex intellectual activity in which we have, in the psychologist Jerome Bruner's well-known phrase, 'gone beyond the given'.

(Davis 1989: 149)

In a sense, this is what Katz wishes to assert in the case of mysticism. Davis in fact claims support for this position, not merely from philosophy, but from psychology too, and gives a number of salient examples to secure the point thoroughly. What she does *not* stress in the above passage, however, is the role that interpretive activity plays not simply in mediating representations of our experienced environment but actually in the part-creation of it. This is certainly the point that Katz wishes to make forcefully and consistently in 'Language, Epistemology and Mysticism' with regard to mysticism. For him, it is the case not just that belief-concepts interpret the mystic's experience after the event, but that in an important sense they shape it throughout to the extent that the experience a mystic has is actually conditioned by the expectations he brings to it as a result of his mystical training and background. The fact that religious backgrounds and belief-systems differ so widely is thus what makes mystics' cross-cultural experiences so *different*.

There is an immediate problem with Katz's reasoning and methodology up to this point, and indeed throughout. Granted, it has become almost a commonplace within philosophy and psychology to assert that apprehension of the world is never direct but always interpreted, that we never see things-in-themselves, and that in and through the act of perceiving the perceiver directly affects and influences what is in fact perceived. Thus, when Katz makes the assertion that all intelligible experience is complex, interpretation-rich and mediated, he is making a relatively uncontroversial claim that draws wide support from a rich range of empirical studies, particularly from within psychology. However, it is surely important to recognize that Katz is attempting to carry over and apply such firmly secured insights to a very unusual context in his paper: that of mystical experiencing, which is typically and by definition said to be a state which bypasses normal modes of sense and apprehension. In the light of this recognition, it is surely right to ask whether or not insights which have been developed via close examination of the normal, everyday, physical world *can* or ever *should* be applied without qualification to states, apprehensions and encounters which do not take place there. Indeed, the NDE is once again a good context within which to make and test this criticism of Katz. For when an NDEr encounters a light – however identified – within an NDE, it cannot be said to be the case that the NDEr is apprehending it via the normal channels of sense perception. Presumably in this highly unusual context the laws of perception that govern the physical world cannot be said to operate; consequently something other than simple physical seeing is at work. And whilst direct apprehension of things-in-themselves is indeed impossible within the normal run of things, it may well be the case that the same laws do not apply in the very different realm of religious experiencing, such as that in which mystical experiences and NDEs may be said to occur.

This said, Katz's argument is an improvement on Lindbeck's in two key ways. First, whilst we saw that Lindbeck provides rather poor empirical data in support of his cultural–linguistic thesis, Katz attempts to defend and illustrate his position via recourse to detailed descriptive analyses of a range of different mystical experiences. This occupies a significant part of his paper, and whilst we have the space only for one detailed example here, it at least gives a flavour of the rigour which Katz brings to his enquiry overall. Why, Katz ponders, do mystics in the Jewish Kabbalistic and the Buddhist traditions have different experiences? When the former achieve their ultimate mystical state – 'devekuth' – they are not absorbed into God as a drop of water would be absorbed into the sea, but rather, enjoy an intimacy with and a clinging to God in which the sense of individual self-identity is retained. The 'I–Thou' sense of encounter is upheld. The 'I' is not lost or submerged in the 'Thou'. Katz compares the attainment of mystical union with God within the Kabbalistic tradition with that encountered within Buddhism. He argues that: 'The pre-conditioning of the Buddhist consciousness is very different from that of the Jewish and this difference generates the radically different mystical experience which the Buddhist aims at and reaches.' For the Buddhist, the attainment of Nirvana, in direct contrast to the Jewish devekuth, is *not* an I–Thou relational state, but one in which individual self-identity is *lost*. This belief is part of the mystic's training and belief, and generates, argues Katz, a powerful expectation that the ultimate state of the mystic's experience will be like this. And thus it turns out to be. A comparison of the experiences reported by mystics from both traditions shows us this plainly, he asserts. In short, the types of experiences which the differing Jewish and Buddhist mystical traditions define as being of ultimate attainment actually *dictate* the form that such attainment will take. It is not the case – and it makes no sense to claim – that an identical experience is being interpreted in two different ways. It is simply the case that the two types of mystics have qualitatively different types of experiences. Katz concludes:

> The absence of the kinds of experience of unity one often, but mistakenly, associates with mysticism, even as the 'essence of mysticism', in the Jewish mystical context, is very strong evidence that pre-experiential conditioning affects the nature of the experience one actually has. Because the Jew is taught that such experiences of unity do not happen for reasons flowing out of the Jewish theological tradition, he does not, in fact, have such experiences.
>
> (Katz 1978: 34–5)

A second aspect of Katz's paper which may be seen as a development from Lindbeck's position concerns the possibility of a transcendent source of origin or trigger for such experiences. As we have already noted, Lindbeck is unclear about this, but hints that naturalistic processes – explicitly, Freud's 'oceanic feeling' – may be at work in the creation of mystical type experiences. Katz is more subtle in this regard, however. He certainly does not wish to claim, as some of his critics have suggested, that the mystics' conceptual vocabularies actually and solely *cause* their experiences. Bagger (1999: 97) has recently cited this misunderstanding of Katz's position as a fundamental weakness of the editor's contribution to the Katz-inspired symposium *The Problem of Pure Consciousness*. And indeed, a careful reading of

'Language, Epistemology and Mysticism' reveals that the author stops short of asserting anything like this position. For example, towards the end of his study he writes, 'We must heed the warning that linguistic intentionality does not generate or guarantee the existence of the "intentional object", but we must also recognize the epistemologically formative character of intentional language mirroring as it does intentional acts of consciousness' (Katz 1978: 63). In other words, language does not solely *cause* mystical experience, but does contribute to its formation as (a particular variety of) mystical experience. As to what *triggers* the experience to begin with, Katz is silent, as perhaps befits the study of mysticism in particular. Nowhere does he appear to postulate a purely linguistic and/or psychological origin, as writers such as Lindbeck and, more recently, Don Cupitt appear to seek to do. Instead, as Bagger asserts, he 'leaves that question for theology, physiology, or neurology and only insists that philosophically the mystical data can reveal no answer' (Bagger 1999: 97).

What he *does* have much to say about, however, are the well-known attempts that have been made by James, Stace and others to draw up a list of common features which may be said to constitute the common core underlying mystics' reports. Of these, perhaps that of Stace is the best known, with its inclusion of the following characteristics:

1 Unifying vision, all things are one, part of a whole
2 Timeless and spaceless
3 Sense of reality, not subjective but a valid source of knowledge
4 Blessedness, joy, peace and happiness
5 Feeling of the holy, sacred, divine
6 Paradoxical, defies logic
7 Ineffable, cannot be described in words
8 Loss of sense of self.
                    (quoted in Beit-Hallahmi and Argyle 1997: 74)

Once again, Katz sees in such attempts as these the imposition of a misleading consistency on what are in reality clearly diverse experiences. Again, there is much that Katz asserts that space does not permit us an exhaustive analysis of, but, in essence, what he draws attention to is the now widely appreciated fact that words only 'mean' things in context. Thus, for example, where James (1960) famously cited four elements – ineffability, noetic quality, transiency and passivity – as constitutive of the core of mysticism, Katz sees problems. For common use of a word like ineffability, he writes, may lead observers to the conclusion that every experience which is referred to as ineffable must be in some sense similar. Katz disputes this contention, arguing that whilst 'two or more experiences are said to be "ineffable", the term "ineffable" can logically fit many disjunctive and incomparable experiences'. For many contradictory experiences – such as dread as opposed to joy – can all be designated as in some sense is ineffable if an experient feels that he or she lacks the adequate language to convey their depth or intensity. Thus: 'an atheist can feel a sense of dread at the absurdity of the cosmos which he labels ineffable, whilst the theist can experience God in a way that he also insists is ineffable' (Katz 1978: 48). Shared use of a word like ineffable in these two very different contexts does not mean that each experience should be designated the same or similar. Indeed, even across religions, the problem exists in a very similar way. Thus: '"ineffable" *nirvana* is not the ineffable *Allah* of the Sufi, nor the ineffable *Allah* of the Sufi the "ineffable" *Tao* of Taoism' (Katz 1978: 48). And so on.

In a similar vein, Katz also singles out the much more detailed lists of claimed common characteristics of extrovertive and introvertive mysticism – such as that of Stace, cited above – which feature the oft-repeated claims that mystical experiences are ineffable and which include a 'sense of objectivity or reality' as part of the shared essence of mystics' experiences. Once again, Katz takes exception to a somewhat indiscriminate use of a word like *reality* which effectively 'lifts' it out of its context as used by each mystic in order to assert the (spurious) presence of cross-cultural commonality. Thus, he writes that: 'While it is the case that all mystics claim that theirs is an experience of reality – actually reality with a capital R – this seemingly common claim provides no basis for Stace's extreme conclusion about the "universal common characteristics of Mysticism".' Why? Again because of the presence of different, seemingly incompatible uses of the word 'reality' across a range of traditions of which Stace is either unaware or which he chooses not to acknowledge. Thus:

while objectivity or reality (Reality) in Plato and Neo-
platonism is found in the 'world of Ideas', these
characteristics are found in God in Jewish mysticism
and again in the *Tao*, *nirvāna*, and Nature, in Taoism,
Buddhism, and Richard Jefferies respectively. It seems
clear that these respective mystics do not experience the
same Reality or objectivity, and therefore, it is not
reasonable to posit that their respective experiences of
Reality or objectivity are similar.

(Katz 1978: 50)

In sum, therefore, Katz is critical of any and all attempts to assert
commonality to experiences on the basis of the presence of
identical or similar descriptors within testimonies which simply
disguise the fact of the real differences that exist between the
experiences they seek to describe. Such a position, for him, simply
fails to pay sufficient attention to the fact that what may be –
indeed often is – occurring is that 'different ontological realities'
are simply 'being covered by the same term' (Katz 1978: 51).

Language, epistemology and the NDE

We must once again return to the central focus of the current
chapter, for in the light of the above discussion we may now be in
a position to ask to what extent it can be said to be the case that
Katz's arguments have made impossible the identification of the
light encountered in so many NDErs' testimonies. In answer to
this, we may begin by returning to one of the questions with which
we began: that is, whether or not any conclusions drawn arising
from his study of mysticism *can be* carried over to the study of
NDEs. What has become clear as a result of this brief overview
is that there seems no reason why they should *not* be. For if
the concept of unmediated experience is impossible, as Katz
asserts, then presumably that is as true for the NDEr as it is for
the mystic. What such a conclusion would mean for the purposes
of the current enquiry is that any attempt at recovery of a pure
experience that is later interpreted by the NDEr in testimony is
flawed from the outset, because it fails to recognize that the NDE
is shaped throughout by concepts and expectations that the NDEr

brings to his or her experience and which therefore structure and help create and shape it.

Indeed, *expectation* has emerged as a crucial shaping force in Katz's analysis of religious experience. This fact becomes very clear towards the close of his paper. Thus, as a result of his overall analysis, he is able to conclude:

> This much is certain: the mystical experience must be mediated by the kind of beings we are. And the kind of beings we are require that experience be not only instantaneous and discontinuous, but that it also involve memory, apprehension, *expectation*, language, accumulation of prior experience, concepts, and *expectations*, with each experience being built on the back of all these elements and being shaped anew by each fresh experience.
> (Katz 1978: 59; emphases mine)

He continues:

> Thus experience of *x* – be *x* God or *nirvāna* – is conditioned both linguistically and cognitively by a variety of factors *including the expectation of what will be experienced* . . . There is obviously a self-fulfilling prophetic aspect to this sort of activity.
> (Katz 1978: 59; emphasis in the original)

We note in these extracts the force of the assertion as it stands. How does it enable us to further explore the experiences of NDErs? We have already noted that such an analysis is problematic within the NDE context because it is often unclear how the NDEr learns the conceptual repertoire of expectations that may be said to have shaped his or her experience. Indeed, we have already noted at least one account (see p. 118) that pre-dates the modern era of near-death studies, and yet looks very much like a contemporary NDE. In addition, we have also had detailed cause to question whether the acknowledged fact that uninterpreted experience is an impossibility within the normal run of things also holds true in the distinctly abnormal context of near-death and mystical experiencing: an assumption apparently held by Katz

131

but not without significant problems. However, examination of yet more NDE testimonies raises further questions about drawing oversimplistic conclusions regarding the relationship of expectation to experience within this context. For what is to be made of the claims of NDErs who report specific *details* of experiences which they simply *did not* expect to have? The question arises precisely because a number of NDErs report just such experiences, sometimes even remarking on the presence of such unexpected elements within their NDEs. Consider, for example, the following testimony-extract:

> At the time of my NDE I was a practising Roman Catholic. Had I died I would most certainly have expected that any visions I had would have related to my faith, and that if I was to see a being of light I would have related it to Jesus or Mary or an angel. As it was, when I suddenly found myself in this gentle glowing light and standing a little below the three beings above me, they appeared as young Indian men, and, though they were dressed alike in high-necked silver-coloured tunics with silver turbans on their heads, I felt they were young Indian princes, or rajas. Two were facing each other and the third facing me. And from a jewel in the centre of each forehead or turban three 'laser' beams emitted, meeting in the centre.
> My whole lifestyle was changed as a result – much reading about various religions and philosophies.
>
> (Fenwick and Fenwick 1995: 81)

Indeed, what is noteworthy about the closing statement within this account is the fact that the *experience* itself sparked an interest in acquiring knowledge about a variety of religions and philosophies which the NDEr manifestly did not possess at the time of the experience. It is clearly not the case here that prior expectation created the possibility and detail of the experience, and even though the respondent does show some awareness of the existence of a 'being of light' motif within such accounts, it is unclear as to whether she possessed this knowledge at the time of her NDE. What *is* clear is that the overall experience she had ran counter to her prior religious expectations – apparently quite markedly. How, one wonders, might Katz account for the presence of features in testimonies like this, features that *surprised* subjects? Indeed, such an observation may be said to lend weight to a criticism of Katz voiced by Forman in which he questions the adequacy of Katz's model for an understanding of *innovation* and *novelty* within traditions of religious experiencing.[5]

Of course, Katz is not alone in holding the position he does. As we have seen, Lindbeck would also wish to assert that cultural–linguistic expectation shapes experience. So too would Don Cupitt, who in a faintly amusing vein has recently noted of Marian apparitions:

> Mary's various personal appearances on Earth . . . must be carefully preplanned from the heavenly end. She must be kitted out for each occasion with the right skin-colour, costume, dialect, message to deliver, and so on; and there must be no mistakes. Think how traumatic it would be if she were to speak the wrong dialect, or to garble her message! Fortunately, one has never heard of a theophany . . . of a denizen of a supernatural world, in which the one who appeared wore the wrong clothes or fluffed her lines. It just doesn't happen, does it?
>
> (Cupitt 1998: 38)

The implication here, as throughout Cupitt's anti-realist reading of religious experience, is that such experiences are products of expectation, without exception. In the context of this quotation, however, consider the following account sent to Osis and Haraldsson by a doctor which details an observation made of the experience of a young woman patient who nearly died in childbirth:

> She thought she saw her patron saint, the one she prayed to. She introduced him to me, thinking he was right beside her. I didn't see a thing! It was Saint Gerard – the 'saint for the impossible.' She was very happy to see him, and somewhat surprised by his appearance: 'Oh, I didn't expect to see you dressed in that clothing!' She said he was dressed in humble attire, like a monk with sandals and a

gray gown. 'I thought you would be dressed in velvet.' She felt he came to help her get well. She still feels he saved her.

(Osis and Haraldsson 1997: 153–4)

Indeed, the suspicion that a careful reading of experients' testimonies reveals a number of instances where features of their religious experiences surprised them – and hence were not a product of language/expectation – grows when other varieties of religious experience are considered. In this context, for example, consider a further – non-NDE – account from the archives of the Religious Experience Research Centre:

> I was listening to some records, when I felt as though something had been put round me; no words can describe the feeling which filled me. I felt that some presence was with me, I had never experienced anything like it before. It was with me about thirty seconds, then it slowly withdrew, but I was never the same person again . . . if you have never experienced anything like this, you could say it was in my imagination, but if you have had such an experience, then I don't have to try and tell you what it is like, as you will know . . . I think I should tell you that I [do not] belong to any religious body . . . I give it no name to you, as I yet cannot give it a name myself.
>
> (Hay 1990: 46)

Once again, it is hard to see how prior expectation could have created the conditions for such an experience, which plainly occurred unsummoned and unexpected and remained afterwards unnamed. As regards Lindbeck's oft-repeated assertion that language is necessary for experience, it is noteworthy that this respondent actually notes a *failure* to be able to name what it was that 'arrived' in the room: even up to the time of writing. Indeed, of relevance to the current discussion, one final account may be noted, again from the archives of the Religious Experience Research Centre and again reproduced by its ex-director David Hay:

> A friend persuaded me to go to Ely Cathedral to hear a performance of Bach's B Minor Mass. I had heard the

work, indeed I knew Bach's choral works pretty well. I was sitting towards the back of the nave. The Cathedral seemed to be very cold. The music thrilled me . . . until we got to the great Sanctus. I find this experience difficult to define. It was primarily a warning. I was frightened. I was trembling from head to foot, and wanted to cry. Actually I think I did. I heard no 'voice' except the music; I saw nothing; but the warning was very definite. I was not able to interpret this experience satisfactorily until I read – some months later – Rudolf Otto's *Das Heilige*. Here I found it: the 'numinous'. I was before the Judgment Seat. I was being 'weighed in the balance and found wanting'. This is an experience I have never forgotten.

(Hay 1990: 71)

We could go on multiplying such testimonies, NDEs and others, which present either particular problems for Katz by containing features which seem to contradict expectation, or which present particular problems for Lindbeck by appearing to precede their means of articulation in language. In both of these respects, of course, they also cause problems for anti-realist interpretations of religious experience, such as those espoused by Cupitt. Katz may respond – as, indeed, might Lindbeck and Cupitt – by saying that the experiences were not consciously expected, but none-theless unconsciously anticipated. In other words, that they were expected by the experients *really*. In response to this contention, however, we might observe that whilst it is clearly permissible to occupy this position, it is somewhat untestable; this at the very least weakens it considerably.

A common core: conclusions

The suspicion dawns, therefore, that not all religious experiences are a product of language and/or expectation. Indeed, the study of NDE and other testimonies, leading to the unearthing of at least some that contain features that were clearly unexpected by their subjects, may be seen in this sense to constitute additional data, providing a cautious counter-note to conclusions drawn about the nature and construction of religious experience within other contexts, such as that of mystical analysis: an important conclusion and achievement in itself. But what of the possibility of a common core to the NDE? Does the weight of the arguments examined within this chapter, with their clear and numerous weaknesses, still preclude it?

Problematical for those who would wish to deny any possibility of a core to NDE testimonies is the simple fact that a core, of sorts, does appear to exist. Even though, as noted extensively above, philosophical and epistemological truthfulness and rigour may warn us to be cautious of claims such as those of Moody that the features of such a core may be straightforwardly discerned and described as they are 'in themselves', nonetheless it seems clear that certain motifs *do* recur within NDErs' testimonies with some regularity, both cross-culturally and pre-Moody. The presence of some kind of light motif seems very widespread, as we have already noted, as does the experience of a period of darkness en route or prior to it.

Indeed, in recent years the darkness motif has drawn welcome attention from researchers, with some of these, such as sociologist Allan Kellehear, wishing to assert it as a general, possibly core feature of NDEs as a result of his own ongoing cross-cultural analysis. Once again, however, we are left with a variety of problems when attempting to account for what the darkness actually 'is', just as we are when attempting to specify the nature and identity of the light. Kellehear, for example, whilst asserting that 'darkness appears to be a cross-cultural experience' (Kellehear 1996: 188), debates whether it is always described as a tunnel. Indeed, in his cross-cultural analysis of NDE motifs in *Experiences Near Death* he cites a variety of testimony-extracts which appear to describe movement through some area or period of darkness but which describe it in various ways. Many of these interpretations turn out to be, perhaps predictably, culture-specific. Thus, for example, a Chinese report exists which describes emergence from a 'dark tubular calyx'. As regards the cultural resonance of this feature, Kellehear notes that: '[The] calyx, of course, is the throatlike part of a flower and complements the lotus imagery of much pure land Buddhist narrative' (Kellehear 1996: 34). Elsewhere, as we have seen, other researchers have drawn attention to the presence of some kind of period of darkness within NDE accounts. Moody cites a tunnel, Ring and Grey cite 'entering the darkness', Sutherland cites movement towards a light as part of her NDE 'deep structure', and so on. In a small survey of African accounts, Morse cites the unusual testimony of a grandmother suffering from a stroke, who stated that:

> During this time I felt I was put into a big calabash with a big opening. But somehow I couldn't get out of it. Then a voice from somewhere said to me, 'Be brave. Take my hand and come out. It is not yet your time to go.'

Again, we note the possibility that an area of darkness – perhaps enclosed or even tunnel-like – is being described using imagery appropriate to an African setting: in this instance the hollow shell of a gourd. Indeed, in this instance, it is worth noting that the whole experience of the respondent ends up being described and interpreted by her in distinctly non-Western terms: 'I believe someone was trying to bewitch me, but found that I was an innocent soul' (Morse and Perry 1992: 122–3). As regards the *interpretation* of the darkness, Kellehear presents the intriguing suggestion that Westerners use 'tunnel' so often because it is a culturally available image that denotes *movement*, not architecture. Noting that 'The tunnel experience is not described in most non-Western accounts, though an experience of darkness of sorts often is', he concludes, persuasively, that as regards Western accounts, 'Shape reflects architecture rather than experience, but it is experience that is being described by NDErs. Because the experience is difficult to communicate, the descriptions will always be rich in interpretations that lean more toward metaphor than toward measurement' (Kellehear 1996: 37).

The presence of even a limited set of apparently cross-cultural elements – such as movement through darkness and light – creates genuine problems for those who plead for a recognition of differences but fail to admit the possibility of commonality-within-difference within near-death testimonies. At the very least, such commonality deserves comment. If the entire population of the United Kingdom were asked to record their dreams in a single night and even if only a million of them recorded such apparently consistent (and ordered) dream motifs as darkness preceding light or encounters with deceased relatives, the consistency would surely be both acknowledged (however else their dreams may have varied) and the whole situation deemed worthy of closer investigation.[6] Clearly, as regards the NDE, the situation cries out for closer cross-cultural analysis and wider-scale study, as Badham has proposed. As regards the current study, however, it is clear as a result of the cumulative weight of evidence considered in the current chapter that a tentative conclusion regarding the possibility of a common core *can* be advanced, although the next chapter will need to take certain aspects of the investigation in further, more psychological, directions.

For this chapter, as intended, has largely confined itself to exploring the epistemological and philosophical issues surrounding the question of the possibility of such a core within NDErs' testimonies, with the aid of extant literature dealing with other types of religious experience. To this end, we have deliberately chosen to focus most of the discussion around the work of celebrated and much-debated exponents of what have been regarded as powerful cases *against* the possibility of such a core either existing or being susceptible to exhaustive and accurate definition. Although careful analysis reveals that Katz leaves open the possibility of some sort of transcendent trigger for mystics' experiences, it is clear from our overview of his work that the power of expectation in shaping such experiences creates real problems for any attempt to discern what that pure unshaped trigger may be said to be. For him, therefore, as for others, the notion of an identifiable common core to be found across the range of claims to such experience is still highly problematical.

However, even given the genuine value of insights into the complexities underlying the composition of experiential testimony to be derived from these writers, it is clear that a case can still be made for the possible existence of such a potentially identifiable core, largely arising from what have been seen to be genuine problems existing within their research. For the current chapter has also demonstrated: (a) the existence of discernible core NDE features in the absence of any awareness or expectation of their occurrence, (b) the presence of *unexpected* elements to some NDErs' experiences, (c) a strong suggestion of *commonality* of NDE motifs such as the traversing of darkness towards light both within and across cultures, and (d) outstanding problems in accounting for the mechanism(s) whereby language shapes or creates experiences such as those of mystics and NDErs. These four crucial areas, it is clear, combine at the very least to make the argument that NDEs are simply a product of language and expectation problematical. They also leave open the possibility that, after all, a core may exist within many NDErs' experiences which is only *later* interpreted by them in accordance with their varying cultural, linguistic and religious backgrounds. To be sure, such post-experiential shaping may still make it difficult to specify what common motifs such as the darkness and the light may actually be: that is, to *identify* them. It is equally clear, however, that to do justice to what has actually been reported by many NDErs regarding the specific details of their experiences demands that we recognize the *possibility* of the existence of a common core underlying their culturally determined attempts to describe it.

As a result of such analysis we may end up with a much more limited commonality or core than has been hitherto suggested by the elaborate models of researchers such as Moody. As a consequence of this, and in place of such elaborate models, we may wish to substitute a much more limited core with fewer elements. This chapter has strongly hinted at two possible candidates for it: episodes of light and darkness. Further specifically cross-cultural analyses may unearth more. As we have seen, much *existing* NDE research to date has specified at least a discernible number of consistently encountered elements as part of an overall core. What it has *not* done – and what this chapter *has* – is to exercise sufficient caution in identifying what these features *really* are in themselves. In one crucial sense, therefore, this chapter stands as a warning against oversimplistic attempts to claim definitive interpretations and identifications of NDE motifs which say more about the identity of those doing the identifying than about the identity of the light itself. As we have already seen, for example, even Moody's description of the underlying 'being of light' within NDErs' interpretations in testimony is itself an (unacknowledged) interpretation. Carol Zaleski's too brief philosophical treatment of the possibility of a common core to NDEs in her otherwise classic study *Otherworld Journeys*, whilst appearing to come down against the possibility of the existence of such a core, at least draws attention to the ubiquity of interpretation within NDE testimony and the culturally determined identification of the light as a 'being of light' in much near-death research. Indeed, this offers a useful comparison with Katz's assertion that when mystical researchers talk of a commonality of encounter with 'Being' within mystical reports *they* are in fact imposing their own interpretation upon its identity and nature, and that

> Substituting what seem to be more neutral terms such as 'Being' . . . proves less helpful than at first appears because 'Being' too is not a free-floating bit of ontological information, but part of the flotsam and jetsam of specific meaning-systems.
>
> (Katz 1978: 56)

Transplanting such an assertion into the context of discussion of the NDE provides further reinforcement to the argument that even 'being of light' will not do as a description of what the light really is in itself.

At the end of this chapter, therefore, the proposal is made that the possibility of a common core remains, and that certain features of it, whilst not permitting of straightforward definition, are at least amenable to detection and general – albeit culturally determined – description. Far from being a product of language and/or cultural–linguistic expectation, these features may indeed constitute part of an *underlying core* to NDErs' reports which are taken up and interpreted by NDErs both during and after their experiences, but which stand prior to and independently of their culturally acquired expectations of what death may be like. What remains problematical, however, is any attempt to state definitively what the elements of that core are, for even post-experiential shaping ensures that the core may appear masked or disguised. Indeed, as regards the light's identity, we cannot even take Badham's subtle approach and attempt to identify it by function, for it appears to do a number of things, as we have also noted: sometimes merely acting as a destination, sometimes lighting the way, sometimes judging, sometimes asking questions, and sometimes simply returning NDErs to where they came from.

To end with such a conclusion is to admit that there may be a point beyond which analysis simply cannot go. *May* be. At least as regards NDEs, however, far from being 'logically and empirically vacuous' (Lindbeck 1984), the assertion of some sort of commonality seems demanded by the evidence as it stands, with detailed epistemological scrutiny turning out, after all, to lend support to the near-death researchers who have wished to assert the possibility of cores and deep structures within NDE testimonies. Of course, we have not yet committed ourselves to answering the question as to what underlies or causes the commonality. A fingerprint of sorts has indeed been detected, but little has, as yet, been said about the possibility of a hand. Thus the question: 'What causes the NDE?' remains. Also remaining, and exposed vividly via a detailed concentration on the claims and testimonies of NDErs, are very real questions concerning the adequacy and effectiveness of constructivist approaches to and understandings of religious experience such as those adopted and espoused by Katz, Lindbeck, Cupitt and others.

In recent years, however, and as might be expected, there has been no shortage of attempted answers to the question of what the core is in itself. As alluded to at the beginning of this chapter, a number of attempts have been made from within psychology and specifically from within neuroscience to account for all features of any proposed common core to NDEs on the basis of what we know about brain structure and its creations of reality, including any possible altered states of reality brought about by the onset of death. In order to probe more fully into the nature *and* origin of NDErs' experiences, and to bring such research firmly into the theological and philosophical domain, it is therefore necessary to introduce such insights more fully into the discussion.

4

OF PLOTS AND MINDS
Neuroscience, narrative and the NDE

Mind models

Talk of a common core to NDEs raises all sorts of questions that a largely philosophical and theological examination of the evidence cannot answer. In particular, it arouses the suspicion that more attention needs to be paid to the role of the *brain* in mediating or possibly creating such experiences. We have already hinted that some researchers have attempted to explain every aspect of NDEs in terms of recognized and understood processes occurring in the brain at or near the point of death. As this chapter will seek to show, many of these researchers have advanced theories which purport to account neurologically for *every* detail of the NDE: from popular motifs such as tunnels and lights through to other commonly encountered elements such as the out-of-body experience, feelings of bliss and joy, and the life review.

Given the importance of neuroscience for the examination and understanding of the NDE overall, it is clear that attention must be paid to this significant body of research. In the process, however, it is anticipated that some may be led into strange and unfamiliar territory, including theologians and philosophers possessing no grounding in the *exotica* of neuroscience, for whom such an enquiry will be completely new. A key objective of this chapter, therefore, will simply be to introduce interested non-specialists from these and other related fields to some of the most important existing neuroscientific literature that has emerged within the last quarter-century of near-death research. It will gradually become clear that this overview raises serious questions concerning the overall effectiveness of every available neuro-scientific hypothesis that has been presented as an explanation of the NDE, and the chapter will therefore raise inevitable questions concerning the adequacy of these hypotheses as complete explanations of NDErs' testimonies. By way of conclusion, insights from disciplines quite separate from neuroscience and inclining once again towards theology and philosophy will be explored: not least those which promise to unravel the complexities underlying the relationship between experience, narrative, testimony and mind.

Neuroscience and the NDE:
'single factor' theories

The history of neuroscientific attempts to explain the NDE is as short as the modern era of near-death studies itself, yet the history they share is a common one. Beginning at the same time as the first wave of studies of NDEs in the mid-1970s, there was a series of initial attempts to discover a neurological explanation of the phenomenon which promised to render redundant any assertions that such experiences were finally providing empirical data proving details of the liberated soul's final journey to the other side. From the outset, these attempts acknowledged that some kind of structured and unusual experience was occurring to large numbers of people at or near the point of death, and that appeals to explanations of this experience which viewed it as a product of either mere imagination or conscious or unconscious fabrication would not do. As noted in chapter 1, Moody's pioneering work quickly gave way to a number of subsequent studies, such as those of Ring and Sabom, which confirmed that some kind of recognizable phenomenon was (a) occurring and (b) was needful of explanation.

A key hypothesis discarded almost from the outset was any attempt to explain the NDE as a simple dream. For one thing, there was an obvious need to explain why, if NDEs were to be viewed in this way, so many persons would have such similar dreams. Further, note was duly taken, again by the earliest researchers, of the repeated assertions from NDErs themselves that their experiences were qualitatively *different* from dreams. Typical of these are two testimony-extracts reproduced by Sabom:

It's reality. I know for myself that I didn't experience no fantasy. There was no so-called dream or nothing. These things really happened to me. It happened. I know. I went through it. Even though I was in a blackout stage I know myself that I went through it.

(Sabom 1982: 227)

I've had a lot of dreams and it wasn't like any dream that I had had. It was real. It was so real. And that peace, the peace made the difference from a dream, and I dream a lot.

(Sabom 1982: 227)

By discounting this initial cluster of theories, researchers created a need to turn to a variety of academic disciplines for answers to the questions posed by the NDE. Psychology was an obvious front runner amongst these: but *which* area of psychology? Psychoanalytically oriented schools, perhaps, which might offer to account for the NDE in terms of processes deployed to deal with the anxieties posed by death's imminence? Or neuroscience, with its emphasis on the exploration of the brain's functioning and/or its various structures? In fact, the vast majority of theories advanced within the last twenty-five years have been taken from the latter, including appeals to the effects of drugs on recognized brain areas, alterations in levels of oxygen and carbon dioxide and their attendant effects on brain function, the release of naturally occurring stimulants and narcotics such as beta-endorphins near death, effects of sensory deprivation on perception in contexts of extreme impairment of faculties, and the possibility of certain types of epilepsy triggered by the onset of death, including, most frequently, those types occurring in selected portions of the brain, usually the right temporal lobe. Whilst some of these have been questioned by ongoing investigation (as we shall see), some have remained popular throughout the history of near-death research as at least *part*-explanations for the detail of the experiences embodied in near-death testimony.

NDEs and drugs

One particular neuroscientific explanation quickly emerged in the early years of near-death research that saw in drugs – and in particular *anaesthetics* – the key to the mystery of the NDE. Early attention focused on *ketamine*, an anaesthetic developed in the early 1960s and given to patients with cardiovascular or respiratory problems for whom other types of anaesthetic were medically unsuitable. Obviously many NDErs might be expected to fall into this category, and from their own reports – sometimes cross-referenced with medical records – it was clear that many NDErs were under anaesthetic at the time of their experiences. Might ketamine, then, be the simple and sole cause and explanation of NDEs? A study undertaken in the 1970s by Lester Grinspoon and James Bakalar at Harvard University found that ketamine produced hallucinations (dubbed 'emergence reactions') in a significant percentage of experimental subjects which included a range of NDE-like features including out-of-body sensations and subjective impressions of journeyings to other worlds (Grinspoon and Bakalar 1979). Grinspoon and Bakalar concluded from their study that emergence reactions to ketamine 'often seem so genuine that afterward users are not sure that they have not actually left their bodies'. In support of their contention, it is notable that subsequent uses of ketamine for purely recreational purposes have produced similarly vivid and subjective sensations, as in this testimony-extract cited by parapsychologist D. Scott Rogo:

> My perceptions were getting disoriented and when I closed my eyes a lot of information started to happen. Colors, patterns, cross-connections in sensory perceptions. Sounds and inner visions got confused . . . I got deeper and deeper into this state, until at one point the world disappeared. I was no longer in my body. I didn't have a body . . . Then I reached a point at which I felt ready to die. It wasn't a question of choice, it was just a wave that carried me higher and higher, at the same time that I was having what in my normal state I would call a horror of death. It became obvious to me that it was not at all what I had anticipated death to be. Except, it was death, that something was dying. . . .
>
> (Rogo 1989: 123)

One obvious objection to the ketamine theory is that not all persons reporting NDEs were or are under anaesthetic, an objection strengthened by the fact that ketamine is no longer in general medical use, whilst persons still continue to report NDEs. Indeed, the fact that a clear percentage of NDErs undergo their experiences having been given no drugs at all might be seen to further militate against any and all pharmacological explanations. As Zaleski has asserted, 'one cannot build a coherent theory of near-death experience on a psychopharmacological basis [because] not all near-death subjects were under medication, and, in any case, the effects of different drugs vary endlessly' (Zaleski 1987: 165). Granted the force of this objection, it is notable that in recent years the suggestion has been made that the body may itself automatically synthesize under certain conditions naturally occurring opiates that mimic the perceptual side-effects of externally induced medications such as anaesthetics. Indeed, in this context, even a modified form of the 'ketamine hypothesis' has reappeared recently, forwarded by research psychiatrist Karl Jansen (Bailey and Yates 1996: 265–77). Noting that ketamine *does* seem to produce many of the effects associated with the NDE, Jansen has argued that the drug acts as a blocker within a brain besieged by dangers resulting from low blood pressure, and in the process protects a group of cells known as NMDA receptors from damage. Perhaps, Jansen has suggested, the body synthesizes a chemical with a similar effect to ketamine for the same blocking purposes when under severe stress – for example whilst near death – producing comparable side-effects. Clearly there is much here that is needful of further analysis, and Jansen is currently working to develop his hypothesis. Objections to it, however, might be expected to stem from the obvious fact that many effects produced by ketamine, such as the feelings of disorientation and horror expressed in the above account cited by Rogo, do not seem to be reported by many NDErs who instead frequently report contrary sensations of greater perceptual clarity and feelings of bliss and peace. In addition, it is clear that even the limited core NDE features examined in chapter 3, such as periods of darkness followed by light, are seldom reported by ketamine users. The problem seems to be, and was recognized early on, that only a theory that can account for every commonly reported feature of the NDE will suffice as an entirely satisfactory, total neuro-scientific explanation of the phenomenon. In recognition of this problem, a number of other neuroscientific interpretations of NDE phenomena were quickly forthcoming.

Anoxia and hypercarbia

Anoxia (also known as *hypoxia*) is a condition in which there is a reduced supply of oxygen to the brain, causing a disruption or cessation of normal functioning and leading to brain toxicity and corresponding altered states of consciousness. *Hypercarbia* is a condition in which carbon dioxide levels in the brain are elevated, producing comparable effects. There is general agreement that a life-threatening crisis event such as a severe accident or cardiac arrest might result in the occurrence of both conditions, largely due to the disruption in normal blood flow rates which would be expected to occur under such – or similar – circumstances. Drawing on this simple recognition, both anoxia and hypercarbia have been advanced virtually throughout the modern era of near-death studies as possible explanations for NDEs. As arguments on behalf of both as causatory agents for the NDE differ widely, it will be useful to consider both separately and in turn.

Anoxia/hypoxia

Writing in 1980, Nathan Schnaper, Professor of Psychiatry at the University of Maryland, suggested hypoxia as one of a small number of 'primary aetiologies' for the altered states of consciousness which he saw as constituting contemporary NDEs (Sabom 1982: 239). In similar vein at virtually the same time, psychiatrist Richard Blacher of the Tufts University School of Medicine asserted in the *Journal of the American Medical Association* that 'people who undergo these "death experiences" are suffering from a hypoxic state, during which they try to deal psychologically with the anxieties provoked by the medical procedures and talk' (Sabom 1982: 209). Blacher's position is interesting here in that it attempts to marry neuroscientific and psychoanalytic interpretations of the NDE into a neat synthesis. Once again, however, the hypoxia explanation – with or without additional psychoanalytic theories – has come under sustained attack. Responding to Blacher in the 4 July 1980 issue of the *Journal of the American Medical Association*, for example, Michael Sabom wrote:

Sensational after-life proclamations by prophets in the lay media cannot be countered with scientific assertions based on anecdotal experience. Such seems to be the case [with Dr. Blacher and his several medical explanations of the experience] . . . Dr. Blacher points out that 'the physician must be especially wary of accepting religious belief as scientific data.' I might add that equal caution should be exercised in accepting scientific belief as scientific data.

(Sabom 1982: 209)

In more recent years, the anoxia hypothesis has come under additional criticism from Peter and Elizabeth Fenwick. Suggesting that a 'properly controlled study' is needed to settle the hypoxia hypothesis one way or the other, the Fenwicks have also questioned it on the grounds that whereas hypoxia would be expected to create confusion and disorientation in a dying brain, NDErs report, if anything, greater clarity and mental lucidity, as already noted. Furthermore, they cite the testimony of an NDEr who, having suffered lack of oxygen at high altitude whilst an RAF pilot, had effectively undergone both oxygen deprivation and an NDE at different times and on different occasions, and who thus constituted his own control experiment for the testing of anoxia as an explanation for the NDE. Part of his near-death testimony – reproduced by the Fenwicks – reads:

I found myself 'floating' along in a dark tunnel, peacefully and calmly but wide awake and aware. I know that the tunnel experience has been attributed to the brain being deprived of oxygen, but as an ex-pilot who has experienced lack of oxygen at altitude I can state that for me there was no similarity. On the contrary, the whole [NDE] experience from beginning to end was crystal clear and it has remained so for the past fifteen years.

(Fenwick and Fenwick 1995: 213)

Despite ongoing criticism, however, the anoxia theory, like the ketamine hypothesis, dies hard. As we shall see, it has been revived in detail and at length by Susan Blackmore in recent years as an explanation of a variety of core elements of the NDE.

Hypercarbia

More than two decades before the modern era of near-death studies, psychiatrist L.J. Meduna attempted to investigate the use of air rich in carbon dioxide for the treatment of certain psychological conditions. In a series of experiments carried out in the 1950s and well before the modern era of near-death studies, Meduna administered to 200 subjects (including controls) a variety of mixtures of inhalations of gas with varying amounts of carbon dioxide, up to a total of 30 per cent. (Normal air contains a far smaller concentration of CO_2.) The results of these CO_2-rich inhalations included startling perceptual alterations, which in many ways parallel several common NDE elements:

> I felt as though I was looking down at myself, as though I was way out here in space . . . I felt sort of separated.
> (Sabom 1982: 242)

> It was a wonderful feeling. It was marvellous. I felt very light and I didn't know where I was . . . And then I thought that something was happening to me. This wasn't night. I wasn't dreaming . . . And then I felt a wonderful feeling as if I was out in space.
> (Sabom 1982: 242)

> I felt myself being separated; my soul drawing apart from the physical being, was drawn upward . . . where it reached a greater spirit with Whom there was a communion, producing a remarkable, new relaxation and deep security.
> (Fenwick and Fenwick 1995: 215)

Clearly, here, we have many of the features which we would associate with contemporary NDE reports, including feelings of disembodiment, autoscopy, feelings of bliss and peace, and encounters with transcendent beings. Other of Meduna's subjects reported additional phenomena, including 'replays' of past memories and bright lights. Furthermore, Meduna even hints at the presence of a common core to such experiences, writing that:

'During the CO_2 treatment, brains of different persons – persons with divergent emotional needs – *produce similar or even identical phenomena. These phenomena, moreover, are not specific to the function of the agent . . .*' (Sabom 1982: 243; emphasis mine). His conclusion, that 'All the phenomena – dreams, hallucinations, eidetic imagery – rest on some underlying physiological function of some brain structures, which function operates independently from what, in psychiatry, is called personality', also serves to reinforce this point (Sabom 1982: 243). Thus, it would appear that not only does hypercarbia produce phenomena consistent with those reported by NDErs but also that it produces consistent phenomena such as would explain a degree of commonality across NDErs' reports. Is it reasonable, therefore, on the basis of results such as those obtained by Meduna to conclude that hypercarbia simply *causes* the NDE?

On the one hand, this would appear to be the case. After all, in a dying organism in which vital functions such as respiration and heartbeat have begun to fail it might be expected that a build-up of carbon dioxide and corresponding lack of oxygen might begin to permeate the system, including the brain. Peter and Elizabeth Fenwick, however, whilst admitting that hypercarbia may simulate certain aspects of the NDE, nonetheless assert that oxygen deprivation would lead to confusion and disorientation: feelings rarely reported by NDErs. In addition, the Fenwicks note that the NDE would be expected to lead to *overbreathing* which would correspondingly *lower* carbon dioxide levels (Fenwick and Fenwick 1995: 215–16). The key argument in opposition to the hypercarbia theory, however, appears to be supplied by Sabom who records the NDE of a man whose blood oxygen and carbon dioxide levels were measured actually *during* his NDE, a procedure allegedly witnessed by him whilst out of body which later showed that 'his arterial carbon dioxide level was actually *lower* than normal' (Sabom 1982: 244; emphasis in the original). From this, Sabom concludes:

> The fact that he had 'visually' observed this blood gas procedure indicates that the blood was obtained at the time his experience was occurring. Thus, in this one documented case, neither a low oxygen level (hypoxia)

nor a high carbon dioxide level (hypercarbia) was present
to explain the NDE. . . .

(Sabom 1982: 244)

Clearly, Sabom rests much here upon one case. His own and
the Fenwicks' objections notwithstanding, hypercarbia seems to
duplicate many of the features normally associated with NDEs.
However, given the existence of 'white crows' such as Sabom's
non-hypercarbic NDEr, the argument that hypercarbia simply
causes the NDE may also need to be treated with caution. Might
yet other explanations of NDEs therefore prove more fully
satisfactory?

Beta-endorphins

In the early 1980s, a new, naturally occurring brain-based pain-
killer, the *beta-endorphin*, was discovered and successfully
synthesized and it was not long before the effects of this substance
in producing feelings of peace, bliss and painlessness were seized
on by some as an explanation of the overwhelmingly positive
nature of most NDEs. In the early 1980s, for example, researcher
Daniel Carr, instructor of medicine at Harvard Medical School,
argued forcefully in the the *Journal of Near-Death Studies* that
endorphins were involved in producing aspects of the NDE (Carr
1982). His and subsequent research in this context has been
taken up most extensively in the recent writings of University
of the West of England psychologist Dr Susan Blackmore, who
has been long associated with ongoing and sustained attempts
to account for every feature of the NDE neuroscientifically
(Blackmore 1982, 1993).

For Blackmore, a massive release of endorphins – termed an
'endorphin dump' – would be expected to produce the very
feelings of peace and mystical euphoria reported by NDErs. For
her, the positive emotions associated with the natural release of
endorphins can be found in a range of other contexts also,
including the collected experiences recorded by Heim of moun-
taineers who fall great heights but sustain no physical injury as a
result of their falls. From these and other comparable accounts of
bliss experienced as a response to sudden psychological conditions

of fear and stress but where no resultant physical damage ensued, Blackmore has concluded that the *psychological* apprehension of life-threatening danger is itself enough to trigger a release of endorphins, explaining in the process the significant numbers of NDEs which have been reported by persons who thought that they were in danger but who suffered no physical injury at all. Eschewing *total* explanations of NDEs in terms of one particular trigger such as anoxia, Blackmore prefers the endorphin theory as a *part*-explanation of NDErs' experiences, turning to other theories in addition (and including anoxia) as explanations of other aspects of the *total* experience. As we shall see, the recognition that only a processional number of causative factors could provide a total explanation of every aspect of the NDE (which itself is viewed as a description of the dying process as seen from *inside* the dying organism) represented a considerable but somewhat late improvement on the single-factor theories which dominated early neuroscientific discussion of the phenomenon. Noting that the word endorphin is a combination of 'endogenous' and 'morphine', Blackmore asserts that this naturally occurring opiate is released into the brain and spinal cord within a range of contexts to enhance feelings of well-being and decrease the adverse effects of physical exertion, including pain and feelings of stress. Joggers and long-distance runners have been found to have raised levels of endorphins in their systems when tested.

Noting that lowered blood pressure – as would be expected to occur near death – has also been seen to trigger release of endorphins, Blackmore additionally suggests that endorphin release may also be implicated in the life review element of many NDErs' experiences. This is because endorphins have also been shown to trigger seizures in the limbic system of the brain which includes the temporal lobe: long suspected as the trigger for a range of religious and mystical experiences and the reproduction of 'lost' memories. For Blackmore, what is crucial to note about the limbic system is the fact that it contains a large number of areas where endorphins and their receptors are most commonly found. One function of endorphins is to decrease the 'seizure threshold' of certain parts of the brain: the level of activity at which a group or area of cells will suddenly begin uncontrollably firing. The result of such disinhibition is epilepsy, but the form and severity that the epilepsy takes will depend on the part of the brain that is affected. As endorphins are found in large numbers in the temporal lobe, it would thus be expected that the epilepsy would be concentrated here, producing corresponding feelings of a mystico-religious nature and the release of hitherto-forgotten or repressed memories but without necessarily any accompanying – and visual – signs of fits or tremors. We shall have much more to say about the role of the temporal lobe in mediating aspects of NDErs' experiences shortly, and we thus reserve greater discussion of Blackmore's contentions in this regard for then.

As may have become predictable at this point of the current discussion, every theory that has been advanced to explain the NDE is rapidly confronted by a range of critiques and counter-claims. In 1982, and soon after the discovery of beta-endorphins, Michael Sabom, ever ready with a counter-argument to every conventional neuroscientific explanation of the NDE, argued that studies in which beta-endorphins were injected into the cerebro-spinal fluid of fourteen pain-ridden cancer sufferers revealed that pain relief lasted from 22 to 73 hours. If endorphins were implicated in the pain relief and bliss felt by NDErs, surely their relief and euphoria should last much longer than it apparently does (Sabom 1982: 235). This seems a strong argument, given that pain and stress usually return to NDErs immediately following their resuscitation, as the following testimony-extracts make clear:

> As I approached more closely, I felt certain that I was going through that mist. It was such a wonderful, joyous feeling; there are just no words in human language to describe it. Yet, it wasn't my time to go through the mist, because instantly from the other side appeared my Uncle Carl, who had died many years earlier. He blocked my path, saying, 'Go back. Your work on earth has not been completed. Go back now.' I didn't want to go back, but I had no choice, and immediately I was back in my body.

I felt that horrible pain in my chest, and I heard my little boy crying, 'God, bring my mommy back to me.'

(Moody 1975: 76)

There was someone there in the light, waiting for me. And then suddenly I was pulled back, away from it, back, slammed into my body again, back with the pain, and I didn't want to go. I just wanted that peace.

(Fenwick and Fenwick 1995: 6)

Karl Jansen (quoted in Bailey and Yates 1996: 274), supporter of the ketamine hypothesis, has recently argued that endorphins are not hallucinogens and thus cannot produce the rich altered states narrated by NDErs. In similar vein, Allan Kellehear has criticized Blackmore's hypothesis, writing that 'it is rare to observe runners experiencing life review, tunnel sensation, and meetings with deceased relatives' (Kellehear 1996: 121). Forceful as both of these critiques may be seen to be, it is clear that Blackmore is not proposing that the effects of endorphins are responsible for every element of the NDE, as we have already had cause to note. More telling is the observation of Peter and Elizabeth Fenwick that most people undergoing stress and coming near death have raised endorphin levels, but only a comparatively small percentage have NDEs. Once again, therefore, as with virtually all of the hypotheses which this chapter has so far considered, more research is clearly necessary.

Temporal lobe seizure

One possible theory which has been advanced as a full- or part-explanation of the NDE, and which our consideration of the endorphin hypothesis has alerted us to, is that which invokes the role of the *temporal lobe* as creating a number of the features which are common to NDEs. Of particular interest here are neuroscientific studies and experiments which appear to suggest that changes in the functioning of the temporal lobes during altered states of consciousness may lead to sudden 'eruptions' of buried memories in ways analogous to those which appear to constitute the life review element of many NDErs' experiences. Certainly, a number of studies, some not necessarily directly concerned with attempting to specifically understand near-death experiences, make the possible connection between temporal lobe disturbance and the NDE a distinct and intriguing one.

Neuropsychologist Oliver Sacks, for example, in a collection of case histories drawn in part from his own clinical practice, cites two patients who consulted him because of the unbidden revival of musical tunes from their past which they could actually hear replayed and superimposed upon – and sometimes, indeed, even *drowning out* – normal, everyday, background sounds (including, at times, their conversations with Sacks himself) (Sacks 1985: 125–42). One woman welcomed these tunes nostalgically as providing a kind of biographical gap-filling exercise for her, due to the fact that the tunes came from a past part of her life about which she otherwise remembered next to nothing. The other woman was disturbed by them, and wanted them to stop. What, Sacks pondered, was causing these women to hear such things?

His extensive knowledge of neuroscientific literature led him to the conclusion that they were in fact suffering from 'musical epilepsy'; more specifically, an epileptic disturbance of their brains located at a precise area: the temporal lobe within the cerebral cortex. For, according to Sacks, such musical 'reminiscences' (as they were dubbed by Hughlings Jackson to whom Sacks pays homage in his paper) 'occur solely in the context of temporal lobe seizures'.

As noted by Sacks, the first person to explore Jackson's reminiscences empirically was Wilder Penfield, whose exploratory brain-mapping techniques half a century ago produced quite startling phenomena which remain much discussed to this day. By applying a mild electrical stimulation to certain parts of the brain, including pre-eminently the cerebral cortex containing the temporal lobe, Penfield was able to evoke apparently random snatches of remembered scenes, some apparently consciously forgotten by his patients. Appropriately stimulated, Penfield's patients might recount, for example:

> a time of listening to music, a time of looking in at the door of a dance hall, a time of imaging the action of robbers from a comic strip, a time of waking from a vivid dream, a time of laughing conversation with friends, a

time of listening to a little son to make sure he was safe, a time of watching illuminated signs, a time of lying in the delivery room at birth, a time of being frightened by a menacing man, a time of watching people enter the room with snow on their clothes. . . .

(Sacks 1985: 131 quoting Penfield and Perot 1963: 595–696)

Before proceeding, it may be useful to place alongside this typical sequence of stimulated past-life memories the detail and description of the life review as recounted, commonly, in some NDErs' testimonies. Compare, for example, the above account with the following accounts:

During this stage, my life just flashed in front of my face. My whole life . . . Things that had happened to me in my lifetime, like when we got married, just flashed in front of my eyes, flashed and it was gone. When we . . . had our first child flashed in front of my eyes. The biggest thing, I guess, and the longest thing that stayed flashing in front of my eyes, was when I accepted Jesus Christ.

(Sabom 1982: 74)

It was really strange where [the life review] started . . . when I was a little girl, playing down by the creek in our neighbourhood, and there were other scenes from about that time – experiences I had had with my sister, and things about neighbourhood people, and actual places I had been. And then I was in kindergarten, and I remembered the time when I had this one toy I really liked, and I broke it and I cried for a long time. This was a really traumatic experience for me. The images continued on through my life and I remembered when I was in Girl Scouts and went camping, and remembered many things about all the years of grammar school. . . .

(Moody 1975: 66)

Compare also with the following account, narrated well before the modern era of near-death studies:

> The course of those thoughts I can even now in a great measure retrace ... a thousand other circumstances minutely associated with home, were the first series of reflections that occurred. They took then a wider range – our last cruise – a former voyage, and shipwreck – my school – the progress I had made there, and the time I had misspent – and even all my boyish pursuits and adventures. Thus, travelling backwards, every past incident of my life seemed to glance across my recollection in retrograde succession; not, however, in mere outline, as here stated, but the picture filled up with every minute and collateral feature. In short, the whole period of my existence seemed to be placed before me in a kind of panoramic review, and each act of it seemed to be accompanied by a consciousness of right or wrong, or by some reflection on its cause or its consequences.
>
> (Blackmore 1993: 183)

At first sight, the recollections evoked by Penfield's exploratory surgical techniques and the life reviews reported by the above respondents whilst near death seem remarkably similar. There is the same sense of involuntary recall, which seems qualitatively different from mere memory and reminiscence, and including – at least in the second account – the same sort of 'flash cut' sequence from memory-image to memory-image with no overt sense of plotting or intentional sequence as was found by Penfield. Indeed, Penfield highlighted the seemingly random sequence of memories which his procedures evoked, Sacks citing his overall conclusion that the selection of memories narrated to him by his patients seemed 'chosen' 'quite at random' (Sacks 1985: 134). However, closer inspection reveals that many NDErs' life reviews are not random sequences of memory-scenes, but, rather, follow a sort of sequence or rationale. The above account from Sabom (1982), for example, appears to highlight selected, important, scenes from within the respondent's life, climaxing with the acceptance of Christ as Lord and Saviour. The third account, cited by Blackmore and narrated by Sir Francis Beaufort who had only narrowly escaped drowning in Portsmouth Harbour in 1795, appears to have arisen with some sort of didactic purpose for him. We recall the closing assertion that 'each act of it seemed to be accompanied by a consciousness of right or wrong, or by some reflection on its cause or its consequences'. Even the second account, cited by Moody, occurs within the context of a form of judgement in which the respondent is shown by the being of light the consequences of each remembered thought and action. These typical examples seem far from random involuntary recollections. Rather, they appear to fulfil some sort of purpose which we might indeed anticipate as being profoundly relevant to the dying process: the recollection of the high spots and/or particularly traumatic episodes of a life looked back upon, perhaps, or the assessment of the morality and consequences of one's actions. This selectivity is well summed up by the following recollection of a key aspect of his life review as narrated by a young victim of a tank explosion in Italy in 1945 and relayed as part of a fascinating account submitted to the archives of the Religious Experience Research Centre in 1977:

> It concerned an occasion when I was about six years old and had recently returned from India, and had gone out to play with a bunch of the local children. One of these children had a dog which delighted in chasing anything that was thrown for it, sticks, stones or if there was anything, a ball I suppose. And I can remember picking up a stone and throwing it across the railway lines – I happened to be pointing in that direction. The dog chased this stone, straight into the path of an express train going from Paddington to somewhere else in the west country I suppose, and it was instantly killed. I'd never played with a dog before in my life up to then: I'd no idea the dog would get hurt otherwise I'd never have done it. But I immediately got a replay of the whole darned thing in detail.

Reflecting on this within the context of his life review, the respondent was given to understand that 'the soul is an indelible record. We can't get at it, but it can be got at and it can be replayed'.[1]

At this point, then, it would appear that despite the apparent similarities between evoked memories derived via stimulation of the temporal lobe and the life review reported by many NDErs, the selectivity and purposive nature of the latter appears to set it apart qualitatively from the former. Yet a closer look reveals that even this apparent contrast may be misleading and thus needful of closer examination and possible revision. For, *contra* Penfield, Sacks asserts that apparently involuntary epileptic discharges within the temporal lobe can in fact give rise to highly *meaningful* memories of great significance to some sufferers. One of his patients suffering from musical epilepsy, for example, heard the tunes of her apparently lost youth which filled, according to Sacks, a 'nostalgic need' at once 'chronic and profound'. Of this lady's lost youth and its relationship to her consequent condition, Sacks writes:

> Orphaned, alone, she was sent to America, to live with a rather forbidding maiden aunt. [The patient] had no conscious memory of the first five years of her life – no memory of her mother, of Ireland, of 'home'. She had always felt this as a keen and painful sadness – this lack, or forgetting, of the earliest, most precious years of her life. She had often tried, but never succeeded, to recapture her lost and forgotten childhood memories. Now . . . she recaptured a crucial sense of her forgotten, lost childhood. The feeling she had was not just 'ictal pleasure', but a trembling, profound and poignant joy. It was, as she said, like the opening of a door – a door which had been stubbornly closed all her life.
>
> (Sacks 1985: 136)

Thus, far from being simply a random musical replay of half-forgotten childhood tunes, Sacks's patient's musical reminiscences served a crucial purpose: a purpose felt all the more keenly when they faded away. Indeed, her sadness when the tunes finally ceased, summed up in her wistful comment that 'The door is closing . . . I'm losing it all again', strikingly parallels the feelings of regret which many NDErs express when their experiences cease and they are brought back to normal life (Sacks 1985: 137).

In further support of his contention that apparently random seizures can in fact produce highly relevant and purposive experiences and feelings, Sacks additionally cites the report of another patient – neither his nor Penfield's – whose epilepsy was triggered by the stress of finding himself alone with strangers. The case, narrated by psychologist Dennis Williams, details an epileptic episode, the onset of which was marked by

> a visual memory of his parents at home, the feeling 'How marvellous to be back.' It is described as a very pleasant memory. He gets gooseskin, goes hot and cold, and either the attack subsides or proceeds to a convulsions.
> (Sacks 1985: 136; quoting Williams 1956: 29–67)

Commenting again on the apparently purposive nature of this experience, given the circumstances of its onset, Sacks remarks that 'I cannot help thinking that if one has to have seizures, this man . . . managed to have the right seizures at the right time' (Sacks 1985: 136). What is also striking about this brief account is how closely it parallels the experiences of NDErs. For, as we have had abundant cause to note, many persons experiencing NDEs experience the onset of their near-death crisis entirely within the company of strangers - 'faceless' medical personnel, perhaps, or strangers at the scene of an accident – before finding themselves suddenly reunited with loved ones in a homely, safe environment which is experienced as a positive, intensely pleasant homecoming. Again, therefore, if we were to invoke disturbances in the temporal lobe as a full or part explanation of the NDE, we might conclude that what we know of temporal lobe epilepsy matches what NDErs report very clearly and closely.

Three further pieces of evidence concerning the nature and functioning of the temporal lobe support this contention. First, we recall Blackmore's argument that endorphins, being found in large numbers in the temporal lobe, may be expected to induce seizure activity here, given their sudden release in times of psychological or physical stress and danger. Second, the Fenwicks acknowledge that the temporal lobe is also highly sensitive to variations in oxygen supply. If anoxia were to occur at or near the point of death, therefore, we would expect it to have a significant effect on functioning in precisely this area of the brain. Third, it is generally acknowledged that sufferers from temporal lobe epilepsy often exhibit symptoms of what is known as *hypergraphia*: the tendency to feel compelled to write at great length about mystical, spiritual and/or conventional religious realities, often fashioning whole cosmologies over time as a result (Kaplan and Sadock 1980: 153). Whilst this is not at all evident as being present within NDErs' testimonies from a reading of studies such as those of Moody, Ring, Sabom and the Fenwicks – in which, as we have already noted, accounts are usually cut up and cited as extracts of fuller narratives – an examination of archival material at the Religious Experience Research Centre reveals a large number of clearly hypergraphic testimonies. Thus, for example, the extract cited earlier of the life review of the man whose stone-throwing as a boy had resulted in the unfortunate death of a dog, whilst containing in a few opening paragraphs some typical NDE features such as the out-of-body experience, tunnel sensation and encounters with deceased persons, also contains some eleven pages of speculative material on the nature of the soul, the purpose of existence, the origin of the universe and the meaning of life. A further exami- nation of the archival material preserved by the RERC reveals that a large number of accounts reveal just this tendency (which is not confined to NDErs). What is most important to note in this context, however, is that hypergraphia has been long recognized as a symptom of temporal lobe epilepsy. Whilst the presence of hypergraphia within NDErs' reports has been hidden from view often because of the editing of accounts carried out by near-death researchers themselves, an examination of original accounts never before seen by a wider scholarly public – such as those in the RERC archives – reveals that hypergraphia is a significant feature of a significant number of accounts. Once again, the temporal lobe seems involved in the NDE, at least by implication. And once again, more research is clearly called for.

Inevitably, the role of the temporal lobe in creating or mediating NDE-type experiences has been strongly debated. Perhaps also inevitably, Michael Sabom has often led the way in this. Taking up and considering the role of the temporal lobe in *Recollections of Death*, for example, Sabom cites a number of reasons why he feels it is not involved. First, he argues that temporal lobe seizures typically involve sensory delusions involving the interpretation of the size and/or location of objects in the environment, auditory illusions and feelings of remoteness and detachment: not at all what is reported by NDErs. Second, he argues that negative feelings usually predominate when seizure activity occurs in the temporal lobe, leading to expressions of fear, sadness and loneliness. Again, he asserts, such negative emotions contrast sharply with the overwhelmingly *positive* feelings of bliss, peace and joy reported by NDErs. Third, he argues that the nature and intensity of visual and auditory hallucinations produced by temporal lobe epilepsy – including horrible and threatening presences and figures or strange music and voices – contrasts sharply with the majority of accounts reported by NDErs. Fourth, Sabom talks about the random nature of many thoughts and emotions evoked by seizure activity in the temporal lobe, including forced thinking and random ideas crowding the mind in an obtrusive and unwelcome way. Again, he asserts, the NDE lacks such confusion and mental congestion, instead being characterized by clarity and mental lucidity. Finally, he cites a further list of other feelings and experiences associated with temporal lobe epilepsy which seem to militate against the notion that disturbances of the temporal lobe are responsible for NDEs. These feelings include:

> [a] buzzing sound in Heschl's gyrus, odors in the uncus, alimentary tract sensations in the insula, tastes in the cortex just above the insula, somatic sensations from the 'second sensory' area above the insula, and head sensations and body sensations in the deep portions of the temporal tip.
>
> (Sabom 1982: 238; quoting Penfield 1955)

Whilst Sabom's list of counter-arguments to the temporal lobe theory of NDEs seems impressive, there are a number of aspects of it that raise questions and doubts. For one thing, it fails to recognize the existence of negative NDEs (which Sabom did not acknowledge at all in his 1982 study, and to which he devotes only scant attention in his most recent work). However, as chapters 1 and 2 of *this* study have already showed, negative NDEs have long been acknowledged, and whilst not systematically studied, may indeed be in part explicable by some of the more negative and unpleasant results of temporal lobe seizure as detailed by Sabom and noted above, such as feelings of fear and perception of figures and presences of a horrible and threatening nature. It is also of note that Sabom's argument that temporal lobe disturbance may create a sensation of buzzing may actually *support* the argument that the temporal lobe is implicated in the NDE. For whilst it is rarely reported and cited in present-day studies of the phenomenon, an intrusive buzzing noise *was* recognized as an NDE feature by many early researchers, and even found its way into Moody's model. Thus, for example, one of Moody's respondents in *Life After Life* reported 'a really bad buzzing noise coming from inside my head' (Moody 1975: 29–30); another reported 'a loud ringing. It could also be described as a buzzing' (Moody 1975: 30), and another reported a similar 'ringing noise brrrrnnnng-brrrrnnnng-brrrrnnnng, very rhythmic' (Moody 1975: 31).

Not all respondents report such a noise. Moody, again in *Life After Life*, cited NDErs who had heard more melodious sounds, one describing 'Japanese wind bells' and another relating that 'I began to hear music of some sort, a majestic, really beautiful sort of music' (Moody 1975: 30). This finding has certainly been replicated many times in subsequent research and is also well-illustrated in another testimony-extract from the archives of the Religious Experience Research Centre:

> It was 1942 – I was then 27 – when, following the birth of my first child, I suffered an embolism of the lung and lay dangerously ill. There was almost no hope left for my life; my husband was with me day and night in the hospital. Then I had the following experience.
>
> I heard music, which seemed to come from a space without limits, of a beauty and tone colour such as I had hitherto never heard. It filled my whole being with rising joy, with a positive feeling of bliss. I am not really particularly musical, but here I was able to hear every single part individually, at the same time in accord in

wonderful harmony, and the most enchanting thing was
that I could easily have conducted this gigantic orchestra:
the instruments were following my will. I saw no details;
it was all only sound. My pain was forgotten – I just
listened with a deep feeling of happiness.[2]

In this context, we do well to recall Sacks's contention that hallucinations of a particularly auditory nature are typically associated
with temporal lobe seizures, and may include snatches of music
– or even complete tunes – either consciously or unconsciously
known to sufferers from temporal lobe epilepsy. Indeed, he highlights Penfield's acknowledgement that temporal lobe stimulation
is particularly associated with auditory disturbance:

> We were surprised at the number of times electrical
> stimulation has caused the patient to hear *music*. It was
> produced from seventeen different points in 11 cases.
> Sometimes it was an orchestra, at other times voices
> singing, or a piano playing, or a choir. Several times it
> was said to be a radio theme song . . . The localisation
> for production of music is in the superior temporal
> convolution, either the lateral or the superior surface
> (and, as such, close to the point associated with so-called
> *musicogenic epilepsy*).
>
> (Sacks 1985: 131; quoting Penfield and Perot 1963;
> emphasis in the original)

Further criticism of Sabom's position vis-à-vis the temporal lobe
and its relationship to the NDE has emerged in recent years from
Blackmore. She has been critical of Sabom, here, at several points,
arguing first that the NDE consists of a process whereby the
stimulus to the temporal lobe is widespread and hence meaningful,
and not localized and meaningless as was the case in Penfield's
studies. Furthermore, whilst acknowledging that fear may be a
characteristic emotion associated with temporal lobe disturbance,
Blackmore argues that Sabom fails to recognize the presence of
other factors at work in the production of the NDE, which may
modify or even override some of the negative feelings which the
disturbed temporal lobe has been seen to evoke. In particular, as

noted above, she points to the soothing effect of beta-endorphins in creating the feelings of serenity and peace reported by so many NDErs. Finally, Blackmore has highlighted the fact that during the NDE there is a 'generalized amplification of activity' of the temporal lobe which may explain why lots of memories, even some unfolding 'in sequence', are evoked during the life review. She has drawn attention to this in response to Sabom's contention that the temporal lobe could not be responsible for producing the life review because stimulation of the lobe involves 'a random, single event of no particular significance': a far cry from the apparently purposive nature of the life review as reported by some NDErs. For Blackmore – echoing contentions which we have already had cause to note in our examination of Sacks's discussion of musical epilepsy – the memories evoked by an epileptic seizure may indeed be purposive, not random, and may correspond to a patient's hopes, fears and preoccupations as these are related to his or her particular context. She concludes:

> This opens the way to understanding how it is that the life review is so personal and so relevant. It is the concerns of each individual and their own personal interpretations that will be evoked when their temporal lobes are affected near death.
>
> (Blackmore 1993: 217)

Despite the presence of apparently strong counter-arguments regarding his own counter-claims, Sabom has in recent years defended the position that temporal lobe disturbance is not sufficient to explain the NDE. Thus, for example, in his most recent study *Light and Death*, he is critical of the temporal lobe hypothesis for failing to do justice to the phenomenology of the experiences reported by NDErs. In this context, for example, he cites the testimony of Dr Ernst Rodin, Medical Director of the Epilepsy Centre of Michigan and Professor of Neurology at Wayne State University who, based on his clinical practice, has concluded in the *Journal of Near-Death Studies* that:

> The hallmarks and nuclear components of NDEs are a sensation of peace or even bliss, the knowledge of having

died, and, as a result, being no longer limited by the physical body. In spite of having seen hundreds of patients with temporal lobe seizures during three decades of professional life, I have never come across that symptomatology as part of a seizure.

(Sabom 1998: 181; quoting Rodin 1989: 255–9)

Sabom adds to this the observation that, whilst Michael Persinger's well-known laboratory experiments at Laurentian University which have artificially stimulated the temporal lobes of hundreds of subjects have produced alterations of mood and consciousness, these remain nonetheless 'fragmented and variable' and not the 'integrated and focused' experiences of NDErs (Sabom 1998: 179; quoting Persinger 1989: 233–9).

Drawing again on recent neuroscientific advances in the understanding of brain function – including anomalous states of consciousness – Sabom has in recent years even questioned the role of endorphins within the overall experience, appealing to studies that have concluded that the role of endorphins in epilepsy remains highly ambiguous and that endorphins might even be effective in *treating* those suffering from temporal lobe seizures (Sabom 1998: 179).

From the combined weight of these arguments, Sabom concludes:

the 'dying brain hypothesis', which attempts to explain the NDE on the basis of endorphins, hypoxia, and temporal lobe seizures, cannot adequately account for the near-death experience. To do so would be like confusing bronchitis and pneumonia – there may be similarities, but the trained medical observer knows that they are fundamentally different conditions with different symptoms and methods of treatment.

(Sabom 1998: 181)

Within this context, and given that we must respect the weight of arguments advanced from all sides by specialists in the areas of neuropsychiatry and related fields, it is notable that Peter and Elizabeth Fenwick, on the basis of their wealth of neuroscientific training, experience and background, also hesitate to embrace the temporal lobe hypothesis. For whilst, as we have seen, they accept that anoxia may indeed affect the function of the temporal lobe, they question whether temporal lobe seizure is enough to explain the NDE completely. One crucial piece of evidence stands out for them, centring on the related issues of NDErs' memories of their experiences and the clarity and coherency of those memories. First, whilst the temporal lobe is highly sensitive to changes in blood gas composition, it is also, as we have abundant cause to note, associated with *memory*. On this basis, the Fenwicks make the simple point that if effects and disturbances within the temporal lobe are the basis of the NDE, then the experience would be expected to be forgotten. The fact that NDErs' experiences are so firmly and vividly *embedded* in their memories militates, for them, against this explanation.

Indeed, Peter and Elizabeth Fenwick, in discussing neuro-scientific approaches to the NDE in their recent study *The Truth in the Light*, make much of the fact that NDErs so vividly remember their NDEs. The physical and psychological trauma occasioned by situations such as cardiac arrests and/or serious accidents, they assert, would be expected to erase any memories associated with such crisis events. Memory, they continue, is 'delicate and easily damaged' and 'does not function in uncon-sciousness' (Fenwick and Fenwick 1995: 205). Therefore they ask, given current neuroscientific understandings of the function of the brain in assembling mental models of the world which are coherent and remembered, how can we explain the cohesion and vividness of the recalled experiences narrated by NDErs? In this respect, they assert: 'From the point of view of both memory and model-building, it should be quite impossible to have an NDE when brain function is really very seriously disordered or the brain is seriously damaged' (Fenwick and Fenwick 1995: 205). None-theless, they conclude, this appears to be precisely what *does* happen in the case of NDErs.

In support of this contention they cite the case – 'One of the most extraordinary we received' – of David Verdegaal. Whilst on a sales trip to Australia, Verdegaal suffered a massive heart attack followed by a stroke. He was rushed to hospital and revived, having apparently undergone an incredible half-an-hour 'from the time of the arrest to the time they finally managed to restart my heart'. Verdegaal then spent two weeks in a coma, before finally reviving with a tale of a detailed NDE, of which the following is a striking segment:

> It was then that the Lord took me by the hand and led me through a garden where surely beauty had found its name. This was an old-fashioned, typically English garden with a lush green velvet lawn, bounded by deep curving borders brimming with flowers, each flower nestling within its family group, each group proclaiming its presence with a riot of colour and fragrance as if blessed by a morning dew. The entrance to the garden was marked by a trellis of honeysuckle so laden that you had to crouch down to pass beneath while at the other end a rustic garden gate led to the outside. It was here that my walk through was to end as I was gently led through to the other side. It was at this moment that the realization that I was going to live came to me and I would have to face the consequences of living. There followed two weeks as I lay in a coma in an in-between world.
>
> (Fenwick and Fenwick 1995: 206)

Finally, Verdegaal emerged from his coma blind and paralysed. Three years later, after extensive rehabilitation with his tutor, Mrs I.L. Cross (who put him in touch with the Fenwicks), he had recovered sufficiently to start work. Peter Fenwick applies detailed neuroscientific insight to this account. We know, he asserts, that the patient suffered widespread brain damage, including areas associated with sight (hence the blindness) and movement (hence the paralysis). A fall in blood pressure, he adds, was probably the most likely cause of the blindness, affecting the so-called 'watershed areas' of the brain and thus leaving Verdegaal unable to make sense of any visual impressions still available to him. What is of crucial importance to note, for Fenwick, is the fact that despite such massive damage, Verdegaal was still able to retain a memory – structured and coherent to the point of constituting a world in which he was able to see and think – of what had happened to him during the near-death crisis. Upon this point, Fenwick remarks:

> Even if we concede that in some mysterious way, a brain which is disorganized to the point of unconsciousness can retain the ability to make coherent models, these should not be remembered. I would not expect David to have memory of anything he experienced during his period of unconsciousness. Even if in some extraordinary way his brain was able to make models during this time, I would expect them to be fragmented, random and unclear. But this was not so. Not only did David retain memories, but they were coherent memories of a fantastic visual world.
>
> (Fenwick and Fenwick 1995: 207–8)

Thus, the Fenwicks move forward any critique of attempts to account for the NDE neuroscientifically – whether these appeal to the temporal lobe or some other single causal factor – in two key, related, ways. First, they raise the question of why the experience is remembered so vividly, when this would in no way be expected, and second, they question why the experience is remembered as an *ordered whole*, and not just as 'disorganized fragments'. To be secure, they argue, any consistent neuroscientific explanation of the NDE must resolve these two, key, issues. Again, therefore, and overall, despite at times appearing as an attractive neuroscientific explanation of the NDE, any theory which invokes the temporal lobe or any other single-factor theory as the key or sole causative agent for the phenomenon must face the real objections to such explanations which still exist from some highly informed quarters. As we have noted in this lengthy section, the temporal lobe represents a charged battleground over which theories of the NDE have been – and continue to be – exchanged. It remains far from certain, however, what the outcome of the battle will be, unless some way can be found to confront and resolve the objections to this and other single-factor theories which we have unearthed from some highly respected specialists.

Multiple factor theories

The evolving recognition that no one single theory of the NDE has been able to satisfactorily explain every aspect of the phenomenon has given rise in recent years to a number of theories which suggest that more than one causative neurological agent is needed to explain the total experience of NDErs. After all, it is now widely recognized that death is a *process*, not simply a single *event*. A brain undergoing the trauma of its own death does not simply switch off; rather, it begins to undergo a series of developing processes that lead to its ultimate, final, expiry. Thus, in place of positing single-factor theories in order to explain the experienced, subjective reality of this process, some theorists and researchers have turned to more elaborate models of process*es* which might be expected to be occurring within a dying brain. By enlisting a number of factors or triggers for a corresponding number of NDE elements, it is proposed that a total explanation of the entire sequence of the NDE – from the sensation of leaving the body through to the NDErs' eventual return – will succeed where single factor theories, explaining only one or two elements, are bound to fail.

Fire in the brain

Psychologist Ronald Siegel, for example, in an entertaining collection of clinical accounts of hallucination drawn from his own research at UCLA, cites the experience of 'Ace', rendered paraplegic by a near-death crisis-event when he fell off a ladder whilst repainting his house. According to Siegel, during his moments of unconsciousness, Ace experienced some commonly encountered NDE elements, including an out-of-body experience, music, a 'long subway tube . . . [with] smooth crystalline walls which glistened with a bright light coming from the end', the presence of 'spirits' and 'souls' and feelings of peace and calm throughout. Interestingly, given our discussion of the temporal lobe, above, Ace related that it was the music of a well-known singer singing a half-forgotten song that brought him 'back' to life. As Siegel narrates: '"Barbara Streisand brought me back", exclaimed Ace with a straight face, "I heard her singing that song about people who need people, and the next thing I know I'm vomiting in the emergency room of the hospital"' (Siegel 1993: 253).

What, ponders Siegel, is the correct neuroscientific explanation for experiences such as that undergone by Ace? Crucially, he rejects any single causative agent in favour of a possible *variety* of causes, some known, and some yet to be discovered. In this regard, he first of all draws attention to the fact that the NDE has much in common with many other hallucinatory episodes, citing a variety of triggers as being common to both. These, he asserts, may include drugs, stress, fever, isolation and fear; remarking that 'Given an infinite variety of triggers, the brain responds with a finite number of responses' (Siegel 1993: 254). Significantly, he adds to his list of causative agents the possibility that psychological factors – and not simply neuroscientific processes – may be at work also, suggesting that anxieties occasioned by the perceived onset of death may stimulate defence mechanisms whereby an individual may attempt to turn away from the dying body in order to enter a psychological state in which the threat subsides or vanishes altogether. This explanation, akin to the phenomenon of *depersonalization*, he perceives as part of the defence reactions which all human beings share and which manifest in situations of life-threatening danger.

In addition to all of these processes, which, crucially, might reasonably be expected to occur *together* at the point of death, Siegel adds the need to take into consideration still further factors to do with the *context* and *setting* within which the NDE begins to unfold. In particular, he notes that the onset of death may itself trigger the surfacing of religious and cultural fantasies from *within* the self which appear to the dying subject as if they in fact are coming from *outside* it. This confusion of inner and outer may be increased, Siegel writes, in situations where the body's senses are either temporarily thrown out of normal modes of functioning, as in the case of drug administration, or – even more significantly for the purposes of explaining the NDE – when systematically shutting down precisely because the process of death has already begun. To illustrate this point further, he gives the example of a man standing at the window of a lighted room and looking outside as night begins to fall. Such a man, writes Siegel,

> is absorbed by the view of the outside world and does not visualize the interior of the room. As darkness falls outside, however, the images of the objects in the room behind him can be seen reflected dimly in the window. With deepening darkness the fire in the fireplace illuminates the room, and

the man now sees a vivid reflection of the room, which appears to be outside the window. As the analogy is applied to the near-death experience, the daylight (sensory input) is reduced while the interior illumination (the general level of arousal in the brain) remains bright, so that images originating within the rooms of the brain may be perceived as though they came from outside the windows of the senses. Thus, when the Book of John tells us, 'In my Father's house there are many mansions,' or when Ace tells us that there are many spirits in the light, there are probably no more mansions and spirits than there are images of those structures in our own brains.

(Siegel 1993: 254–5)

According to the case study presented, Ace's wife remarks at this point that Siegel's interpretation of her husband's experience makes it sound like a dream. In reply, Siegel only partly accepts the description, preferring to view the experience as '"a waking dream . . . jarred loose by the shock of the accident and organized by the nervous system in such a way to keep the personality of the victim intact"'. In this sense, the NDE is 'really there', but 'in mental not physical space'. Siegel stresses that the limits of the experience we can reasonably expect to have must on this reckoning correspond to what we have in our mental space. Thus, he declares to Ace, '"In a million near-death visions, I could never meet your brother unless I knew what he looked like or sounded like in the first place. And you could never see or hear my deceased father"' (Siegel 1993: 255).

Some of this is already familiar. What Siegel has significantly *added* to the current phase of the discussion, however, is a vivid illustration of how multiple factors and triggers may combine to create the NDE. To the existing list of single factors such as the effect of drugs, for example, Siegel adds the possibility of psychological defence mechanisms induced by death anxieties, the presence of afterlife imagery occasioned by the fact of the perceived onset of death itself, and the shift from models of reality driven by outer images and sensations to models driven by 'inner space'. This significant shift, he argues, is created by the fact that whilst the senses may begin to fail, the inner world might still continue to function: at least for a while. Overall, and in conclusion, it is clear that Siegel does not see in experiences such as Ace's the possibility of proof of life after death (or, indeed, of the reverse), but rather, as providing us with an unusual opportunity to see how a number of factors combine at the end of life to create the illusion of other worlds. However, the reality that death might well be the end is, for Siegel, interestingly confirmed by his research into the communicative skills and abilities of animals. Thus, at the very end of his case study involving Ace, he narrates how he told Ace and his wife the story of attempts to teach a gorilla to communicate using signing. As Siegel concludes the story:

> I described how a team of psychologists taught a gorilla to communicate with American Sign Language. Once he acquired a basic vocabulary, the gorilla showed that he had sophisticated thoughts about life and death. There was great wisdom in his signs, especially when asked, 'What is death?'
>
> I signed the answer he gave. My palms were turned up, fingers pointing away from my body. Then I moved my hands together so they touched, rotated them inward, and moved them apart until the palms faced downward. The sign meant *finished, the end*.
>
> (Siegel 1993: 256; emphasis in the original)

Dying to live

The most complex and comprehensive neuroscientific inter-pretation of the NDE to have appeared in recent years, by common consent, is that proposed by University of the West of England psychologist Susan Blackmore. Over the course of the last fifteen years or so, Blackmore has continued to advance her 'Dying brain hypothesis': a series of multiple causes constituting the neuro-scientific basis of near-death experiences, delivered within the context of an overarching recognition that only a thesis which combines a different cause for each particular element of the NDE can hope to constitute a total neuroscientific explanation of the entire phenomenon. To this end, she combines a number of causes for each aspect of the NDE (from the sense of separating from the body, to feeling peaceful and blissful, to moving through the tunnel towards light, to experiencing a life review and finally to resuscitation and recovery) into a complete framework designed to account neuroscientifically for every specific feature of what is in fact a *composite* – and not a single – experience. As her starting point, therefore, she rejects any theory that sets out to claim that the NDE 'proves' the existence of a soul ontologically distinct from the body and capable of surviving its death. Indeed, such a dualistic concept of selfhood, for Blackmore, fails to do justice to what much contemporary theorizing about the self – both philosophical and psychological – has concluded about what human consciousness is and where it may be said to reside. In common with the Fenwicks, and drawing heavily from the writings of theorists such as philosopher Daniel Dennett, Blackmore argues that our sense of selfhood should be seen as a *model* constructed by the brain from data derived from memory, expectation, the senses and imagination. To this end, she rejects, with Dennett, the old 'Cartesian theatre' model of selfhood: the idea that 'I' am an observer located somewhere inside of me looking out at the world as if in some sort of theatre watching the play of life unfold. Instead, she perceives the self's conception of being a self within what is popularly known as reality as a *model with no core*, immortal or otherwise. There are faint strains of the Buddhist conception of *anatman* in Blackmore's thinking here, well summed-up by the final line of her book *Dying to Live* in which she concludes that 'We are simply here and this is how it is. I have no self and "I" own nothing. There is no one to die. There is just this moment, and now this and now this' (Blackmore 1993: 264).

As may have become clear from these contentions, Blackmore perceives our sense of reality to be composed of the model of conscious experiencing which is most stable at any given time. Thus, she writes that 'the system takes the most stable of its models and attributes to it the status of "real"' (Blackmore 1993: 161). As noted above, in normal everyday functioning that model is a rich composite which consists of information processing from a range of sources: *inner* (memory, imagination, expectation) and *outer* (the senses of seeing, hearing and so on). Both are normally combined in ways we are not entirely conscious of, but the result is a liveable model of self in the world which we call real.

But what, she wonders, might occur at or near the point of death when the senses which mediate the 'outer' components of the reality-model begin to fail? How might the self become constituted, or reconstituted, then? Clearly, within such a context, she asserts, we would expect a number of processes to start occurring. In particular, we might expect the normal, everyday, self-model – with its attendant conception of what constitutes the real world – to begin to break down. As the outer senses begin to fail (with hearing usually the last sense to cease functioning) the brain struggles to construct a model of reality which is still coherent and liveable by drawing on inner data, and using memory, expectation, and imagination in particular for this purpose. Further, the model also begins to be constituted by inner processes that are now experienced as outer events, such as changes wrought in the visual cortex by processes such as anoxia and alterations in functioning of the temporal lobe brought about by massive endorphin release. Such inner processes within such altered states of consciousness are experienced by a dying subject as if they are actually outer events, in ways directly comparable with Siegel's analogy of a man in a lighted room looking out over a darkening world, as examined above. Crucially, the composite model of reality which such processes combine to produce is, for Blackmore, no more or less real than the normal everyday model which combines inner and outer data. For they are both 'a fiction created to make sense of the world' (Blackmore 1993: 223). It is just that the altered state of consciousness into which the dying begin to pass is powered progressively less and less by outer stimuli and more and more by inner stimuli as the dying process advances. This, for Blackmore, explains why NDErs are so insistent that their experiences were more real than dreams. For the system, whilst dying, still valiantly attempts to restore a sense of reality in the best way it can, once again calling reality that which is the most stable model of reality it has. If such is now mainly made up of inner processes, these are experienced as no less real than those which normally constitute the self's everyday model.

Complex as all of this is, it is essentially only the framework within which the detail of Blackmore's thesis is worked out. What that detail consists of is a description of the processes which might be expected to occur within a dying brain and which therefore constitute the data which power the altered model of reality lived in – albeit temporarily – by the dying. Thus, for example, Blackmore considers the out-of-body component of the NDE. What inner processes might be at work here? Recall: any explanation that appeals to the possibility of ontological separation of soul and body is ruled out a priori. So how might Blackmore's thesis attempt to account for the out-of-body experiences of the following NDErs, drawn once again from the archives of the RERC? The first account dates from 1915, when the respondent was seriously injured whilst laying mines beneath the German trenches on the Somme:

> Relief from pain was profound. I seemed to float above the first-aid men who were still trying to keep me alive. I tried to tell them there was nothing more they could do. Somebody said 'he's gone' and my body was carried out of the over-crowded dugout. For a moment I saw it lying half-naked on the pile of dead just behind the trench. Light snow was falling, and began to cover it. Then suddenly, I was free, poised in the silence of a timeless universe.[3]

The second account is taken from a much larger testimony, already quoted in part, from a soldier injured in a tank explosion in Italy in 1945:

> I could literally feel myself pulling out of my own body. There was a very definite sensation of relief of pressure. Eventually I pulled quite clear of the body and floated up to the ceiling where I turned and lay parallel with the ceiling with my back to it looking down at my own body lying on the bed. I was aware of the two men in the beds each side of me, but not particularly interested in them. I looked at myself, thought 'That's strange!' and passed straight through the ceiling.[4]

For Blackmore, both of these experiences would become explicable once it is accepted that the self's sense of location is a construct, a composite model drawing on inner and outer stimuli.

Near death, she writes, body image begins to break down, in large part due to the progressive loss of sensory input. Struggling to construct a coherent model of selfhood – including the *location* of that self in the world – the brain might be expected to turn to data derived from memory; for 'Memory can supply all the information about your body, what it looks like, how it feels and so on. It can also supply a good picture of the world. "Where was I? Oh yes, I was lying in the road after that car hit me" – or, we might add in the case of the above accounts, lying wounded behind enemy lines or in bed after the tank exploded' (Blackmore 1993: 177).

In support of the contention that memory provides the body's location within an NDE, Blackmore cites another vivid image from Siegel illustrating how it is that memory images are constructed from a *bird's eye view*:

Do you see the beach as though from where your eyes would be? Or are you looking from above? Many people recall such scenes in a kind of bird's eye view. It seems likely, therefore, that in the event of nearly dying, or any other circumstance in which the normal model of reality has broken down, such a bird's-eye memory model may take over as 'real'.

(Blackmore 1993: 177)

What are we to make of this set of contentions regarding the out-of-body component of many NDEs? It certainly sounds attractive, attempting as it does to posit a simple explanation of the phenomenon without invoking metaphysical hypotheses involving immortal souls for which, according to Blackmore, there is apparently no real proof. One possible powerful objection to it, however, concerns the set of startling claims made by some researchers – most notably University of Connecticut psychologist and near-death researcher Kenneth Ring – that during near-death episodes NDErs make observations of things around them whilst unconscious which later turn out to have been veridical and which they could not have seen either physically or imaginatively. Outstanding amongst this clutch of cases are instances in which such apparently veridical observations were made by blind and in some cases *congenitally* blind persons. These claims sound so staggering, and contain such potentially enormous implications not just for Blackmore's research but for a wide range of other fields also, that we shall reserve further and more detailed discussion of them for the following chapter.

Explaining the tunnel and the light

Of course, Blackmore also needs to explain the presence of all of the other commonly encountered elements of the NDE, quite apart from the out-of-body component, without invoking non-naturalistic hypotheses, and this she duly does. As we have already had cause to note, for example, she invokes the role of beta-endorphins as the cause of the feelings of bliss and peace reported by NDErs. The temporal lobe is invoked to explain the life review, with the soothing effects of beta-endorphins being seen to cancel out the feelings of fear and disorientation often produced by disturbances in this area of the brain. The phenomenological similarities between the experiences of NDEs and the experiences of users of drugs such as LSD are stressed throughout. What, though, of the two core elements which the previous chapter of *this* study examined in considerable detail: the tunnel experience and the encounter with light?

Three things, she asserts, make for a good theory as regards an explanation of these and the other features of the entire NDE. First, a good theory must be specific. In the case of the tunnel, for example, 'it should be one that explains why there is specifically a tunnel near death and not something else' (Blackmore 1993: 75). Second, a good theory does not simply invent other worlds or transcendent forces to explain unusual events such as those encountered by NDErs during their experiences. As we have already seen, that is why the invocation of any variation on Platonic or Cartesian dualism in order to explain the out-of-body experience is ruled out a priori. In fact, the dualism implied in any attempt to explain the tunnel as a sort of passage to the other world is ruled out, for Blackmore, precisely because it is prey to the same kind of psychological, philosophical and conceptual confusion to which body–soul dualism falls victim. Third, she asserts, a good theory should make testable predictions. In each of these areas, she writes, most existing explanations of the tunnel and light phenomenon fall down. As regards the tunnel, for example, Blackmore contends that it cannot be any kind of real tunnel connecting this world to the next because if such were the case we would expect to be able to see, detect or measure it. Furthermore, she adds, 'if two worlds are fundamentally incommensurable there cannot be anything that goes from one to the other' (Blackmore 1993: 77). Neither, she asserts, can the tunnel be seen symbolically, as has been contended by researchers such as Celia Green and Kenneth Ring, for this begs the question as to why this symbol should be evoked or produced rather than some other. Thus, she argues, if, as has been contended, the tunnel is intended to symbolize the transition from this world to some other place, why are other symbols of transition not reported, such as doorways, arches, chasms and so on? Further, Blackmore rejects any theory that sees in the tunnel and light some sort of final memory or replication of the birth canal with the light of the world being reached at the end. To begin with, infants would not have the cognitive capacity to store such memories at such an early stage of development. In addition, she asserts, there are vast differences between the tunnel apparently traversed by NDErs and what a baby might experience as it moves slowly through the birth canal. Thus, she writes:

> the birth canal is nothing like a tunnel with a light at the end and the foetus does not float gracefully nor rush rapidly down the middle of it. It is an extremely tight fit, squashed to a very short length, and the foetus is pushed out with the top of its head usually emerging first, not its eyes. It takes a vast leap of the imagination to make the two comparable, and yet this theory has produced a welter of 'New Age' ideas and techniques.
>
> (Blackmore 1993: 79)

Finally, and as seemingly conclusive counter-evidence to the claim that the NDE is birth revisited, Blackmore cites her own comparative study of persons born normally and by Caesarean section. Surveying the reports of 254 persons of whom 36 had been born by Caesarean section, she notes that the 36 did not report statistically any more or less NDEs than those born normally (Blackmore 1993: 79–80).

How, then, does Blackmore account for the tunnel and light within her own neuroscientific model? First, she notes that tunnels and tunnel-like phenomena are a common feature within a range of conditions, including epilepsy, migraine, meditation and relaxation, when pressure is applied to both eyeballs, when falling asleep, and when certain drugs such as LSD have been ingested. Indeed, she asserts, approximately one-third of persons have reported a tunnel sensation at some point during their lives, albeit within a range of contexts. It is no surprise that this image has, therefore, been the subject of sustained study over the years. Thus, for example, Heinrich Kluver at the University of Chicago in the late 1930s noted four 'form constants' which he perceived as typically occurring during the hallucinations of experimental subjects, and which included tunnels, spirals, lattices and cobwebs. Commenting on the occurrence of such forms, Blackmore concludes: 'Their origin probably lies in the structure of the visual cortex, the part of the brain that processes visual information' (Bailey and Yates 1996: 291). Indeed, she cites support for just such a conclusion from the work of Jack Cowan, neurobiologist at the University of Chicago. Using mathematical mapping of the processes whereby the external world is perceived and reproduced on the visual cortex via the retina, Cowan has proposed a theory in recent years for the tunnel and light effect encountered in NDErs' testimonies which has been adopted, tested and fine-tuned by Blackmore herself.

Brain activity in the visual cortex, Cowan has argued and Blackmore notes, is usually kept in a stable state due to the function of certain cells which inhibit the action of others. This process of inhibition usually prevents random firing, but in the presence of certain conditions such as anoxia or drug intoxication with hallucinogenics we might expect the process to be interrupted, causing disinhibition and hence *random* firing in the cortex. Of course, as we have already had cause to note, one process that might be expected to occur during a near-death episode is the onset of anoxia, with attendant effects including disinhibition within the visual cortex. Cowan argues that such disinhibition would produce 'stripes of activity' that move across the cortex which can in fact be mapped using complex mathematical formulae. Using such mapping, it can be further shown that such striping would produce a subjectively 'visual' sensation of concentric rings or spirals. 'In other words', comments Blackmore, 'if you have stripes in the cortex you will seem to see a tunnel-like pattern of spirals or rings' (Bailey and Yates 1996: 291).

What preliminary comments might we make about Blackmore's explanation of the tunnel and light motif thus far? To begin with, her thesis certainly might reasonably explain the following tunnel-like experience reported by a Moody NDEr:

> There was a feeling of utter peace and quiet, no fear at all, and I found myself in a tunnel – a tunnel of concentric circles. Shortly after that, I saw a T.V programme called *The Time Tunnel*, where people go back in time through this spiralling tunnel. Well, that's the closest thing to it I can think of.
>
> (Moody 1975: 33)

Thus far, therefore, Cowan may be seen to have provided a theory that accounts for at least some features of the tunnel and light sensation reported by NDErs. But, Blackmore acknowledges, there are some problems with his theory also. For one thing, how might it attempt to account for the bright light reported at the centre of the tunnel by some NDErs? For another, whilst Cowan's work may indeed account for some constancy of reported imagery across some NDE reports, why is it, Blackmore ponders, that NDErs do not report *other* imagery associated with such disinhibition, such as Kluver's other form constants which include lattices and cobwebs?

In order to extend and hence improve Cowan's work, therefore, Blackmore has proposed a streamlined theory. Here, she simply suggests that where the visual cortex is disinhibited, all cells begin to fire randomly, producing neural 'noise'. By mapping what this might look like, Blackmore proposes that because far more cells are devoted to the centre of the visual field than to the periphery, more randomly firing cells will appear at the centre of the field than at its edge. Indeed, using a computer programme to produce a simulation which replicates what this might look like to a dying subject, Blackmore has produced a series of visual images that does indeed look like a dark tunnel with a glowing, growing light at the end. Drawing her conclusions from this, Blackmore asserts that: 'I imagined the effect would appear like a flickering speckled world which gets brighter and brighter towards the centre. Again, this is like a tunnel form' (Blackmore 1993: 84).

Further, Blackmore's fellow Bristol researcher Tom Troscianko has proposed a refinement of her contentions in this regard by suggesting that an increasing amount of disinhibition in the cortex may lead to an ever-increasing amount of neural noise which might be expected to produce the effect 'of a light at the centre getting larger and larger and hence closer and closer' (Blackmore 1993: 85). This, together with the brain's bias towards forward movement, might explain not simply the tunnel and light phenomenon but also the reported sensation of moving *through* a tunnel towards an approaching – and hence growing – light, Blackmore asserts. It may, she adds, also explain why persons apparently move along the tunnel at different speeds ('If the movement is induced merely by the . . . noise then it depends on the amount of noise. The more noise, the greater the speed'), why early research findings suggested that stroke victims report no tunnel sensations (stroke damage to the visual cortex may prevent the processes required to produce the sensation) and why so many NDErs report that however bright the light was, it did not hurt their eyes ('Naturally, it would not hurt your eyes because your eyes are not involved in any way'). Finally, the theory also accounts for why the experience eventually ends:

> According to this theory the tunnel would usually come to an end with all the cells finally ceasing to fire. Alternatively, if the oxygen supply happened to return before this stage was reached, the inhibition would resume, the light dim, and the movement reverse. In this case one would presumably have the sensation of going back down the tunnel.
>
> (Blackmore 1993: 86)

This certainly sounds like a persuasive neuroscientific explanation of two key features of many NDErs' testimonies. How well, therefore, does it stand up to critique? First, we might question once again whether such a model is adequate to explain the varieties of experiences actually reported by NDErs. Presumably, if Blackmore's theory is correct we should expect to find the darkness described as a tunnel invariably and cross-culturally. Is this, however, the case? Whilst she claims that the tunnel is indeed a cross-cultural NDE element, Blackmore's contention in this regard has been questioned in recent years by a number of researchers who have failed to find it in a variety of non-Western accounts. Allan Kellehear, for example, has recently refuted it for lack of evidence, accusing Blackmore of asking Indian respondents loaded questions in order to obtain a description of the darkness they encountered during their NDEs which corresponds to the 'tunnel' form so crucial to her thesis. He has also been critical of her attempt to draw conclusions regarding the universality of the tunnel from a single study whereas other cross-cultural studies have signally failed to find it, either in many non-Western accounts generally or in Indian accounts in particular. Indeed, Kellehear, as a result of a recent overview of cross-cultural studies of the NDE and his own cross-cultural analysis of near-death testimonies from a range of non-Western cultures, has recently been drawn to assert that 'I have not been able to find the tunnel as a descriptor in any NDE account from societies dominated by archaic or primitive religions' (Kellehear 1996: 188). In fact, according to Kellehear, the life-review motif is also a notable absentee from many non-Western accounts, including sample groups from Guam (in which tunnels were also absent), Native America (in which the tunnel also failed to be reported), Aboriginal Australia (no tunnels) and Maori New Zealand. The tunnel was also absent from a study group of cases from Melanesia (Kellehear 1996: 22–41).

Interestingly, commenting on the marked absence of the specific *tunnel* feature in so many non-Western accounts, Kellehear remarks that whilst the specific tunnel *shape* is not reported, 'a period of darkness may be'. This experience, he remarks, 'is then subject to culture-specific interpretations: a tunnel for Westerners, subterranean caverns for Melanesians, and so on' (Kellehear 1996: 35). Indeed – and most intriguingly – Kellehear makes the suggestion that 'tunnel' is used as a descriptor by many Western NDErs first because it is a common Western symbol that denotes movement through a space of darkness (and is thus freely available and particularly suggestive to Westerners as an interpretation of their experience due to their familiarity with tunnels) and second because they are using such an image to denote such *movement* and not to denote architecture or actual shape. This is a crucial distinction, Kellehear remarking that: 'Shape reflects architecture rather than experience, but it is experience that is being described by NDErs. Because the experience is difficult to communicate, the descriptions will always be rich in interpretations that lean more toward metaphor than toward measurement' (Kellehear 1996: 37).

Indeed, we can say much more here about the non-occurrence of *tunnel* as a descriptor of either shape or architecture of the experience of darkness by concentrating, ironically, on large numbers of *Western* reports. For what is notable here is the number of accounts that fail to describe the darkness as in any way tunnel-like, with some respondents going out of their way to *avoid* the use of the word tunnel. Consider, for example, this account from one of Sabom's respondents:

> I was travelling through a tunnel. It didn't look like a tunnel, but when you're in a tunnel, all you see is blackness around you. If you move very fast you can feel the sides moving in on you whether there are sides or not because of the darkness.
>
> (Sabom 1982: 63)

Such a frank admission and description seem to support Kellehear's contention regarding 'tunnel' as descriptor of movement, not shape, very succinctly and well. Elsewhere, however, it is notable that a variety of interpretations of the experience of being in the blackness which describe it in several ways are used by Westerners, ranging widely and including 'dark, black vacuum', 'utterly dark black void', 'floating and tumbling through space', 'a deep, very dark valley', 'a narrow and very, very dark passageway', 'rushing through space at a great speed', and so on. Nowhere in these and many other comparable accounts is tunnel used. More disturbingly for Blackmore, however, are the number of accounts which describe darkness *but no light*. In addition to some of those already quoted above, these include being in 'a total dark soundless void', 'a black space', 'I was in what felt like outer space' and a large number of accounts which describe darkness but no illumination or indeed any features of any description. Further, we might consider the large number of cases that describe darkness with no light but with no *movement* of any description either, of which the following is typical:

> Everything was black. Then a floating sensation, like spacelessness like they have in a space program. I wasn't floating in any direction, but it was like I was hanging there.
>
> (Sabom 1982: 63)

Finally, we might additionally consider accounts where some sort of traversing of darkness towards light *is* reported, but where the light is not described as occupying the centre of the visual field. In this regard, for example, consider the following:

> I was rocketing through space like an astronaut without a capsule, with immense speed and great distance. A small group of circles appeared ahead of me, some tending toward the left. To the right was just a dark space.
>
> (quoted in Bailey and Yates 1996: 219)

What are we to make of this somewhat large and representative sample of Western cases which either fail to describe the darkness as tunnel-like, which fail to describe movement or light, or which describe light which seems not to occupy the centre of the darkness? One thing that all the accounts have in common, of course, is that they all seriously call into question the adequacy of Blackmore's model when it is called upon to account for many NDErs' actual descriptions of their experiences. For in view of our above analysis of her position regarding the neuroscientific basis of the tunnel motif, it is clear that her theory demands that all descriptions of episodes of darkness are in fact descriptions of movement through a tunnel towards an ever-growing light. We recall: for Blackmore, it is the light at the apparent 'end' of the tunnel that gives the whole a tunnel-like shape, and the increasing size of the light which gives the impression of movement. Clearly, therefore, accounts which describe darkness but no light, darkness but no movement, or lights at the side of the darkness (rather than at its centre) must demand some sort of neuroscientific explanation other than that which Blackmore provides. For her model cannot satisfactorily explain these, and appears, in fact, to be contradicted by them.

As she herself admits: a good theory is specific. Thus, as we have already had cause to note, for Blackmore any theory adequate to explain the tunnel must describe why it is referred to as a tunnel and not as something else. In view of the testimony-extracts reproduced above (all drawn from existing Western studies of NDEs), together with the limited cross-cultural study of the tunnel motif carried out by scholars such as Kellehear, we may question whether her theory is specific enough to account, phenomenologically, for the great number of Western and non-Western accounts which fail to include either specific descriptions of tunnels or which fail to include descriptions of darkness, light and movement as constituting one, single, whole. Perhaps in attempting to produce a neurological trigger that explains the specific *tunnel* feature, Blackmore has allowed herself to be overly influenced by some near-death researchers' composite NDEs – such as Moody's model – which also use tunnel to define what is in reality an extremely diverse range of darkness features. Furthermore, this apparent shortcoming of Blackmore's neuroscientific interpretation of the period of darkness encountered by many NDErs reminds us once again that explanations of NDE elements must do justice to the descriptions of those elements *given* by NDErs. It is no good producing an explanatory neuroscientific framework to explain features of an experience that are not always – or even often – reported. At the very least, however, we may note in closing that Blackmore's explanation of both tunnel and light motifs demands that both are reported together, with the apparently growing neural noise at the centre of the visual cortex being itself responsible in large part for movement along the dark tunnel. Where darkness is reported in the absence of light (or vice versa) it would appear that her explanation for both – indeed, the movement through one towards the other – cannot stand.

Neuroscientific shortcomings

In one sense, the apparent force of the above criticisms is unsettling. For Blackmore's neuroscientific attempt to account for each feature of the NDE is, as we noted at the beginning of our examination of her claims, the most comprehensive explanatory model that currently exists. Exposing the weaknesses of it, therefore, at once exposes the shortcomings of our collective knowledge of neuroscience in one, crucial, area. As we have already had detailed cause to note, serious reservations have been expressed concerning just about every feature of Blackmore's neuroscientific NDE model, including her explanations for the out-of-body element, the feelings of peace and joy reported by NDErs, and her citing of the temporal lobe as implicated in the life-review sequence. The above analysis has additionally cast doubt on her explanation of the darkness and light motif. Indeed, a suspicion begins to dawn that there are real grounds for doubting neuroscience's ability to account for the occurrence and distinctive features of the NDE in other ways also. Recall, for example, Fenwick's surprise regarding the fact that the NDE is remembered *at all* by NDErs, let alone remembered so very vividly. Recall too his surprise at the fact that what is remembered is not 'random and unclear' but apparently structured and sequenced: not at all, he contends, what we would expect of an unconscious and disorganized brain.

In this context, and by way of conclusion to this chapter, we might usefully return to recall a central contention of this study overall: that NDErs' experiences are inevitably encoded in testimony, and that therefore their narratives are all we have as evidence for the occurrence and detail of their experiences. In view of this consideration, we might begin by highlighting some penetrating questions regarding the adequacy of *any* neuroscientific explanation – whether utilizing single- or multiple-factor theories – to account for NDErs' *stories*. For as Zaleski has asserted and as we have had abundant cause to note:

> The otherworld journey . . . is at its very roots a story. In order to fulfill its narrative purpose of engaging interest and its didactic purpose of impelling the audience from ideology to action, it must portray the afterlife as an active

realm, and the soul as a protagonist whose experiences epitomize and interpret those of earthly life. If the soul must take on the shape of the body for that purpose, then so be it; if near-death visions had to conform to the requirements of abstract philosophical theology they would make dull stories indeed.

(Zaleski 1987: 193)

We might add here, as Zaleski does not, that if near-death visions had to conform to the requirements of contemporary neuroscientific theorizing and model building then they would make equally dull stories. More correctly, however, it would be true to say that such conformity would rob them of their narrative form – and impact – altogether. For models of mental processes, even complex models of unusual processes, are not stories, and in the case of the claims to their unusual experiences made by NDErs, stories are all that we have.

Such considerations may usefully set the agenda for the remainder of this chapter and its eventual conclusion. For as may have become clear from the above, a crucial question which the student of testimony may wish to ask in the light of the existing discussion is that which seeks to ascertain exactly how *models* of neurological processes – processes either currently known or, as we have seen in the case of the NDE, largely unknown – provide an adequate and exhaustive explanation of NDErs' *testimonies*. Do they provide – or, indeed, can they ever promise to provide – a complete explanation and/or interpretation of these 'travellers' tales', or must we look elsewhere for a fuller and more complete explanation: perhaps even to disciplines outside neuroscience altogether which nonetheless have a long and respectable history of dealing with testimony?

Indeed, further questions and issues present themselves when we recall that testimony is what analysis of the NDE is ultimately called upon to explain. We might ponder, for example, whether a concentration on the complexities underlying the production of NDE *narratives* may enable us to complete, or even correct, current neuroscientific NDE *models*, with all their weaknesses, controversies and shortcomings. Such pondering may even prompt examination of whether theology and philosophy, with their rich range of tools developed for just such an examination of testimony to a diverse range of experiences, religious experiences included, might have something to offer here. At the very least, we should expect our understanding of NDErs' testimonies to be deepened as a result of such wider, cross-disciplinary analysis. At most, however, we might hope that, say, *theology's* long engagement with testimonies to religious experience might have something to offer neuroscientific model-builders such as Blackmore and Fenwick, and may even answer some of the questions which their own studies have left currently unanswered.

Yet further, but related to this complex cluster of issues, we might consider the *epistemological* questions and problems which surround the relationship of neuroscientific models to NDErs' narratives. How, for example, might we attempt to understand the transition from neurological process(es) to individual experience to final testimony as found within contemporary near-death literature? Zaleski has already highlighted the intricacies of this process as it is found within *medieval* vision literature, commenting that 'the vision story does not jump in one bound from the visionary's oral report to the narrator's pen', and we once again recall to mind her penetrating observation that

> we cannot simply peel away the literary wrapper and put our hands on an unblemished event. Even when a vision actually did occur, it is likely to have been reworked many times before being recorded. The vision is a collaborative effort, produced by the interaction of the visionary with neighbors, counselors, the narrator, and other interested parties. One cannot point to the moment when the vision changed from a matter of personal confession into a public project; rather, it is built up in layers placed over one another like a series of transparencies. Though a bottom layer of actual experience may be present in some (but certainly not in all) vision stories, its contours are nearly indistinguishable from those of the superimposed images through which we discern it.
>
> (Zaleski 1987: 86)

We have already noted how telling this observation is. Yet it is clear that there are a variety of ways in which we might extend and test it by concentrating attention more specifically on contemporary claims to near-death experience. Can we, for example, discern the same or similar processes of composition and redaction by studying the genesis, evolution and development of modern NDE reports? Standing nearer to these than we do to medieval vision stories, might it be possible to discover the moments and stages through and by means of which the 'bottom layer of actual experience' makes the transition to 'personal confession' and eventual 'public project' within any given twenty-first-century near-death report? Given the interdisciplinary methodology which the current study is attempting to deploy consistently, we might at least try to bring to bear on contemporary NDE reports a sophisticated and extensive understanding of epistemology and narrative analysis which allows us to discover the means whereby a stream of apparently mental processes – however neuroscientifically understood – becomes a contemporary NDEr's final testimony. For these are also important issues which have not yet been addressed by those within the context of near-death studies, or indeed by those outside it who nonetheless share an interest in unravelling the complexities underlying the phenomenon of near-death reports. To this cluster of questions surrounding the essentially narrative nature of the near-death phenomenon we now, therefore, turn, in a closing attempt to resolve some of the deep and unresolved issues which this chapter has highlighted as needful of deeper discussion and, perhaps, final resolution.

In search of narratives

In our analysis above of Penfield's experiments with artificial brain stimulation, we noted that electrical stimulation of the temporal lobes produces disorganized fragments of memory: flash cut scenes of random episodes from a subject's past which suddenly resurface with no apparent organization or purposive order and sequence. We have already seen what such flash cut reminiscence looks like. Another extract from Penfield's notes of his experiments makes this even clearer. Subjects, he noted, produced bizarrely unlinked and disorganized fragments from memory including, in one case, a time of standing on the corner of Jacob and Washington, South Bend, Indiana . . . of watching circus wagons one night years ago in childhood . . . a time of listening to (and watching) your mother speed the parting guests . . . or of hearing your father and mother singing Christmas carols.

(Sacks 1985: 131)

It is interesting to compare these jumbled fragments of memory with a textual extract from a very different source: a piece taken from Dr Johnson's notes describing his French travels:

There we waited on the ladies – Morville's – Spain. Country towns all beggars. At Dijon he could not find the way to Orleans – Cross roads of France very bad. – Five soldiers. – Woman. – Soldiers escaped – The colonel would not lose five men for the sake of one woman. – The magistrate cannot seize a soldier but by the Colonel's permission, etc., etc.

(Hauerwas and Jones 1989: 100)

What these very different extracts have in common, despite differences of context and content, is their plain lack of narrative structure. If anything, they resemble bare chronicle rather than proper narrative, although even here it is stretching somewhat the meaning of chronicle to make Penfield's artificially induced memories fit this description. Certainly, however, neither extract appears to resemble anything approaching a testimony of any description, let alone those specific types of testimonies narrated by NDErs. What, therefore, is missing from such extracts which would be necessary to *turn* them into narrative testimonies?

In recent years, a great deal of attention has been paid from within both philosophy and theology to the distinctive characteristics of narrative, as well as to the ways in which life as lived and experienced shares these characteristics. Whilst isolating and carefully defining what all of the distinctive features of narratives are, the crucial role of *plot* in producing both story and intelligible human experiencing is highlighted throughout a variety of studies concerned to probe this relationship. Thus, for example, theorists such as Paul Ricoeur, David Carr, Alasdair MacIntyre and Stephen

Crites (quoted in Hauerwas and Jones 1989: 69) – amongst others – have all asserted that experiencing (and interpreting) human consciousness shares in many respects the structure of a narrative. Additionally, and in various ways, they have all asserted that it is by taking up and experiencing events, persons and situations encountered during the course of our lives into coherent and consistent narratives that we render them *meaningful* and *intelligible*. Thus, for example, attention is often drawn to the fact that our lives' consistencies, intelligibilities and continuities through time are sustained because we are able to discern the *plots* that hold everything together. In this sense, it is further argued, it is legitimate to talk of selves-as-*stories*; of the story of our lives, or of the self as narratively constituted. David Carr, for example, drawing in part on the work of Paul Ricoeur, draws useful attention to the way in which life, like story, is always *plotted*. Accepting Ricoeur's definition of 'emplotment' as a 'synthesis of heterogeneous elements', Carr asserts that this, essentially, is the way in which human life is in fact structured and experienced. 'Is not life itself', he asks rhetorically, 'already precisely a synthesis of the heterogeneous?' (Wood 1991: 160–1).

Similarly, Alasdair MacIntyre has asserted that the perception of intentionality and intelligibility within the actions and experiences of others is only made possible because of the narrative order within which such actions and experiences take place and within which they are perceived. We thus 'live out' narratives, MacIntyre concluding that 'Stories are lived before they are told – except in the case of fiction' (Hauerwas and Jones 1989: 97), and citing – with approval – Barbara Hardy's contention that 'We dream in narrative, daydream in narrative, remember, anticipate, hope, despair, believe, doubt, plan, revise, criticize, construct, gossip, learn, hate, and love by narrative . . .' (Hauerwas and Jones 1989: 97). Further, Stephen Crites asserts that we continually engage in a fundamentally narrative ordering and organization of consciousness, not merely because our experience of living – of *being* – requires it, but because our (narrative) consciousness itself is shaped by the master stories of our surrounding culture. Thus, there is a crucial sense in which our sense of self-as-story is shaped by the stories within we live, move, and, indeed, into which we were born. Finally, and in similar vein, Ricoeur himself asserts that we can even go some way towards becoming the *authors* of our own lives by applying the plots of stories which are important to us to our own dynamic, developing, narratives-in-progress. The need for this may be particularly acute, he maintains, at times of crisis where such a process of intertextuality may play a crucial role in making sense of a world gone suddenly and temporarily wrong.

How might this brief but fundamental recognition of the structure of human experience as plotted (and hence rendered intelligible and navigable) help us to understand the NDE? How, for example, might it enable us to fine-tune or even overthrow some of the neurological insights into the origin and content of NDErs' testimonies which this chapter has been concerned to explore? Taking Blackmore's model (with all its faults) of the neuroscientific processes underlying the NDE as our starting point, we may simply suggest, first of all, that our recognition of the narrative ordering of selfhood goes some way to explaining why it is that the NDE (unlike, say, the random stimulation of the temporal lobes) possesses a narrative structure. For, like all experience, the unusual state of the self experienced very near the point of death requires to be rendered intelligible, and we must note carefully what it is that requires translation into intelligibility. It is precisely that sequence, or process, of events that begins to occur when the normal model of reality is replaced by the very different sequence that sets in when the brain begins to die: perhaps including dysfunction of the temporal lobe, hypercarbia, anoxia, changes in the visual cortex, and so on. Recall: despite all of these unusual changes to the system's ordinary state of consciousness, Blackmore asserts, the brain continues valiantly the attempt to reconstruct a liveable and intelligible model of reality – a self, in short.

However, it is clear that the self thus (re)constituted is a plotted, *narrative* self. This much is clear from the testimonies of near-death survivors themselves: they return from death with *stories* to tell. Yet this recognition of the fundamental role of plot in constituting and rendering intelligible such a journey is missing from Blackmore's dying brain hypothesis, but entirely consistent with what we would expect if narrative is so fundamental to any intelligibly experienced state of the self. In the dying process, plot still glues everything together, and in so doing renders the self-model intelligible. *Indeed, what is missing from Blackmore's 'dying brain hypothesis' is precisely that synthesis of hetero-geneous elements which Ricoeur and Carr have seen as so constitutive of our fundamental experience of reality.* As we can see, in seeming support of their shared position, we find that in dying, as in living, we are still constituted by a fundamentally narrative ordering of experience.

Indeed, here we could make a second, related, point. Could it be that the casting of the NDE into such a narrative form serves a function within the dying process itself, either by increasing the very possibility of survival or by securing some other crucial objective? As we have noted, above, for thinkers such as MacIntyre and Hardy it seems that in order to live we must render intelligible the actions and intentions – friendly or hostile – of others. This, as we have also seen, is accomplished through a narrative ordering of the events of our lives. But what of those apparently private episodes near death, where the only companion (or adversary) is death itself? Could a narrative ordering of experience have some survival value here, say by casting into a (familiar) narrative environment the important – literally life-and-death – decisions which need to be taken? In support of this contention, we may pause to consider some further testimonies which highlight the aspect of choice within the NDE itself. For many NDErs seem to reach a point – dubbed the 'barrier' or 'border' by some researchers – which represents the climax or deepest part of their story and where a decision needs to be made:

> I was somewhere lying down. Behind me were a whole bunch of people in white. They were talking to me. In front of me were two buttons, a red one and a green one. The people in white kept telling me to push the red button. But I knew I should push the green one because the red button would mean I wouldn't come back. I pushed the green one instead and woke up from the coma. I don't know why I knew that the red button was bad. But it was, because I'm still here.
>
> (Morse and Perry 1991: 39)

194

Others also have spoken of a crucial decision in which life and death were almost literally hanging in the balance, or dependent on a simple but intelligible and narratively rendered choice. However, some near-death survivors report episodes in which a choice to live or die seems possible, with the options seemingly weighted in favour of *death*. Thus, for example, some NDErs tell of the same symbolic barrier or border being reached – usually again as the climax of their total narrative – at which the choice of life or death is apparently offered with death portrayed as the most attractive option:

> I was suspended over a fence . . . On one side of the fence
> it was extremely scraggly territory, mesquite brush and
> generally a junky place you wouldn't want to be. On the
> other side of the fence was the most beautiful pasture scene
> I guess I have ever seen in my life or even imagined . . . [It
> was] a three- or four strand barbed-wire fence . . . The
> fence was a definite dividing line, with the beautiful green
> grass coming right up to the fence and stopping . . . The
> left was the world, here, the world. The scraggly dirty place
> is where I live . . . The other place is where I am going.
>
> (Sabom 1982: 68)

It is clearly difficult to see the survival value of this scenario. In fact, the episode looks suspiciously like an attempt to assist the subject to choose death over life. Perhaps we may be led to assert that the object of casting the life-or-death decision in such a form may be to *ease* the transition from life to death. Either way, we may reasonably conclude that casting the life-or-death decision as the climax of an unfolding narrative is of benefit to the NDEr by making the unfamiliar familiar, and thus providing it with intelligibility and comprehensibility which actually serves to aid choice: either for survival or for death. Sometimes, it may indeed be the case that the latter option represents the best outcome.

Narrative, testimony, memory

Despite the possibility that the casting of NDE elements during the near-death crisis event into an intelligible narrative may help the

NDEr negotiate the crisis, there remain questions concerning how the NDE reaches its final, fixed form. Simply stated: does the NDEr return with a story entire, or is there any sense in which its composition is completed retrospectively? This point is needful of discussion, particularly when we recall Zaleski's detection (see p. 87) of just such a process of ongoing and retrospective composition underlying the construction of the experiences embedded in the testimonies of medieval otherworld visionaries. As a result of this process, Zaleski asserts, the medieval other-world journey narrative, far from being a purely personal confession, was in fact a complex collaboration in which redaction may be seen to have emerged from several sources, including neighbours, counsellors and other interested parties. Can we discern a comparable process of composition or sequence of redaction underlying contemporary NDE reports?

Certainly, attention has been drawn to the fact that NDErs' stories do not attain their final fixed form during the near-death crisis event itself. Robert Kastenbaum, for example, has alluded to the *retrospective* composition of NDErs' testimonies, asserting that their eventual stories are in fact products of their central nervous systems' ongoing attempts to deal with the anxiety, stress and disorganization which coming so close to death must inevitably create:

> The worst of the stress and disorganization is over. Intense feelings and images have been generated, but these do not add up to an integrated memory. The central nervous system starts to work on these residual feelings, trying to reduce the tension associated with them. Sometimes this can best be accomplished by elaborating a kind of 'story' in which all the parts more or less fit. At a more remote point in time, the survivor will then be equipped with what he considers to be a mental record of the specific experiences he went through at a specific time. Actually, what he has is the elaboration of an integrated memory story by higher levels within his nervous system, using various 'raw materials' that include, but are not necessarily limited to, what was experienced during the crisis itself. The memory conforms, then, to the general principles of

mental organization and may be of great interest for a number of reasons. But it does not necessarily correspond to what the person experienced during the peak of the crisis.

(Kastenbaum 1984: 24–5)

This is an important set of observations for a number of reasons. For in addition to highlighting the fact that NDErs' testimonies are indeed retrospectively composed, it also arouses a suspicion that what NDErs recall – and hence narrate – about their experiences may in fact be different to what they *actually* experienced during their near-death crises. Indeed, such a recognition adds significant weight to the conclusion reached in the last chapter that attempting to ascertain what really happens to NDErs – what the core elements of their experiences actually are in and of themselves – may be nigh on impossible to determine. It is also supported by some well-known studies of memory which also draw attention to the fact that what is remembered about an experience or situation may not actually accurately correspond to what was experienced *at the time*.

Elizabeth Loftus, for example, long recognized as an authority in the field of the study of memory, has concluded that 'It may well be that the legal notion of an independent recollection is an impossibility', asserting that the memory functions more like the 'village story-teller' than a 'tape recorder', and adding that 'we can and we do so easily forget. We blur, shape, erase, and change details of the events in our past. Many people walk around daily with heads full of "fake memories"' (Frazier 1991: 54ff.). Indeed, for Loftus, memories are retrospectively composed in often highly complex and shifting ways, making access to 'the truth' of a given experience or situation largely impossible to determine:

As new bits and pieces of information are added into long-term memory, the old memories are removed, replaced, crumpled up, or shoved into corners. Memories don't just fade . . . they also grow. What fades is the initial perception, the actual experience of the events. But every time we recall an event, we must reconstruct the memory, and with each recollection the memory may be changed

– colored by succeeding events, other people's recollections or suggestions . . . Truth and reality, when seen
through the filter of our memories, are not objective facts
but subjective, interpretative realities.

(Loftus and Ketcham 1991: 20)

Such observations have been given added weight in recent years
as a result of failed legal actions taken against persons wrongly
accused of child abuse. Indeed, a recently recognized psychological condition, 'false-memory syndrome', has arisen out of just
such observations as those of Loftus that memories of events may
hardly correspond – or not correspond at all – to actual past
events.

Of course, many false memories of child abuse have arisen
within a therapeutic context. Yet therapists have ironically long
known that memories which emerge during therapy and/or counselling may be unreliable. This makes access to an individual's
actual past – crucial to the success of psychotherapy – extremely
difficult if not impossible, as psychotherapists from various
schools have frequently freely acknowledged. As Carl Rogers, for
example, asserts:

We can *never* know the past. All that exists is someone's
current *perception* of the past. Even the most elaborate
case history, or the most complete free association about
the past, reveals only memories present now, 'facts' as
perceived *now*. We can never know the individual's past.

(Zeig 1987: 185)

The fact that at least some false memories have arisen within
the context of the relationship between analyst and analysand
arouses a suspicion that at least some of the detail of a faulty
recollection may be supplied by others. Returning to Kastenbaum's
above assertion of the unreliability of NDErs' memories, however,
it appears that for him the NDEr composes his or her retrospective
testimony largely alone. Is it therefore the case that NDE memories
belong in a different category and should be seen as entirely private
creations? What, for example, of the possibility that NDErs'
memory-stories *also* have at least some of their detail supplied by

others? In this context, for example, consider an interesting confession made by Raymond Moody in an appendix to his second study of NDEs, *Reflections on Life After Life*, where, commenting on his interviewing methods, he admitted that:

> I always start with as neutral a question as possible, for instance, 'Could you tell me what happened to you?' In a couple of cases I did ask very loaded questions. This was because the persons being interviewed were still in hospital beds recovering from the illnesses which had led to their 'deaths'. They were in a great deal of pain and yet obviously wanted very much to talk. *I led them on a bit, I confess, because I wanted in a way to get the interviews over with as quickly as possible so that they would be more comfortable.* In these cases, I asked them about whether certain elements of the composite near-death experience had been present in their experiences. However, if they did not recall them, they said so. This, in a way, gives me encouragement.
>
> (Moody 1977: 131–2; emphasis mine)

This is in some ways a remarkable admission from the acknowledged founding father of near-death studies, and one which raises a number of questions. One particularly interesting question it may provoke is that of the exact number of respondents Moody *did* lead on. His assertion that it was 'a couple' raises the question as to why, therefore, he felt it was necessary to make the admission at all. For out of the more than 150 NDErs interviewed by Moody over the course of *Life After Life* and *Reflections on Life After Life* – a number which increased during research for the latter book and which Moody freely admits he finally lost count of – the leading of 'a couple' of people on would surely have had little effect on the final analysis. At the very least, however, the suspicion remains that information could have been supplied by the interviewer to at least some respondents which may have been instrumental in the composition of their final narratives. It also raises the question as to how far interview techniques devised and implemented by *other* near-death researchers may run the risk of similarly supplying information extraneous to – even perhaps alien to – their respondents' own memories of their experiences.

Students of testimony, particularly theologians familiar with the mass of literature surrounding the subject of religious conversion, may begin to feel on familiar territory here, not least because of their recognition of processes such as intertextuality underlying the content and structure of a range of religious texts, the testimonies of converts amongst them. Indeed, much more recent studies from within the sociology of religion offer abundant evidence of the paradox that a convert's allegedly private encounter with God is in fact a very public creation, shaped through and through by the collective context in which it is received, composed and ultimately articulated. In accounting for the distinctive features of Jehovah's Witnesses' testimonies, for example, sociologist James Beckford has noted in a well-known and influential study of conversion rhetoric that new converts to the movement:

> [D]raw upon their knowledge of the organization's formal rationale when seeking to make practical sense of the conditions under which their conversion allegedly took place. This knowledge serves partially to constitute their own experiences as a form of appropriate conversion.
> (Beckford 1978: 29)

Furthermore, attention has also been drawn, once again from within the context of the study of conversion, to the ways in which *giving* a testimony shapes and reinforces it. In this respect, for example, Lewis Rambo, in a classic multidisciplinary investigation of the phenomenon, has concluded, first, that biographical reshaping in the light of their ongoing new experience results in converts' reshaping of 'the past through selection, arrangement and modification of life experience in light of . . . [a] . . . group's discourse', and second, that such a revised understanding of their lives' stories are reinforced by the giving of that testimony before other, like-minded, souls within the group. Thus:

> Research indicates that what people profess before a group consolidates belief. Through a subtle interplay between speaker and audience, people come to believe what they

say . . . [Thus] . . . Public testimony serves a dual purpose. It helps converts solidify commitment through biographical reshaping, and it also confirms and reminds the group of the validity of its worldview and methods. Audience and speaker form a powerful matrix of support and reinforcement.

(Rambo 1993: 142)

This assertion has, we may usefully note, potential insight to shed on testimonies other than those of converts. For NDErs also have ample opportunities to give their near-death testimonies to like-minded persons at meetings very similar to those at which converts narrate the stories of their salvation before believing communities. Since 1977, the International Association for Near Death Studies (IANDS) has existed to perform a range of functions for both NDErs and non-NDErs who share an interest in the phenomenon. These include descriptions of 'typical' NDEs, organization of conferences, pastoral advice for the terminally ill and/or their carers, publication of the *Journal of Near-Death Studies*, advice as to what to do if you or a loved one suspects that you have had an NDE, and the regular updating of an IANDS web site. One thing that existing and new NDErs are encouraged to do via the site is to join a local Support Group, usually arranged on a geographical basis, in which visiting speakers and NDErs may meet regularly to share the details of their experiences and the ongoing changes which these may have brought about in their lives. As we shall see in the next chapter, some key NDErs whose testimonies have influenced crucial and ongoing pieces of research by IANDS-affiliated near-death researchers were referred to those researchers in and though local IANDS support groups and their members. We will thus have much more to say about IANDS in the next chapter.

It is already clear, however, that the existence of such support groups provides ample opportunities for the giving – and hearing – of testimonies, with all the attendant possibilities for processes of biographical reshaping, deepening of commitment, and reinforcement of group belief which exist for converts testifying before believing communities, as noted by Rambo and others. Once again at this point we are clearly confronted by an area in which much more research needs to be carried out. Fruitful directions for future – particularly sociological – investigations may, for example, focus more widely on the ways in which IANDS chapters function as believing communities analogous to those found within mainstream religions, on the ways in which the dynamics and processes underlying the composition of NDErs' testimonies resemble those underlying other types of religious experiencers such as converts and, indeed, on the ways in which the testimonies of both NDErs and religious converts share structural (and possibly other) similarities. For now, however, we may simply note that a cumulative case for asserting that the composition of contemporary NDErs' testimonies may pass through various stages and contexts of composition *en route* to completion, together with the recognition that this may in numerous ways affect their recall and narration of what 'really' happened to them during their near-death crisis events, is further strengthened by applying insights from different fields of investigations (such as those of Rambo in the area of conversion) to the somewhat less explored area of near-death studies.

Memory revisited

Our detour through the role of plot in constructing a testimony, together with our brief exploration of the ways in which the self's story is reshaped in various ways by the processes inherent in both its recollection and expression, returns us to some fundamental questions regarding the NDE which, as we have seen, neuroscience has been unable to answer. We have already noted how the recognition of the ubiquity of emplotment within the phenomenology of intelligible human experiencing may help correct and complete explanations of the NDE such as that offered by Susan Blackmore in her 'Dying brain hypothesis'. Yet other problems and limitations still remain with other comparable studies which we are now potentially in a position to resolve. For Peter and Elizabeth Fenwick, for example, what is currently inexplicable about the NDE viewed neuroscientifically is both its coherency and its vividness in memory. Are we now in a position to resolve *this* puzzle? Clearly we are, if we accept that an NDEr's testimony receives its final fixed form at some distance in time from the actual near-death event. For this chapter has shown that it is clearly probable that both the structured story which at least some NDErs tell and its vividness and clarity may both stem from a variety of sources other than the purely private experiences of the NDErs themselves. As we have been seeing, for example, both plot and detail may potentially hail from a wide range of sources, including subsequent attempts by the central nervous system to deal with the shock and trauma of nearly dying, the behaviour of near-death researchers themselves as they attempt to draw out a story along already existing and fixed lines, and the processes which have been seen to exist when the NDEr's story is told and retold before groups (which may themselves interact in the process of composition and reshaping of the original traveller's tale). When we add to this sequence the recognition that memory is fluid, dynamic and ongoing, and not just a static, fixed, once-for-all recollection of things past, we begin to see the very real potential that exists both for the construction of an extremely coherent and integrated story and why such a story should come to assume such vividness and detail.

The conclusions to which we have been led do not, of course, automatically lead to the grand conclusion that all neuroscientific attempts to contribute to the understanding of the NDE are bound to be inadequate and should henceforth be abandoned. Certainly, what we have demonstrated is the fact that they are bound to be limited by the fact that they posit models in order to explain experiences, or worse, that they advance such models in order to explain testimonies. What is being additionally asserted is that a concentration on how all experience is required to be plotted in order to become intelligible, together with a recognition that the composition of testimony, like memory, is complex, dynamic and public, leads us to a point beyond the limitations of existing neuroscientific explanations of NDEs. This is not at all to suggest that NDEs may not turn out to be based on modified neuro-scientific processes occurring within a dying organism. Once again we are reminded of the need for more research. Just because all existing attempts to account in detail for all of the features of such a process are not yet in place does not mean that they never will be. For, like memory, neuroscience too is dynamic, developing, ongoing.

One further question remains, however, untouched at the end of this chapter which will be needful of attention in the next. For what might we make of explanations for NDErs' experiences which attempt to bypass neuroscience altogether? A variety of these have been advanced throughout the history of near-death studies, and, as we have already had cause to note, most of them appeal to some sort of body–soul dualism which is alleged to be demonstrated by the fact that during an NDE some of the self seems to separate from the body, first to apparently view it from outside and then to depart for some other world. That such alleged observations may be based on nothing more than memory and imagination is frequently countered by assertions that they are sometimes of things which could not have been seen unless the subject was, literally, outside his or her body. Indeed, recent years have seen a number of remarkable claims concerning aspects of NDEs reported by severely visually impaired people (including the blind and even congenitally blind) which include apparently visual capabilities such as the viewing of resuscitation attempts and even features of the topography outside the hospital altogether. Such claims, if true, would of course render obsolete each and every attempt to account for the NDE neuroscientifically. For theologians and philosophers also, these claims might reasonably be expected to be of tremendous interest and clearly deserving of closer scrutiny. To an examination of such we now, therefore, turn.

SECOND SIGHT?

NDEs and the blind

Close encounters of the disembodied kind

One of the most remarkable and widely cited cases within near-death literature concerns one 'Maria', whose NDE began after she was rushed to Harborview Hospital in Seattle suffering from a heart attack and subsequent cardiac arrest. In an experience that has been extensively quoted since its initial appearance in 1984, Maria, having apparently separated from her body during her arrest, claimed not simply to have witnessed the resuscitation attempts that were being made upon her but also to have floated during this time *outside* the hospital altogether. Taking full advantage of the sudden freedom which her temporary out-of-body condition afforded her, she continued to float up until she reached the third floor of the North Wing of the building. There, resting on a ledge outside one of the windows, she spied a single tennis shoe. Having been resuscitated Maria remembered, as she later described it, her 'eyeball to shoelace' encounter, and when the opportunity presented itself told the full story of her experience to Kimberly Clark, her critical care social worker. In doing so, she also asked Clark to find the shoe in order to confirm that she had, indeed, left her body at the time of her experience. Clark followed Maria's instructions as to the location of the shoe, later recalling:

> With mixed emotions I went outside and looked up at the ledges but could not see much at all. I went up to the third floor and began going in and out of patients' rooms and looking out their windows, which were so narrow that I

had to press my face to the screen just to see the ledge at all. Finally I found a room where I pressed my face to the glass and saw the tennis shoe! My vantage-point was very different from what Maria's had been for her to notice that the little toe had worn a place in the shoe, and that the lace was stuck under the heel and other details about the side of the shoe not visible to me. The only way she would have had such a perspective was if she had been floating right outside and at very close range to the tennis shoe. I retrieved the shoe and brought it back to Maria; it was very concrete evidence for me.

(Wilson 1997: 98)

Taken at face value, Maria's experience sounds extraordinary indeed. Even standing alone, it appears to provide convincing, corroborated evidence that during her NDE, a part of her was able to function and move about independently of her stricken body. However, Maria's remarkable experience does *not* stand alone. For in addition to her case, a number of others collected by a range of researchers have, on occasion, revealed further experiences of apparently corroborated veridical observations made by persons during NDEs and other out-of-body experiences. Many of these sound as impressive as Maria's encounter with the shoe and have been reported for a number of years. Respected paranormal investigator Celia Green, for example, gives a number of such cases in her own classic study of out-of-body experiences. The first of these (as also quoted on pp. 24–5) involves a post-operative subject's experience that occurred when

I was in hospital having had an operation for peritonitis; I developed pneumonia and was very ill. The ward was L shaped; so that anyone in bed at one part of the ward, could not see round the corner.

One morning I felt myself floating upwards, and found I was looking down on the rest of the patients. I could see myself; propped up against pillows, very white and ill. I saw the sister and nurse rush to my bed with oxygen. Then everything went blank. The next I remember; was opening my eyes to see the sister bending over me.

I told her what had happened; but at first she thought I was rambling. Then I said, 'There is a big woman sitting up in bed with her head wrapped in bandages; and she is knitting something with blue wool. She has a very red face.' This certainly shook her; as apparently the lady concerned had a mastoid operation and was just as I described.
She was not allowed out of bed; and of course I hadn't been up at all. After several other details; such as the time by the clock on the wall (which had broken down) I convinced her that at least something strange had happened to me.

(Green 1968: 121)

Another patient, having undergone standard and apparently complication-free surgery for displacement of a foot, wrote:

Before coming round I saw myself up in a corner of the room and I was looking down upon the hospital bed. The bedclothes were heaped up over a cradle and my legs were exposed from the knees down.

Around the right ankle was a ring of plaster and below the knee was a similar ring. These two rings were joined by a plaster strip each side of leg. I was struck by the pink of my skin against the white plaster.

When I regained consciousness two nurses were standing a {sic} foot of bed looking at the operation, one quite young. They at once left the private ward and I managed to raise myself up and look over the cradle seeing again exactly what I had seen when still 'out'.

Being a hot day was perhaps why the bed clothes had been pulled away from my legs and were heaped over the cradle. The particular way in which the plaster had been applied was plainly seen from my position in the corner of room and the contrast between pink skin and white plaster was striking.

(Green 1968: 123)

There are, of course, a number of problems in accepting such claims – old and new – at face value. Indeed, by and large, sceptics are not impressed, preferring instead to interpret such experiences as arising out of the influence of a variety of factors including confabulation, imagination, distorted retrospective reporting of events, altered states of consciousness and even downright fraud.[1] Indeed, there is something to be said for this position, particularly when it is considered that many researchers involved in investigating such claims made no subsequent attempts to substantiate them for themselves. Impressive as her study is, Celia Green, for example, made no attempt to follow up and interview the witnesses involved in the often impressive and detailed testimonies presented there. A review of other, comparable literature containing similar claims reveals that this is the case there also.

In fact, when attempts *are* made at detailed follow-up and investigation of such cases, these frequently reveal many of the claims made to be either weak or false. Psychologist Susan Blackmore's attempts, for example, to gain more detailed information regarding Maria's sighting of the tennis shoe were unsuccessful, as were all of her attempts to gain 'properly corroborated cases' which could not be accounted for by non-paranormal explanations. Indeed, in the conclusion to this aspect of her study *Dying to Live*, she writes of the occurrence of apparently paranormal perception during NDEs that:

> It is my impression that it probably never does happen. Certainly I have found no evidence, yet, that convinces me that it does. I may still find it. However, for the moment at least, these claims present no real challenge to a scientific account of the NDE.
>
> (Blackmore 1993: 134–5)

NDEs in the blind

The reader may be reminded at this point of William James's contention concerning his own quest to find a genuine *medium* in the closing years of the nineteenth century. In this regard, James wrote that: 'If you wish to upset the law that all crows are black, you must not seek to show that no crows are; it is enough if you can prove one single crow to be white' (quoted in Wilson 1987: 169). Whether or not James ever found the mediumistic equivalent of a white crow is a matter of some conjecture. Certainly, however, at the beginning of the twenty-first century, the quest to find the NDE equivalent of a white crow – a case that proves beyond a shadow of a doubt that persons can and do leave their bodies during episodes of apparent clinical death – shows no sign of abating. Cardiologist Michael Sabom, for example, has recently produced a seemingly impressive new case including a female respondent's description of a type of bone saw with which she was entirely unfamiliar before she 'viewed' it whilst clinically dead. The subject was undergoing a new surgical technique nicknamed 'standstill' by doctors in which her body temperature was lowered to 60 degrees, her heartbeat and respiration deliberately stopped, and all blood drained from her head. Thus rendered clinically dead, the subject was then to have a life-threatening basilar artery aneurysm removed from her brain. Following the successful surgery, the subject, a thirty-five-year-old musician named Pam Reynolds, recalled that during her operation – at a point subsequently confirmed to be when the surgeon was about to drill through her head with a Midas Rex bone saw – she suddenly heard a sound:

> It was a natural D. As I listened to the sound, I felt it was pulling me out of the top of my head. The further out of my body I got, the more clear the tone became. I had the impression it was like a road, a frequency that you go on ... I remember seeing several things in the operating room when I was looking down. It was the most aware that I think that I have ever been in my entire life ... I was metaphorically sitting on [the lead surgeon's] shoulder. It was not like normal vision. It was brighter and more focussed and clearer than normal vision ... There was so much in the operating room that I didn't recognize, and so many people.
>
> (Sabom 1998: 41)

Later on in her experience, Reynolds would undergo other elements of a remarkably detailed NDE including a journey through a 'tunnel vortex', the hearing of her dead grandmother's voice, an encounter with numerous figures in an 'incredibly bright' light, a remarkable encounter with a number of other deceased relatives who fed her with 'something sparkly', and an eventual return to her body, described as 'like diving into a pool of ice water'. Interesting as all of this sounds, what was *especially* noteworthy about the case for Sabom was the subject's 'bird's eye' description of the Midas Rex bone saw, a surgical instrument about which she had no prior knowledge:

> The saw thing that I hated the sound of looked like an electric toothbrush and it had a dent in it, a groove at the top where the saw appeared to go into the handle, but it didn't . . . And the saw had interchangeable blades, too, but these blades were in what looked like a socket wrench case . . . I heard the saw crank up. I didn't see them use it on my head, but I think I heard it being used on something. It was humming at a relatively high pitch and then all of a sudden it went *Brrrrrrrr!* like that.
>
> (Sabom 1998: 41)

How to account for such a remarkable description by an unconscious non-specialist? At first Sabom was baffled, especially when the subject's description of the saw turned out to contain *in*accurate details of certain aspects of the groove and its location. Perhaps she had simply given the best description she could of the saw as seen from an unusual vantage point in the midst of the duress of being suddenly fully aware in the midst of an operation. In the end, he was forced to conclude that the case was ambiguous. Whilst for some, he wrote, Reynolds's observations would help clinch the argument for genuine out-of-body experiences in life-threatening situations, for others it would be dismissed together with comparable cases as wholly hallucinatory or simply based on fantasy. In fact, the jury is still very much out over this case and similar aspects of Sabom's data regarding apparently accurate visual observations of surgical procedures made by NDErs. Suffice to say that, taken together, the body of evidence from this and similar cases seems for those who take such data at face value to constitute an impressive body of evidence for which explanations – whether conventional or non-conventional – have yet to be fully found.

There is, however, an apparently even more impressive set of cases which at the beginning of this new millennium lay serious claims to the status of near-death research's white crows. For in very recent years there have been a number of extraordinary cases of out-of-body episodes during claimed NDEs in the *blind*, including those of persons blind from birth. Foremost amongst the researchers who have been concerned to investigate these and similar cases is University of Connecticut Psychologist Kenneth Ring, who, together with co-researcher Sharon Cooper, has claimed to have researched in extensive detail a number of such cases.

Issues for theology and philosophy

There are a number of reasons why philosophers and theologians might wish to consider carefully unusual claims of apparently impossible observations made by NDErs, both blind and sighted. For if the research conducted in this area should turn out to produce verifiable and accurate observations of events such as surgical resuscitation procedures narrated by unconscious sighted, blind and congenitally blind persons, it would lend powerful evidence in support of the argument that the self cannot simply be equated with the brain and/or other bodily functions, but rather possesses the ability to function independently of the body and its senses. Indeed, as we have noted in previous chapters, such observations – if proven to be accurate and veridical – would provide powerful new evidence for the reality of some form of body–soul dualism, together with support for the notion that the self may be in some sense immortal: a claim that many of the world's major religions and philosophies have consistently maintained. It may, of course, be argued that *any* verified account of out-of-body observations, whether reported by the blind, the congenitally blind, or the sighted, might serve to demonstrate the reality of some form of dualism. However, as Ring and his co-researchers have noted, the occurrence of such cases in the *blind* – and particularly in the *congenitally* blind – provides evidence of a particularly 'hard' type. Thus, for example, Ring has recently written that this particular subset of out-of-body experiences may come to represent 'a kind of ultimate test for the validity of veridical perceptions during NDEs – as well as a challenge for skeptics' (Ring and Valarino 1998: 73). Given the implications that would arise if such cases *should* turn out to be sound, we might usefully extend the sphere of Ring's challenge to include philosophers and theologians also. And at the very least, such intriguing claims of temporary sight restoration or bestowal to blind persons during their NDEs may surely promise to richly repay detailed analysis and discussion: for philosophers and theologians certainly, but also for those seeking to explore the mechanics of perception and the mysteries surrounding the brain's role in making sense out of what we view through our eyes within the ordinary run of everyday events when we are far from death.

The question becomes, of course, whether the evidence for these extraordinary happenings is of a quality sufficient to establish a case for theology, philosophy and other disciplines to seriously consider. Only if it *does* turn out to be of sufficient quality will such responses be necessary, but if a case *could* be made, it would clearly be necessary for such disciplines to incorporate this research into any future thinking – with momentous consequences. Regardless of the ultimate strength or weakness of the evidence, it is clear that those working with the dying in both medical and pastoral contexts have a clear and vested interest in keeping abreast of these interesting developments. In what follows, therefore, I intend to present the evidence arising from cases of NDEs reported by the blind and congenitally blind, to assess its quality, and to explore the implications of the debate for those who are perennially concerned to explore the nature and limits of the self and the possibility of that self's access to otherworldly realities. In attempting to do all of this, the current chapter will also constitute the first serious attempt from within academic philosophy and theology to respond to the extraordinary claim that during their NDEs, the blind can suddenly, temporarily and apparently miraculously, see.[2]

In search of evidence

Rumours of out-of-body observations made by blind persons during NDEs have existed for a number of years, and a number of major researchers working in the field of near-death studies have claimed to have encountered such cases. Of apparently impossible veridical perceptions reported by some of her near-death subjects, for example, leading thanatologist Elizabeth Kubler-Ross has stated:

> We asked them to share with us what it was like when they had this near-death experience. If it was just a dream fulfilment those people would not be able to share with us the colour of the sweater we wear, the design of a tie, or minute details of shape, colours and designs of the people's clothing. *We have questioned several totally blind people who were able to share with us in their near-death experience and they were not only able to tell us who came into the room first, who worked on the resuscitation, but they were able to give minute details of the attire and the clothing of all the people present, something a totally blind person would never be able to do.*
>
> (Wilson 1987: 155; emphasis mine)

This claim, taken from a tape-recorded lecture given by Kubler-Ross, does not appear in the published account of the lecture in her study *On Life After Death* (Kubler-Ross 1991). One obvious problem with it, of course, is the lack of any accompanying corroborative evidence in its support. Indeed, this is also a problem with *other* claims of sight reported by blind NDErs that have appeared in recent years. Raymond Moody, for example, failed to give corroborative evidence in support of a similar claim of sight in a blind NDEr which appeared in one of his own early studies (Ring and Cooper 1997: 103). Similarly, researcher Fred Schoonmaker has claimed one case of a congenitally blind NDEr who was accurately able to describe the number of people present during his resuscitation and the particular nature of the procedures involved. Urged by other researchers to publish this case, Schoonmaker declined. Again, corroborative evidence was therefore not forthcoming (Blackmore 1993: 133).

In 1989, however, physician Larry Dossey, long interested in the possible relationships between spirituality, religion and medicine, published the following account of an NDE in a congenitally blind woman named Sarah who apparently 'died' during a routine gallstone operation. Gallstones having been removed, and having recovered from the trauma of apparent clinical death, Sarah reported seeing something that, in Dossey's words,

> amazed her and the rest of the surgery team as well – a clear, detailed memory of the frantic conversation of the surgeons and nurses during her cardiac arrest; the OR layout; the scribbles on the surgery schedule board in the hall outside; the color of the sheets covering the operating table; the hairstyle of the head scrub nurse; the names of the surgeons in the doctors' lounge down the corridor who were waiting for her case to be concluded; and even the trivial fact that her anesthesiologist that day was wearing unmatched socks. All this she knew even though she had been fully anesthetized and unconscious during the surgery and the cardiac arrest.
>
> (Dossey 1989: 18)

Then Dossey adds: 'But what made Sarah's vision even more momentous was the fact that, since birth, she had been blind' (Dossey 1989: 18).

Psychologist Susan Blackmore recognized the need for verification of Dossey's case of blind Sarah and in March 1991 wrote to him to ask for Sarah's address and requesting any corroborative statements which Dossey might possess from the OR team involved in the resuscitation. In her study *Dying to Live*, Blackmore reproduces part of Dossey's candid reply:

> 'Sarah's' story was a composite – the only composite story in the entire book, *Recovering the Soul*. My reasons for composing her were to dramatically illustrate the key features of non-local ways of knowing – ways that seem (to me) fully documented in the experiences of diverse numbers of human beings. The 'fact' that Sarah was congenitally blind was a way of illustrating that non-local ways of gaining information bypass the senses and are ultimately independent of the brain.
>
> (Blackmore 1993: 131)

In short, Dossey made Sarah up to illustrate what he thought were cases that had been adequately documented elsewhere. In fact, as Blackmore asserts, they had not been. Indeed, at this point in the search for documented cases of NDEs in the blind, Blackmore reproduces an extract of a letter sent to her by Kenneth Ring, himself keen to uncover such cases. Ring wrote:

> In short, as much as this is the lore of NDEs, there has never, to my knowledge, been a case of a blind NDEr reported in the literature where there was clear-cut or documented evidence of accurate visual perception during an alleged OBE. . . . I wish there were such a case – we'd all love it. I'm sure that's why people like you and me wrote to Dossey with such alacrity. It *seemed* exactly what we'd been looking for. . . .
>
> (Blackmore 1993: 133; emphasis in the original)

Ring's response to non-cases such as Sarah's was clearly one of disappointment. However, as we will now see, his subsequent quest to discover a hard and verifiable case was shortly to take a series of highly unusual turns.

The odyssey of Kenneth Ring

As previously noted, since his own interest in NDEs was piqued by reading Raymond Moody's *Life After Life* in 1975, researcher Kenneth Ring has devoted himself to exploring a number of aspects of the NDE and is currently recognized as one of the world's leading near-death researchers. Whilst examining the transformative effects undergone by NDErs as a result of their experiences for his 1984 NDE study, *Heading Toward Omega*, Ring began to discover a small number of testimonies which seemed to indicate that perceptual abilities could be temporarily *heightened* during NDEs. In one case, for example, one of Ring's respondents described an experience that began when she heard her doctor pronounce her dead. Then:

> Bang, I left! The next thing I was aware of was floating on the ceiling. And seeing down there, with his hat on his

head, I knew who he was because of the hat on his head
. . . it was so vivid. I'm very nearsighted, too, by the way,
which was another one of the startling things that
happened when I left my body. I see at fifteen feet what
most people see at four hundred . . . They were hooking
me up to a machine that was behind my head. And my
very first thought was, 'Jesus, I can see! I can't believe it,
I can see!' I could read the numbers on the machine
behind my head and I was just so thrilled. And I thought,
'They gave me back my glasses.'

Things were enormously clear and bright . . . From
where I was looking, I could look down on this enormous
fluorescent light . . . and it was so dirty on top of the light
. . . I was floating *above* the light fixture . . . and it was
filthy. And I remember thinking, 'Got to tell the nurses
about that.'

(Ring 1984: 42–3, emphasis in the original)

In recent years, Ring has gone on to make much of observations
such as respondents noticing the dust on top of light fittings
in order to make his case for the veridicality of out-of-body
perceptions during NDEs. He has, for example, devoted a chapter
to it in a recent general study of NDEs, *Lessons from the Light*,
with his co-author Evelyn Elsaesser Valarino (Ring and Valarino
1998: 55–71). His ongoing discovery of what appear to be rather
persuasive accounts of out-of-body perceptions reported by the
blind, some during seemingly well-documented NDEs, have
constituted some of the most interesting aspects of his research to
date. In 1997, for example, together with co-worker Sharon
Cooper, he published a detailed, groundbreaking and highly
original study of NDEs in a total of thirty-one blind and severely
visually impaired respondents. This first appeared in the official
IANDS *Journal of Near-Death Studies*, whilst a more popular
version, 'the first extensive nontechnical account of our findings',
would later appear in Ring and Valarino's 1998 study and later
still would appear as a book on the subject in its own right entitled
Mindsight, written by Ring and Cooper and published in 1999
(Ring and Cooper 1997; Ring and Valarino 1998; Ring and
Cooper 1999). In order to collect their cases of NDEs in the blind,

Ring and his co-researchers turned to various sources and avenues of information. They placed an advertisement in *Vital Signs*, an informal newsletter published by IANDS, in order to locate some of their respondents, whilst also contacting a total of eleven 'national, regional and state organizations for the blind'. In addition, they alerted their colleagues in the field of near-death studies about their quest to find and study NDEs in the blind, and requested referral of any appropriate cases. By the time of their 1997 study, Ring and Cooper had screened a total of forty-six respondents and eventually interviewed thirty-one of these. By the time of the 1999 study, *Mindsight*, a small number of additional cases had appeared, with one of these being extensively described and analysed before being retracted by Ring and Cooper, who informed readers via an *errata* sticker in the front of the book to disregard it entirely. In fact, the 1999 study offered little valuable additional material in the way of either case studies or analysis and continued to lean heavily on the cases found in the original, groundbreaking 1997 article. To date, this remains the most scholarly and academic of all of the pieces written by Ring and his co-researchers on claims of NDEs in the blind, and for this reason it will constitute the main focus of this chapter, which will also draw additional comment from the other main sources, as appropriate.

Case studies

The thirty-one chosen interviewees for the original 1997 study conducted by Ring and Cooper had all reported remote perception of themselves and their surroundings during out-of-body experiences, either in connection with an NDE or outside an event of life-threatening danger altogether. All but three found out about the appeal through one of the channels Ring had used for his requests for referral of potential subjects. Of these thirty-one interviewees, fourteen were congenitally blind, most without even light perception at the time of their experiences. An additional eleven were adventitiously blind (that is, they lost their sight after the age of 5 years). The remaining six were individuals who, whilst not completely blind, suffered from severe visual impairment at the time of their out-of-body experiences. Of the thirty-one interviewees eventually chosen for the study, twenty-one were NDErs, of whom ten were congenitally blind, nine adventitiously blind, and two severely visually impaired. Because of the constraints of space, Ring and Cooper only presented one case in depth, following it with 'a synopsis of a second comparable case', and including briefer presentations of other cases of visual perception by OBErs and NDErs which offered the possibility of corroboration from others present whilst the alleged perceptions took place. Ring summarizes the conclusions of the study as follows:

> Our findings with respect to this issue are unequivocal: blind persons, even those blind from birth, recount experiences that clearly conform to the familar prototype of the beatific NDE first popularized in Moody's book *Life After Life* [that is, they contain the same elements of out-of-body experience, ineffability, feelings of peace and serenity, encounters with lights, and so on]. Their narratives, in fact, tend to be indistinguishable from those of sighted persons with respect to the elements that serve to identify the classic NDE pattern.
>
> (Ring and Cooper 1997: 108)

As regards the possibility that the blind can, indeed, temporarily *see* during out-of-body and near-death episodes, Ring and Cooper are equally unequivocal. 'Our interviews', they write,

> with both NDErs and OBErs offer abundant testimony that reports of visual perception among the blind are common, that their impressions concern both things of this world and otherworldly domains, and that they are often clear and detailed, even in narratives furnished by those who have been blind from birth.
>
> (Ring and Cooper 1997: 119)

Of obvious and primary importance here is an analysis of the case studies which Ring and Cooper present as a result of their research and upon which they base such remarkable findings.

Vicki Umipeg

The most detailed account presented is that of Vicki Umipeg, a 43-year-old congenitally blind married mother whose NDEs (she reported two) took place at ages 20 and 22 respectively, and who was referred to the researchers, interestingly, by Kimberly Clark, the critical care social worker who had found Maria's shoe on the window ledge of Harborview Hospital, and who had met Umipeg at an NDE support group organized by Clark. It is the *second* of Umipeg's two NDEs to which Ring and Cooper devote attention in the study, and which will thus be important to examine here.

By another interesting coincidence, Umipeg's experience – like that of Maria as recounted by Clark and discussed above – took place at Harborview Hospital in Seattle. At age 22, she was a nightclub singer and one night after performing was involved in a car crash and rushed to the hospital. Although she had no recollection of the journey *to* the hospital, Umipeg suddenly 'saw' herself *in* the hospital, lying on a metal table:

> I knew it was me . . . I was pretty thin then. I was quite tall and thin at that point. And I recognized at first that it was a body, but I didn't even know that it was mine initially. Then I perceived that I was up on the ceiling, and I thought, 'Well, that's kind of weird. What am I doing up here?' I thought, 'Well, this must be me. Am I dead? . . .' I just briefly saw this body, and . . . I knew that it was mine because I wasn't in mine. Then I was just away from it. It was that quick.
>
> (Ring and Cooper 1997: 110)

Ring and Cooper continue to detail Umipeg's experience as it unfolds. In *Lessons from the Light*, Ring includes an interesting transcript of one of their interviews with her. Umipeg describes her vain attempts to communicate with the doctors and nurses:

> I knew, too, the feelings they were having. From up there on the ceiling, I could tell they were very concerned, and I could see them working on this body. I could see that my head was cut open. I could see a lot of blood. . . .
>
> (Ring and Valarino 1998: 76)

219

Interestingly, Ring notes that although Umipeg saw a lot of blood, 'she could not tell its colour' (Ring and Valarino 1998: 76). However, the subsequent interview transcript reveals a number of startling perceptions, recounted in seemingly great detail:

KR: After you failed to communicate to [the doctors and nurses] what's the next thing you remember?

VU: I went up through the roof then. And that was astounding!

KR: What was that like for you?

VU: Whew! It's like the roof didn't . . . it just melted.

KR: Was there a sense of upward motion?

VU: Yes, um-hmm.

KR: Did you find yourself above the roof of the hospital?

VU: Yes.

KR: What were you aware of when you reached that point?

VU: Lights, and the streets down below, and everything. I was very confused by that.

KR: Could you see the roof of the hospital below you?

VU: Yes.

KR: What could you see around you?

VU: I saw lights.

KR: Lights of the city?

VU: Yes.

KR: Were you able to see buildings?

VU: Yeah, I saw other buildings, but that was real quick too. . . .
                                              (Ring and Valarino 1998: 76)

After this, Umipeg ascended yet further and found herself in a 'tube', then moved through it towards a light, and finally found herself in 'an illuminated field, covered with flowers . . .'. She then met two schoolfriends, 'long deceased', together with relatives and acquaintances – similarly deceased – from her former life. However, before she could communicate with them, a 'brilliant figure' (whom she 'intuitively' understood to be Jesus) blocked her way and told her that she must return to life in order to bear children. At hearing this, Umipeg had mixed feelings. Although she wanted to stay with Jesus, the promise of children excited her. Before leaving the heavenly realm, however, she was given the chance to understand 'the significance of her actions and their repercussions' by way of a 'panoramic review of her life'. Finally, she found herself back in her body, with '"a sickening thud" like a rollercoaster going backwards' (Ring and Valarino 1998: 77).

During their discussion of the Umipeg case, Ring and Cooper allude to a point that they will expand upon later in considering explanations for all of the apparently remarkable perceptions of their blind NDErs: the *impossibility* of the hypothesis that a purely naturalistic explanation for the reported events is to be preferred. Reproducing another detailed transcript of their interviews with Umipeg, they consider the possibility that the experience may, after all, turn out to have been a simple dream. But again, the very fact that Umipeg suffers from congenital blindness seems to militate against this:

Interviewer:	How would you compare your dreams to your NDEs?
Vicki:	No similarity, no similarity at all.
Interviewer:	Do you have any kind of visual perception in your dreams?
Vicki:	Nothing. No color, no sight of any sort, no shadows, no light, no nothing.
Interviewer:	What kinds of perceptions are you aware of in your typical dreams?
Vicki:	Taste – I have a lot of eating dreams. And I have dreams when I'm playing the piano and singing, which I do for a living anyway. I have dreams in which I touch things . . . I taste things, touch things, hear things, and smell things – that's it.
Interviewer:	And no visual perceptions?
Vicki:	No.
Interviewer:	So that what you experienced during your NDE was quite different from your dreams?
Vicki:	Yeah, there's no visual impression at all in any dream that I have.

(Ring and Valarino 1998: 78)

As we shall have cause to note shortly, Ring will take up and consider a range of other naturalistic hypotheses for cases like that of Vicki Umipeg, before ultimately deciding that a very *new* hypothesis is called for in order to account for experiences such as hers.

Brad Barrows

Ring and Cooper's second detailed case study, that of Brad Barrows, is in many respects similar to Vicki Umipeg's. Like Umipeg, Barrows is congenitally blind, and had no physical vision at the age of his NDE, which took place when he was 8 years old and a student at the Boston Center for Blind Children. Describing the onset of his NDE, Barrows recounted to Ring and Cooper a sudden sensation of rising up from his bed and floating towards the ceiling. He saw his roommate get up from his bed to get help for him, a fact that his roommate apparently later confirmed. As Ring and Cooper describe the next stages of Brad's experience, he 'then found himself rapidly going upward through the ceilings of the building until he was above the roof. At this point, he found that he could see clearly.' Outside the hospital, Brad's vision indeed seemed totally restored, and once again bears comparison with the quality and detail of Umipeg's observations. 'He estimates', write Ring and Cooper,

> that it was between 6:30 and 7:00 in the morning when this happened. He noticed that the sky was cloudy and dark. There had been a snowstorm the day before, and Brad could see snow everywhere except for the streets, which had been plowed, though they were still slushy. He was able to give us a very detailed description of the way the snow looked. Brad could also see the snowbanks that the plows had created. He saw a street car go by. Finally, he recognized a playground used by the children of his school and a particular hill he used to climb nearby.
> (Ring and Cooper 1997: 113)

After this, Barrows entered a 'tunnel' and emerged from it into 'an immense field illuminated by a tremendous, all-encompassing light. Everything was perfect'. Next, Barrows became aware of beautiful music, and 'a glittering stone structure so brilliant that he thought it might be burning hot'. He entered it and encountered a man 'from whom emanated an overwhelming love'. The man ended Barrows's account by nudging him back into his body. Finally, like Umipeg, Barrows had rather a rude awakening back to life, 'finding himself in bed gasping for air, attended by two nurses' (Ring and Cooper 1997: 113).

Preliminary comments

A number of features of these two accounts press for comment at this point. They are, by Ring and his co-researchers' own judgements, 'certainly among our most impressive cases' (Ring and Valarino 1998: 81). Indeed, the detail of these two accounts that they present significantly outweighs the detail which they devote to their other cases, both in the technical presentation given in the *Journal for Near-Death Studies*, the later presentation given in *Mindsight*, and the chapter devoted to the subject in Ring and Valarino's *Lessons from the Light*. As the two most detailed and impressive cases presented by Ring and his co-researchers, therefore, they demand an appropriately detailed response, and for this reason we shall devote most attention to them shortly within the context of our attempt to produce an appropriate theological and philosophical rejoinder. Fortunately in this regard, however, Ring and his co-researchers also assert that these cases, though impressive and detailed, are 'entirely typical of our sample as a whole in that our blind respondents, as a rule, tend to describe NDEs that are no different from those reported by sighted persons' (Ring and Valarino 1998: 81). Indeed, many of the other cases interviewed by Ring and Cooper simply serve to confirm their overall findings. In each case, remote perception both of this and other worlds seems, impossibly, to occur in blind OBErs and NDErs, some of them congenitally blind. Claims are made that in some cases this receives confirmation from others present at the scene (a point to which we will need to return). In each case this perception seems, ultimately, to be not simply a restoration of vision to the blind and congenitally blind but even an *improvement* upon what normal vision would be expected to be like. We have already noted that as far back as 1984 Ring was presenting data which seemed to indicate that poor vision could be temporarily improved during an NDE. An examination of his latest findings reveals more claims of a similar nature.

Thus, Ring and Cooper write that 'our scrutiny of these transcripts frequently revealed a multifaceted synesthetic aspect to the experiencer's perception that seemed to transcend normal sight' (Ring and Cooper 1997: 134). As proof and illustration of this, they offer a number of testimony-extracts, of which the following is representative:

> I was hovering over a stretcher in one of the emergency rooms at the hospital. I glanced down at the stretcher, knew the body wrapped in blankets was mine, and really didn't care. The room was much more interesting than my body. And what a neat perspective. I could see everything. And I do mean everything! I could see the top of the light on the ceiling, and the underside of the stretcher. I could see the tiles on the ceiling and the tiles on the floor, simultaneously. Three hundred sixty degree spherical vision. And not just spherical. Detailed! I could see every single hair and the follicle out of which it grew on the head of the nurse standing beside the stretcher. At the time I knew exactly how many hairs there were to look at. But I shifted focus. She was wearing glittery white nylons. Every single shimmer and sheen stood out in glowing detail, and once again I knew exactly how many sparkles there were.
>
> (Ring and Cooper 1997: 139)

Overall, therefore, what is being claimed is that sight is not simply restored or bestowed during these special cases, but that it is sight of a kind that transcends the usual limits of perception, *even in the sighted*.

Giving sight to the blind

Such a claim may give food for thought to those working in a number of different academic fields, psychology foremost amongst them. For it may have become apparent that the cases presented by Ring and Cooper are in many ways analogous to a group of case studies of perception in the once-blind which exists in a very different context: that of those persons whose sight is restored after an operation to remove a cataract or other visual obstruction. Indeed, in a small number of cases, doctors have managed to give sight to those congenitally or adventitiously blind, thanks to modern – and in many cases pioneering – surgical operations.

Such cases make for fascinating reading and are well documented, particularly in medical literature and in studies dealing with the psychology of human perception. Classic studies by Gregory and Wallace (1963), Valvo (1971) and, more recently, Sacks (1995), amongst others, have all detailed the often remarkable – and sometimes tragic – results of subjects whose sight has either been restored after a long period of blindness or given for the first time by doctors using advanced medical procedures. Indeed, thanks to advancing medical technology, such cases may be expected to increase in future years, and more, comparable, studies may therefore be anticipated.

One celebrated case reported by Gregory concerns one S.B. who received corneal grafts at age 52, but for whom perceptual normalcy was never fully possible, and for whom visual perception of even something as straightforward as a lathe – a tool with which he was fully acquainted by touch – was an impossibility. An impossibility, that is, until he had actually *touched* it:

> We led him to the glass case, and asked him to tell us what was in it. He was quite unable to say anything about it, except he thought the nearest part was a handle ... He complained that he could not see the cutting edge, or the metal being worked, or anything else about it, and appeared rather agitated. We then asked the Museum Attendant for the case to be opened, and S.B. was allowed to touch the lathe. The result was startling; he ran his hands deftly over the machine ... Then he stood back a little and opened his eyes and said: 'Now that I've felt it I can see.' He then named many of the parts correctly and explained how they would work, though he could not understand the chain of four gears driving the lead screw. ...
>
> (Gregory 1987: 94)

Subsequently, S.B. became severely depressed by his new-found abilities, a depression that ultimately contributed to his untimely and premature death a mere two years after his sight-restoring operation.

Elsewhere, Valvo cites the case of a patient blinded at 15, who, given his sight back twenty-two years later, reported that:

> During these first weeks [after surgery] I had no appreciation of depth or distance; street lights were luminous stains stuck to the window-panes, and the corridors of the hospital were black holes. When I crossed the road the traffic terrified me, even when I was accompanied.
>
> (Sacks 1995: 114)

Interestingly, of course, the perceptual confusion reported by this subject contrasts sharply with both Vicki Umipeg and Brad Barrows, who, as reported by Ring and Cooper, appeared virtually immediately to gain the ability to perceive accurately just such things as hospitals and streetlights with virtually no difficulty whatsoever (except for an immediate and initial sense of 'frightening' disorientation in the case of Vicki Umipeg, which was quickly followed by the ability to see lights and buildings outside the hospital apparently with great clarity). Indeed, a case reported by Sacks of 'Virgil', who was given his sight back after virtually a lifetime of blindness, contrasts sharply with the claims of Ring and Cooper's blind respondents to see and identify their *doctors* immediately. At the age of 50, his bandages finally removed and newly sighted in one good eye, Sacks describes Virgil's immediate perceptions and reactions:

> There was light, there was movement, there was colour, all mixed up, all meaningless, a blur. Then out of the blur came a voice that said, 'Well?'. Then, and only then, he said, did he finally realize that this chaos of light and shadow was a face – and, indeed, the face of his surgeon.
>
> (Sacks 1995: 107)

Sacks compares this experience with that of S.B.:

When the bandages were removed . . . he heard a voice
coming from in front of him and to one side: he turned to
the source of the sound, and saw a 'blur'. He realized that
this must be a face . . . He seemed to think that he would
not have known that this was a face if he had not
previously heard the voice and known that voices came
from faces.

(Sacks 1995: 108)

I have reproduced these interesting testimony-extracts in some
detail for the purposes of comparison with cases such as those of
Vicki Umipeg and Brad Barrows, and to point out the contrasts
which obviously exist between testimonies in which sight is
physically restored to the blind and the testimonies of blind
NDErs who report out-of-body perceptions. Sacks makes the
useful – and popular – suggestion that the results of sight-restoring
operations demonstrate that seeing is done not simply with the
eyes, but with learned concepts through which we make sense of
the information that our eyes send to our brains. Thus, he writes
in connection with the Virgil case that:

When we open our eyes each morning, it is upon a world
we have spent a lifetime *learning* to see. We are not given
the world: we make our world through incessant experience, categorization, memory, reconnection. But when
Virgil opened his eye, after being blind for forty five years
– having had little more than an infant's visual experience,
and this long forgotten – there were no visual memories
to support a perception; there was no world of experience
and meaning awaiting him. He saw, but what he saw had
no coherence. His retina and optic nerve were active,
transmitting impulses, but his brain could make no sense
of them. . . .

(Sacks 1995: 108)

Indeed, like S.B., Virgil was frequently only able to correctly
identify an object after he had built up a *conceptual* awareness of
it by touching it, or something similar. To this end, after his
operation, Virgil began collecting – and frequently touching –

miniature models of things such as toy cars, toy animals and models of buildings in order to be able to identify their full-size and real-world counterparts.

In search of new paradigms?

Ring and Valarino make only scant reference to this cluster of known medical cases analogous to their own NDErs' testimonies in *Lessons from the Light*, and there is only passing acknowledgement of the case studies reported by Sacks *et al.* in the more technical presentation of the data given in the *Journal of Near-Death Studies* and *Mindsight*. There seems, however, to be a reason for this. For Ring and Cooper are convinced that no extant naturalistic explanations of the mechanisms of perception are sufficient to account for the experiences which they have uncovered. Thus, they claim, the normal channels and mechanisms of perception are bypassed in near-death episodes, to be replaced by a new mode of perceiving which they term 'transcendental awareness' and 'mindsight'.

In part, one suspects that such a new mechanism is required precisely because their data conflict with comparable cases such as those of S.B. and Virgil. In addition, however, they have already alluded to the fact that perceptual abilities experienced by NDErs seemingly undergo an almost miraculous enhancement that places them far *above* the abilities of even the most perfectly sighted. Further, they need some sort of perceptual hypothesis that bypasses the possibilities of other naturalistic explanations such as blindsight and skin-based vision, which are ruled out in the case of Ring and Cooper's subjects on the grounds that most were unconscious and in hospital beds at the time of their NDEs. Indeed, all conventional hypotheses which might be introduced to explain out-of-body perceptions – both visually and conceptually – would seem to be contradicted by the unusual *perspectives* from which, as we have seen, they usually proceed: that is, outside the self, usually from above, and often some distance above any surrounding action and activities going on. In the case of Umipeg and Barrows, for example, there would seem to be no conventional naturalistic explanation which would account for them suddenly 'floating' through a hospital ceiling and witnessing things outside the hospital altogether, such as snowbanks, street-lights and traffic.

Thus it is that, in the concluding sections of their investigations, Ring and Cooper explore the exciting possibility that wholly *new ways* of perceiving have opened up – albeit temporarily – to NDErs. To this end, they consider a number of possible modifications to existing ways of thinking about the self and its perceptual abilities and potentials in order to explain their findings, drawing for these on contributors to the field of 'New Paradigm Science' such as Kenneth Arnette, Amit Goswami and Jenny Wade. Essentially, they suggest, we need to consider a number of 'common postulates' held in common by these thinkers concerning the essential nature of human consciousness. One is that 'consciousness itself is primary and the ground of all being'. Another is that 'consciousness is nonlocal': that is, that it is nonbounded by time or space and is in fact 'unitive'. ('There is only one consciousness, which we call mind.') All of these are given little elaboration, and the reader is referred by Ring and Cooper to the texts they have cited by Arnette *et al.* for further detail (Ring and Cooper 1997: 145ff.). Interesting as all of this may be, it is the final postulate that Ring and Cooper present which seems to link the others, and which is of particular interest as regards the question of dualism. It is, as Ring and Cooper state, 'that consciousness may and indeed must sometimes function independently of the brain'. Indeed, for them: 'This is a key assumption, especially for understanding how the blind may become aware of something that seems like visual perception', and they continue:

> Thus, what we have here is an adumbration of a process that begins with Mind fully independent of brain becoming self-referential, that is, becoming identified with consciousness itself, and then converting this noumenal consciousness into a dualistic modality that generates the familiar phenomenal world. What we have called transcendental awareness is at least the beginning of the reversal of that process by which, even though traces of an everyday dualism remain, the individual is enabled, however temporarily, to experience the world from a

perspective independent of brain functioning and the operation of the senses.

(Ring and Cooper 1997: 144)

In conclusion, Ring and Cooper are well aware of the implications of this, particularly in the light of their own research:

> What the blind experience is more astonishing than the claim that they have seen. Instead, they, like sighted persons who have had similar episodes, have transcended brain-based consciousness altogether and, because of that, their experiences beggar all description or convenient labels. For these we need a new language altogether, as we need new theories from a new kind of science even to begin to comprehend them. Toward this end, the study of paradoxical and utterly anomalous experiences plays a vital role in furnishing the theorists of today the data they need to fashion the science of the 21st century.

(Ring and Cooper 1997: 146)

Evaluating the evidence

These are bold claims. Indeed, we have examined the work of Ring and Cooper in some detail not simply because it is far and away the most extensive investigation of NDEs in the blind ever carried out, but because their conclusions, if correct, would seem to challenge – and possibly overthrow – conventional ways of thinking about the self, consciousness, life and death. This, in turn, would be expected to be of considerable importance not simply in fashioning new science, and in particular new *neuroscience*, but new philosophy and theology as well. At this point in our investigation, therefore, we must return to the questions with which we began: how good is the quality of the evidence presented in the literature, and what issues for philosophy and theology in particular does it raise?

To begin with, a number of issues arising out of the research undertaken by Ring and Cooper call for comment and closer examination. This is particularly the case when we return to consider their two most impressive case studies – those of Vicki

230

Umipeg and Brad Barrows. As regards these, it might first be asked: how *convincing* is the evidence that during their NDEs, some sort of hitherto-impossible perception was suddenly opened up to them? Several issues press for comment here. First, it is notable that, although 33 at the time of the interview, Barrows's experience occurred when he was 8 years old. Although recent years have seen a flurry of interest in the NDEs of children, a researcher critical of Ring and Cooper's work might seriously question whether the testimony, twenty-five years after the event, of an episode that occurred to an 8-year-old boy, should qualify as one of their two most impressive cases. As regards the Umipeg case, on the other hand, although the NDE to which Ring and Cooper devote attention took place during adulthood, it is notable for some unusual inconsistencies, particularly as regards the nature of the seeing involved. Thus, although it is claimed that Umipeg's 'mindsight' allowed her a rich visual perception denied to her by her usual physical state, it is curious that colour was not part of the experience. We recall the contention that she could 'see a lot of blood', with Ring's comment that 'she could not tell its colour – she still has no concept of colour, she says'. Ring and Cooper make much of the fact that mindsight is an improvement on physical sight, as we have already had cause to note. We recall their contention that it is *more* than simple physical vision; indeed, that it is an 'omnidirectional awareness . . . a type of knowledge that stretches our concept of ordinary "vision" beyond the breaking point' and even 'a state of consciousness in which . . . things present themselves in true Blakean fashion, "as they are, infinite"' (Ring and Cooper 1997: 139). It is curious, therefore, that it lacks the simple colour red. Indeed, in the light of this, we might be forced to conclude that far from representing an *improvement* on existing ways of seeing, it might be seen as a distinct *weakening* of them. Indeed, we may further question the claim that some sort of perception of the 'real, "infinite" nature' of things *is* being disclosed to these temporarily mindsighted NDErs at all. For, in addition to lacking basic colour, their perceptions during these episodes also seem to be very *mundane*: doctors, hospitals, streetlights, snowploughs, slush and so on. A critic may be forgiven for wondering at this point whether this is really what we would expect to see if we were suddenly to awaken to a wholly new state of consciousness with our doors of perception cleansed. Surely – at the very least – we should expect in such a situation to see in colour. Indeed, we might reasonably expect to appreciate more, deeper and greater colour in such a condition, not less colour or none at all.

Further, the reader may wonder at the statistical improbability of some of the events that Ring and Cooper present. NDEs seem quite rare, despite the recent publicity that has surrounded them. In this context, for example, it is worth noting that a recent study organized by British theologian Paul Badham and neuroscientist Peter Fenwick, which attempted to gain empirical support for the hypothesis that something leaves the body during an NDE, foundered because of a paucity of cases in the hospital chosen for the study (Badham 1997: 14). To find NDEs in the *blind*, therefore, would seem to be an incredibly difficult task. That Ring and Cooper found twenty-one such cases is an extraordinary achievement. That one of their two best cases was referred by the same social worker as was involved in the celebrated 'tennis shoe' case, and indeed came from the *same hospital*, seems most striking – and incredibly statistically improbable.

Corroborative evidence

To their credit, Ring and Cooper recognize that a genuinely empirical study of NDEs in the blind which is concerned to establish whether genuinely veridical perception takes place during such episodes must concern itself in part with finding *corroboration* of such perceptions from others present. The problem with this, as they acknowledge, is to find witnesses who can independently corroborate what NDErs, apparently, see, and to find them in some cases several years after the episodes took place. However, as a result of their research, Ring and Cooper *do* appear to have managed to find a small number of such cases. Again, however, a critical reading of the quality of the data presented reveals the need for caution in accepting them unreservedly. One presented case, for example, was not collected by Ring and Cooper, but was passed to them by another researcher, and appears to have not been followed up. Another, however, is worthy of more detailed comment because it is presented in some detail, although it involves an OBE not associated with any apparently life-threatening condition, and does not, therefore, relate to sudden sight during a full-blown NDE. It concerns one 'Frank', who had been blind for ten years at the time of his experience, and who had in fact reported several OBEs (although it is unclear whether sight occurred in some or all of them). On the morning of a friend's wake, Frank had asked a friend to purchase a tie for him to wear. The friend bought the tie for Frank without telling him anything about it and he put it on. For some reason he then lay upon the couch. In his own words:

> I was laying down on the couch and I could see myself coming out of my body. And I could see my tie. The tie that was on. And it had a circle on it – it was red – and it had a gray circle, two gray circles on it. And I remember that.
>
> (Ring and Cooper 1997: 120)

Subsequently, Frank revealed that he described the design of the tie to the friend, who was surprised at his correct description of it. The transcript of the interview as presented by Ring and Cooper continues:

Interviewer: And do you remember what the tie looked like even now?

Frank: Yeah. It's a rose-colored tie with circles on it and dots in the middle of the circle. Whitish/grayish circle around there. And it's a beautiful tie, 'cause every place I go they remark on it. So she [the friend] said to me, 'Who told you?' And I said, 'Nobody.' I said, 'I just guessed.' I didn't want to tell because, like I said before . . . you can't say things to certain people.

(Ring and Cooper 1997: 121)

In search of corroboration for Frank's apparently impossible observation, Ring and Cooper tracked the friend down, and Cooper proceeded to interview her concerning her recollection of the incident. From Cooper's notes of the interview, we read:

I independently called [Frank's] friend who said she did purchase a tie for Frank that day and did pick him up for the wake. However, she didn't have a clear recollection of the sequence of events that day to confirm the accuracy of Frank's story and didn't remember the exact design and colors of the tie. She added that Frank is a down-to-earth guy who in her experience does not embellish stories. And even though she couldn't independently corroborate his account, she tended to think he was probably accurate in recounting the details.

(Ring and Cooper 1997: 121)

Although Ring and Cooper present this as a 'corroborative' case of sight during a blind respondent's out-of-body experience, it is clear that it is not. The witness does not remember clearly the events or the tie. She thus cannot corroborate the detail of the episode in question, but merely presents a testimony to Frank's apparent truthfulness and simply thinks that he was 'probably accurate' in the details he gives. Even Ring and Cooper are forced to conclude that 'we lack the crucial confirming facts we need from the witness involved . . .' (Ring and Cooper 1997: 121). Once again, therefore, we must exercise care with the quality of the data presented. We have already noted that Ring and Cooper make some bold claims on the basis of their research, even to the effect that 'new theories and a new kind of science' may need to be fashioned as a result. More cautious commentators may be forgiven for suggesting that much stronger data are needed before they agree that existing scientific paradigms need to be hauled down and new ones erected. Again – and at the very least – there is a need for further, independent, research into such cases before we begin to consider the need for a new 'science of consciousness'.

NDEs in the deaf?

As we have seen, Ring and Cooper have advanced two terms to describe the new perceptual abilities which they believe to be temporarily reported by some blind NDErs and OBErs. In their paper for the *Journal of Near-Death Studies*, they favour the term 'transcendental awareness'. In the later publications, as we have

234

seen, this is dropped in favour of the shorter 'mindsight'. The second, later, term is interesting, as it suggests the notion that the new state of consciousness is primarily sight-driven. Indeed, if the reports of blind NDErs are to be accepted at face value, some sort of preternatural seeing *does* seem to be a key part of the experience. However, we may question whether sight *alone* would be expected to be a part of any new kind of 'superconsciousness'. We may wonder, for example, if other perceptual abilities – such as hearing, touch or taste – might equally be enhanced, together with sight. Indeed, in considering other perceptual skills in the light of the NDE, we might begin to wonder whether comparable cases of miraculously restored senses are reported in NDErs with different perceptual deficiencies and handicaps. What, for example, of research into sudden *hearing* during NDEs reported by the deaf or even the congenitally deaf? As far as I am aware, no such studies exist. But if we are genuinely to attempt to test the hypothesis that some sort of developed state of consciousness occurs at or near the point of death, and which brings with it a restoration – and improvement – of physical skills either impaired or absent altogether during life, then clearly we must consider the possibility of such reports. At the very least, a study of cases of sudden hearing during NDEs reported by the congenitally deaf would help add to the argument that some sort of transcendental awareness awaits us after death, and would thus strengthen some of Ring and Cooper's contentions yet further.

Blindness at Bethsaida

Further questions present themselves at this point, however. For it may now become useful to examine how philosophy and theology might begin to respond to the remarkable claims that we have been in the process of uncovering. Given the nature of these, it would appear that all sorts of questions have been raised which theology and philosophy may be in a good position to answer. Can they therefore make a contribution to any serious discussion of the research as it stands at present? Do they *need* to? And if they *do*, what particular issues raised by the study of NDEs in the blind might be said to be of particular relevance to these related disciplines?

To begin with, we may pause again to consider the quality of the evidence to which theology and philosophy are being invited to respond. As we have had cause to note, although at first sight the evidence for mindsight seems good, upon closer inspection there are significant weaknesses even in the most apparently 'impressive' cases. Indeed, sceptics might want to argue that, at the very least, the jury should remain out over these claims until such a time as further, more convincing cases may emerge. On this basis, therefore, theologians and philosophers might want to conclude that no evidence of sufficient quality has emerged so far to warrant their serious attention. Indeed, in keeping with one of the central aims of this book, a key purpose of this chapter has simply been to present such research to a theologically and philosophically orientated readership who may not hitherto have been aware that it existed, but who may now be in a position to assess realistically whether it constitutes a case which needs to be taken seriously or whether, conversely, it can simply be discarded.

However, further studies may yet turn out to more convincingly replicate some or all of the findings claimed by Ring and his co-researchers concerning restoration of sight to the blind during NDEs and related episodes. If such should occur, it might reasonably be concluded that there is after all some sort of case to answer. Theology, in this instance, might be expected to explore scriptural evidence for the existence and interpretation of such apparently miraculous sight restoration, and for Christian theologians in particular the miraculous accounts of restoration of sight to the blind performed by Jesus and recorded in the New Testament might be expected to be one obvious and important resource. Mark 8:22–6 is of obvious significance here, recording as it does that:

> They came to Bethsaida, and some people brought a blind man and begged Jesus to touch him. He took the blind man by the hand and led him outside the village. When he had spit on the man's eyes and put his hands on him, Jesus asked, 'Do you see anything?'
> He looked up and said, 'I see people; they look like trees walking around.'

> Once more Jesus put his hands on the man's eyes. Then his eyes were opened, his sight was restored, and he saw everything clearly. Jesus sent him home, saying, 'Don't go into the village.'

In view of the earlier discussion regarding the results of sight-restoring operations on the blind, this man's initial confusion regarding what he is looking at rings true to what we might expect to be his experience, assuming, of course, we take the narrative with a literalness that not all commentators would accept. Taken as a literal description of a surgical procedure – albeit a highly unusual and miraculous one – it may be argued that Jesus has to perform an essentially two-stage healing in order to get the man to see clearly: first, a healing of the eyes, enabling the blind man to *look*; then an inner healing within the brain – a sort of conceptual healing – enabling him to *see*. And this two-stage progression, as we have seen, is what is actually needed in many cases where sight is given to the congenitally blind or restored to the long-term blind.

However, there is one crucial difference between New Testament accounts such as the above and the cases presented by Ring and Cooper. For these researchers, as we have had abundant cause to note, do not interpret their findings along purely physicalist lines, but instead seek to present an argument for some sort of mind–body *dualism*, turning to New Paradigm Science in order to interpret the full meaning and implications of this. It is clear that such a model of personhood might give theologians and philosophers, together with members of a variety of faith communities, some pause for thought, particularly in relation to any future afterlife. As chapter 2 has already shown, for example, interpretations of NDEs within certain Buddhist traditions do not invoke dualism at all and instead view such experiences as occurring in purely mind-dependent realms (Rinpoche 1992: 319ff.). For many Western philosophers and psychologists, although dualism has a long and venerable history, it seems to have few supporters today, with some notable exceptions. Certainly in the realm of psychology, thinkers such as Daniel Dennett and Antonio Damascio find the 'Cartesian theatre' model of the mind extremely difficult to accept, and have correspondingly presented powerful arguments that favour monism and psychosomatic unity (Dennett 1991; Damascio 1994). From within a very different context, many adherents from within the religious traditions bounded by classical theism would wish to assert that far from simply possessing immortality as a sort of birthright, human beings must await the *bestowal* of life after death on the last day as a gracious act of God, and would therefore be suspicious of any assertions regarding human immortality which understood it as some sort of autonomous possession. The belief of many within such traditions is that life after death proceeds by way of *resurrection*: the raising to life by God of an embodied – albeit transformed and glorified – self prior to judgement. Christianity, for example, may not seem to lend itself to the kind of dualistic model of selfhood apparently presented in many NDErs' testimonies, including, of course, those of the blind, with their particularly strong dualistic implications.

One possible response to this objection might be to claim that NDErs are seeing glimpses, not of a final state after resurrection, but of an intermediate state between death and final judgement in which the newly liberated soul continues to enjoy experiences and sensations. This claim is held in various and diverse ways by large numbers within all of the traditions of classical theism who believe that there is, in essence, a temporary state of disembodiment between physical death and final resurrection. For a few contemporary theologians and philosophers too, such as Roger Trigg and John Hick, this scenario is perfectly plausible, and they join a very long and venerable theological and philosophical tradition which has consistently wished to assert that human beings are made up of more than just a body (Trigg 1988; Hick 1985). However, *another* possible and alternative response to this intermediate state hypothesis might be to question whether NDEs do, indeed, *demonstrate* a form of dualism in which the soul survives the death of the body or whether they merely *presuppose* it. As we have seen, there are numerous problems with the quality of the data presented by Ring and Cooper which may caution against too-ready acceptance that what their respondents have revealed to them simply proves dualism or disproves monism. In view of this, it is surely legitimate to assert that instead of invoking any hypothesis which involves some sort of dualism as a way of interpreting their data, some other hypothesis might more effectively be invoked which explains them more satisfactorily, such as the possibility that they have been contaminated in some way, or that imagination or retrospective composition of NDErs' narratives is what is really responsible for their testimonies. In support of this contention, we may consider whether any form of mind–body dualism is possible at all, particularly in the continued absence of convincing parapsychological evidence which would strengthen the case *for* it, together with the very many objections to it which exist within contemporary philosophy and psychology (Hastings 2000: 516–17). In such a situation of academic doubt combined with the continued lack of good, hard, evidence, the dualistic hypothesis cannot be said either to explain or to be in some sense proved by the testimonies of NDErs (blind NDErs included). If such should turn out to be the case, some other hypothesis will need to be invoked in order to satisfactorily explain the cases under discussion. John Haldane, who has occupied just such a position, presents it succinctly when he writes of NDEs that: 'Whatever the nature of the evidence it cannot lend support to a view whose falsity has been established, and in such an event therefore some other explanation is called for' (Haldane 1989). Of course, future studies of the experiences of NDErs may turn up stronger evidence for dualism than that which currently exists. In this case, there may well be a need for major rethinking about the nature of mind, selfhood and the prospects for immortality. Until such evidence arises, philosophers and theologians are surely right to cast about for alternative explanations of the data as presented by Ring, Cooper and Valarino.

A final judgement?

One further, final, issue pressses for attention here. Ring has made much in recent years of the life review which is contained in many NDErs' accounts of their experiences. As has already been noted in this chapter, Vicki Umipeg, for example, was given a review of her life by 'Jesus' at the end of her NDE, in which she saw apparently everything from her birth up to the time of her near-death episode within a 'complete panoramic view of her life' whilst 'the being gently commented to help her understand the significance of her actions and their repercussions'. Such a gentle, non-judgemental, form of review is fairly typical of other cases presented in the literature, and has been given extended treatment in recent years by Ring and his co-workers, most recently in *Lessons from the Light*.

The presence of such a form of judgement apparently following directly after the cessation of an NDEr's life might represent a further issue that may give theologians pause for thought. For this seems a far cry from the Jewish, Christian and Muslim belief that judgement will only occur on the last day, when the dead are finally raised by God. By contrast to this, in NDErs' testimonies, there appears to be no sense of the sleep in the earth prior to resurrection that we find described in, say, Daniel 12:2 or 1 Thessalonians 4:14–15. Instead, judgement within these contexts seems to occur virtually immediately after death in many near-death reports: not at all what we find in the eschatologies of classical theism.

What might theologians make of this apparent discrepancy? Again, little in the way of response has so far been forthcoming. Of course, it is just conceivable that there are two judgements: the first a friendly warning before the earth-shattering solemnity and finality of the second one. However, there appears to be no scriptural basis for this in any of the sacred texts of classical theism, and it is notable that belief in an imminent as opposed to an end-time judgement has recently been traced back as far as the third century by theologian Carol Zaleski, who detects it in the Western apocalypse *Visio Pauli* (Zaleski 1996: 72; Fox 2000a: 9ff.). Whatever – if anything – theologians might ultimately make of such a discrepancy, it has clearly been with us for a long time.

Conclusions: beyond reasonable doubt?

This chapter has attempted to provide an overview of all of the research to date concerning NDEs in the blind, in order to present it to a broadly philosophical and theological readership who may not be aware of its current state. It has also begun an attempt at a critique of the research, particularly that of Ring and Cooper who have produced far and away the most detailed study that currently exists. It has ended by suggesting some avenues of response which theology and philosophy may wish to consider. Throughout, the strong suggestion has been made that philosophers and theologians may wish to hold fire on deeper, more sustained engagement with the research, pending future studies of a higher, more critical standard which may – or may not – replicate some of the remarkable claims which are currently being made by a comparatively small number of near-death researchers.

Indeed, and overall, much of this chapter may appear to have been deeply critical of most if not all of the current research in this area, and of Ring and Cooper in particular. I should like to end, therefore, with a final qualification of the position which my own response to their claims has led me to take. Thus, although this chapter has attempted to show that they have *failed* to provide successful proof that during their NDEs the blind are able to see, the bold and brave endeavour which Ring and Cooper have made to discover convincing cases is clearly laudable. For dualism remains an unproven hypothesis which may yet be decided by the kind of research they present. In *Mindsight*, for example, they allude to yet another case where a woman, apparently blind from birth, was suddenly able – *unlike* Vicki Umipeg – to distinguish and apparently correctly indentify the differences between yellow, purple and pink flowers. The presentation of such eyebrow-raising data reveals courage and conviction on the part of the researchers, and a readiness to respond to future critiques of their work which must surely follow.

There is a sense, however, in which much psychical research must assume some sort of dualism (together with the existence of some sort of immortal essence or soul) in many of the fields in which it operates: whether it seeks to prove out-of-body experiences and communication via channels from the dead, or whether it seeks to probe for veridical evidence of certain types of ghosts and apparitions or the existence of past lives via techniques such as regressive hypnosis. In each area of investigation, however, real doubt still remains as to the quality and correct interpretation of the evidence presented, even as parapsychological research enters yet another century of discussion and debate, over a hundred years after the founding of the first Society for Psychical Research in 1882. Indeed, it is true to say that controversy rages within parapsychology with an intensity that few other areas of academic enquiry can match, the very fact of such ongoing dissension and disagreement only serving to underline the ambiguity of so much of the evidence presented. In such a climate, research such as that presented by Ring and Cooper can only be welcomed. For whatever its ultimate shortcomings, it points the way ahead, seeking to provide a firm empirical footing for some extraordinary – but potentially immensely significant – claims. Whilst it may not be the case that a new science is needed to explain such alleged anomalies, it may turn out to be the case that the twenty-first century finally puts their existence on completely undisputed ground. Only good research can do this. Ultimately it will take bold hypotheses and brave endeavour such as that launched by Ring and Cooper which may yet enable parapsychology to discover its white crows, pushing the argument for claims such as the existence of the soul, together with the promise of sight to the blind, beyond the doubt which still remains.

6

THE RERC STUDY

Introduction

Located within the Department of Theology and Religious Studies at the University of Wales, Lampeter, the Religious Experience Research Centre (RERC) currently contains over 6,000 accounts of religious experience: conversion testimonies, descriptions of encounters with numinous presences, feelings of supernatural fear and horror, descriptions of answered prayer, encounters with unusual lights, and many others. Such an unusual collection has itself an unusual history. Its originator was a zoologist, Sir Alister Hardy, who was born in Nottingham in 1896. Hardy, an outstanding academic who was to receive a knighthood in recognition of his research into marine biology, developed early in his life a particular concern to explore the newly emerging theory of evolution and the implications arising from it for a range of areas of human experience, not least those of religion and spirituality. When his early academic studies were interrupted by the outbreak of the First World War and Hardy was called up for active service he appears to have made some sort of vow to 'what I called God': if he was to survive the war, he would devote himself to an attempt to bring about a reconciliation between humankind's spiritual and religious awareness on the one hand and Darwinian theory on the other. Hardy happily did survive the war, and by the mid-1920s had been appointed chief zoologist on the exploratory vessel *Discovery*. It was at this point that the case collection of religious experiences housed at the RERC archives was to have its genesis.

Before sailing on the *Discovery*'s various expeditions, Hardy wrote to the General Press Cutting Association in London requesting articles on religion, God, faith, prayer and the relationship between science and religion. As an addendum to this list, Hardy added: 'Anything in fact of a religious or spiritual nature', before setting out the sorts of things he was *not* interested in, including church notices, reports of sermons, clerical obituaries or anything of a spiritualistic or psychic nature. He lodged this request for the first time in 1925, and it led to subsequent, repeated and more direct approaches to various newspapers for particular types of personal, vivid, immediate religious experiences which usually took the form of a question: 'Have you ever been aware of or influenced by a presence or power, whether you call it God or not, which is different from your everyday self?' By the summer of 1968 Hardy had amassed an amount of material large enough to require some sort of base or centre to house it all in and permit work to start. He approached Manchester College, Oxford, which gave him two rooms to help further his research, and with the aid of various grants from charitable trusts he was able to open, at the age of 73, what was originally called the Religious Experience Research Unit, in September 1969.[1]

In the more than thirty years since its inception, the number of accounts in the collection rose significantly. Although from the outset he appears not to have wished to collect accounts of paranormal experience, a number of these were sent to him anyway, and by the time that he wrote an analysis and classification of his first 3000 accounts in *The Spiritual Nature of Man* in 1979 Hardy had already found enough accounts of apparitions, telepathy and precognition to give numerous examples of such experiences. A number of studies were to follow including those from scholars such as Timothy Beardsworth, David Hay and Michael Jackson, all keen to extend the explorations of religious experience which Hardy had begun into areas including religious education and psychiatry. In recent years, the unit – now rechristened the Religious Experience Research Centre – has continued to conduct research, and the collection of cases continues. The majority of these are in the form of testimonies, usually included in or added to letters giving brief information about the subject's background and the context of his or her particular experience.

Whilst subjects who have submitted accounts are obviously self-selected and thus present a 'skewed sample' of reports which makes them impossible to use in a number of statistically rigorous contexts, nonetheless they remain, as Verena Tschudin has written in a recent collection of accounts published by the Centre, 'marvel-lously spontaneous and varied accounts, rich in subject and in variety of language, [with] each account expressing its own completeness at the time of writing' (Maxwell and Tschudin 1990: 5).

Although Hardy was well aware of the existence of phenomena such as near-death and out-of-body experiences, he made no systematic attempt to study these. Indeed, there is a suggestion that he felt that the exploration of such experiences was not the Centre's concern or at least not its primary focus, and he was content simply to file them.[2] However, during the writing of this book, the possibility presented itself that they might provide a rich resource with which to further explore NDEs. To this end, a search of the archives was begun in the hope of finding a useable number of accounts. In the event, the search proved successful. Nearly 100 usable accounts were uncovered, of which virtually none had been examined or reproduced in any published source. Indeed, some could be dated to the earliest years of the RERC, and had thus lain, untouched, in the archives for over thirty years. It was an exciting time of discovery that promised to significantly enhance *Through the Valley of the Shadow of Death* by providing a rich database with which to test some of the conclusions drawn in earlier chapters. In all cases, the accounts, nearly all in the form of letters to the Centre and many addressed to Hardy himself, are reproduced in the following pages without corrections either to original spelling, grammar or punctuation.

Methodology

Initially, however, collection of the accounts presented several problems that needed to be addressed before genuine analysis could begin. It immediately became clear, for example, that whilst much interesting material was found, no account – predictably – was discovered which fitted entirely the original 'Moody model' with its fifteen elements, as discussed in chapter 1. However, even finding accounts that matched subsequent and more modest models, such as those of Ring and Grey, proved problematical. For whilst it was possible to find some accounts in which respondents *were* near death and had unusual experiences, it was usually the case that they would report only a small number of elements: an out-of-body experience, perhaps, or entry into darkness, or an encounter with a benign light. Indeed, one key objective of the study soon became to see how many accounts matched to any significant extent existing model NDEs as proposed by other researchers; consequently no account that included any element of either Moody's original model or the model of any subsequent researcher was excluded from analysis. Proceeding on this basis, the ensuing search of the archives revealed the presence of ninety-one usable accounts in total, although not all of these occurred when subjects were near death, as will shortly become clear. Although at first sight this might appear to constitute a relatively small database, within the context of many existing studies of NDEs it is in fact quite large. Ring's original study, *Life at Death*, for example, drew on only fifty-four case histories fcr its analysis, Grey's *Return from Death* used forty-one, Sutherland's quantitatively sophisticated 1990 study of NDE 'fruits', *Reborn in the Light*, drew on fifty cases, whilst Morse's 1991 study of NDEs in children, *Closer to the Light*, drew far-reaching conclusions on the basis of a sample of only twelve cases (Ring 1980; Grey 1985; Sutherland 1992; Morse 1991). Viewed against this background, therefore, the RERC study could justifiably claim to be based on a comparatively large collection of cases.

The collection of data on specifically *near-death* experiences was complicated, however, by the fact that it was often difficult to determine where an episode of life-threatening danger began and ended. In some cases – such as haemorrhage during childbirth or being blown up by a mine during wartime – it was fairly easy to determine that a subject may have been near death or clinically dead at the time of his or her experience. But in other cases – such as recuperating in hospital some days after an accident or operation or where an illness had passed its peak but convalescence was still necessary – it was much more difficult to determine whether clinical death had temporarily occurred, or even whether subjects had been subjected to any degree of life-threatening danger at all. Did experiences that arose within these contexts count as

NDEs or not? For as is well known, persons suffer sometimes catastrophic relapses in the days following operations or accidents, and some relatively simple illnesses can impose enormous strains even when the worst of their suffering has passed. In order to resolve this issue, it was decided to replace the designator 'near-death experience' (NDE) with 'crisis experience' (CE) which, for the purposes of the RERC study, would be used to designate an experience that occurred to a subject either clinically dead, near death or in some other crisis situation in which a threat to the subject's life had occurred but its peak had *apparently* passed. In this way, it was also hoped to avoid the risk of excluding a potentially significant report from analysis as a *near-death* report merely on the grounds that it was difficult or impossible to determine the immediate presence or otherwise of a threat to that subject's life. To this end, all accounts were gathered from the archives in which a subject reported the presence – immediate or past – of a life-threatening crisis event which precipitated his or her experience: no matter whether that experience included out-of-body experiences, darkness, lights, meetings with deceased relatives or merely one of these features. Being thus obtained, accounts were scanned for all fifteen of Moody's original elements, as well as for any new elements that had emerged in studies produced subsequent to *Life After Life*. As a result of using this selection process, thirty-two CE accounts were uncovered and examined.

Using these search criteria, however, still left outstanding problems. For it became clear very quickly that a large number of accounts existed in the archives in which no life-threatening crisis event was either present or recently past, and yet in which there appeared a range of traditional NDE elements, including out-of-body experiences, tunnels, lights and so on. In fact, as was to become apparent, there were *more* of these accounts than CE accounts. What should be done with them? Ignore them because their subjects were not near death, or include them on the grounds that they resembled – in some cases quite vividly – NDEs? In the event, it was decided to *include* such reports, using the designator 'non-crisis experience' (non-CE) to refer to them. Fifty-nine such accounts were eventually collected, and upon analysis it became clear that subjects carrying out a range of activities, including sleeping, resting, meditating and walking, reported experiences very similar to subjects who were apparently near death. Indeed, the comparison of these two distinct but similar groups of testimonies became another major aim of the study, setting it apart in one crucial respect from any major study of NDEs that had gone before. Obviously, the CE testimonies stood closer to what have traditionally been dubbed NDEs by virtue of the overall contexts in which they occurred. But, as became clear, a number of non-CE testimonies resembled NDEs in very many ways, inviting discussion, analysis and an attempt at explanation.

Having collected a usable database, the next phase of the study was concerned with the formulation of the remainder of the questions which analysis would attempt to answer. The sheer number of out-of-body experiences found within the archives – reported by significant numbers of CE and non-CE subjects alike – was deemed too large to devote extensive attention to, meriting, as it did, a separate study in its own right, and one which remains a fruitful area for another researcher to attempt. However, given the discussion in chapter 5 above of some of Kenneth Ring's more recent and controversial claims surrounding the verified existence of out-of-body perceptions in the blind, it was decided that an analysis of accounts for evidence of veridical observations made by the blind or visually impaired was particularly important. In the event, any account which involved observations obtained out-of-body and later found to be correct was deemed significant, and it was whilst searching for accounts that involved any possibility of *corroboration* that a small number of *shared* experiences were discovered: experiences almost unknown in the existing literature. Elsewhere, a number of other questions suggested by previous chapters of this book presented themselves for discussion. In the analysis that follows, these are taken up and explored in turn, the codes in brackets after each testimony-extract referring to their computerized number within the RERC archives.

Negative experiences

Previous chapters of this book have already explored some of the complexities surrounding the question of negative, or 'hellish' NDEs, a question which features particularly prominently in the work of researchers such as Maurice Rawlings in the US and

Margot Grey in Great Britain. As has been noted, both researchers uncovered enough cases of such experiences in the course of their studies to draw various conclusions from them. Rawlings viewed such episodes (representing 27.5 per cent of his total case collection) as evidence of the truth of the Biblical accounts of hell as a place of punishment for the unsaved, and Grey attempted a variant of Ring's five-stage NDE model in order to accommodate and explain the 12.5 per cent of negative accounts from within *her* total case collection (Rawlings 1978; Grey 1985). Indeed, as a result of his own ongoing research, the frequency of accounts of negative near-death experiences was 'moving towards being 50–50', according to Rawlings in his foreword to a 1997 study of NDEs: a significant percentage indeed (Kent and Fotherby 1997: xi).

It has also become clear throughout the current study, however, that not all near-death researchers have been agreed upon the existence of such a sizeable number of such cases. Moody, for example, makes no mention of them in any of his books. Ring accords them no significant treatment. A 1982 Gallup poll revealed that only 1 per cent of 102 cases examined were negative or hellish in nature (Rogo 1989: 141). Similarly, Michael Sabom reported no cases of negative NDEs in his 1981 study *Recollections of Death*, whilst his most recent study *Light and Death*, although admitting of their existence, was to reveal only two out of a total sample size of forty-seven NDEs examined (Sabom 1982, 1998: 170). As a result of these different conclusions, it was decided that one prime objective of the RERC study would be to look for negative NDEs, with a view to ascertaining if they existed anywhere in the archives and, if so, how many of them there were.

CE cases

In order to begin to answer these questions, a simple analysis of the feelings described by respondents as occurring during their experiences was derived from the thirty-two CE testimonies. One of the most striking conclusions from this analysis turned out to be the discovery of the overwhelmingly *positive* nature of the experiences described. In the vast majority of cases, feelings of calm, peace, bliss and joy dominated throughout, as in the following:

All the time I was up there I never felt afraid, or alone.
There was someone or something which was up there.
A presence that radiated love, joy, warmth and deep
awesome spiritual feeling. All the feelings that are good
as life were up there ... It was the most beautiful
experience I have ever had, and I will always cherish it.

(3817)

I have often asked myself subsequently: How can a
human being on the threshold between death and life
suddenly be so happy?

(3725)

I almost feel as if I were in a state of grace.

(3538)

I was awakening to an intensity of joy I have never since
experienced.

(2817)

I remember being up above myself, in a great light, and
saying 'It's so beautiful up here in the light'.

(3674)

As I looked I began to realize that what I was seeing was
something beyond any experience I had ever had and
while I lay there I felt I was shedding all pain and worries
and I was overcome by a sense of profound peace and
happiness; nothing seemed to matter any more.

(1406)

By contrast, only a small number of cases – two in total – revealed
the presence of negative or unpleasant emotions and sensations
throughout the experience. Of these, one appears to have been
triggered by the administration of drugs given to combat TB, and
is described vividly by the respondent as being

absolutely terrifying. As terrifying as the London Blitz.
And there was no rescue except within oneself. In my

250

panic, from which no this-world-person could save me, I sought out every good thing I could think of – good memories – good poems (Chesterton's 'The Donkey') – and doing good things for other people in the ward, even if it were no more than helping an old lady to the loo and back . . . And flowers meant much to me. They mean less now, when I'm 'sane' again. I used the Lord's Prayer, with my silent inner-voice. . . .

(1443)

Another respondent, coming close to death during childbirth, described a combination of hopelessness, sadness, terror, awe and loneliness, in an experience which began with her viewing her own body from outside during a Caesarean section:

Later I was removed to a distance from the world so that I was able to see our world and at the same time experience another dimension. On looking back at the world I was given the knowledge that the world was totally unimportant and insignificant – the idea that God is the *only* thing that matters. On realising this hopelessness I felt at once both a profound relief but also a terrible sadness at the apparent futility of all our strivings.

I was surrounded by a power of such total domination and power that I was terrified. I was literally in awe – I believe I experienced the enormous power of God. All around me a word boomed out. I cannot remember what this word was but it seemed as if the whole of Creation truly emanated from this one word. I really understood the meaning of the phrase from the Catholic Mass, which says 'From age to age He gathers a people unto Himself.' At a distance, far far away from me were these 'gathered souls' – not visible forms but all joining in glorifying God. The noise was tumultuous. I was a long way off, suspended in terrible isolation because I was not ready to join them because of my imperfections. My loneliness was absolutely acute and I longed to join them.

(3885)

One further finding of particular note concerned the *mixed* nature of some of the experiences reported. Hitherto, near-death research had tended to draw a sharp dichotomy between *positive* and *negative* NDEs. The RERC study, however, revealed four CE cases in which *both* positive *and* negative feelings were experienced. One woman who nearly died during childbirth, for example, revealed that at first

> I was not afraid, and was not at all tense. Suddenly I felt as though I were being sucked down into a great whirling void, in which sound was not sound but a tremendous vibrating hum, and I felt a sense of abject fear. I remember thinking very lucidly, that I was being foolish and this must be how the anesthetic took affect. I waited for this feeling to abate, but it seemed to grow increasingly stronger. The point was reached when I felt sure that my senses or body could tolerate no more, and just at that time, the tremendous humming diminished and the sensation of being drawn at tremendous speed slowed.

At this point, however, the feelings experienced by the respondent underwent a major change. Surrounded by light and suddenly aware of invisible presences, she described how:

> It is terribly difficult to put into words the emotions experienced at this point, but I can only try. I suddenly felt an almost overwhelming sense of warmth, of well being, and felt myself to be being enveloped in or with an overpowering love, as though I were being caught up in something so beautiful, emotionally speaking, and yet not having any real understanding of why this was so or how I knew it was so.
>
> (3522)

In similar vein, another respondent described a development of feeling within an experience that began negatively in terror but ended on a distinctly positive note, with a revelation of God's love. Ill and fearful as a result of long-term chemotherapy which

252

had plunged her into intermittent bouts of depression, she wrote
that on one occasion

> Once again in despair I began to pray silently, 'God help
> me. Please, God help me.' As I repeated the plea, I
> thought, 'I wonder what God really looks like?'
> *Instantly*, I felt myself being lifted out of my body and
> carried up – up. In terror, I screamed for help. In my
> nightmares, Norman [her husband] would hear me
> moaning and awaken me. But this time, no one heard me
> – up and up I was carried, until with a shattering of light
> I entered another world (room?) and found myself face-
> to-face with God. A shimmering circle of light like the
> one which separated one world from the other, encircled
> his face – which I recognized as the face of my beloved
> therapist.
> It was then that I realized that God is love. His face
> reflects that face which the individual loves. For me – love
> needs no visible body, only that which I trust and accept
> as it is – because the person exists, (or has existed, as in
> the case of my parents, whom I loved so dearly). – In the
> morning I awoke refreshed but somewhat peevish at
> Norman because he had not 'come to my rescue' upon
> hearing me scream.
>
> (3678)

In just one case where a mixture of feelings was reported, the
order of the above accounts was reversed and an experience which
started out positively ended negatively. Following one of a series
of operations to treat Crohn's disease, the respondent began
feeling numbness. Then:

> Everything became much quieter and there was an
> atmosphere of calmness. Spiritually I rose and was able
> to see myself several feet below. Thereafter I seemed to
> travel through golden-coloured space (like the light that
> comes from the sun). I felt comforted and a warmth and
> a glow surrounded me.

In her testimony, these initial impressions were then followed by a series of apparently unconnected experiences. A trip into space was followed by a vision of wars, suffering and confusion, followed by an experience of déjà vu ('In the middle of this I realised that I had had this experience many times before and only wondered why I had not remembered it'), followed in turn by a vision of the extinction of the earth, described as 'a flicker – similar to a candle which soon went out'. The experience finally ends on a note of distinct fear:

> I looked up into space and entered a black hole. There were people there – I don't know where they came from. It was rather strange – they couldn't move – even blink – everything stayed the same for about one hundred years – I did too. I became frightened. I wondered if it was because we were being punished – I still do not know.
>
> (3764)

Non-CE cases

Analysis of the fifty-nine non-CE testimonies from the RERC archives revealed a distinctly similar set of findings. Once again, it was clear that the vast majority of subjects reported over-whelmingly positive feelings, as typified by the following extracts:

> I became aware that there was a faint light in the room which deepened until the room was full of a deep golden light, & I knew I was in the presence of an immense power & love, & I felt the peace of God, which does indeed pass all understanding. I have never lost that inner peace.
>
> (2479)

> The next thing I knew I felt a great love, an immense happiness, an excitement.
>
> (3428)

> [T]he light was like nothing on earth, it was all around and uplifted me with an indescribable feeling.
>
> (2062)

AND THEN IT HAPPENED – an overpowering feeling of love and joy encompassed me – a tremendous sense of elation such as I had never encountered before, overcame me. I was in ecstasy – in perfect union with God. The emotion was so strong and unexpected, that I was at a loss to comprehend its meaning.

(3442)

I sat down again and kept my eyes on the light. I have never, before or after, felt such a sense of peace and comfort. I felt a powerful presence in the bedroom and I knew that I would be given Divine strength to carry on with my duty to the end.

(2026)

Following this came a feeling of liberation; utter contentment, delight, ecstasy; whatever it was, I have never felt so wonderfully happy in my whole life. I could feel a smile spreading over my face and my eyes lighting up. It was obviously apparent to others too – they must have sensed something for I found them looking at me with something akin to awe.

(1148)

I was charged with a feeling of such vibrant happiness and contentment that I have not experienced before or since (13 years has passed since this took place).

(3451)

Indeed, of this group, only three respondents reported negative feelings throughout their experiences, with a further five reporting a mixture of positive and negative elements. The most obviously negative account was reported by a woman who had a vivid out-of-body experience in a sleeping carriage on an Indian train in 1942. *En route* to Bareilly Junction, where she needed to change trains for Kathgodam, the subject prepared for bed and retired, 'emotionally exhausted and . . . "wishing I were dead" as I lay down'. Having fallen asleep immediately, the subject underwent an out-of-body experience. It was not, however, a pleasant one:

A terrible feeling of utter hopelessness and of death came over me. I supposed myself to be dead. All 'I' seemed to be was an 'EYE'. I could see everything quite clearly in the railway compartment including my own body and I seemed to be suspended in space, and had a feeling of 'deadness', yet I was AWARE of every detail of my physical surroundings, on the assumption that 'I' was up there by the light.

(514)

Two further accounts, both associated with music, fell into the 'negative' category also. In the first of these, the subject reported listening to Brahms's First Symphony when

a chord sounded and at once I was removed from my normal life. My whole physical being was dissolved and I knew that I was in reality a spiritual creature who only had the semblance of a body. I was, quite obviously, the note of music. Not only that, but I was also the light that shone a clear blue just to the left of my mental vision. Being thus totally non-physical scared me and at once I was reunited with my ordinary self and for some years preferred to forget the incident.

(3670)

In the second account, the subject was engaged in singing the *Sanctus* of Bach's Mass in B minor in Central Hall, Westminster, when she felt herself to be floating

well above the choir, somewhere under the domed roof. I presumed that my body was still standing in the soprano ranks, and decided that I had better rejoin it in case it fell over while I was not there to control it – which would have seriously disrupted the music. So I went back, partly disappointed and partly relieved to have a good excuse to terminate an experience so unusual as to be faintly alarming. Whether or not I continued singing all the while I am not sure; I think it likely that the experience was 'out of time' and that there was no break in bodily continuity.

(3769)

Of the non-CE accounts that combined positive and negative elements, four became more positive as they unfolded. Of these, the most vivid involved a hotelier who had fallen asleep whilst resting on a couch and woke to a most extraordinary experience. In fact, this testimony is a good example of a large number of accounts derived from the RERC archives which included NDE elements undergone in circumstances far removed from those of life-threatening danger. The hotelier's experience contains no less than nine of Moody's fifteen model NDE elements, beginning with one of its most rarely encountered elements – the noise:

> I had gone to bed around 3 p.m and had fallen asleep. Then I actually woke up. I was completely wide-awake and very alert. The next moment I was aware of strange reeling sensations in my head, like two separate forces one on each side of my head and there was also a vibrating buzzing in my ears. This was very powerful. I was frightened and tried to lift my head from the pillow. This was impossible to do. The whizzing through my head was somehow like a great centifugal force pushing me deeper into the pillow (I was on my back). The ringing/buzzing in my ears seemed to get louder and more forceful and really hurt and by this time I was terrified.

In despair, the subject found herself praying to Jesus, although she had abandoned churchgoing some fourteen years before. Abruptly there then followed a vivid out-of-body experience, described in overwhelmingly negative terms:

> The next thing I was aware of was that I was hovering over the bed. This really was weird – I was so clear minded but so bewildered. I didn't seem to be anything except pure mind and awareness. I tried to reason out what I was doing up there without any body and then the thought came to me 'I'M DEAD!' Horror struck, I then thought 'this is what it's like to die; how can I possibly be dead when I'm able to think about it and be here over my body – I can't be dead.'

A sense of darkness and despair continues to prevail, as she describes how:

> Next, I felt a terrible aloneness, the likes of which I have never ever before felt in my life . . . I was in darkness, alone, lost, and I did'nt know where to go, what to do or if anything existed and I'm certain that I touched Hell although I did'nt think of that then. This heavyness was on me and then I 'saw' my two little boys. Their faces seemed to come before me and one was then nearly six and the other nearly 3. That was when a terrible sadness came onto me. This was a different feeling again to the previous one. It had a quality of inexpressible heartbreak and I pray I shall never again ever feel that dispair. I felt that I was so necessary to my children and how much I loved them. The next emotion that entered into my consciousness was a knowledge, not a spoken message, more like a telepathic exchange and I was 'informed' that I would not be leaving my boys but would return to them.

It is at this point that the narrative undergoes an abrupt shift. Hitherto, as we have seen, the descriptors used by the subject to describe her feelings throughout her experience have included those communicating a vivid sense of fear, terror, bewilderment, horror, aloneness, lostness, weight, sadness, heartbreak and, finally, despair. Abruptly, however, the mood shifts when the subject next describes how immediately following her 'telepathic' communication:

> I was . . . completely submerged and covered and filled with a 'LOVE' beyond all our understanding and comprehension. An intense overwhelming unselfish, pure and all embracing understanding 'LOVE and PEACE' . . . There was full acceptance of what I was and what I had ever done. This was so profound and awesome but comforting and total; I was melted into it and knew that this was the 'WHOLE'.

The abrupt change into an overwhelmingly positive experience continues over into its next phase, where the subject enters a transcendent realm:

> I found I was on a hill-top. It was lovely, the sun was shining and the grass seemed so green. Everything seemed more intense and denser. I saw a small stone building like a sheep shelter with an opening of a door and a window (no door or window was actually in). I went to this place and entered. A woman was standing inside. She was middle-aged, very dark and masculine built. I had never seen her before but must add that I have seen her since in a strong dream. She was just standing there with her arms folded, she looked firm. Into my mind came the thought 'You must leave now and go back'). I really did'nt want to come back. I was quite prepared to leave everything and everyone here and I was fully able to realize that this meant leaving the boys too, but I wanted to remain there. Again the strong thought came to say I must return at once. The next thing I knew was that I was wide awake and <u>so</u> filled with happiness and joy and strength.

Indeed, afterwards, the memory of the experience clearly remained vivid and real, and ultimately the whole experience turned out to be impossible to share:

> This great inner joy stayed with me for days. I tried to tell my husband but could tell that he thought I had been dreaming. I then tried to talk about it to a friend, but when I saw the look which came upon her face, I stopped.
>
> (3843)

Comment

The findings of the RERC study with respect to the existence of negative NDEs and NDE-like experiences as revealed by the CE cases examined are unremarkable in serving to simply reinforce existing studies' conclusions that most *reported* cases are over-whelmingly positive in nature. Of course, this does not necessarily indicate that negative experiences are in the overwhelming minority, and may simply be indicative of the fact that respondents are more likely to report positive experiences than negative ones. Further, the low percentage of negative cases as compared to the total number of CE and non-CE cases examined reflects the composition of the RERC archives viewed as a whole. Thus, for example, a 1998 study by Danish anthropologist Merete Demant Jakobsen of a wide variety of negative spiritual experiences within the archives – including episodes such as 'experiences of evil in the room where one is sleeping', 'experiences of evil present in a place', 'evil present in or entering into a human being' and 'evil intent in another person' – discovered a total of only 195 such negative accounts out of a total of over 4,000 archival testimonies examined (Jakobsen 1999). As with the present study, it is impossible to determine whether such a very low percentage supports the contention that positive spiritual experiences outnumber negative ones, or whether they are simply more likely to be reported. At the time of writing, no single study of NDEs has concentrated solely on negative experiences: reflecting, perhaps, the difficulty researchers encounter in finding enough such cases and representing yet another avenue for future research.

The darkness

Recent years have seen a flurry of controversy surrounding the darkness motif encountered by many NDErs and variously described in their testimonies. Chapter 3 alluded to this, noting Allan Kellehear's contention that 'tunnel' is frequently used as a descriptor for an apparently universal experience of traversing darkness by many Western NDErs as a way of describing *movement* rather than *architecture*. In addition, as also noted, Kellehear has further maintained that whilst an experience of darkness is indeed encountered cross-culturally within near-death testimony, the descriptor tunnel seems confined 'largely to societies where historic religions are dominant' – perhaps because the tunnel-shape is more frequently encountered in such societies and is thus more readily to hand as way of describing the sensation of moving rapidly through darkness (Kellehear 1996: 188). The underlying supposition here appears to be that whilst an experience of darkness is apparently a universal feature of NDEs (and hence transcends cultural background and expression), its means of interpretation and hence description appear culturally conditioned, and may thus reflect cultural background, experience or even expectation. Therefore, in attempting to account for why the descriptor 'tunnel' is seldom or never encountered in NDEs reported from within hunter-gatherer cultural contexts, Kellehear asserts that 'Those in hunter-gatherer societies tend not to encounter this symbol regularly, so this would lead us to assume that this descriptor will be rarely chosen . . .' (Kellehear 1996: 188). By contrast, NDErs from within cultural contexts dominated by historic religions are more frequently exposed to tunnels, being long-term settlement cultures 'where tunnels are well known technologically, architecturally, and intellectually' (Kellehear 1996: 188). Thus, he concludes, we would expect to find the darkness described as a tunnel more readily and frequently within these cultures, perhaps explaining why Western studies of NDEs *do* appear so frequently to contain NDE testimonies in which the darkness is indeed described as a tunnel.

Such controversy surrounding the precise description of an allegedly universal darkness motif, together with the availability of its means of expression, is of more than just passing, surface, interest. Rather, it goes to the heart of the most exhaustive existing neuroscientific attempt to account for both the tunnel and light elements of many NDErs' experiences. As noted in chapter 4, Susan Blackmore's neuroscientific analysis of the NDE asserts that the effect of anoxia upon the visual cortex may create a subjective impression of moving through a tunnel towards an ever-growing area of brightness. As also noted, such a theory requires, first, that the tunnel should always be associated with a steadily growing light 'feature' at its centre (in order to create the sensation of movement) and, second, that the darkness should always, invariably, and cross-culturally be experienced and hence described as a *tunnel*. For neuroscience, whether concerned to explore the NDE or some other feature of brain activity, would at the very least wish to assert as a fundamental fact of nature that all brains are identically neurally wired. Where the darkness is not described as tunnel-shaped, where darkness is reported without light, where light is reported without darkness (or a tunnel), or where light is reported but either not growing or not located centrally within the darkness, then some explanation other than Blackmore's is clearly called for.

Chapter 3 concluded on the basis of the descriptions of darkness contained within existing studies of NDEs that some other explanation was called for. The RERC archives were found to contain a number of accounts allowing the opportunity to further test Blackmore's hypothesis by affording access to an original and unexamined group of testimonies: some containing descriptions of darkness, with a few even pre-dating the modern era of near-death studies and therefore standing before and apart from any possibility that their subjects could have known that tunnels leading to lights might reasonably be expected to occur near death as a result of their prior acquaintance with NDE literature. The RERC study sought on the basis of such accounts to analyse the frequency of the occurrence of darkness within its database, to analyse the ways in which the darkness was described, and to look for the frequency of 'tunnel' as a descriptor for it. As will become clear, its findings were to turn out to be as interesting as they were unusual and unexpected.

CE cases

The hunt for a darkness and/or tunnel feature within the RERC archives raised a further methodological problem which needed to be addressed before analysis could proceed. For what should be done with accounts that included descriptions of a seemingly similar – perhaps identical – experience but which used words such as 'void', 'whirlpool', 'passage' or 'shaft' to describe it? Nowhere here is it absolutely clear that a tunnel is being variously described. Neither is it clear that in each case the feature is black or dark. This being acknowledged, the question arose as to whether such accounts should be included in an analysis ostensibly designed to measure whether an experience of darkness was being universally and invariably described as tunnel-shaped or not.

In order to resolve this problem, it was decided that any accounts which included descriptions of a tunnel, a period of darkness – whether traversed or not – or a motif comparable to either a tunnel or an episode of darkness should be included. After all, a real suspicion exists that the use of descriptors such as 'shaft' or 'passage' may indeed indicate that something like a tunnel or a period of darkness is being described. Overall, no data which might usefully and safely be included were excluded, but extreme caution was retained regarding the obvious dangers involved in grouping testimonies containing different descriptors under the same band of headings (a danger which, as chapter 1 showed, was not recognized by some of the earliest and most influential near-death researchers, to the subsequent detriment of early near-death research). At the very least, recognition of this issue surrounding the collection, classification and analysis of subjects' experiences served as a salutary reminder within the study that qualitative analysis of testimony is not, nor can ever claim to be, an exact science.

Using the above criteria, a total of eight CE accounts were found to include a significant darkness, tunnel, or related motif needful of closer examination. Of these, six also contained reference to an encounter with a light of some sort, whilst two did not. Further, of the eight subjects reporting this feature, only two used the descriptor 'tunnel' whereas the rest used other terms. In addition, two of the eight accounts were submitted to the archives before 1975. These were especially interesting, given that the respondents could not have known at this time that tunnel was a popular descriptor as part of many experiences which are now widely thought to occur at or near death.

Of the two accounts making use of the term 'tunnel', one gave a particularly detailed description (see p. 118) very consistent with what Blackmore's visual cortex theory requires. Occurring during childbirth, the respondent's experience (written in August 1971) began when

> Everything whirled and blackness formed a tunnel, a long long tunnel with an opening at the other end which glowed with a bright light.
>
> Down, down into the whirling blackness. It seemed a long time before I reached the opening and found myself floating gently in a warm soft mist, all golden as with sunlight, soft music and a feeling of complete happiness

and such peace that passes all understanding, was mine, faces came out of the mist smiled and faded away.

(2733)

The second use of the descriptor 'tunnel' was contained in a very long and detailed testimony – already cited in part – submitted to the archives in 1977 as a taped transcript of an experience undergone by a soldier as he recovered from injuries sustained when his tank was hit by anti-tank fire during the closing months of the Second World War. Later, in Forli Hospital, Italy, 'smothered in bandages', his experience began when he found himself leaving his body and viewing it and those of two other patients from above. Then, he 'went straight into pitch darkness'. As the account continues:

> I had the feeling that I was confined, as one would have in a tunnel. I don't know how long this state lasted, it wasn't hours or anything of that sort, it was only a matter of minutes, and I became aware of a light in the distance. That gave me an orientation point, and I realized that I was floating on my back, feet first, down towards this light. The light slowly and steadily got brighter as it would if you were walking down a tunnel approaching the end and as I got near to this tunnel end, I slowly rotated into an upright position facing the light. I was still definitely floating, I was well clear of any surface beneath me. I came out of the tunnel effect into a subdued light, like the sort of light you will get on a late spring, early summer morning just after sunrise when there's a certain amount of mist, around.

(3766)

Again, movement occurs along an apparent tunnel-shape in the direction of a steadily growing light that occupies its centre and appears to grow as the subject approaches it. Indeed, it is notable that the respondent actually remarks that the presence of light at the end of the tunnel provided him with an 'orientation point' as regards his own position and the direction in which he was travelling. Here also, therefore, Blackmore's hypothesis appeared supported.

More problematical for it were the remaining six cases. Of these, two were found to use the descriptor 'space' to describe the episode of darkness. The first of these, already referred to in part above as occurring when the subject was seriously ill after abdominal surgery to treat Crohn's disease, described an out-of-body experience after which she

> seemed to levitate into space and could see the whole of the Universe. First I could see the moon with life on it – I looked again and then there wasn't. I could only see it as we know what it looks like through television etc. I was able to see many planets (with life) – when I looked again there was nothing. The atmosphere seemed continually to change from being able to see things and feeling warmth and comfort as if there was some power turning things on and off. I heard the stars (but could still hear what was going on around me on earth while all this was happening). Out there in the universe everything was magnificent and perfect and whole – not as we see it but . . . words just fail me – it was too incredible to describe.
>
> (3842)

A second CE subject who described an episode of darkness in terms of space had a series of unusual experiences after a difficult operation whilst recuperating in hospital, making only a passing reference to 'movement at great speed through space' (3771). The significance of the word 'space' to describe the darkness encountered in these experiences will be returned to when the non-CE accounts derived from the archives are examined, below.

Of the remaining four accounts, another of the two pre-1975 testimonies containing the darkness motif described a sensation of 'being sucked down into a great whirling void', complete with a loud humming and a sense of disorientation and fear, *en route* to an encounter with a 'brilliant light', with 'even greater light . . . radiating from somewhere ahead' (3522). It was unclear from this account, however (already partly referred to, above), whether the light was first perceived when the subject was 'inside' the void or whether she had a sense of its growth in size respective to herself before she found herself surrounded by it:

As I began to lose consciousness, sound grew dimmer but I was not afraid, and was not at all tense. Suddenly I felt as though I were being sucked down into a great whirling void, in which sound was not sound but a tremendous vibrating hum, and I felt a sense of abject fear . . . [Then, abruptly] . . . I felt myself to be surrounded by or with brilliant light, and even greater light seemed to be radiating from somewhere just ahead. I felt as though I were being led forward, although I was not conscious of walking, nor could I actually see anyone. I was conscious of sound (rather muted and musical, but not music). I had a distinct awareness of not being alone, but no actual vision of anyone else.

(3522)

Another account described the sensation a subject had of leaving his body whilst whirling around but moving not downward, as in the above account, but *upward* through some sort of whirlpool:

It was a most strange feeling and words cannot describe it properly. It was as if I was whirling about in a whirlpool as I left my body. As I reached the ceiling I stopped (not of my own power) and looked at my peaceful body on my bed. Then I carried on with my journey.

(3817)

Finally, of the two remaining accounts, one, already cited above, contained the description of a woman who experienced a vivid sense of being 'suspended in terrible isolation' but moving in no direction whatsoever and kept apart from a group of gathered souls (as a result of her own unfitness for entry into Heaven) who were praising God – once again implying the presence of some sort of void phase of darkness or blackness without actually specifying in any detail that this was actually so. A final account clearly stated an area of darkness, but one which the subject did not appear to move *through* and which she was not apparently located *within* either. Under anaesthetic for a major operation, her account described how she at first found myself bound tightly in white bandages, lying on a marble slab, way up in the sky. I could turn my head only, and could see the traffic and buildings, below. It was dark and raining, down there. The street and car lights were on and I saw a newsvendor selling papers. Then, *from the darkness before me*, I saw an evil-looking old woman coming towards me with a large stiletto in her hand. I heard her say: 'If I cut her in her side, she will die.'

I tried to move, but could not. I had no feelings of fear or anything, come to think of it. Then, beside me, appeared this bright light. I looked up, and saw an angel, quite 12 feet tall. I could not look at it for long, it was so bright. Then my dead daughter's voice came clearly: 'You must go back, Mummy, you must go back.'

'I cannot move, Angela', I said, and the evil woman was very near, now.

'You <u>can</u>, Mummy', my daughter's voice was emphatic and urgent. 'You can move. You must go back. <u>YOU ARE STILL OF THE EARTH</u>.'

I made a superhuman effort to roll off the slab, and did so before the old woman stabbed me. Then I found myself rolling gently down snowy slopes into oblivion.

(2799; emphasis mine)

Non-CE *cases*

Analysis of the fifty-nine non-CE cases included in the study yielded a total of sixteen which contained either specific reference to a tunnel, a period of darkness, or some other comparable motif which it was determined may have been implied by respondents as a result of the language used in their testimonies. Interestingly, in addition to the descriptor 'tunnel' (which was used by four respondents), a frequent and obviously favoured descriptor was again 'space': a word that was specifically encountered in no less than nine testimonies. Of course, words only derive their specific meanings from their contexts, and unlike 'tunnel', 'space' can have a number of meanings, being used to denote – amongst other things – an area between points or locations, a blank area between words, a dark expanse between planets or galaxies, or an unspecified interval of time. How, therefore, did the more than 50 per cent of non-CE subjects who favoured this descriptor *use* it?

Most frequently – in a total of four cases – respondents' use of 'space' seemed to indicate that *outer space* was being described. Thus, one subject wrote:

> I had just retired to bed and had settled down, when suddenly on closing my eyes, I suddenly felt very light and could see above the earth. I could see the earth, also the darkness of space and stars, and then suddenly the earth was getting further and further away from me. Then I was back in my own room. It happened very quickly. I was not asleep for I told my husband what I experienced.
>
> (4061)

In similar vein, a second subject reported how

> I was feeling well. I was standing in my living room . . . In an instant I was on another plane in another world, I found myself out in space or what space may be like many miles from earth. It was not as you see space when you look up at the sky. It was as though I saw the whole universe at once, but much condensed, as if I was looking through the wrong end of a telescope. I was there in spirit form. I could not have been there in any other way. I was seeing with my normal eyes, I felt exactly as myself. I did not see any part of myself or anything of the human world. When I arrived in this place I was looking upwards. I could see a mass of space before me, it was moving slowly upward. The atmosphere was of very little density. . . .
>
> (3428)

A third account, which was induced by the subject as a result of self-hypnosis, began by him mentally picturing a 'spot of Light'. Then

> [I] . . . Start to move toward the light & find that I am held back by some force, (Pulling me back, and actualy stopping me). Still in control of my facultys. I reason that

to proceed, I must picture/create a door in space and step
through. I will then be free to proceed. This I did – (Note,
I only had to think of the door and it was there, But it was
a door that one thinks of as an Airlock type door. As in a
Space Ship etc) I opened the door & stepped though, I
was then free & travelling through Space at a tremendous
velocity. I went to the beginning of Creation. I saw
primeval matter & Star dust, I mingled & was One with
all Creation. I WAS GOD – Yet I was I. I was One
with Space, Time Eternity. As soon as this was realized, I
was thrown back to my phisical body with tremendous
force. In fact my body bounced in the bed & it felt as
though I had been Electrically shocked. I lay for quite
some time pondering on what had happened to me.

(4075)

A fourth account combined use of 'space' and 'tunnel', resulting
in a description in which the subject, as a result of group meditation
during a week's retreat, underwent an experience in which

I was travelling through space gazing at spheres revolving.
At close inspection it appeared that each world was made
up of small pinnacles ajacent to one another. I found
myself entering into one of these and all was dark except
for a faint beam of light ahead towards which I moved. I
appeared to be in a tunnel but gradually the solidity of the
walls became transparent, and I found that adjacent
passages held their own occupants and although there
was no communication at first awareness developed
and finally the walls disappeared and fellowship and
communication was complete.

(3913)

The remaining subjects who specifically described space as part
of their experiences gave generally insufficient detail to determine
what kind or type of space was being depicted. A woman who
had a vivid out-of-body experience during a three-day retreat in
which she was attempting to resolve marital difficulties reported
how:

Suddenly, and without any warning whatsoever, I felt myself moving or floating off into space. It was almost as if I were a bird and had wings and was soaring upwards. My spirit rose swiftly and silently to a; height where I could see my body on the bench far below in deep contemplation.

(3442)

Another respondent submitted a brief experience in which she described how she 'Appeared to be suspended in space but united with Mother. We appeared to be "one". Our head & shoulders appeared visible but not the rest of the body' (Mother had recently died) (3569).

A further subject – in language strongly suggestive of but not directly alluding to outer space – described an out-of-body journey towards a light in which he 'soared way up into the blue sky, beyond the clouds and across the infinite reaches of space' (3451).

And another subject reported an experience in which she was resting after a busy morning, when

Suddenly I had the feeling that I was leaving my Body – I can't describe the glorious feeling for the few moments that I seemed to float into space or as I then thought my spirit into Heaven.

(3874)

Finally, a respondent who underwent her experience whilst sleeping first felt a powerful feeling

in which I was 'dead' but only in the physical sense; in fact I was somewhere in dark space, feeling very alive indeed, and also feeling the invisible presence of 'God', whom I asked to take away everything that was inessential, but let me keep the essential. Upon which a huge storm arose, and as it buffeted 'me', I could feel that all kinds of superfluous, inessential components of my self were being blown away, as easily as dead leaves, and when the storm suddenly stopped, I felt essentially 'whole' and unharmed. It was a shattering and marvellous experience which greatly helped to remove some of my remaining fears and apprehensions.

(505)

Of the four non-CE respondents who specifically used the descriptor 'tunnel', two did so in association with mention of light also. In addition to the account cited above in which a woman meditating on retreat moved through a tunnel towards a 'faint beam of light', a further subject – a nun – described a vivid dream which is reproduced here in full:

> I found myself standing, with a companion, on the bank of a broad river which ran through beautiful countryside. Ahead of me the river narrowed, and in the distance I could see that it passed through a rocky tunnel on the other side of which there shone a brilliant warm light.
>
> I noticed that at the sides of the river the water moved very slowly indeed, and that underneath there lay many black pebbles. The pebbles gradually became cleaner as they reached the centre of the river, where the water flowed rapidly, bearing completely clean pebbles along in the force of the current towards and through the tunnel.
>
> I asked my companion what this meant, and he explained that the pebbles were souls who had died. The black ones were those soiled by sin and the water cleansed them and gradually moved them as they became cleaner into the rapids in the centre. There they were carried through the tunnel into the presence of God. It was impossible for a black pebble to pass through that tunnel, but it was certain that the water's of God's river would cleanse them in time and guide them to the entrance and on into his glory.

(4020)

The two remaining accounts using the descriptor 'tunnel' did so without any mention of light. One described a dream in which the respondent had dinner with a doctor in a 'short tunnel' looking out over a landscape covered by a roof 'like the roof of a Cathedral' and including Mary, Joseph and Jesus in the sky. A further account is of note in that 'tunnel' was not the subject's originally chosen descriptor, but was acknowledged as suitable upon subsequent exposure to literature dealing with NDEs. In it, the respondent related how, on the night her grandmother was cremated:

> I was lying in bed with my eyes closed, I was finding it hard to sleep. I eventually realized that although I was wide awake, I couldn't move, speak, or open my eyes. I could feel my boyfriend asleep next to me, and I wanted to tell him something awful was happening to me, I was terrified, I was then aware of watching myself in the bed, from a corner of the room, but not from myself, it was as if I was floating between 2 bodies, my own, in the bed, and another, standing watching me. I then felt as though I was floating on what seemed like a black stream, and I was being taken along with the current, I felt as though I was drowning. I tried to fight and struggle because I was so scared, but I was still paralised, although by this time I was very confused and am not exactly sure of what was happening. I think I was floating in the 'other body' because every so often I would, for a split second be back 'in myself', in the bed, then I would be back to the drowning sensation, I don't know how long It Went on, and I tried to fight but eventually I was exhausted through the sheer effort of trying to open my eyes and move my muscles. And I gave in, when I stopped trying to fight I found that the sensation wasn't unpleasant at all in fact it was the most wonderful feeling, I felt absolute relaxation and peacefulness all of a sudden I felt as though I understood everything. Then I was back in my own body when I opened my eyes, I was crying, but with overwhelming relief, I said 'God wanted to show me what it was like to die' to my boyfriend, flopped with exhaustion and went straight to sleep.
>
> (4052)

In addition to being highly unusual, this account is also notable for the additional comment made by the respondent at the very end, in which she adds some closing comments regarding the nature of the 'black stream':

> I have had no further experiences like this, but after reading the article in Woman, I had to write and tell you what had happened, as the 'near-death' feeling of travelling down a dark tunnel was so close to my own feeling. I have never read anything or come into contact with this subject before, so to read that description, was very reassuring.
>
> (4052)

The issuing of follow-up questionnaires in order to clarify details of accounts submitted to the RERC archives has only been carried out in a very few more recent cases, and thus testimonies from respondents – many of them, it is assumed, long dead – were all that the current study was able to analyse. The above account is interesting, however, in that it is assumed that few researchers, without the benefit of the final clarificatory comment or any additional information from a follow-up questionnaire, would have read 'floating on what seemed like a black stream' as an attempt to describe the experience of travelling down a dark tunnel. It may well serve as a reminder, therefore, that the darkness motif (the phrase itself an interpretation), whether or not universally tunnel-shaped, is indeed capable of being described by a very wide range of complex and inventive descriptors. It may also serve as a reminder of the ways in which exposure to near-death literature may consciously or unconsciously provide experiencers with a range of descriptors for their experiences which may not originally have occurred to them to use: whether or not – as in the above case – such descriptors later encountered turn out to be adequate to the task of describing a given element of their experiences.

Before moving on to a discussion of this section's findings, brief mention can be made of the remaining accounts that employed neither 'tunnel' nor 'space' to describe the darkness. Of these, one described an experience 'just before waking' which included a 'dark passage' and a light – but without locating the light at the end of the passage. In it, the subject was dreaming that I was walking down a long dark passage where I became aware that beside me was a pale golden glowing cloud, and within this – but not seen – was a tremendous Presence. My own consciousness opened out to this and received a clear sense of a boundless personality, endlessly strong & at the same time endlessly gentle, understanding and all-powerful. I was filled completely with joy – so to speak dissolved in bliss.

(1408)

By direct contrast, another account – cited above and involving the resting hotelier of account 3843 – found in the darkness not a positive presence but a negative sense of lostness, isolation and confusion: 'I was in darkness, alone, lost, and I did'nt know where to go, what to do or if anything existed . . . I'm certain that I touched Hell.' Standing somewhere between these two extremes was the experience of a young man who, under the influence of LSD, 'seemed to have arrived at a cul-de-sac'. He simply adds: 'I waited' (3941). Finally, another positive experience described a woman's encounter with a 'shaft of brilliant Light' down through which she travelled one morning en route to rejoin her body which she had apparently left whilst asleep. In the absence of further information, it is unclear whether the shaft was made of light or whether it was in fact a dark shaft illuminated by a tunnel located somewhere near by, perhaps at the end. Again, however, it is notable that the experience is described in overwhelmingly positive terms:

I felt a sort of click as I entered my body & woke at once to full consciousness with a truly heavenly feeling of Joy which stayed with me 2 or 3 days. All I could recall of my excursion was a vivid feeling of Joy, Love & Light – I just revelled in it. I didn't want to talk about it & as I was living alone I didn't need to.

(3671)

Comment

In only two of the CE cases could Blackmore's model be reasonably made to explain an experience *as actually described* (2733, 3766).

Instead, whilst the tunnel-and-growing-light motif was indeed encountered in a quarter of the accounts examined, three-quarters suggested a much more diverse set of potentially related but in no sense identical or consistent experiences. The occurrence – or lack – of *movement* through the tunnel portrayed in the narratives examined is also worthy of comment here, for once again it appears clear that diversity rather than unanimity typifies them. Thus, for example, two respondents' narratives revealed that their subjects were in fact stationary within the darkness (2799, 3885), two depicted movement upwards (3817, 3764), two depicted movement downwards (2733, 3522), one described 'slow and steady' movement *down* a tunnel but could well have been attempting to describe horizontal movement (3766) and one, whilst specifying movement at great *speed* through space, did not reveal anything about direction, inclination or angle (3771). Indeed, at this point it is difficult even to detect a unity *underlying* the diversity of descriptions of movement in the above accounts (as might be the case, for example, if the same experience was being interpreted and hence described in different ways), save that some sort of description of transition from one place to another might be being attempted. However, even this hypothesis is negated by the existence of two accounts where no movement at all was described. Indeed, recognition of the diversity of descriptions of the *role* of the darkness motif within respondents' overall experiences would seem to rule out any and all attempts at defining its essential nature by examining its *function*.

The situation becomes more complex still when the fifteen non-CE accounts are added to the analysis. To begin with, it has been clearly shown that frequently encountered CE elements such as tunnels, periods of darkness, and even journeys through outer space are reported in a variety of contexts in which subjects are not in any situation of life-threatening danger whatsoever. Tunnels were reported by two subjects in dreams (3459, 4020) and by one subject – retrospectively – during a sleepless night (4052). The influence of LSD caused one subject to find himself in a dark cul-de-sac (3941). One subject travelled along a 'shaft of brilliant light' one morning just *before* awakening (3671). Another respondent encountered a sense of desolation in darkness just *after* waking from an afternoon sleep (3843), whilst another travelled above the earth into space, having just retired to bed at night (4061). Three experiences were self-induced as part of either self-hypnosis (4075) or guided meditative practices (3913, 3428). Two further experiences appear to have occurred purely spontaneously (505, 3606). In the remaining accounts it is not clear what respondents were doing at the time. At the very least, however, recognition that NDE features such as the darkness or tunnel motif frequently occur within a wide variety of non-life-threatening contexts requires that any neuroscientific theory called upon to explain them must do so within these contexts also. Researchers such as Ring (1984) and Grey (1985), to their credit, have realized this, and chapter 1 examined their contentions that severe disruptions to normal breathing patterns – such as would be expected to occur both near death and within certain meditative practices – may indicate the types of mechanisms involved. Such a theory would certainly explain most of the CE accounts studied here, together with the non-CE experiences which occurred during meditation. It might even posit a testable explanation for the occurrence of darkness and light motifs during sleep by referring to conditions such as sleep apnoea that deprive sufferers of oxygen at certain intervals during sleep unless corrected. The breathing disruption hypothesis, however, appears unable to account for experiences which occur spontaneously or in other contexts where breathing is normal and undisrupted, and thus remains incomplete as a total explanation of all subjects' experiences, both within the RERC study and elsewhere in the annals of near-death studies.

Before moving on, mention must be made of the curiously high incidence of descriptions of *outer space* encountered in this phase of the investigation. As noted above, no less than four non-CE subjects specifically described either travelling to or through outer space, or being in some sense suspended within it. A further five subjects used the word 'space' but in a less specific way. Of the CE subjects, one made specific reference to levitating into space where she could see the moon and stars: implying once again that outer space was being traversed (3764). A further subject, whilst describing rapid movement through space, gave no clear descrip-tion of it (3771). At the very least, however, we have a total of five CE and non-CE accounts out of a total of twenty-four which describe an encounter with some sort of darkness motif in terms seemingly suggestive of a visit to outer space: more than 20 per cent of the total. When other more general descriptions of 'space' are included in the analysis, it becomes clear that respondents used it no less than eleven times within the twenty-four accounts examined. It was therefore encountered in nearly half of them, and easily outnumbered the descriptor 'tunnel' (which was specifically used only six times in total). Is this finding significant, anomalous, coincidental or simply absurd?

It is certainly not without precedent. Carl Jung has described in his autobiography *Memories, Dreams, Reflections* an experience similar to some of those encountered above which occurred as he lay 'in a state of unconsciousness' in which he 'experienced deliriums and visions which must have begun when I hung on the edge of death'. It occurred whilst he was hospitalized with a heart attack which had occurred subsequent to an accident in which he had broken his foot, in 1944. The account continues:

> My nurse afterward told me, 'It was as if you were surrounded by a bright glow.' That was a phenomenon she had sometimes observed in the dying, she added. I had reached the outermost limit, and do not know whether I was in a dream or an ecstasy. At any rate, extremely strange things began to happen to me.
>
> It seemed to me that I was high up in space. Far below I saw the globe of the earth, bathed in a gloriously blue light. I saw the deep blue sea and the continents. Far below my feet lay Ceylon, and in the distance ahead of me the subcontinent of India. My field of vision did not include the whole earth, but its global shape was plainly distinguishable and its outlines shone with a silvery gleam through that wonderful blue light. In many places the globe seemed coloured, or spotted dark green like oxidized silver. Far away to the left lay a broad expanse – the reddish-yellow desert of Arabia: it was as though the silver of the earth had there assumed a reddish-gold hue. Then came the Red Sea, and far, far back – as if in the upper left of a map – I could just make out a bit of the Mediterranean. My gaze was directed chiefly toward that.

Everything else appeared indistinct. I could also see the snow-covered Himalayas, but in that direction it was foggy or cloudy. I did not look to the right at all. I knew that I was on the point of departing from the earth.

Later I discovered how high in space one would have to be to have so extensive a view – approximately a thousand miles! The sight of the earth from this height was the most glorious thing I had ever seen.

(Jung 1963: 320–1)

Clearly, any suggestion that whilst near death or in other contexts persons – or aspects of persons – can literally leave the earth, either to view it from space, or to observe other planets, stars or galaxies from a point apart from it, sounds simply absurd. Yet this would appear to be what at least some persons – past and present – have asserted, and it was certainly one of the most striking and unusual findings of the entire RERC study. If such experiences are to be understood as being either dreams or visions – and even Jung, an expert on *both* dreams *and* visions, seemed confused as to what *his* experience was – it may usefully be asked why this particular dream or vision recurred so often in the analysis of the RERC archives. Yet, tantalizing as it may be, any attempt to answer this question might more usefully be reserved until more accounts are found, in other studies or generally elsewhere. For prior to the current study, this unusual and specific feature of NDEs and NDE-like experiences has gone virtually unremarked in the literature: indeed the ever-growing field of near-death studies remains one in which – with a few exceptions – claims of journeys to other worlds through *tunnels* still seem to predominate. At this point, the current study must part company with this literature, having found descriptions of tunnels to be in the minority, having also found that other descriptors are more frequently chosen as preferred ways of describing experiences of darkness, voids and – in some cases – transitions to other realms. More cases of NDEs or NDE-like experiences which include journeyings to outer space might at some point in the future permit a more thoroughgoing, structured and systematic attempt to grapple with what currently appears as a strange – even bizarre – anomaly, restricted to this one, single study. The discovery of no further accounts of this nature may of course reveal that the RERC studies' finding of a large number of descriptions of outer space was itself simply anomalous, and hence deserving of no further discussion.

Transformations

Chapter 1 noted that examinations of the transformative effects created apparently as a result of undergoing an NDE can be seen to have constituted something of a second wave, or subdiscipline, within near-death studies: with a history beginning at the publication of Kenneth Ring's *Heading Toward Omega* in 1984 and continuing through to the present day. As that chapter also noted, further detailed studies that have sought to analyse the transformative effects of the NDE include those of Margot Grey (Grey 1985), Melvin Morse (Morse and Perry 1992) and Cherie Sutherland (1992). What is perhaps most significant about these is the degree of unanimity which exists within them regarding the precise nature of the changes most frequently claimed as resulting from NDEs. Thus it is that NDErs contend that their NDEs have made them less afraid of death, more convinced of the existence of reincarnation, less conventionally religious but more spiritually sensitive, more concerned with social as opposed to political issues, and more psychically talented. NDErs also consistently report a range of changed attitudes to themselves subsequent to their NDEs, commonly claiming to have attained higher degrees of self-worth, greater levels of self-understanding, diminished concerns regarding others' opinions of them, heightened desires to help people, and greater abilities to love and empathize combined with higher capacities for tolerance. This being said, however, strains in relationships that NDErs had with others prior to their NDEs have also been a finding of many transformation studies, with increases in divorces and other familial strains typically reported. Given this ongoing concern within near-death studies to analyse and quantify a range of life-changes claimed by NDErs, the RERC study sought to determine whether any of the RERC subjects reported any fruits resulting from *their* experiences. In this way, it was hoped once again that existing studies' conclusions could be checked and independently verified. This aspect of the study was particularly assisted by the fact that such a high percentage of subjects – forty-two out of the ninety-one combined CE and non-CE testimonies – reported that their lives had indeed been changed, often permanently and usually for the better, as a result of their experiences.

CE cases

Of the seventeen CE subjects who made specific reference to life-changes induced by the experiences they described, six claimed a decreased fear of death as one of these, usually as a result of a new or enhanced conviction that death was not the end of consciousness altogether. Typical of such claims were the following:

> I still feel very grateful and humble for this experience, certainly have no fear of death, knowing it is as simple as walking from one room to another.
>
> (2733)

> The next time I am called upon to meet death I shall have no fear.
>
> (3538)

> <u>Never never</u> fear death. It is <u>Heaven</u>.
>
> (4072)

Indeed, the overwhelmingly *positive* nature of the transformative effects described above turned out to be typical of the CE cases taken as a whole. Thus, for example, two subjects reported that their experiences had created or reinforced their belief in the existence of God. One wrote that 'I was left with a strong conviction that I had experienced something that I could not explain in everyday terms and it fortified my belief in God' (1443).

Another wrote:

> Except for this experience . . . I would say my life has been very average, and I rather like it that way. I was raised within a family who believed in a rather strict upbringing of the children, but not overtly so, in God as our source

of spiritual comfort, and in honesty, whatever the cost. I think I could have been considered devout prior to this experience, but not fanatically so. I had sometimes wondered if God were God, if faith was based upon truth or not. Since this time, I am sure with a sureness which couldn't be shaken He Is.

(3522)

One respondent graphically illustrated the positive nature of his experience by describing as its main fruit the impression it left upon him as being the most beautiful experience he had ever had:

All the time I was up there I never felt afraid, or alone. There was someone or something which was up there. A presence that radiated love, joy, warmth and deep awesome spiritual feeling. All the feelings that are good as life were up there. But things like time did not matter, nothing that was here on this material planet mattered up there. It was like being in a different dimension. It was the most beautiful experience I have ever had, and I will always cherish it.

(3817)

Two accounts made specific reference to paranormal conse-quences arising from their experiences. In one case, the subject reported an instance of miraculous healing apparently produced as a result of her near-death episode:

Midnight 26 Jan. 79 I lay very ill in bed in hospital. It was my birthday and the place was a beautiful sight with flowers & 'get well' cards all around. I could not walk or even move myself in bed without the nurses' help. So ill I felt I was dying & prayed to God. A deep feeling of <u>Love</u> enveloped me and I found myself in a new world – pastel colored & lovely where I was able to walk about. My father & mother (long ago deceased) welcomed me to my surprise. It was with a heart full of praise to God that I realized I was walking there. Suddenly I said 'I can walk' & it seemed my body and spirit came together again &

I moved my legs in bed, then got out and walked about. The Specialist who saw me next morning was astounded and asked me to come to a meeting of young doctors & show them how I could walk. I did so and I understand it was all recorded in 'Case History' of the Ferntree Hospital. Dr. Gaye wrote the name of the trouble as <u>Polymyelitis Rheumatism</u>. Very few cases of healing known in Australia & few in England.

(3692)

A second subject (writing in August 1971 and thus well before the connection between the NDE and psychic development was made by Ring and others) related in more general terms the acquisition of 'psychic' gifts during her experience, which at first were resisted and only later embraced:

It was nearly a year later that I began to be made aware that I had been given a gift of Psychic dimensions. I did not welcome it and was in fact frightened of the very idea. I tried this new awareness, to close my ears and eyes, and could not. I sought consultation with a trusted minister as well as our family physician and received their assurance that both my mental and physical, as well as spiritual side was quite normal, and I was advised at that time to allow this gift to develop in a natural way or to fade, whichever might be the case. After a great deal of soul searching, I followed this advice, and retain this gift now, and while it is a strong gift, I do not believe I have yet known its' fullest measure. This is another story and quite long, so there isn't really any need to go into it here.

(3522)

At the end of this overview of the positive fruits claimed by the majority of CE subjects, brief mention can be made of the only two cases which related effects which were negative or which left subjects feeling either disconcerted or indifferent about their experiences. The first of these, related by a woman who nearly died from TB in 1965, contained the candid admission that

At the time, I promised myself that if ever I got better, I'd never forget. Well, I haven't entirely forgotten – but I have tended to discard it – you know – I was ill – I'd had all those drugs – and when the drugs were withdrawn, I got 'normal' again . . . Sceptical as ever.

(1443)

The second account, that of a woman whose experience took place in hospital in Australia, is unusual in that in the midst of an apparently near-death episode which began with an out-of-body experience, the subject moved through the ceiling and found herself:

> on a battlefield, where the whole place was piled with dead men, & Russian tanks & machinery (I knew they were Russian, because of the writing on the tanks). Then I was in a hospital, which seemed to be run by nuns. There was a woman who was having a baby & she was screaming, & the nuns were being horrible to her – stuffing a pillow on to her head to stop her cries. Then I was back in my bed again.

Commenting on this aspect of her experience, the subject asks 'Was all this hallucination due to drugs?' before adding 'Whatever it was, I know I felt very ill afterwards, & for months I seemed to be obsessed with all the horror that was going on in the world' (3583).

Non-CE cases

Out of the twenty-five non-CE subjects who made specific reference to life-changes induced by their experiences, seven included a decreased fear of death as one of these, usually as a result of a new or enhanced conviction of the existence of the indestructible human soul, or spirit. Typical expressions from within this group of testimonies included:

> Death is not to be feared. It is the end of one life stage. The soul will live on.

(3428)

I feel I have had proof of life after death, and that we have a spiritual as well as a physical body.

(3462)

Since this happened to me, my great fear of death vanished. I know one's Soul/Spirit/Higher Consciousness lives on forever.

(3843)

I do not think I would have had things otherwise, because the experience has given me an incomparable gift – the sure KNOWLEDGE of what lies beyond the transformation that men call death!

(3941)

As was the case with the CE accounts examined, good, positive fruits dominated the non-CE case collection also. One subject, for example, in language reminiscent of that most optimistic of Christian mystics, Mother Julian of Norwich, wrote that

I think it was several weeks later that I remembered [the experience] suddenly & felt so thankful that the memory of it came back to me – for it gave me a feeling that, in the end, all would be well.

(3611)

In similar vein, a person who had a vivid experience whilst meditating was able to write of his out-of-body experience and subsequent revelation that 'It is still the most important thing that ever happened to me, and governs my whole attitude to life' (3451).

Two non-CE respondents used very similar language to describe a fruit that was not reported by the CE subjects examined in this phase of the study: a sense of belonging to something greater than themselves created in them as a result of their experiences. Thus, for example, a subject who had a very vivid out-of-body experience during a Managerial Grid Course lecture concluded from it that

I'm wondering if what actually happened to me was that
I reached a higher level of consciousness which liberated
me from myself and made me a part of something greater.

(1148)

Such a sentiment compares well with that expressed by another
respondent who received from her experience the fruit of
'belonging', writing that

Since the phenomenon, I have had a sense of belonging,
as if I were related to every rock, tree, flower, mountain,
cloud, animal and person. I am truly concerned about
them and I feel a great love for everyone and everything
in the universe. In other words, I am in attunement with
my world, which is the whole world.

(3442)

Two respondents reported positive after-effects, but ones where
the effects were short-term only, lasting hours or days rather than
having a permanent impact on their lives. One of these, dated 28
September 1969 and therefore one of the earliest accounts ever
submitted to the archives, related how, after a vivid experience of
light, the respondent

settled down in bed but was fully aware that an aftermath
remained and continued for several weeks. It was a sense
of warmth and glow, of utter contentment mixed with
an expectancy and hope that the experience might be
repeated.

(147)

In similar vein, a subject whose experience occurred during
Buddhist meditation recorded a similar short-term side-effect:

For two days afterwards everything I did, even what
would normally be boring drudgery, filled me with the
greatest delight. I felt it didn't matter what happened to
me; everything was very good.

(3519)

285

By contrast, an apparently long-term solution to an acute problem was reported by a subject whose experience – a very vivid out-of-body experience – occurred during a period of grieving for a dead child and longing for one to take his place. As a result of her experience, the subject felt able to write, simply: 'My longing for a child just disappeared' (3865).

As with the CE accounts examined, the development of psychic abilities as a result of an experience was reported in the non-CE group also, but by only one subject. Following a vision including an encounter with robed figures in a light which occurred whilst the respondent was resting, he was subsequently able to report that

> From then on I can talk to people who have passed on. I have what I shall call my 'everyday people' who hang [out] with me, look out my eyes, & are learning as I'm learning (Spirits).
>
> (3944)

Finally – and again as with the CE collection of accounts examined for signs of transformation – a small number of non-CE subjects reported negative or indifferent fruits. Of these, one, whose experience occurred whilst she was sleeping, wrote that: 'The incident had no effect on me, except to make me quite sure that in sleep our spirits can leave our body and return' (3470). Another, whose experience also occurred during sleep, simply added at the end of his experience a note of reluctance to talk about what had happened, commenting that 'I didn't want to talk about it & as I was living alone then I didn't need to' (3671).

Comment

One obvious conclusion to have emerged from this phase of the RERC study concerns the large number of subjects in both CE and non-CE groups who reported a diminished fear of death resulting from their experiences. Of the CE subjects who included a description of some aspect of transformation triggered by their experiences, 35.29 per cent mentioned decreased fear of death within their testimonies, and this compares favourably with the

28 per cent of the non-CE subjects who also reported this motif. One conclusion that might be drawn from this is that it is not necessary simply to come close to bodily death whilst undergoing an experience with typical NDE features (such as an out-of-body experience) to emerge with a reduced fear of death afterwards. Rather, having an experience which may *appear* to the subject to point to the possibility of immortality – such as an OBE whilst resting or sleeping, leading to the conviction that the soul can function independently of the body – may suffice to instil in him or her an often strong and permanent belief that personal death is not the end. Whether or not such a dualistic view of personhood is correct or even philosophically or psychologically possible is not the issue here. Instead, the conclusions that subjects themselves draw from their own experiences are what really matter. And often their experiences are so vivid as to provide, for them, a solid basis for drawing conclusions across a range of important, existential issues: including the question of their own immortality and its relationship to the way they live and understand their lives *before* their deaths. This is well summed up in the words of a subject whose own out-of-body experience prompted him, as a GP, to collect cases of his own and to draw conclusions from them, in which he became convinced that

> this other body is the real self, Spirit, God, or whatever you like to call it. It is harnessed at birth, and released at death (and occasionally temporily) released and returns, as in illness or accident . . . I feel that religion is merely an attempt to discover this real self, and without the personal experience, it is possibly not possible to find it. It is so completely divorced from any other experience in living.
>
> (3437)

Overwhelmingly, the positive nature of transformative effects created by NDEs and noted in previous studies was confirmed by the RERC study. As has been noted, only two of the CE subjects reported anything other than positive, beneficial fruits arising from their experiences. The overwhelmingly positive nature of the transformations wrought by experiences with NDE-like features within the non-CE group of testimonies was also seen during this phase of the study. It is worth noting, however, a range of trans-formative fruits reported in the studies of Ring, Grey, Morse and Sutherland which did *not* appear to be reported by subjects in the RERC study. Thus, for example, no account examined alluded to any specific shift away from conventional religiosity towards a more general spirituality as a result of their experiences: a major trend in the studies of Ring *et al*. Similarly, no testimony examined described an increased involvement with social issues as a result of a CE or non-CE, again in contrast to many other existing studies. There was also a general failure to report any changes in attitudes towards themselves by subjects in the RERC study: save, as already noted, a diminished fear of death and a corresponding rise in belief in the soul's immortality.

Common elements

A further aim of the RERC study was to attempt to test the findings of existing research by assessing the accuracy of existing NDE models, beginning with the detailed fifteen-element model presented by the 'early' Moody but including the more cautious models of later researchers such as Ring and Grey also. By so doing, it was hoped to contribute to the ongoing discussion as to whether NDEs might be revealing a common spiritual essence, accessed by all at the point of death and pointing, perhaps, to a common spiritual core within all of the world's religions and spiritualities. Taking the groups of CE and non-CE testimonies in turn, Moody's original model was first used as a template, and each account compared with it for both similarity and dissimi-larity. One area of particular interest concerned the *number* of elements of Moody's model that each account contained, and this in turn raised a cluster of related questions that this aspect of the study was concerned to tackle. Would, for example, any testimony examined yield all fifteen of the Moody model's original elements? What would turn out to be the average number of elements contained in both CE and non-CE study groups? Would CE accounts contain more or fewer elements than non-CE accounts? And would any element of any model – whether that of Moody or any of the researchers who came after him – be found in no accounts at all, or in so few as to make their inclusion in any model of archetypal NDE elements dubious or problematical? As elsewhere in the RERC study, the conclusions drawn regarding the possibility of commonality across accounts proved interesting and, in certain respects, somewhat surprising.

CE cases

Certain conclusions regarding common features contained within the CE testimony-group have already been drawn in this chapter. Thus, the frequency and nature of descriptions of feelings evoked by experiences, the darkness described in them, and the transformations in the lives of subjects outlined in their accounts have already been commented on in detail. For this reason, it is not necessary to make any additional remarks here regarding four elements of the original Moody model: 'feelings of peace and quiet', 'the dark tunnel', 'effects on lives' and 'new views of death'. What, however, of the model's other features?

Out of the total of thirty-two CE accounts found in the archives and included in the study, none contained all fifteen of the elements of Moody's original model. The maximum number of features in any one account examined was ten, in a testimony submitted to the RERC in August 1971, and hence pre-dating the coining of the term 'near-death experience' by some four years. The average number of elements in any one CE account was 3.3. Two features were absent from any report: no respondent, for example, reported reaching a *border or limit* separating this life from the next, although, as will shortly become clear, one account came close to this assertion. Additionally, no report contained Moody's fifteenth element, that of *corroboration*. Of course, the extent to which a subject's testimony can provide corroboration of itself (as it seems to be being made to do if Moody's fifteenth and last element is taken at face value) is problematical on a number of grounds and because of this it will be reserved for later discussion, below.

Hearing the news

Of the elements that were reported in only a handful of cases, only one respondent described the element of hearing the news of his death, a disconcerting feature of a report submitted by an ex-soldier who sustained massive injuries in a mine explosion during the First World War:

> Relief from pain was profound. I seemed to float above the first-aid men who were still trying to keep me alive. I tried to tell them there was nothing more they could do. Somebody said 'he's gone' and my body was carried out of the over-crowded dugout. For a moment I saw it lying half-naked on the pile of dead just behind the trench. Light snow was falling, and began to cover it. Then suddenly, I was free, poised in the silence of a timeless universe.
>
> (2817)

The life review

Another infrequently encountered feature of the reports was the life review, reported in only two cases. In the first of these, which occurred shortly after the explosion which gave rise to the above account, the subject comes close, without actually describing it, to a feature analogous to the otherwise absent border element, writing that:

> Suddenly, interrupting enlightenment, I felt the intrusion of the past. Though perfectly free in this new-found at-one-ment with reality, I remembered the human relation-ships left behind. I was an only child, engaged to marry, and expecting to return to college after the war. Here was a moment of decision to be handled. I could go forward with growing spiritual awareness or back to embodi-ment. The grace of free-will left the choice to me. As I pondered the alternatives the motives influencing thought took shape and colour around me. They were displayed without comment in a before-now-after continuum in which I saw where each one led. Both good and bad motives were dispassionately exposed. An imperfect thought took deformed shape, but was instantly cancelled when I saw how it was wrong or inadequate. The criteria

of timeless Truth were mine to use. I knew I could either go forward or back. I saw where either way led, and what the alternatives implied.

(2817)

The second life-review element was interestingly also reported by a combat near-fatality, this time a soldier wounded in a tank explosion in the Second World War, whose experience has already been partially examined above (p. 264). Recovering in hospital afterwards, the subject recounted a most complex NDE in the midst of which he realized that

the soul would be, or at least could be, used as a basis for judgement. And this was immediately taken up and I was given a replay of an action of mine that I had forgotten, which is now fresh in my memory, and that I would rather forget. It concerned an occasion when I was about six years old and had recently returned from India, and had gone out to play with a bunch of the local children. One of these children had a dog which delighted in chasing anything that was thrown for it, sticks, stones or if there was anything, a ball I suppose. And I can remember picking up a stone and throwing it across the railway lines – I happened to be pointing in that direction. The dog chased this stone, straight into the path of an express train going from Paddington to somewhere else in the west country I suppose, and it was instantly killed. I'd never played with a dog before in my life up till then: I'd no idea the dog would get hurt otherwise I'd never have done it. But I got an immediate replay of the whole darned thing in detail. I could remember all the details, and basically what it means is that the soul is an indelible record. We can't get at it, but it can be got at and it can be replayed. And the connotation is, that when we die . . . and our souls go this place of assessment, that we will be required to provide answers for various questions and if we try to evade the issue or dissemble in any way, they will simply give us an instant replay of the facts as they happened.

(3766)

The noise

Three subjects described noise or music as a feature of their experiences. Of these, one bore direct comparison to the buzzing or ringing sound isolated by Moody, and recounted so vividly in George Ritchie's *Return from Tomorrow* (Ritchie and Sherrill 1978). The subject – who nearly died whilst giving birth and whose account has already been quoted from at length – described at first a 'tremendous vibrating hum' which frightened her. This reached a pitch of intensity before diminishing, by which point she found herself 'surrounded by or with brilliant light', sensing also a presence with her, and being 'conscious of sound (rather muted and musical, but not music)' (3522). More precise descriptions of actual music were given by the remaining two respondents. One described – albeit briefly – a 'tumultuous' noise of invisible 'gathered souls . . . joining in glorifying God' whilst she hung suspended in isolation unable to join them (3885). Another, giving somewhat more detail, described how suffering from an embolism of the lung after the birth of her first child

> I heard music, which seemed to come from a space without limits, of a beauty and tone colour such as I had hitherto never heard. It filled my whole being with rising joy, with a positive feeling of bliss. I am not really particularly musical, but here I was able to hear every single part individually, at the same time in accord in wonderful harmony, and the most enchanting thing was that I could easily have conducted this gigantic orchestra: the instruments were following my will. I saw no details; it was all only sound. My pain was forgotten – I just listened with a deep feeling of happiness.
>
> (3725)

Ineffability

A rather higher number of CE subjects – six out of the thirty-two examined – described their experiences as being in some sense ineffable: surpassing their abilities to put them into words. A paradoxically detailed and somewhat lucid description of the ineffability of his experience comes from the First World War mine victim whose life review was examined, above:

> Words are so limiting. How can they describe this burning confrontation which is as vivid today as it was fifty-odd years ago? I try to make little comparisons with worldly joys, but these are so trivial. Relaxing in a warm bath after a hard game; swimming at night in a phosphorescent tropic sea; finding the trail again after being lost in the jungle; seeing light at the end of long research; waking pain-free after an operation; being helped in my gardening by a friendly blackbird; listening to the Sahara as it settled for the night after a day's searing heat – such glimpses of the underlying peace which accompanies Love's release from fear or stress can come to all of us. They bring assurance to those who think. They wake joy, but are only faint echoes of my out-of-time communion with the heart of joy Itself in ecstasy of becoming, the new birth.
>
> (2817)

Other references to the ineffability of their experiences included those given by subjects in the following – briefer – terms:

> During the convalescence I was given experiences which are beyond description – but I will try.
>
> (3956)

> I hope that I have been able to convey my feelings to you in a clear way. It has been most difficult to put into words, an experience which was a deeply personal one and has not been shared until this time.
>
> (3522)

> Out there in the universe everything was magnificent and perfect and whole – not as we see it . . . words just fail me – it was too incredible to describe.
>
> (3764)

> I looked down and saw myself, dark blue & grey in the bed. I felt no pain. I heard soft voices, as though they were

discussing something – there were no doctors at my bedside!! I felt the most wonderful feeling of love, peace, beauty. Our earth words just cannot describe what I felt. There is no word <u>here</u> for it. No emotion to describe it.

(4072)

Meeting others

A total of twelve CE subjects described meeting others in their accounts. Of these, two described meeting both religious figures and non-religious figures (i.e. family, friends or strangers), two described encounters with religious figures only, and eight described meetings with non-religious figures only. Of the encounters that included religious figures, two included encounters with Jesus. In one of these, the subject was unconscious and suffering from septicaemia after an emergency operation when she recalled

> walking through a very beautiful field. At the end, what appeared to be small church Jesus came to the door, he put out his hand, and bade me go back. I awoke to find doctors around my bed. I asked the time, to be told, 2.30 A.M. I found out later at that time my mother had been praying for me.
>
> (3753)

Another account – again including religious figures only – involved a subject waking, in hospital in intensive care,

> to be most conscious of four nuns (not earthly) standing silently in vigil to one side of the room I occupied. There was a most wonderful atmosphere of sanctity, and I mentally said to myself, 'If ever I was at the other side of the world, say in Australia, and knew I was about to die, I would wish to return to this very room to do so.' I again fell asleep and when I awoke four hours later the nuns has disappeared and the atmosphere of sanctity had completely vanished.
>
> (3914)

One further account included a meeting with an unusual quasi-religious figure who welcomed the subject to a transcendent realm and gave him a short tour, before introducing himself with the title of 'Patriarch'. In the account, the hospitalized subject found himself emerging from a tunnel to find a 'vast crowd of people in the distance'. Looking at the crowd, he noted that:

> They looked dead, but not really dead. They looked more like they'd been switched off, with the exception of a fair sized group immediately to the front of me. They had the impression of being very preoccupied and very worried. Certainly not interested in me, and there was no reason I suppose why they should have been, but it is unnatural to approach a group or anybody without someone in the group looking at you. They didn't even look at me. The exception to this was three people right in the edge of the crowd immediately in front of me. A distinguished elderly gentleman. A very composed and peaceful looking woman and a young fellow who seemed to be about twenty-eight years of age. He was well-built. He looked to be a very fit and happy sort of individual. I suppose the woman was around thirty-five and the elderly gentleman was somewhere around sixty-five or seventy. I came to a stop about six feet away from these three people and they said 'Welcome!'

Almost immediately, the subject then became aware of a commotion at the periphery of his vision, 'like a dog going through a wheatfield. You could see the movement, but you couldn't see the cause of it. This continued approaching until eventually an incredibly old man literally popped out of the crowd, looked at me, and said "You're early!"' Led through the crowd by the old man, the subject was then taken to a 'place of assessment' in which he was finally able to weigh up the leader in more detail, before describing him in the following terms:

> [H]e was old, he gave the appearance of being infinitely wise, and what was very obvious was that he had a very steely determination. I suppose this was evident in

everything he said and the way it was expressed: nothing was wishy-washy, nothing was left in doubt. I couldn't say exactly how old he was, but I got the impression he was so old that age didn't matter any more. As for the subsequent information, I got the impression he had been asked exactly the same questions so many times that he'd welcome someone with a few original questions. And it was fairly obvious he wasn't using his full capacity of reason and explanation. He was almost bored in fact. Despite that, he was still very much on the ball and the steel of determination was there.

Curious as to the identity of the figure, the subject engaged in persistent questioning as to the man's true identity, before receiving an answer – of sorts:

> After much persistence on my part this leader character, more or less to shut me up I think, more than anything else, and in response to my query as to who he was, said 'Call me Patriarch'. It seemed as good a name as any, so it stuck.
>
> (3766)

Perhaps rather disappointingly, the remainder of the CE accounts in which figures are described as being encountered by their subjects lack the extraordinary detail and descriptive power of the above account. As already noted, eight out of the twelve CE accounts that included a meeting with others made reference to them as being either family, friends or strangers. Five of these subjects encountered relatives: two seeing dead relatives, one seeing a relative who was apparently still living, and two hearing – but not seeing – their dead relatives. Of the accounts including dead relatives who were *seen* by their subjects, one contained a brief description of a seriously ill woman's appearing, in 'a new world' in which 'my father & mother welcomed me to my surprise' (3692). The second contained the following moving description by a woman 'very near to death when I had bronchial pneumonia':

I was lying in bed with one of my daughters by my side
& I was holding her hand. Suddenly the whole room filled
with light. There was a wonderful sense of peace and
beauty. I had no feeling of pain or discomfort. A little way
from me I 'saw' my husband and my mother waiting to
help me when I needed them. I felt conscious of holding
my daughter's hand & I said to her, 'Shall I go now?' She
said 'Do you want me to go?' I thought for a moment &
then said, 'No, I don't think so.' Alison said to me 'There
are three things you said you wanted to do – why don't
you do the first of them?' (which was to go to sleep). This
I did, being quite aware I was not going with my husband
& my mother at that time.

(3538)

One further account including a 'visual' encounter with a
relative concerned a woman's meeting with her mother who was
alive at the time. In it, the subject, on drugs in hospital,

lay still for a long time and one day suddenly saw the vision
of my mother by my bedside, (she was alive at the time and
many miles away caring for my family). She was beautiful
in the vision, dressed in her usual black garb.

(3511)

The remaining two accounts including reference to encounters
with relatives described auditory impressions only. Of these, one
was submitted by a woman whose experience took place during
a severe bout of influenza. In it, the subject described how

I saw my own body on the bed . . . I had the feeling of
great peace, and being bathed in a wonderful light. With
great reluctance, obeying the voices of those who had
cared for me in the past, and who had since 'died' (i.e. my
Father, a favourite teacher, and my nurse when a child
amongst others), telling me I had to 'Go back' as 'my
work was not finished here', I say again with great
reluctance I returned to the body on the bed, and thereafter recovered. Still today on living by the sea, I can still

feel the joy and peace of that moment, when floating at high tide, on a slight sea swell, right in the rays of the sun. It's Heavenly!

(3912)

A second experience including reference to auditory communication only concerned another woman, this time under anaesthetic, whose dead daughter spoke to order her back to life. In her testimony she writes, simply, 'Then my dead daughter's voice came clearly: "You must go back, Mummy, you must go back"' (2799).

The remaining respondents' accounts of encountering others described presences, meetings or observations of persons not known to them or recognized by them either as religious figures with whom they were familiar during earthly life or as other figures known to them prior to their temporary deaths. One account made reference to 'gathered souls' only seen at a distance, praising God (3885). Another subject encountered zombie-like people in a 'black hole', motionless and unblinking (3764). A more detailed account made initial reference to an invisible presence fulfilling the role of guide: 'I had a distinct awareness of not being alone, but no actual vision of anyone else.' As the experience progressed, the subject

became aware that I was being discussed, by whom or what I had no idea . . . I felt that whoever had been my guide had drawn aside and waited, also listening. Then very distinctly, I heard the words, 'She is to return; it is not her time for crossing. The gift of life is regiven for her children's sake. Take her back.' Whose voice it was, I do not know.

The account ends:

For the first time I could see my guide and felt rather than heard the words addressed to me, which were, 'Return to your family, there will be another time for you here. Wear well the mark upon you, it will remain, and you can not remove it, however you try.' I realized a sense of desolation, but before I could protest, I felt the light fading

and knew again the sensation of being pulled into a totally
dark void of accelerated motion and sound. Then there
was absolute nothing. How long it was after this that I
became fully aware of myself, I have no way of knowing.

(3522)

The being of light

As we have seen, within the evolving history of near-death studies
concentration on the light or 'being of light' (Moody's eighth
element) has often taken centre-stage. This emphasis is particularly
underlined by the titles of books which have sought to show that
the light is in some sense the central or most important part of
NDEs, and the last decade or so has seen a flurry of books with
titles such as Peter and Elizabeth Fenwick's *The Truth in the Light*,
Cherie Sutherland's *Reborn in the Light*, Kenneth Ring and
Elizabeth Valarino's *Lessons from the Light* and Michael Sabom's
Light and Death. The RERC study of CE accounts revealed
thirteen testimonies (40.6 per cent) in which a light motif appeared,
but one very striking and immediate finding to arise from analysis
of these concerned the *in*frequency with which the light was
described as having any definite and recognizable personality. This
finding was particularly significant, given the fact that in so many
other studies – such as those cited above – the light appears to fulfil
the function of judge, divine presence, psychopomp, or identifiable
religious figure. This was clearly not the case with the RERC study,
in which the light manifested or contained an identifiable presence,
personality or role in only two out of the thirteen CE accounts
in which it figured. However, analysis was complicated by the
fact that whilst a definite and recognizable presence was only
manifested in the light on two occasions, a very significant number
of other respondents – no less than eight out of the remaining
eleven – reported usually overwhelming sensations of love, peace
or calm either *within* or coming *from* the light, indicating that it
was the source of a range of identifiable feelings and therefore in
some sense the possessor of personality.

Of the two subjects who recognized a definite identity in the
light, one woman's account – already examined in detail above –
included a description in which it in some sense embodied her

(still-living) therapist, albeit elevated in her experience to God-like status and described in vivid terms:

> up and up I was carried, until with a shattering of light I entered another world (room?) and found myself face-to-face with God. A shimmering circle of light . . . encircled his face – which I recognized as the face of my beloved therapist.
>
> (3678)

A second account identified the light as an extremely tall angel who appeared in the midst of an experience in which the subject was menaced by an evil-looking woman who had emerged from an area of darkness:

> I tried to move but could not. I had no feelings of fear or anything, come to think of it. Then, beside me, appeared this bright light. I looked up, and saw an angel, quite 12 feet tall. I could not look at it for long, it was so bright.
>
> (2799)

As regards the eight accounts which did not clearly ascribe a specific identity or personality to the light but which *implied* some form of personality by virtue of the effect it had on the subjects themselves, there was general agreement that the light contained or bestowed extremely positive feelings. One of these described an experience in which light was the only feature commented upon, and which appeared to the subject from just outside his visual field, following an operation in the spring of 1940:

> Fairly early in the morning about two or three days after the operation I was lying in bed, alone in the room, looking out of the window which was to the right of my bed. As my room was on the first floor my view was restricted to the sky and the tops of some trees; it was a sunny morning.
>
> After a little while I got the impression that the light towards the left hand side of the window was unnaturally bright as if there was some powerful source of light nearby but out of my field of vision.

As I looked I began to realize that what I was seeing was something beyond any experience I had ever had and while I lay there I felt I was shedding all pain and worries and I was overcome by a sense of profound peace and happiness; nothing seemed to matter any more.

Indeed, as a result of this experience, a curious postscript was to follow, worth reproducing in full:

Shortly after this experience, which only lasted a few minutes, my doctor and the nurse came in to pay me their usual morning visit and I noticed that the doctor gave me a very curious look; he seemed surprised and somewhat taken aback and instead of the usual: 'Well, how are you today?' he said nothing to start with. After examining me and having the usual chatter with the nurse, he made some remark to her to the effect I was certainly looking much better, to which she agreed, at the same time giving me an odd look, as if she was surprised at what she saw.

(1406)

Elsewhere within the CE accounts examined, encounters with the light appeared similarly beneficial, as in the following examples:

After a minute or two I came out of my body and floated to the foot of my bed, looking down upon my body. I saw a stream of golden astonishing light flowing with great speed up my body. The most remarkable thing about [it] was the complete feeling it gave me of extraordinary calm. I looked for a little while and then went back to my body.

(1439)

I felt I was being welcomed with love and I wanted to move nearer to the source of this light, but there was a sense of waiting all around me. . . .

(3522)

It seemed a long time before I reached the opening and found myself floating gently in a warm soft mist, all golden as with sunlight, soft music and a feeling of complete happiness and such peace that passes all understanding, was mine, faces came out of the mist and faded away.

(2733)

I suddenly became very numb although I was still aware of what was going on around me. Everything became much quieter and there was an atmosphere of calmness. Spiritually I rose and was able to see myself several feet below. Thereafter I seemed to travel through golden-coloured space (like the light that comes from the sun). I felt comforted and a warmth and glow surrounded me.

(3764)

I had the feeling of great peace, and being bathed in a wonderful light.

(3912)

In addition to all of these very similar descriptions, a further account described light suddenly illuminating a subject's room with a brightness seemingly invisible to others who were gathered around her bed. Again, the light brought with it 'a wonderful sense of peace and beauty', and the ill and bedridden respondent reported suddenly feeling neither pain nor discomfort. At the same time as the light's arrival came an appearance of the subject's deceased husband and mother also, although it is not clear whether or not she actually saw these in the light, or whether the light somehow bore their identity, or whether they were themselves glowing brightly and hence providing the illumination. The experience (3538) is noteworthy, however, in that the light was only witnessed by the dying subject, and not by those in attendance on her. As we shall shortly see when we turn to examine the non-CE accounts for common elements, a small number of cases exist in which both the critically ill *and* their carers are apparently able to see what appears to be the same light illuminating the natural environment at the same time.

What has become plain is the fact of the overwhelmingly positive – and hence beneficial – role that the light plays within CE experiences. Indeed, on only one occasion does the light appear in anything like a negative guise, with one respondent – in hospital for a serious operation – making a passing reference to an impression she had whilst recuperating that 'I had the feeling of light which I could not bear, which was attacking me' (3771). However, reference may usefully be made here to the remainder of CE cases (two) where no particular emotions or feeling tones were attached to the light. In fact, in both accounts the role of the light appeared to be simply to illuminate a transcendental, 'heavenly' environment, such as in the following experience:

> Up and up I went until I reached the place were I was being directed to by some unknown force. It was a beautiful place. A brilliant blue sky, and a strong brightness as if the sun was shining, but I looked around and saw no sun. I looked around and saw miles upon miles of beautiful sand, and upon the sand I saw small houses, oblong shaped . . . Then I was guided to a huge cathedral, it's size was enormous, much bigger than our Anglican Cathedral, here in Liverpool. I looked up the top and saw a dome shaped ceiling, with beautifully decorated walls, and at the top you could see the blue sky through the windows.
>
> (3817)

Non-CE cases

As with the CE cases examined above, certain conclusions regarding common features contained within the non-CE testimony-group have also already been examined during the course of this study. Thus, the frequency and nature of descriptions of the negativity or otherwise of experiences, the nature of the darkness described within them, and the transformations in the lives of subjects outlined within subjects' accounts have already been discussed in detail. Again, therefore, it is not necessary to make any additional remarks here concerning the elements of Moody's original model covered under the headings: 'Feelings of peace and quiet', 'The dark tunnel', 'Effects on lives' and 'New views of death'. What, however, of the model's further features?

To begin with, it is notable that two elements of Moody's original model which were encountered in the CE study group were completely absent from the non-CE cases examined. Of these, one was obviously *hearing the news* of one's own death, as would be expected given that none of the non-CE subjects were near death at the time of their experiences. The other absent element – also absent from the CE case collection – was the *border* or *limit*. A further feature present in the CE testimony group but absent in the non-CE group was the *life review*. As with the CE group, examination of the *corroboration* element will be reserved for more detailed discussion later. However, from this preliminary analysis of missing elements it is once again clear that no testimony contained all fifteen elements of Moody's original model. The maximum number of features in any one account was nine, and the average number of elements in any one non-CE account was 2.9.

The noise

Of the elements that were reported in only a few cases, only three subjects described any kind of *noise*. One, in a most unusual experience to be considered in more detail below, described 'being a part of a rushing, wind-like sound', recalling Moody's subject in *Life After Life* who described the noise as being 'like the wind (Moody 1975: 30). A further respondent reported during an out-of-body experience that 'the whole atmosphere was filled with what I can only call "praise" . . . It was as if everything was ringing and singing with joy' (3420), whilst another – whose account has already been cited in greater detail, above – reported a far less melodic group of sounds during an initially terrifying out-of-body experience at the point of waking:

> I was completely wide-awake and very alert. The next moment I was aware of strange reeling sensations in my head, like two separate forces one on each side of my head and there was also a vibrating buzzing in my ears. This was very powerful. I was frightened and tried to lift my head from the pillow. This was impossible to do. The whizzing through my head was somehow like a great centifugal force pushing me deeper into the pillow (I was on my back). The ringing/buzzing in my ears seemed to

get louder and more forceful and really hurt and by this
time I was terrified.

(3843)

Ineffability

A correspondingly small number of subjects – six – referred to
the *ineffability* of their experiences, using phrasing very similar
to that used by the CE subjects. One subject, whose feelings and
discoveries during a spontaneous out-of-body experience were
subsequently to free her from a deep depression, described the
most profound phase of her experience as containing a feeling of
deep love, peace and wholeness which she was simply 'unable
to fully express' (4067). A respondent who underwent a vivid
experience of a journey into a darkness lit by a 'silvery-white
light' where he communed with souls and made many discoveries
concerning the meaning of death and the purpose of life introduced his narrative with the comment that:

> It is very difficult to describe in words all that happened
> . . . I find it very difficult to do so. I find it hard to describe
> on flat paper the feeling and the impact of finding yourself
> in another world, on another plane, on a spiritual
> excursion.
>
> (3428)

Two further subjects expressed difficulty describing the immediate
after-effects of their experiences also. One person who entered a
dark passage in the company of a pale glowing golden cloud
containing a presence one morning before waking wrote that after
she awoke, 'I lay for some time still filled with the quite indescrib-
able sense of joy & bliss & lightness which gradually faded' (1408).
Another respondent describes an experience of leaving his body,
gaining knowledge and encountering a light spontaneously 'as I
walked near Main & Bowery Streets at noon in Akron, Ohio',
ending with the comment that 'This lasted briefly but made an
unforgettable impression – difficult to describe' (3425). A further
subject made similarly brief reference to the difficulties inherent
in describing her experience: 'I don't know how else to describe

it . . . the blessing, can I call it, or glory of communion with God [?]' (3865). Another wrote, simply, 'In recollection, it is difficult to be exact. At the time one had no terminology for this kind of experience' (3523). In sum, and overall, it is clear that, as with the CE subjects, non-CE subjects on occasion also expressed great difficulty in finding words to describe their experiences.

Meeting others

A significant number of RERC accounts described experiences in which subjects, apparently far from death, encountered deceased relatives, religious figures or strangers, often during out-of-body experiences or journeys to other realms containing tunnels, lights and other NDE-like features. Out of a total of thirteen such accounts, five occurred when the subject was either waking from sleep or when the subject had just awoken. The remainder occurred in a variety of contexts, including deep sleep, astral projection, meditation exercises and – in one case – within an apparently spontaneous out-of-body episode. Of the figures encountered in these thirteen accounts, seven were unknown to the subject, four were recognized as religious figures, whilst two accounts included encounters with relatives. The following is an example of an experience which occurred shortly after waking, in which the experient, a widow, encountered her recently deceased husband:

> I woke up one sunday morning nearly 3 years ago on September 6th. The sun was streaming in my bedroom, I looked at my watch to see if it was time to get up to do some gardening before breakfast. I had been deeply shocked by my husband's death as we were devoted to each other; & I was working continually to stop myself thinking. My watch showed me it was 6.30 A.M. and I decided I had better not get up for a little while, else I would wake my daughter & her husband with whom I was staying. So I laid down again, then I felt an extra-ordinary feeling on the inside of both of my feet, as if something was loosening & was trying to get free. I wondered what was happening to me. Then I felt a sensation as if a rubber glove was being pulled off me but

on the inside, & the next second I was floating up through cloud smoothly & without effort. I was amazed at this & wondered what was happening to me & was looking up all the time. Then I stopped & saw my husband surrounded by cloud, but I saw him very clearly just above me. He held out his arms to me as if imploring me to go to him and I wanted to go to him. But then I thought of my daughter who had recently married, but had not then settled down as it was very early days, so I spoke to my husband and told him I couldn't leave her yet, as I felt she still needed me. The next instant I was back in my bed as usual, but marvelling at what had happened. . . .

(3462)

Another subject, whose experience also occurred just after waking and included out-of-body sensations, a loud buzzing and a journey through darkness followed by an experience of overwhelming love and peace, describes a visit to a 'hill top' and an encounter with a woman – apparently a stranger – as the very last 'phase' of her richly detailed account:

It was lovely, the sun was shining and the grass seemed so green. Everything seemed more intense and denser. I saw a small stone building like a sheep shelter with an opening of a door and a window (no door or window was actually in). I went to this place and entered. A woman was standing inside. She was middle-aged, very dark and masculine built. I had never seen her before but must add that I have seen her since in a strong dream. She was just standing there with her arms folded, she looked firm. Into my mind came the thought 'You must leave now and go back'. I really did'nt want to come back. I was quite prepared to leave everything and everyone here and I was fully able to realize that this meant leaving the boys too, but I wanted to remain there. Again the strong thought came to say I must return at once. The next thing I knew was that I was wide-awake and <u>so</u> filled with happiness and joy and strength.

(3843)

307

One of the most unusual non-CE experiences in the archives, which also occurred shortly after the subject had awoken, involved a detailed encounter with a cloaked stranger and included an out-of-body experience, feelings of intense love and an approach towards a brilliant light:

> Some years ago I awoke quite suddenly in the early hours, and in the half light I saw a cloaked and hooded figure standing by my bed. There was no aureola, nor any illumination whatsoever surrounding this figure, in fact it appeared to be an ordinary person apart from the cloak and hood.
>
> Then I had the feeling that my whole being was drawn in a great sense of Love out towards this figure; and when this Being raised an arm over my upper body (I do not know if it was part of the cloak that overshadowed me, or, believe it or not, a wing), I had the sensation of being a part of a rushing, wind-like sound. Then my consciousness, my spiritual self, or atman, call it what you will left my physical body and I felt myself rising into a light, a warmth, an overwhelming sense of Ultimate Being that increased as I rose upwards towards that cloaked arm, or wing. It would be impossible to describe to you the nature, or the brilliance of that Light as it increased in what must only have been milliseconds. Just when my Ego, my spiritual being, was on the point of no return to the physical level of consciousness I experienced the sensation of rising up against the 'wing' of the Being's arm, almost with a bump, and I returned most unwillingly, as if pulled by a powerful elastic, back into the body on the bed.
>
> (4067)

Jesus and Mary appeared to another respondent, who described her experience as occurring 'between sleeping and waking' but avers that it was 'different to a dream'. In her account, she told of how

> At a great distance, I saw, in a beautiful golden light, the figure of Jesus and his Mother. I can't remember any

details – in fact I was in danger of forgetting the experience, so bogged down was I with my negative emotions. I think it was several weeks later that I remembered it suddenly & felt <u>so</u> thankful that the memory of it came back to me – for it gave me a feeling that, in the end, all would be well.

(3611)

Three accounts included meetings with others during experiences that occurred whilst the subject was meditating or attempting astral projection. One subject wrote of the climax to a period in which he had been attempting 'to separate the spirit from the "flesh" to obtain proof that there are two sides of me' as occurring when

sitting in an easy chair I suddenly began to drift upwards, my spirit body a replica of the physical body, but somehow more solid and free. As I started to drift upwards I looked at my physical body (in the easy chair). I had the feeling that I had died. Soon after registering this feeling I 'landed' somewhere in Spirit-land, with buildings, grass, churches, & more wonderful than any place I have been to here on earth – I entered a door of a large building and saw my brother and father who had been dead for several years and held a conversation with both about my mother who at that time was alive. Thereafter I made numerous journeys into Spirit-land using my will to direct me where I wanted to go. I have learnt much in the Halls of learning in Spirit-land and hold conversations without using words.

(3454)

Another subject, also practising astral projection, described numerous visits to the 'next plane', in one of which he was taken to 'a combination of Cathedral and University' in order to hear an oration given by 'Teacher Masters with the faces of Gods' (3470). A further subject, practising group meditation, found herself in a tunnel and aware of occupants of separate tunnels:

I appeared to be in a tunnel but gradually the solidity of the walls became transparent, and I found that adjacent passages held their own occupants and although there was no communication at first awareness developed and finally the walls disappeared and fellowship and communion was complete.

(3913)

Joyous communion with others was also reported by the following subject whose experience followed a period of seeking after truth which included – at points but not immediately prior to his experience – episodes of meditation:

The next thing I knew I felt a great love, an immense happiness, an excitement. I had been joined by others. I saw no one, I saw nothing, this was an emotional not a visual experience. We were a small group three or four of us together, I believe four, I had been joined by these other souls and my look at heaven had gone. I felt the presence of these other souls our spirits mingled. We were all sharing the same experience, seperate but as one. We shared a great excitement, a great love, the highest emotional feeling possible, we were 'bubbling with joy together' it was as though lovers who had been apart for a very long time had found each other. It was a wonderful feeling, so intense that it was a noisy joy. I felt then and feel now that there was a childlike innocence and purity in this joining together of souls.

(3428)

Of the remaining accounts in which other figures or beings appear to have been encountered by subjects, one, submitted by a schoolboy, contains an experience which occurred during what the subject described as a vision/dream, suggesting that the episode occurred whilst he was sleeping and yet had a quality that set it apart from a 'mere' dream. In it, the schoolboy describes how

One night, I sensed myself going on a long 'journey'. All the time, I was watching my body do everything as if it were another person doing it. Anyhow, I arrived, petrified. Jesus was wearing a long watery-yellow robe, with a purple strip on it. He had brownish hair, with a long, flowing brown beard. He radiated love, joy and peace. When He saw that I was petrified He said in a gentle, loving voice, 'Don't be afraid, Julian. We won't hurt you'. Immediately I was no longer scared in any way. He was shining brightly, with a halo. There was one bishop next to Jesus, and two next to God. Jesus told me that He and God had been studying me carefully, and I could become a vicar, if I wanted to. Jesus said that He and God would like it very much if I did. But, the choice was mine, He said, and I should make the decision myself, as it was my life. He said goodbye, and then, the next thing I knew, was I was being woken up by my matron, at school.

(4036)

Another experience which occurred whilst the subject was dreaming, but which was described by her as 'the most vivid and real dream I have <u>ever</u> had', involved a meeting with a doctor in a tunnel, together with a vision of Mary, Joseph and Jesus. The account includes the following description:

There was a long episode at the beginning which I can hardly remember, but the general impression was that I was living in a 'grey' town. It was full of people who were crippled in some way, either mentally or physically. The men looked defeated, the children were excessively cruel to one another. I had been invited to lunch with a doctor who lived at one end of this town. I remember walking down the street to see him, and passing one of the other two doctors in the town, these other two were 'grey' men. The doctor I was going to see was different – and how!

We sat down to lunch in a short tunnel. The doctor lived with his old father in a house the other end of the tunnel which was part of a <u>quite</u> different region – like paradise. I was sitting at the 'paradise' end of the tunnel while my doctor friend was carving a bacon joint. I looked up into the clear blue sky and saw an arched roof effect upon which was a collection of beautiful patterns and colours, like a kaleidoscope.

I said to the doctor, 'Look, the sky is like the roof of a cathedral'. But he couldn't see what I could see. I was disappointed by this, but assumed that the reason he couldn't see it was that he had grown used to it through living there. I also saw Mary, Joseph and the infant Jesus in the sky, but he could not see these either.

(3459)

Finally, one account in which the subject became aware of the presence of 'heavenly beings' occurred during a spontaneous out-of-body experience, in a field, at lunchtime, during the Second World War:

Suddenly the whole atmosphere was filled with what I can only call 'praise'. It was as if everything was ringing and singing with joy. I was dimly aware of something like vague heavenly beings near me. I felt as if I could touch them, although I was only conscious of vague shadowy forms. In a flash I knew that I was part of something that always had been and always would be. Then it seemed as if with this realization I came back to normal into my body again.

(3420)

The being of light

As with the CE accounts examined, analysis of the fifty-nine non-CE accounts revealed a significant number containing a light motif: twenty-nine in total, constituting 49.1 per cent of the entire non-CE case collection. However, and once again in common with the CE accounts examined, the light was only described as having a definite and recognizable personality in a small number of cases: five in total. Of these five, the light was identified as God in one case, both Jesus and Mary in one case and as Jesus in a third. In the remaining two cases, whilst the light was clearly described as having personality or simply as 'living', no actual identity was unambiguously ascribed to it. However – and once more in common with the CE case collection – a very substantial number of subjects, whilst ascribing no definite identity or personality to the light, nonetheless reported often overwhelming sensations of calm, peace, beauty or love created in them by their exposure to it: once again indicating the possibility that the light was the source of a range of identifiable feelings and thus in some – perhaps indefinable – sense the possessor or source of personality.

Of the two subjects who reported the light as being Jesus, one was the schoolboy whose account was related at length above and who encountered Jesus in a 'vision/dream' in which he appeared 'shining brightly, with a halo' (4036). The second described the appearance of both 'Jesus and his Mother' who manifested themselves to the subject 'in a beautiful golden light' (3611). A third account, which contains the experience of another schoolboy who at the beginning of his summer holidays began to have a number of 'disturbing thoughts' concerning the meaning of life and the nature of God, includes the following episode in which answers to his deep questions began, apparently, to be revealed to him:

> I began to grasp, for the first time, exactly what God was; at one level, he was a human being . . . at another level, an all pervading Energy which encompassed, and was part of, the whole universe, of every living thing, including myself; and also, the Creator of the Universe. It was so amazing that I was communicating with this all-pervading Energy force as an equal – and in doing so, I too was encompassing the universe, becoming a part of everything around me. I found myself liberated from the confines of my body; no longer bound by skin . . . I soared way up into the blue sky, beyond the clouds and across the infinite reaches of space. Now, it was all infinite bliss, infinite light – infinity was no longer an enemy but a friend – I had been looking at Hell, a dark threatening universe without God; but now, I was one with God, the life force, light was permeating the universe; God/Life/Light, the three are all one – with them, the universe is Heaven; without them, Hell.
>
> (3451)

Of the two accounts in which the light was described in terms which suggested either that it had personality or that it was in some sense alive, one included an out-of-body experience in which the subject, coming *close* to equating the light with God,

> was enveloped (I can only call it that) and lifted high above the high bank and tall hedge on top, as though by unseen and unfelt hands, enveloped in a wonderful living brilliant light ... It seemed an eternity I was held aloft with the most wonderful glow of peace and awareness of the wonder of God.
>
> (3679)

A second account, which told of a woman's experience one morning just before waking, described the light vividly in terms of possessing a particular personality, whilst once again stopping short of providing any unambiguous definition of that personality's full identity:

> One morning apparently just before waking, I was dreaming that I was walking down a long dark passage where I became aware that beside me was a pale golden glowing cloud, and within this – but not seen – was a tremendous Presence. My own consciousness opened out to this and received a clear sense of a boundless personality, endlessly strong & at the same time endlessly gentle, understanding and all-powerful. I was filled completely with joy – so to speak dissolved in bliss.
>
> There was a sense of coming home, or coming back to something or someone once well known, which made everything else of no importance beside it. I felt a great longing to share this with other people & childishly begged this Presence to go to others & leave me if necessary now that I knew it.
>
> How long this state lasted I do not know as there was no sense of time, but on finding myself awake in bed I lay for some time still filled with the quite indescribable sense of joy & bliss & lightness which gradually faded.
>
> (1408)

Intriguingly, the subject adds in the very next paragraph of her letter (addressed to Sir Alister Hardy after he had apparently given a talk at Hampstead Parish Church) that 'I found myself realizing quite certainly whose presence I had been in, & I still cannot doubt it in spite of the amazement of such an experience happening to me!' It is tempting to speculate here as to whether she is attempting to communicate that it was indeed *God* whose presence she had been in, but, coming as it does from a person who had heard Hardy speak in church, it is conceivable that other identities may also be implied, such as Jesus or Mary. It is also tempting to speculate as to whether the subject – aged 63 at the time of her letter which includes the experience that she had 'just over a year ago' – was actually at the beginning of the process of dying in her sleep during this experience before, fortunately, being able to reverse the process in order to wake normally.

As with the CE accounts examined, a very large number of non-CE accounts made clear references to the positive feelings engendered in their subjects as a result of their being close to, or actually inside, the light, without actually identifying it, implying personality but not unequivocally stating it. A wide number of contexts were cited by non-CE subjects regarding the occasion of their experiencing this unidentified but extremely benign light, including contemplative silence, prayer, meditation, listening to music, drug intoxication, walking in the country, being anxious and sleeping. Sometimes the light was encountered in conjunction with an experience of darkness, sometimes during an out-of-body experience, and sometimes in conjunction with one or more other NDE-like elements. A range of descriptions of the positive feelings engendered by the light in this large group of respondents included the following:

> I have never, before or after, felt such a sense of peace and comfort.
>
> (2026)

> The most devastating was the feeling of love it was so intense that I rocked from side to side in my chair. It reached such a peak of intensity that I remember saying, 'I think I'm going to die, I think I'm going to die'. I could

not feel my body as a body, it was just a sensation of love and light. I heard and felt my hair crackle like static electricity and as if the entity knew I had taken as much as I could and physically . . . began to withdraw.

(3875)

The light that we had all been following had drawn us together to this point but suddenly between myself and the source of the light a black cross was stretched. There was no way through unless I embraced this evil symbol. My reluctance stiffened into resolve and there was a momentary loss of consciousness and then I stepped into the joy of union with the light.

(3913)

I had an overwhelming feeling of cleansing and uplift and was left in a state of excited serenity, and friendliness to everyone.

(3950)

I was naked & knew I was perfect, & the air was warm – the whole thing was so incredible & I kept repeating 'this is it, this is it'. I was aware so strongly that this was all-important & terribly personal. The sense of time-lessness was very strong: it seemed to last a long, long time but I can't remember the exact time but I returned to normal very gently. I can say truthfully that now I do not fear death.

(4058)

Comment

Three elements of Moody's original model have not been included in this analysis of CE and non-CE common elements. One of these – 'Telling others' – was deliberately omitted on the grounds that it is difficult to determine what exactly was meant by it in Moody's original study, or, indeed, what has been meant by it in much research since. To date, it has been used by Moody and others to cover a wide range of effects engendered by having an NDE, including a desire not to tell others of the experience, a desire to tell others, disbelief from others (often the medical profession) or fear of being misunderstood or ridiculed. All of these responses, in varying degrees, were found in both CE and non-CE groups. The following are examples:

> I have not mentioned this to anyone before (except a close friend). I am not unbalanced, and certainly would not lie about it. My great fear was that no-one would take me seriously, but I swear it did actually happen.
>
> (3764)

> It seemed impossible that other people didn't see these things – at first I thought I must be having common 'religious' experiences, but soon knew I must not speak of them, they were mine alone.
>
> (3956)

> One cannot talk of this experience to all and sundry, but I did tell my nephew who is an Anglican Priest.
>
> (2010)

> I could no longer claim personal communion with the universal life force, but retained a belief in everything that I learnt . . . and still feel a need to communicate this experience to the people I meet. It is still the most important thing that ever happened to me, and governs my whole attitude to life.
>
> (3451)

Problematical for similar reasons is another element of Moody's model, 'coming back', which once again is something of a catch-all category embracing a wide diversity of reports in which respondents firmly do not wish to return to life, want to be returned, are sent back with a task or message, describe in some detail the mode of their return, or simply wake up to find themselves once again alive and embodied. All of these modes of coming back were also detected across the CE and non-CE accounts examined in the RERC study:

I realized a sense of desolation, but before I could protest, I felt the light fading and knew again the sensation of being pulled into a totally dark void of accelerated motion and sound. Then there was absolute nothing. How long it was after this that I became fully aware of myself, I have no way of knowing.

(3522)

With great reluctance, obeying the voices of those who had cared for me in the past, and who had since 'died' (i.e my Father, a favourite teacher, and my nurse when a child amongst others), telling me I had to 'Go back' as 'my work was not finished here', I say again with great reluctance I returned to the body on the bed and thereafter recovered.

(3912)

[I]t seemed my body and spirit came together again & I moved my legs in bed, then got out and walked about.

(3692)

I was aware that the operation was drawing to a close and I re-entered my body again.

(3885)

A third element of Moody's model also presented problems for analysis, although for different reasons. In *Life After Life*, Moody presented a small number of cases in which corroboration of NDErs' claims – particularly as regards observations made by them whilst physically unconscious yet apparently out of body – was itself claimed. On the basis of these, he was to conclude:

Can any of these reports be checked out with other witnesses who were known to be present, or with later confirming events, and thus be corroborated?
In quite a few instances, the somewhat surprising answer to this question is 'yes'. Furthermore, the description of events witnessed while out of the body tend to check out fairly well. Several doctors have told me, for

example, that they are utterly baffled about how patients
with no medical knowledge could describe in such detail
and so correctly the procedure used in resuscitation
attempts, even though these events took place while the
doctors knew the patients involved to be 'dead'.

(Moody 1975: 99)

As this book has shown at various points, corroboration of
NDErs' claims has been sought in a wide variety of ways. In
addition to asking them for descriptions of their resuscitation
procedures and then checking these off against medical records of
the same procedures as Michael Sabom has done, other researchers
such as Paul Badham and Peter Fenwick have attempted in
recent years to locate distinctive designs in high locations around
operating theatres in the hopes that NDErs, whilst out of body, will
'remote view' and identify them correctly. Most controversially of
all, we also recall Kenneth Ring's research with blind NDErs.
Clearly, this is a potentially hugely significant area of research, and
much more work needs to be done. Unfortunately, the RERC study
could not claim to make a particularly useful contribution to it. All
that was available to work with in the RERC archives were the
anonymous testimonies – usually letters – of experients themselves,
with no possibility therefore afforded of follow-up interviews with
anybody else present at the various out-of-body or near-death
episodes described. Indeed, even if such had been possible, the
situation would have been complicated by the fact that many of
the accounts examined, including those of many elderly people,
were several years old.

However, this being said, some accounts were still noteworthy
within the context of the quest for corroboration of subjects'
reports either because the subjects themselves had made attempts
subsequent to their experiences to check information obtained
during them, or because of the presence of pieces of detail which
suggested that some sort of genuine observation apart from the
body had been made by some respondents in at least some
situations. Obviously, an NDEr's testimony cannot provide
corroboration of itself. Nonetheless, the information included in
a small number of accounts was deemed interesting enough to be
presented and briefly examined.

Thus, for example, a particularly detailed out-of-body account was notable for the vividness of the respondent's description of herself as seen from above, and not – as normally – in the mirror:

> One night, not long after we were married, Malcolm and I were lying in bed. He had fallen asleep with his right hand clasping my left. I was drowsy but not asleep. I found myself out of and above my body but unable to get away from it; I couldn't move further away than the length of my left arm. I shook and pulled it but couldn't get free. I looked down to see what was holding me and saw Malcolm's hand clasping mine. But something was wrong. Did I look like that – was that really me? Black curly hair lay on the white pillow. Yes, my own hair was black. The face was sunburnt. Yes, I had been out in the sun. The nose? Was my nose that shape? I didn't think it was – surely the tip of it should have been slightly tilted the other way? One eyebrow was higher than the other but somehow that didn't look quite right either. Yet it must be me because there was Malcolm holding my hand and looking just as I was accustomed to seeing him. Again I tried to free myself but with no success and I must have sunk back into my body and gone to sleep.
>
> When I awoke in the morning I remembered what had happened in the night. I hurried to look at myself in a mirror and examined my face. It looked just the same face I was accustomed to seeing. Why, then, when I had been out of my body had it looked different? Why had not Malcolm also looked different. The explanation was, of course, that when I had been out of my body I had seen myself left and right as others saw me and not as I appeared to myself in a mirror image.
>
> (3526)

Vivid as this description is, regrettably the subject fails to mention how so much detail was available to her at night and thus presumably in darkness or at least semi-darkness. It has long been established within paranormal literature, however, that unusual illuminations of the environment often accompany sightings of things such as apparitions.[3] Perhaps a similar principle is at work here.

Another account, also occurring at night but under more normal lighting conditions, was reported by the respondent whose experience in a sleeping carriage on a train in India in 1942 has already been partially referred to. Once again, the account is notable as being an out-of-body experience containing impressive detail, and is therefore worth reproducing at length:

> About 9.30 p.m when the light was fading I made ready to sleep which involved going into the toilet which was connected with the compartment (no corridors on those trains), but remaining clad in my blue overall slacks and blouse. When I came back into the compartment, I found the other occupants had already switched off the main lights and there remained the usual central overhead blue light glassed in a circular cover. I had already opened my bedding roll (we ALL travelled with these in India in those days), and I lay down on my bottom bunk to sleep. I was pretty well exhausted emotionally and I remember 'wishing I were dead' as I lay down. It should be said that I wore my hair in plaits (and still do) round my head in 'Gretchen style' and while I had 'done my hair' in the toilet, I had pinned it up again, for I had no wish to display myself with 'hair down' . . .
>
> I fell into an immediate sleep: the next thing I 'knew' was that I, my Consciousness, was gazing down at my own body lying on its face on the lower berth and my Consciousness noted that my hair plaits had slipped from my head at the back where I'd pinned them and that my body was FACE DOWNWARDS. 'I' or my consciousness, tried to 'turn' and managed to do so, in so far as I was aware of the Blue Light precisely to my right, 'I' was within a few inches of it, right up at the top of the railway compartment. 'I' then observed the male occupants of the compartment and the precise way they were lying asleep in the dim light. A terrible feeling of utter hopelessness and of death came over me. I supposed myself to be dead. All 'I' seemed to be was an 'EYE'. I could see everything

quite clearly in the railway compartment including my own body and I seemed to be suspended in space, and had a feeling of 'deadness', yet I was AWARE of every detail of my physical surroundings, on the assumption that 'I' was up there by the light.

Then suddenly, the thought of my children came to me and I longed to 'get back' into my body which I could see so clearly lying on its face down there on the berth, the hair plaits slipping away from the back of the head and the face in the pillow and the legs slightly parted in a sprawling position, and the right elbow sticking out . . . over the edge of the bunk . . .

The next thing I knew was a slight tingling sensation and I became aware of the top centre of my physical head and gradually sensation returned to my recumbent body on the bunk. My <u>body was face downwards when I returned to it</u>. I became fully awake. I looked at my watch, it was within ten minutes of the time we were to arrive at Bareilly Junction in the small hours. My companions were sleeping utterly. I rose, folded up my bedding roll and collected my cases as the train slowed down in the night and got out when it stopped in the darkness at Bareilly Junction.

(514)

One additional small subcategory of testimonies in which corroboration of a subject's experience was at least implied involved a very few episodes which were located in the archives which appeared to be *shared* by more than one person. Only three accounts fell into this category, all non-CE, but all worthy of brief mention here. In one, the subject had just settled her terminally ill aunt down for the night and had sat by her bedside on a chair, when:

Why, I do not know, but my eyes seemed drawn to the corner of the room. There, at the top of the wall shone a small light which slowly grew in size and brilliance. I could not withdraw my gaze but I had no sense of fear. I determined to be quite practical and made myself look out of the window, thinking that an outside light might be reflected in the bedroom but there was no outside light. I sat down again and kept my eyes on the light. I have never, before or after, felt such a sense of peace and comfort. I felt a powerful presence in the bedroom and I knew that I would be given Divine strength to carry on with my duty to the end. I felt an exhileration, a peace and well-being and I knew that I had been given a manifestation of God's care for me, unworthy though I was. I went to sleep, calm and re-assured, knowing that the burden was no longer mine.

Corroboration that something had, indeed, appeared – or was appearing – in the corner of the room is hinted at as the moving narrative continues:

There was an unexpected sequel to my experience.

On the following night, when I had again attended to my patient, I noticed that she did not, as usual, close her eyes. I followed her gaze and was surprised to realise that she was staring up above at the very place where the light had shone for me. I asked my Aunt what she was looking at. She replied: 'Nothing.'

I said: 'Come on. Tell me. What do you see up there?'

She replied: 'I'm not going to tell you. It's a secret.'

My aunt died a few days later. I am convinced that we were both, however unworthy, privileged to be granted this manifestation of Divine help in our hour of need.

(2026)

Two further, comparable, accounts hint at the possibility that aspects of unusual experiences associated with a dying person can be shared by a second, healthy, party. In one, an out-of-body experience appears to be shared:

I should like to recount one very strong experience of this kind which deeply affected me, and which seems to me religious in my sense of the word. I was visiting a very dear, very old friend, whom I was not able often to see.

She was then approaching ninety years old. At the moment of departure I was strongly conscious of her extreme frailty, so that it almost seemed as though I felt it in my own body. I was conscious also of her inevitable nearness to the end of her life, and of the mystery of mortality especially in its relation with a personality so rich as hers. As though it carried with it the meaning of intimacy, this consciousness seemed to take on a life of its own, to become a kind of actuality in which the seperateness of her identity and mind dissolved, but were not lost. I had put my hand on her shoulder, and at once I felt, for an extraordinary and timeless moment, out of my body, in some serene, ineffable dimension of being that was beyond us both.

(3523)

A second, similar, account, is more dramatic and direct:

My husband a Doctor had been ill on and off for some time but had recently recovered and had been given a good report from the Doctors. Suddenly the following day he returned home from the hospital and suddenly fell sideways. I held him in my arms and felt I was almost able to go with him – I was almost through the door, and I found myself mentally pushing someone away fighting them, then the door was slammed in my face and he was dead. Afterwards I felt I had been fighting either God or the Devil.

(3580)

Interestingly, what he calls the 'empathic near-death experience' in which 'someone at the bedside of a person who is dying' is temporarily enabled 'to participate empathetically in the dying experience of that other person' has been presented by Raymond Moody in his most recent study of NDEs, *The Last Laugh*, as a 'new kind of near death experience' (Moody 1999: 4–5), and is one which has attracted the interest of a number of additional researchers also, including P.M. Atwater (Atwater 1994) and Allan Kellehear.[4] It remains to be seen whether a sufficient number of accounts of such experiences will emerge which enable closer analysis to take place. As things stand, exploration of such an unusual category of NDE is still very much in its infancy.

Summary

Alister Hardy, whose initiative and industry in creating the RERC archives served in large part to make this chapter possible, has been described as being 'like a fisherman casting his net upon the waters, but instead of coming up with a few well-defined fish, [finding] he had caught a great array of glittering creatures that did not seem to fit his preconceived grouping' (Maxwell and Tschudin 1990: 6). In a sense, viewing the accounts which have constituted the RERC study as diverse creatures which challenge existing classifications, categories, models and taxonomies is useful and has been justified by conclusions which have been reached and which may be summarized by way of conclusion in what follows. A number of directions for future research have also suggested themselves over the course of the RERC study, which may also be usefully summarized as potential starting points for future and possibly more detailed studies.

One conclusion which gradually became clear as the study progressed was that the inclusion of non-CE accounts within it was both useful and revealing. For as we have had abundant cause to note, persons report experiences with virtually the whole range of NDE features – with the exclusion of the border and the life review – within a very wide range of contexts far removed from those involving life-threatening danger. We recall the figures quoted earlier: the average number of Moody's original fifteen NDE elements in the CE and non-CE accounts examined were 3.3 and 2.9 respectively: a difference of only 0.4. Perhaps it is safer in future studies and in view of this fact to abandon the use of the term 'near-death experience' altogether as a descriptor for a class of experiences involving the recurrence of certain key elements such as out-of-body experiences, episodes of darkness, meetings with deceased relatives and encounters with benign and comforting lights. As we have seen, such experiences can occur in a rich range of contexts, including walking, resting, meditation and simple sleep, in which the subject is seemingly in no physical danger at all. Whilst this fact has certainly been noted within near-death studies, receiving comment in the evolving studies of Ring, Grey and the Fenwicks, the RERC study has demonstrated vividly, quantitatively and conclusively that the parallels and similarities are striking indeed. Such a finding has implications for a wide number of issues within near-death studies, including all present and future neuroscientific attempts to explain the NDE naturalistically. For it is now clear that any neuroscientific model which is offered to account for each specific feature of the NDE must also be sufficient to explain testimonies containing a large variety of NDE elements which arise from situations where there is no threat to life – either real or perceived – at all. Clearly this is an important issue, and one which raises all sorts of questions regarding the likelihood that persons resting, meditating or sleeping can suddenly and apparently inexplicably experience endorphin dumps, temporal lobe seizures, anoxia and changes in the visual cortex sufficient to create experiences involving feelings of peace, journeys through darkness and encounters with bright lights. It is just this range of experiences in persons far removed from death that psychological analysis must also explain, if it is to present neuroscientific models sufficient to explain near-death experiences which occur in situations where death is, in fact, very far away.

The fact that a recognizable number of features recurred in a great many experiences within the RERC study suggests that classifying them under a single heading – whether NDE, CE or something else – is justified: at least up to a point. However, it has already been noted that only a small number of the fifteen elements of Moody's original model were found in the experiences of subjects either clinically dead, critically ill, or far from physical danger. In view of this, perhaps a more modest and cautious model – such as Ring's five-stage model including peace and a sense of well-being, separation from the body, entering the darkness, seeing the light and entering the light – is to be preferred to Moody's more elaborate and complex scenario. This has been the opinion of other near-death researchers such as Margot Grey, and is a finding supported by the RERC study, although it is of note that few, if any, respondents included in the study actually *entered* the light they saw and felt, suggesting that even a modest model such as Ring's may need to be trimmed further in order to do adequate justice to NDErs' reports. The RERC study suggests that closure on this issue is at least premature, and also suggests that there is still much to do as regards what actually does, and does not, constitute an NDE, an issue that is complicated by the already acknowledged presence of a large number of NDE-like elements in contexts where the subject was in no physical danger at all.

Another area of complexity regards the identification of the darkness motif reported in a substantial number of accounts. The discovery that this was described so often in terms suggestive of outer space was perhaps the RERC studies' most unexpected and startling finding. As was concluded earlier in the study, speculation as to the meaning of this unusual discovery is also premature until other studies can confirm or overrule it. As things stand, however, the RERC study suggests that researchers should now be on the look out for it, whatever its eventual significance and meaning may turn out to be. If it *is* found elsewhere, the hunt for cultural analogues and historical antecedents will be on. To a certain extent, it is already suggested by studies of shamanic experiences within certain cultures which appear to contain an intriguing number of NDE-like features, including journeys away from the earth and into space. Rasmussen, for example, has drawn attention to the ecstatic experiences of a range of Eskimo shamen whose journey-ings in search of sick tribal members' souls may take them into space, on visits around the earth or to the moon (cited in Eliade 1964: 289–92). Indeed, such a comparison between the experi-ences of NDErs and shamans is further suggested when the contexts in which shamanic trances are entered is considered. Of the *angakok*'s entry into this state, Eliade has written that:

> Sometimes the shaman's otherworld journey takes place during a cataleptic trance that has every appearance of death. Such was the case with an Alaskan shaman who declared that he had been dead and had followed the road of the dead for two days; it was well trodden by all those who had preceded him. As he walked on, he heard continual weeping and wailing; he learned that it was the living mourning their dead. He came to a big village, which was exactly like a village of the living; there, two shades took him into a house. A fire was burning in the

middle of it, with some pieces of meat broiling on the coals, but they had living eyes that followed the shaman's movements. His companions told him not to touch the meat (a shaman who had once tasted food in the land of the dead would find it hard to return to earth). After resting for a time in the village, the *angakok* pursued his journey, reached the Milky Way, followed it for a long time, and finally came down on his own grave. When he re-entered his body it came back to life, and, leaving the graveyard, he went to his village and narrated his adventures.

(Eliade 1964: 291–2)

To be sure, the sheer complexity and diversity of shamanic practices and reports of otherworld journeyings makes over-simplistic comparisons between their experiences and those of NDErs problematical. As well as flights to outer space, for example, shamans in various cultural contexts enter other worlds via descents into the sea or into the centre of the earth for various purposes. Few – if any – NDErs report anything like such experiences. Nonetheless, parallels between certain elements narrated by NDErs and the experiences reported from within at least some shamanic contexts suggest that there may be some usefulness in pursuing the comparison. The fact that the NDE is so inherently transformative may even suggest a comparison with experiences surrounding shamanic *initiation*. In a wider context, discussions of the intriguing possibility that the NDE represents a contemporary resurgence of shamanism in a variety of secular Western contexts – its democratization, perhaps – raises all sorts of very interesting issues surrounding the directions which twenty-first-century spirituality is likely to take. All of these issues may usefully be reserved for future researchers – *if* the RERC studies' conclusions in this regard should turn out to be anything other than anomalous.

Another conclusion clearly drawn concerns the overwhelmingly *positive* nature of the experiences described. In very many cases, as we have seen, subjects in the midst of episodes of life-threatening crisis are literally transformed by encounters with benign presences, often described in terms of their brightness and calming effects. Lives are frequently and dramatically changed by such experiences – whether they contain lights or not – and fear of death often decreases significantly: even if subjects were not near death at the time their episodes occurred. What the light really is in itself may be impossible to determine: that was certainly the conclusion of chapter 3 of this book, and the findings of the RERC study have not shed any real additional light on the subject. However, the consistently positive and unforgettable nature of the experiences engendered by exposure to the light cannot be passed over without a final comment. Whatever its true identity may turn out to be, the light seems invariably to be good *for* us and *to* us: at least, that has been the testimony of a large number of respondents examined over the course of these pages. It is surely impossible to remain unmoved by such accounts. For many, it may have become equally impossible to remain entirely fearful of death, in the face of such abundant testimony which suggests that dying may, after all, be gain.

7

BUILDING BRIDGES OR FIGHTING WARS?

Religion, spirituality and the future
of near-death studies

Religious wars

In the summer of the year 2000, at the beginning of a new millennium, a quarter of a century after the initial publication of Raymond Moody's *Life After Life*, a spate of articles appeared in the *Journal of Near-Death Studies* (*JN-DS*) surrounding the outbreak of so-called 'religious wars' within the 'NDE movement'. These lengthy articles filled two complete numbers of the *Journal* and revealed that a number of the world's pioneering near-death researchers had arrived at major disagreements concerning, of all things, religion. The first shots in the conflict had in fact been fired two years previously by Michael Sabom in his book *Light and Death*. In it, readers who had been impressed by his religiously neutral and theologically non-partisan earlier work, *Recollections of Death*, may have been surprised to find that the same author was now espousing a particularly conservative Christian interpretation of NDEs. In fact, a major inspiration behind *Light and Death* was Sabom's concern about the directions that near-death studies had been taking in the years between this and his previous work. What surprised many about Sabom's latest book, however, were the adverse comments aimed in it at some of his co-researchers. Fellow NDE pioneer Raymond Moody, for example, was criticized for his experiments with mirror-gazing at his self-constructed psychomanteum at his home in Alabama, experiments which constituted the subject matter of his 1993 study, *Reunions*, and which provoked Sabom's comment that 'The Raymond Moody I knew was a medical doctor, not a witch doctor' (Sabom 1998: 145). Sabom was also to describe as a 'dog-and-pony-show' a spiritualistic-style meeting in which Moody had appeared on an Atlanta stage with one George Anderson who claimed to be able to bring messages for the audience from the 'other side' (Sabom 1998: 144).

Even more damning was Sabom's criticism of the work of two other pioneers of near-death studies: Maurice Rawlings and Kenneth Ring. Whilst Rawlings was criticized for alleged mis-handling of data and a subsequent failure to correct his mistakes in future studies even when these were pointed out to him, Ring was criticized for a range of things. On one level, Sabom appeared to have misgivings about the nature of the selection and interviewing of respondents chosen by Ring to provide data for his previous books. As regards *Heading Toward Omega*, for example, Sabom was to allege in *Light and Death* that:

> A highly select group of 20 or so near-death experiencers was interviewed by Ken 'to glean the real, hidden meaning of these NDEs.' These interviews consisted of 'informal but far-ranging conversations' during which 'strong feelings of love' were exchanged – emotions that Ken later admitted 'transcended the usual relationship between interviewer and interviewee'.
>
> (Sabom 1998: 134)

As regards the relationship of Ring to the wider world of near-death studies, Sabom was to make further critical allegations, even to the extent of claiming that Ring was proposing a 'new religion' of 'spiritual universalism' to be built on the foundation of the findings of much near-death research, especially his own (Sabom 1998: 135). Indeed, Sabom was also highly critical in *Light and Death* of Ring's and IANDS's own 'compromising' influence over the directions taken and subsequent conclusions drawn by friends and fellow NDE researchers such as Margot Grey, Chuck Flynn, Cherie Sutherland and Phyllis Atwater (Sabom 1998: 137).

In the summer 2000 issue of the *Journal of Near-Death Studies* Kenneth Ring responded at length to many of these charges. In a paper entitled 'Religious Wars in the NDE Movement: Some Personal Reflections on Michael Sabom's *Light and Death*', Ring vigorously refuted many of Sabom's accusations, denying the charge that he wanted to start a new religion, refuting the allegation that he had somehow assumed the *de facto* leadership of near-death studies, whilst objecting throughout to the style and tone of Sabom's latest work. Much of the paper, however, was devoted to Ring's *own* observations and regrets regarding the direction and position taken by near-death studies over the question of religion. In particular, he cited the directions taken by many Christian responses to the NDE, singling out Maurice Rawlings for special criticism. Agreeing with Sabom that Rawlings's work displayed 'methodological weaknesses, shoddy scholarship, and blatant religious bias' (Ring 2000: 237), Ring argued that Rawlings's lack of theological impartiality and his (mis)use of the NDE for apologetic ends

> does not exactly add anything of value to the field of near-death research; on the contrary, it only detracts from it by serving as ideological fodder – *disguised* as research – for the religious wars that elements of the conservative Christian community wish to wage on the NDE movement.
>
> (Ring 2000: 239)

Elsewhere, and in similar vein, Ring was to criticize the 'overt religious fervour' of many IANDS meetings, commenting, with obvious disdain, 'I sometimes have the feeling I am at a kind of revival meeting' (Ring 2000: 234–5). Overall, he regretted the fact that 'the body of the NDE, like some sort of sacred relic or corrupted corpse, is fought over by warring parties either for rights of possession or unceremonious burial' (Ring 2000: 240), and ended with some suggestions for future directions in which religion might respond to the claims of NDErs, particularly those which sought to avoid 'partisan denominationalism' in favour of a recognition that the phenomenon 'shines with the Light that ultimately leads us back to God' (Ring 2000: 243).

In the same *Journal* issue, Sabom replied to Ring's criticisms of his latest work. Responding to fifteen excerpts from Ring's paper, he reasserted his original positions, including his claim that Ring was attempting to start a new kind of religion and his original observations regarding the influence of Ring upon the direction taken by much near-death research within IANDS. In particular, Sabom drew attention to the need for a thoroughly Biblical interpretation of the NDE, writing towards the close of his response to Ring that 'the truth of the Bible is my one presupposition' as regards the meaning and true nature of NDEs (Sabom 2000a: 268). Poignantly, Sabom closed on a regretful, personal note to Ring that 'our differences have severely strained our friendship'. 'Although we disagree on major issues involving the NDE', he added, 'I have always valued you as a friend and gifted researcher. I look forward to our meeting again' (Sabom 2000a: 269).

The next issue of the *JN-DS* appeared to offer little hope of this. In the fall 2000 issue the *Journal* was again given over almost entirely to the ongoing 'religious wars', with an opening article by Gracia Fay Ellwood responding directly to Sabom's closing article from the previous issue. Here, commenting on the Ring–Sabom dialogue of the summer, Ellwood observed that religious tensions within near-death studies appeared to 'have exploded into hostile exchanges', before examining a number of Sabom's contentions from her own perspective of academic theology (Ellwood 2000: 6). In particular, she argued that the Bible is 'highly ambivalent' on the subject of psychic phenomena. Sabom's position both in *Light and Death* and his *JN-DS* article had been that the Bible forbade deliberate engagement in such practices and condemned any attempts made to contact the dead spiritualistically or by some other comparable method (Ellwood 2000: 18). Ellwood's response to this was to cite the complexities involved in interpreting what the Bible says on such matters, whilst contesting the position that the Biblical and religious prohibitions which *do* exist – such as those found in Exodus 22:18 and Micah 5:12 – should be allowed to hinder any vital area of research: including that undertaken in an attempt to discover the fate of the soul after death. She also maintained that certain scriptural passages, such as Jesus's knowing the thoughts of others (Luke 9:22) and his calling of the dead back to life (Mark 5:21–42), express an ambivalence concerning the subject of psychic experience which appears to offset somewhat the prophetic prohibitions (Ellwood 2000: 18).

In common with Sabom, Ellwood recognized in her piece the need for some sort of yardstick and criterion against which to interpret the true meaning and value of the NDE, but questioned the hermeneutical adequacy of Sabom's position regarding the straightforward use of the Bible and the example of Jesus for this purpose, arguing that

> the huge body of mainline Biblical scholarship shows that this supposedly clear and objective criterion is profoundly multivalent [and] that the Biblical Jesus is in fact a number of interpretations, some mutually inconsistent, based on memories two or three decades old of the works and teachings of a founder who did not record his own message. . . .
>
> (Ellwood 2000: 14)

Overall, her conclusion suggested her own ambivalence about the meaning and implications – theological and otherwise – of a phenomenon that was now causing so much dissent amongst its earliest and still most respected researchers.

Sabom's own response to Ellwood – in the same issue – simply served to underscore how high feelings were now running within the ongoing debate. Containing none of the cautious ambivalence of Ellwood's own contribution, Sabom's piece consisted mainly of a reiteration and attempted reinforcement of his previously expressed positions in *Light and Death* and the previous issue of the *JN-DS*, whilst clearly demonstrating the distances that had by now come to separate the various camps. Sabom's conclusion, that 'there is only one God and one truth, and His truth is revealed in the Bible', showed that he had not modified his position in the light of Ellwood's attempt to bring a degree of hermeneutical sophistication to the debate (Sabom 2000b: 42). In addition, he re-emphasized his earlier contentions that some NDErs and others who deliberately seek experience of a psychic or spiritualistic nature may well make contact with deceiving demons. 'To dismiss casually', he wrote, 'the very real possibility, if not probability, that "familiar spirits" appearing during an NDE may in fact be demonic deceptions is to ignore the evidence blindly' (Sabom 2000b: 31). Indeed, in addition to drawing attention to what he clearly perceived as the dangers inherent in such allegedly occult involvement, Sabom also reiterated his position in reply to Ellwood that Truth and Salvation are exclusively found in and through Jesus Christ. Whilst acknowledging that differing denominations may indeed 'embrace diverse approaches' to this, Sabom repeated his consistently maintained position that '*only* Jesus Christ is Lord, and that *only* through Christ is salvation received' (Sabom 2000b: 37).

Playful paranormalism

By the autumn of 2000, therefore, it appeared to observers that the religious war might either rumble on indefinitely or become mired in the winter mud with its participants as far apart as ever. To add to the debate, however, Raymond Moody had the previous year made a contribution of his own to the *fin de siècle* interpretation of the NDE and related phenomena in his book *The Last Laugh*. Here, the founding father of near-death studies showed himself to be at odds with a number of participants in the wider NDE debate, including some religious participants, and he began his work by bewailing the dead-ends which twenty-five years of study of the NDE had produced. Indeed, no less than three responses to the phenomenon, he argued, have got us nowhere throughout the whole history of the NDE movement. The point of *The Last Laugh*, as he was to make plain at the outset, was to break up the 'logjam' and get things moving again.

Throughout this study – arguably his most controversial to date – Moody was to expend considerable frustration at the failed responses to the NDE phenomenon that had prevailed throughout the previous twenty-five years. These responses – from professional parapsychologists, sceptics and fundamentalist Christians alike – have all combined, wrote Moody, to seal up the study of NDEs in a number of blind alleys that have only served to *prevent* academics from understanding such experiences for what they really are. On one level, he wrote, *parapsychology* has made the NDE the subject of a number of academic careers that would be abruptly terminated if an answer to the enigma that it poses were ever to be found. On another, the professional sceptics who comprise groups like the Committee for the Scientific Investigation of Claims of the Paranormal were also castigated for subscribing to a narrow 'scientism' masking a deeper 'social crusade' which contained 'a sinister, authoritarian, design' (Moody 1999: 49). Fundamentalist Christians, however, drew Moody's fiercest criticism, being variously described as 'goshawful deadfannies, stiffs, bores, nuisances, uptight dogmatists, broken records, and wet blankets', not least because of their insistence that the NDE may represent a satanic ploy designed to lure the unwary into what is in reality a deceiving, demonic light (Moody 1999: x).

Moody's suggested way ahead for near-death studies was what he dubbed 'playful paranormalism'. This would, he wrote, free the log jam created by the 'rules of engagement' hitherto adopted by the 'dead end' parties and thus, in turn, take the study of the paranormal generally and NDEs in particular in new and more fruitful directions. What these might be, however, seemed unclear. Playful paranormalists, he wrote, are those for whom the paranormal is seen primarily as *entertainment*. However, there is more to it simply than this, for such a view of paranormal-as-play may also enable us to discover something about a realm which he described, somewhat ambiguously, as being 'alluringly unknown' (Moody 1999: 87). Seen in this way, for Moody, what begins as entertainment may actually culminate in *revelation*.

Followers of Moody's published output since *Life After Life* may have detected in *The Last Laugh* something of a major shift: particularly in his declaration that, as regards NDEs:

> I never assumed myself to be reporting the experiences of people *after* death, nor have I ever reached the conclusion that because people were having certain kinds of experiences when they were near to death, an ongoing 'life' after death had now been proven beyond question.
>
> (Moody 1999: 8)

Indeed, in *The Last Laugh*, he himself went to major lengths to *disavow* such a notion. In fact, he wrote, it was just such a set of observations and conclusions as those presented in *The Last Laugh* which the publishers would *not* allow him to present in his earlier books. So insistent was he that this should be understood, that he declared 'Effective immediately, *The Last Laugh* should be incorporated into the earlier book [*Life After Life*] for all purposes of reading, discussion, or scholarship' (Moody 1999: ix). Henceforth, therefore, it seemed that he wanted it to constitute a little annexe or appendix; Moody declared that 'I'll accept responsibility for *Life After Life* only insofar as it is read and interpreted in the broader context provided by this new, required, supplement' (Moody 1999: ix).

What was the reader to make of all of *this*, coming as it did from the man who had done more than anybody else to familiarize the twentieth century with the phenomenon of the NDE and whose seminal first study had contained, as we have seen, the bold claim on its cover that it contained 'actual case histories that reveal there is life after death'? In the light of the erupting religious war, supporters of his position might have agreed that polarized and entrenched opinions can do little to move the understanding and interpretation of the NDE in fruitful and productive directions, yet there was something about *The Last Laugh* that was deeply unappealing, even unsettling. Moody was surely right, for example, to decry the failed attempts to explain the NDE which had led to the dead-ends he described. Yet his preferred way out of it might have appeared to some to be unconvincing. Undoubtedly the paranormal *is* entertaining, as Moody avowed. Yet surely there is more to it than this, particularly when it is considered that its exponents – including supporters of the view that during an NDE *something* leaves the body – attempt to make empirically verifiable claims about possible supernatural realities. Serious scientists are surely right to take such claims seriously, and even, if persuaded, to test them as appropriate. Moody appeared to denounce such approaches, however, describing parapsychologists as 'pseudo-scientists [who] espouse a system of methods and assumptions they erroneously regard as scientific' (Moody 1999: ix). It is unfortunate that here – as elsewhere throughout *The Last Laugh* – Moody offered no examples of 'pseudo-scientists' working in the field. A critic might have been forgiven for concluding, however, that such subtleties as this were simply lost on Moody, so anxious was he to criticize – often, as in the case of fundamentalist Christians, quite distastefully and crudely – those positions which he was at pains to contrast with his own.

Most significantly, however, Moody signally failed to tell the reader precisely what 'wonderfully fresh knowledge' of the 'alluringly unknown' might be revealed via playful paranormalism. Like so much else in *The Last Laugh*, this was passed over virtually in silence, with no examples cited and not even a set of notes and references to give the reader a sense of where to look. In his preface to the book, Neale Donald Walsch, author of the equally controversial *Conversations with God*, thanked 'Raymond' for 'once again leading the way' (Moody 1999: vii). Critics of Moody's latest book might have been forgiven, however, for viewing it as tasteless, badly written, under-referenced and lacking in concrete examples or supporting evidence for its frequently controversial claims.

Building bridges

In its sustained denunciation of fundamentalist Christian responses to NDEs, *The Last Laugh* had also, intentionally or unintentionally, fired its own salvos within the religious wars. Moody, however, was to play no part in the flurry of academic exchanges that continued in the pages of the *JN-DS*. Instead, as we have seen, this was to be left to others, primarily Ring and Sabom. Indeed, in the light of the apparently deep divisions which separated these two most respected figures in the field of near-death research, and considering the amount of debate which their very public disagreement had begun to generate, it seemed that as regards matters of religion and theology the field of near-death studies was beginning to resemble a house divided against itself. And there, currently, the matter still largely stands.

To a certain extent, the fault for this must lie with philosophy and theology and their failure to engage in any sustained way with the findings of near-death studies. Indeed, this failure called forth, in part, the current work. In bringing it to a close, therefore, it will be useful to point to where it has attempted to build some much needed bridges between religion, theology, philosophy and the NDE. As a result of *this*, it may also be possible to determine where additional bridges may also be built. For one conclusion that this study has led to is that there are vast areas of research into the mystery and complexity of the NDE still to be done. In closing, therefore, it seems both useful and appropriate to end by proposing where *future* bridges may be built: between the parties involved in the so-called religious war, between religion, theology, philosophy and the NDE, and between knowledge of the NDE already gained, and knowledge of the NDE still to be found.

A matter of interpretation

Much of the debate surrounding the NDE, it is clear, has centred on the issue of its correct *interpretation*. Indeed, many of the arguments we have encountered have revolved around the correctly perceived need for an adequate theological and/or spiritual lens through which to view and explain all aspects of the phenomenon. The wider-angle view presented by the current study, however, has in fact shown the situation to be much more complex than this. For whilst the range of existing religious and theological responses can indeed be fitted into the confines of a single chapter, that chapter (chapter 2) showed that even such a limited range was, in fact, very wide in scope: in places moving way outside the West's Christian traditions altogether. As was seen, NDEs and NDE-like experiences can be accommodated and interpreted within a global range of philosophical, religious and other traditions, many of them appealing to quite different and divergent scriptures and traditions and ranging from Mysticism, Eastern Orthodoxy and Conservative Christianity through to Orthodox Judaism, Gnosticism and Tibetan Buddhism. It is certainly difficult, as that chapter made clear, to reconcile such a diverse range of traditions and world views into an overarching interpretative framework: one that, somehow, does justice to them all.

Indeed, and in part arising from these simple recognitions, two conclusions arise. First, it is clear that NDEs cannot unambiguously be used as apologetic tools for the propagation of any one particular religious or spiritual tradition or be somehow fitted into any one tradition to the exclusion of all others. Instead, the NDE appears upon analysis to be inherently *protean*: either by virtue of its ability, somehow, to accommodate itself to a variety of different and conflicting religious traditions or by virtue of its being adopted and interpreted by them in accordance with their own distinctive theologies and world views. Attempting to adjudicate between differing religious cooptions and/or interpretations of the NDE is fraught with obvious difficulties in this regard: again because of the very real differences which exist between the traditions in which the NDE is found and because of the apparent impossibility – unless an exclusivist position such as Sabom's is adopted – of finding some criterion or standpoint from which to interpret the NDE which stands, somehow, above them all.

Of course, this recognition does *not* automatically imply that no one tradition's interpretation – and hence understanding – of the NDE can be said to be better than any other. If, for example, NDEs should turn out eventually to *prove* rather than *presuppose* some form of body–mind dualism, then religions and/or spiritual traditions which recognize and support *this* view of personhood might be said to be better positioned to understand the NDE correctly than those which incline towards monism: or at least be better placed to use the NDE as an apologetic tool for the defence of this particular aspect of their teachings. But this is a big 'if', as the current study has also shown.

Mindsight

For as we have seen, despite a quarter-century of near-death studies, the question as to whether the NDE *does* prove some form of body–soul dualism has yet to be fully answered to everybody's satisfaction. This needs to be spelled out loudly and clearly: *twenty-five years after the coining of the actual phrase 'near-death experience', it remains to be established beyond doubt that during such an experience anything actually leaves the body.* To date, and claims to the contrary notwithstanding, no researcher has provided evidence for such an assertion of an acceptable standard which would put the matter beyond doubt. This fact alone, together with the confidence with which at the end of the current study it can be asserted, should itself be something which gives theologians and philosophers in particular pause for thought.

As its own contribution to this crucial area of enquiry, the current study chose to focus on a small but fascinating body of research surrounding what might usefully be described as hard cases in this regard: research deriving from veteran NDE researcher

Kenneth Ring and co-researcher Sharon Cooper claiming that during their NDEs blind and in some cases congenitally blind persons have received the temporary gift of sight. If true, such claims promise to put the existence of some sort of extra-bodily aspect of the self – together with the possibility of its surviving the death of the body – beyond reasonable doubt. For this reason, the evidence presented in support of this set of startling assertions was examined in detail. As a result, what had initially seemed to be extremely promising and potentially revelatory research turned out to be incapable of providing adequate support for the assertions it made, and this, as chapter 5 showed, for a variety of reasons which were presented there in detail. Overall, despite exhibiting considerable bravery in conducting and publishing research surrounding such startling claims, it was clear that upon analysis Ring and his collaborators had failed to clinch beyond reasonable doubt what at first sight seemed to offer some of the most convincing evidence that NDEs *do* indeed prove – and do not simply presuppose – an actual ontological distinction between body and soul.

Neuroscience and the NDE

Whilst such a conclusion may be expected to be of considerable disappointment to those who see in the NDE proof positive of survival of bodily death, those proponents of the view that the NDE takes place, somehow, in the mind's eye may perhaps view it in some small sense as vindication for *their* position. This, as we have seen, has certainly been the position of neuroscientists such as Ronald Siegel and Susan Blackmore who have sought to explain the NDE by recourse to a series of ever more sophisticated neuroscientific hypotheses. For critics of such a position, however, these attempts to account for every feature of the NDE by recourse to neuroscientific mental models are reductionist at best. At worst, they may be viewed as yet one more attempt by sceptical researchers to deny the existence of any phenomena that do not fit into conventional, narrow, naturalistic and materialistic ways of seeing and understanding the world.

However, the current study may be seen to have given such critics some cause for celebration. For, as chapter 4 showed, despite a quarter-century of discussion surrounding the precise neurological mechanism underlying the NDE, no currently existing single-factor theory such as the influence of drugs or anoxia is sufficient to explain every feature of the core NDE phenomena as they are reported worldwide. Neither, as that chapter also showed, can the multiple-factor models presented by Siegel and Blackmore explain every feature of the experiences reported by many thousands of NDErs. And as the RERC study confirmed, whilst Blackmore's NDE model may indeed be neuroscientifically consistent, it is unable to account phenomenologically for the experiences of a large number of NDErs. And this cluster of findings needs to be spelled out loudly and clearly too: *at present, no total neuro-scientific 'explanation' of even the most basic and consistently encountered features of an NDE is sufficient to adequately explain them.* Of course, this is not intended to imply that no neuroscientific model will ever emerge which explains the core elements of the NDE to everybody's satisfaction. It *does* remain the case, however, that no contemporary neuroscientific framework currently advanced in order to explain the NDE is able to explain very many experiences reported by NDErs. Thus, whilst NDEs remain theoretically explainable by science, they are at present *un*explained by it.

One reason for this, quite apart from the simple shortcomings of the current models advanced by neuroscientists, is the fact that such models are being pressed into service in order to explain *stories*, and as chapter 4 again showed, NDErs do not return from 'death' with models or neuroscientific composites but with *testimonies*. At the very least, therefore, any hypothesis or series of hypotheses which attempts to explain the NDE but which fails to consider the intricacies involved when experience makes the transition from event(s) to testimony may be said to have over-looked the very real complexities involved in such a process. Within this process, it may even be said to be the case that interpretation of the NDE takes a new twist: for now, well-recognized phenomena such as *emplotment* and *intertextuality* may need to be considered: phenomena, that is, recognized in academic provinces far removed from neuroscience, but closer to the domains inhabited by philosophers and academic theologians with their own rich academic traditions of interpreting and appropriating testimonies of various kinds – including those dealing with journeys to other worlds.

Otherworld journeys

Such recognitions have certainly not been lost on the handful of academic theologians and religious studies specialists who *have* responded to the NDE. Of these, as we have seen, Carol Zaleski seeks like many neuroscientists to locate the NDE within the mind's eye, but her preferred way of expressing this is in terms of the culturally conditioned religious imagination which perennially creates and shapes other worlds for us to live in. To be sure, Zaleski is aware, as many neuroscientists are not, of the role of factors such as intertextuality and emplotment in the composition of many kinds of testimony, near-death testimony included. Thus, her understanding of the processes which underlie the compo-sition of otherworld journey narratives – particularly those of medieval visionaries – includes the shaping of such texts by those to whom the story is told *en route* from deathbed to testimony, together with the role of culturally sanctioned religious expecta-tion in the production of visionaries' final stories. However, despite her reticence to commit herself unreservedly to a natural-istic interpretation of near-death testimonies and her sustained attempt to avoid reductionism, it is difficult to escape from the conclusion that her relegation of the NDE to the religious imagination *is* a tacit acceptance that the NDE, after all, exists only in the mind's eye. Such agnosticism notwithstanding, a key contribution that Zaleski has made to our understanding of the NDE, as chapter 2 again showed, is her locating of the NDE in a realm which avoids both a philosophically unacceptable dualism on the one hand and a simple discarding of the data on the other. Instead, by seeking to locate the NDE within the realm of the culturally conditioned religious imagination – and as, essentially, a culturally created and sanctioned artefact of that imagination – Zaleski has opened up a rich seam of investigation for theology to mine. For as she is fully aware, theology has a long and full tradition of investigating the symbols, stories and themes which the human religious imagination has long composed, revived and renewed. Indeed, it is precisely within this context that she locates theology's own distinctive role within near-death studies. For here, she asserts, theology truly comes into its own as a discipline for detecting the vitality of the symbols and stories which emerge and in turn feed the religious imagination.

Within this context, as we have seen, theology therefore becomes for Zaleski therapeutic instead of theoretic. In this way, she writes, 'it is easier to come to terms with religious change while maintaining respect for tradition' (Zaleski 1987: 194). Clearly, such a sensitivity to a range of areas in which theology maintains such expertise may be expected to reveal rich insights into a wide range of religious and spiritual writing, including near-death testimony. Indeed, Zaleski's own theological response to the NDE is proof and evidence of this, as chapter 2 again showed. At the end of this study, however, we might reasonably conclude that in granting theology such a carefully defined role, and by freeing it from the relationships which it has traditionally enjoyed with other, related, disciplines, Zaleski has in fact defined theology's and religious studies' part in the investigation too *narrowly*.

For as previous chapters of this book have revealed, these disciplines can do far more than assess the potency of religious symbols and symbol-systems, particularly when they choose to work in concert with their sister-disciplines. Theologians, for example, can collect data of their own and conduct their own critical investigation of near-death claims, as Johann Christophe Hampe has done and as the RERC study attempted in chapter 6. Sensitivity to phenomenological approaches to religious texts – including testimonies – can help ensure that neuroscientific model-building restricts itself to producing theoretical frameworks which do justice to experiences people actually report and have. Narrative theology can explore ways in which emplotment turns experience into story. Psychology of religion can make its own contributions to exploring naturalistically the aetiology of the NDE, responding and contributing to the valuable insights provided by secular neuroscience. Sociology of religion can investigate the social and cultural forces that call forth the need for new myths when old myths lose their power. Philosophy of religion can test the epistemological accuracy and phenomenological cogency of the claim that a common core underlies the variety of reported religious experiences across cultures, including, of course, the NDE. And so on.

The RERC study

Without near-death testimonies, there would, of course, be no such thing as near-death studies. The request for *further* evidence of such experiences, such as a piece of the pearly gates or a photograph of any NDEr's claim to an encounter with deceased relatives, sounds as absurd as it surely is. In the light of the recognition that *testimonies* to NDEs are all we possess, near-death researcher Robert Kastenbaum is surely right to draw attention to the crucial issue of whether an NDE is, in fact, an experience or a *report* of an experience. His conclusion, that it is the latter, opens up, for him and for us, a number of crucial questions. 'A report', he writes, 'is a communication', and as such has been constructed according to certain rules. Investigators who begin with this recognition are therefore rather like students of other types of religious testimonies, such as those given by converts, who heed James Beckford's advice to view such narratives not as portals revealing raw experience but as accomplishments of actor/narrators who have composed their self-stories as a result of radical transformations of identity (Bailey and Yates 1996: 250).

In a very real sense, Kastenbaum's challenge to researchers to be aware of the nature of the material with which they are working has been heeded throughout this work. A further suggestion from Kastenbaum, however, that the centrality of such data to NDE research invites ongoing *collection* of NDE testimonies has also been heeded. Thus, the RERC study was devoted to the collection, sorting and analysis of a large number of original NDE accounts, some more than thirty years old. As a result of this analysis, further bridges between the domains of existing near-death research and theological enquiry were opened up. In particular, it became possible for research findings produced from within near-death studies connected with groups such as IANDS to be checked against a different and very distinctive database: that of the Religious Experience Research Centre.

The findings of the RERC study confirmed in many ways some crucial contentions of existing near-death research. Like many other comparable NDE research studies, for example, the RERC study found few negative NDEs. It also confirmed the large body of existing research that has shown overwhelmingly positive fruits manifesting in the lives of NDErs and caused by their NDEs. Common elements found across a large number of cases were also discovered, with reports of out-of-body experiences, feelings of bliss and peace, and encounters with light significantly prevalent. To be sure, the *degree* of commonality discerned across the crisis accounts examined within the study revealed a small average number of Moody's common elements per testimony. In view of this, the study concluded that more general models of NDEs such as the five-stage model advanced by Kenneth Ring and confirmed by Margot Grey might be prefered to Moody's more complex model. Nonetheless, and without reproducing the entire findings of the RERC study, it is useful here to reiterate the study's concluding assertion that a recognizable number of NDE features were found to recur in a great many experiences. Given this finding, it is of importance within the overall conclusion of the present study to draw attention to the fact that a number of structured, relatively consistent testimonies, resembling in several crucial respects what have come to be known as near-death experiences, were revealed by the RERC study: a significant finding, even if taken singly and by itself.

The RERC study also appeared to *disconfirm* some popular notions surrounding NDEs. Significant in this regard were the large number of recognizable NDE features which also occurred in circumstances apparently far removed from bodily death. The implications of this, whilst already discussed at length, are surely significant for future research, not least for future attempts to model the NDE neuroscientifically. The descriptor 'tunnel' for the experience of darkness was also challenged, confirming a similar contention made by sociologist Allan Kellehear but countering the popular notion that NDEs provide concrete illustration of the old adage that there is, indeed, light at the end of the tunnel. Indeed, the findings of the RERC study were distinctly anomalous in this sense, revealing that 'outer space' was a descriptor favoured above more traditional descriptions, such as tunnels and shafts. Also anomalous was the finding that experiences could be mixed in feeling-tone, with negative experiences becoming positive as they unfolded in a small but potentially significant number of cases.

Avenues for future research

The contention that some NDEs may become more positive in feeling-tone as they unfold opens up a testable hypothesis for future research. For it may be the case that there is a direct correlation between complexity – depth – of experience, and its overall mood. Such a hypothesis, whether right or wrong, is surely testable, both in the light of existing data and data still to be collected. Indeed, one further consistent assertion made throughout this book has been that there is still a colossal amount of near-death research to be done by persons working within very many academic disciplines. In describing the bridges which the current study has been attempting to build, it is perhaps fitting at its close to suggest some bridges which remain to be built: not least between NDE research as it stands and NDE research still to be done.

As will have become clear, the current state of near-death studies is such that our understanding of NDEs when viewed from certain key academic perspectives is either incomplete or needful of greater depth of analysis and investigation. Neuroscience is the obvious example here, yet there are many other areas of ignorance that might also be listed. The intriguing number of shared NDEs, in which persons attending the death of another share certain experiences such as the appearance of an unusual light, offers the possibility, at least to a certain extent, of corroboration of NDErs' experiences. Specific additional collection of this variant of NDE testimony may provide fresh avenues for future research. Corroboration of the frequently reported out-of-body aspect of NDErs' experiences might also be obtained via large-scale, systematic research of the type suggested by theologian Paul Badham and discussed in chapter 2; that is, the locating at vantage points on and around operating theatre and intensive care ceilings of distinctive objects which, whilst normally invisible, would be visible to persons who were, somehow, able to leave their bodies and move freely around. Despite criticisms levelled at existing attempts to prove such possible dualism through recourse to hard cases such as those of blind NDErs, this study has in no sense brought closure to the debate surrounding the question as to whether NDEs prove the existence of the human soul or not. Indeed, the question remains very much open, and still awaits definitive closure. Experiments of the type proposed by Badham would appear to promise to settle the matter for good. Indeed, perhaps the most surprising gap in the quarter-century history of near-death studies is that which surrounds this very obvious avenue of investigation. It is to be hoped that the next quarter-century of near-death studies might go some way towards rectifying the startling lack of research in this and similar regards. Collection of more NDE hard cases, including those of blind NDErs, will surely also help resolve issues surrounding the dualism question, as well as providing potential support (or disconfirmation) of the existing studies in this regard of Ring and Cooper.

Chapter 2 highlighted another significant gap in the current understanding of NDEs in its noting of the surprising fact that a significant number of religions (and theologians) have simply failed to respond to the claims of NDErs. As a result of this, near-death studies has not been able to benefit from the rich perspectives upon NDEs which might have been expected to emerge from within some of the world's great religions such as Judaism, Islam and Hinduism. This has been to the detriment of our overall understanding of the phenomenon, for such old and venerable traditions contain their own wide range of theological tools and resources that might usefully be applied within the distinctive context of contemporary near-death studies. Islam, for example, has long recognized the depth, validity and significance of approaches to God which have arisen within the Sufi mystical tradition. As a result, Muslim theologians have devoted great skill and energy to the investigation of mystical experience within this context. The application of such interpretative tools to the NDE, or even a comparison of the experiences of Sufi mystics with those of NDErs, awaits attention, and contemporary Muslim theologians are ideally placed to take up the task. It is to be hoped that in the next quarter-century of near-death studies these and other exciting challenges will be tackled and fully met.

Indeed, the comparison of the NDE with other types of religious experience is another area of investigation that might justifiably be said to be in its infancy. As this study has showed, attempts at comparisons between NDEs and other types of religious experience – such as Judith Cressy's attempt at comparing the experiences of contemporary NDErs with the historical experiences of Christian mystics – have been made but infrequently. Chapter 3 of this book opened up the exciting possibility that a cross-cultural common core to the NDE may indeed exist, and, contesting the view that the NDE is simply a product of language and expectation, concluded that such a core may exist independently of culture and tradition. Despite the acknowledged difficulties of asserting what that core is in itself, such a conclusion surely invites a further comparison between NDEs and other types of religious experience. For perhaps a discernible common core can be found across a *range* of religious experiences, including NDEs, and not just within and between the testimonies of NDErs themselves. Surely, the existence of such a core would be a tremendous and potentially hugely significant discovery in itself. The attempt to compare a range of testimonies to different types of religious experience in search of such a core would also require a number of skills which would mark out theologians as particularly suited to the challenge, not least because of their sensitivity to phenomenological approaches to testimony and their knowledge of the wide variety of religious experiences which exist. However, this is not just a challenge and opportunity for theologians alone; for many other academic disciplines possess a wide variety of tools ideally suited to the investigation and comparison of testimonies to religious experiences within and across traditions.

This conclusion, in turn, serves to reinforce the view that the NDE has been ignored within many disciplines ideally suited to its investigation. David Hufford's seminal folkloristic analysis of supernatural assault traditions – the so-called 'Old Hag' phenomenon – within Newfoundland and across cultures revealed some years ago that a common core to such experiences exists which cannot be ascribed either to cultural diffusion or prior acquaintance with the tradition (Hufford 1982). Fascinating as this fact is in itself, Hufford's study also stands as a first-rate example of the role that folkloristics can play in the analysis of testimonies to anomalous experience. Yet folkloristics also stands as a discipline that has yet to respond to the NDE. This is unfortunate, given the vast amount of experience which folklorists possess in the composition of questionnaires, the handling of testimony, the quantitative analysis of data, and the comparison of reports to religious and supernatural experience within and across traditions: all things which Hufford's seminal study demonstrates very well.

Perhaps the biggest question that the present study has left unanswered and one which contemporary researchers in a variety of fields have yet to fully explore is that which surrounds the *timing* of the contemporary wave of interest in NDEs. Put simply: why now? One possibility may be that the current popularity of a wide range of paranormal claims, including NDEs, reflects a wider Western obsession with personal spirituality and transformation, typified by the massive growth in the market for books on self-help and New Age therapies. Another suggestion, offered by sceptical researchers such as those who comprise the Committee for the Scientific Investigation of Claims to the Paranormal (CSICOP), has been that the public's acceptance of a whole range of 'New Age' and paranormal claims is in large part due to a failure to teach science and critical thinking properly. Although CSICOP's concern in this regard is with failures within the *American* educational system, it is not difficult to see how the argument could be extended to help explain the popular acceptance of paranormal claims in the West generally. In addition, some sceptics have also criticized irresponsible behaviour on the part of the Western mass media which exploit the public's apparently insatiable interest in such things (Fox 1996: 27). Jostein Gaarder, whose philosophical novel *Sophie's World* became an unexpected global best-seller in the 1990s, echoes the sceptical position forcefully when he describes New Age literature as 'pornography', reflecting the view of its critics that it is not fit for consumption by normal, well-balanced, healthily educated individuals (Gaarder 1995: 357).

Interesting as this position is, other writers have suggested deeper, potentially more revealing reasons behind the popular appetite for such things. Harold Bloom, for example, sees in the fascination with the New Age generally and NDEs in particular a contemporary mass-market resurgence and debasement of older, Gnostic, claims. Writing in *Omens of Millennium*, for example, he has recently argued that:

The 'near-death experience' is another pre-Millennium phenomenon that travesties Gnosticism; every account we are given of this curious matter culminates in being 'embraced by the light', by a figure of light known to Gnostic tradition variously as 'the astral body', the 'Resurrection Body' or Hermes, our guide in the land of the dead.

(Bloom 1996: 32)

Telling us nothing about the fate of the soul after death, the NDE nonetheless tells a lot, he writes, about how yet another mass consumer 'industry' has sprung up to cater for a mass audience hungry for a 'travesty of ancient verities' (Bloom 1996: 134). Indeed, 'Industry it certainly has become' writes Bloom,

just as the purveyors of angels are a growth item. We now have IANDS (the International Association for Near-Death Studies) which offers maroon T-shirts, and features a logo that intermixes Moody's tunnel with the Taoist emblem of yin and yang. The quarterly put-out is called *Vital Signs*; there are workshops, conventions, study groups, and much else. This sounds rather like a novel by Aldous Huxley or even Evelyn Waugh, but is merely another instance of American millennial hysteria.

(Bloom 1996: 135)

Bloom's response to such 'shenanigans' is somewhat nostalgic: a return 'to the great texts of a purer Gnosticism and their best commentators' (Bloom 1996: 33).

Now that the old millennium has passed, it will be interesting to see whether the omens that Bloom feels to have heralded its passing will vanish also. A wider and potentially more enduring explanation for the NDE's popularity is provided by Allan Kellehear, whose study *Experiences Near Death* (1996) has recently sought in part to locate the NDE within the context of a rich range of changes to have affected Western society since the 1960s, changes which continue to exert a powerful influence upon a number of popular beliefs including those concerning a possible afterlife. Kellehear suggests that a range of factors must be considered to have combined to create fertile ground for the growth of the NDE's popularity in recent years, including the growth of a culture in the West which is now less death-denying than before the 1960s and which has witnessed a massive expansion of the technological abilities to resuscitate the clinically dead. These factors, he writes, have produced a culture that is now more than happy to hear stories from the increasing numbers of people who have almost passed through death's door before 'returning'. In addition, such a culture, with its stresses on the importance of both individuality and personal choice, has ensured that new options for belief in the afterlife are freely available to and embraceable by all, with important decisions about the meaning of life and death being increasingly left to individuals, themselves increasingly suspicious of the old institutional authorities and no longer willing to grant them exclusive, unconditional, obedience. Indeed, such a society, he writes, is increasingly eclectic, encouraging individuals to do their share of 'existential browsing' before deciding which world view (or death view) suits them best. We are thus free to shop around for that which will orientate us to what we perceive to be of ultimate concern, and one result of this may be the mix and match spirituality which is so characteristic of the New Age and its openness to anything that supports tolerance and pluralism. In fact, in an intriguing contention, he goes so far as to suggest that:

> The NDE is the quintessential postmodern idea of death – eclectic in imagery; philosophically accessible to a wide range of beliefs without being particularly harmful to any of them; and critical of broad, singular, and simplistic ideas, whether materialist or religious. It is not an innocuous idea of death but rather a highly adaptable, and hence highly attractive, set of images.
>
> (Kellehear 1996: 91)

Recalling Bloom's critique of the NDE's debasement of earlier, more venerable traditions, we may wonder in the light of this claim whether the NDE is truly capable of being critical of any kind of belief: material, religious or otherwise. Nonetheless Kellehear returns us via a very different route to a key conclusion of the current study: that the NDE is essentially *protean*, offering support to those who favour *inclusivist*, rather than *exclusivist* positions as regards the status of truth-claims made by religions.

Certainly, writes Kellehear, the NDE offers a particularly appealing – some would say beguiling – view of the afterlife to those who find that they cannot wholeheartedly embrace the dogmas of any particular tradition, particularly those that have traditionally presented fearful or frightening pictures of the life to come. He notes that many of the early researchers such as Moody and Ring signally failed to unearth any off-putting negative, hellish NDEs at all. In addition, he writes, the traditional conceptions of the afterlife as a place of stern judgement are replaced in NDE literature by a gentler scenario in which bad deeds cease to be punishable offences and become instead learning experiences. The fact that the heavenly realms described by NDErs, complete with deceased relatives, libraries and green fields, offer such familiar and welcoming scenes has also done much, he writes, to enhance the popularity of the afterlife vistas they contain. So too has the positive view of death which NDEs have brought, complete with the 'powerful image of a possessive and generous being of light' in place of more traditional images of 'dark and cold, with the pallor of sin and the uncertainty of judgement hanging over every traveller' (Kellehear 1996: 80–99).

Contentions such as those of Kellehear and Bloom invite us to view NDEs as *mirrors* reflecting the changing patterns of popular beliefs within the West over the last few decades: a far cry from seeing them as *windows* affording us privileged peeks into our post-mortem destiny. Indeed, this being said, future avenues of research may yet again be seen to exist within this context: this time ideally suited to those with the skills to extend this line of enquiry yet further by exploring the intriguing but as yet largely untested hypothesis that the NDE offers us nothing less than a modern *myth* of death.[1] This opportunity – for cultural anthropologists and students of mythology quite as much as for social scientists and future theologians – would begin with the recognition that the NDE may be telling us far more about this world than other worlds; telling us also that those twentieth-century specialists in the field of mythology such as Joseph Campbell and Carl Jung were right to argue so consistently and so passionately that we have not, after all, abandoned our myth-making past.

There are aspects to the NDE *corpus* that do not lend them-selves easily to the simple view of seeing in this growing body of literature evidence of modern – or postmodern – mythology in the making. Eliade's contention, for example, that the essence of mythology lies in *cosmogony* appears to refute the view of NDE-as-myth, for the current contemporary interest in NDEs seems to reveal a wide popular interest in our individual *destinies* rather than our collective *origins*. Absent too are any traces of rituals that have grown up around the NDE. A myth that is not, somehow, embodied in ritual is a curious myth indeed: yet save for the giving of public testimonies to NDEs at IANDS meetings, there seems little or nothing in the way of ritual accompaniment to the NDE.

This being acknowledged, however, other aspects of the NDE phenomenon seem to support much more closely the contention that we are indeed viewing mythology in the making. At a basic level, NDEs, like myths, are narrative in structure. More specifi-cally, however, the NDE shares with myth a concern to unlock the mystery of death. Indeed, no less an authority than Joseph Campbell placed the need to transcend death at the heart of humankind's need for myth, writing that the 'recognition of mortality and the requirement to transcend it is the first great impulse to mythology' (Campbell 1972: 22). So too is the need to legitimize and to understand certain crucial aspects of the social order by anchoring them to primal or eternal orderings and decrees: in Zaleski's words, answering the question '"Where am I now in relation to the north, south, east and west of the cosmos, the yesterday and tomorrow of history, the higher and lower ranks of being?"' (Zaleski 1987: 203). Her use of the personal pronoun here obscures a little the fact that myths have usually done this on a communal, culture-wide level: however, we have already seen that her own work supports this position. Allan Kellehear is also once again worth listening to here, particularly his attempt in *Experiences Near Death* to explore the kind of 'transcendent societies' disclosed in NDE narratives. Drawing on a popular typology of ideal societies developed by J.C. Davis, Kellehear has sought to determine which of a number of paradigmatic societies the worlds disclosed to NDErs most closely approximate to

(Kellehear 1996: 100–15). Discarding the 'poor man's paradise' of the *cockayne* society, the work-free leisure-dominated *arcadian* society, the individually determined *perfect moral commonwealth* and the apocalyptically transformed saved society of the *millenarians*, Kellehear concludes that the Transcendent Society most frequently disclosed to NDErs most closely matches Davis's fifth category: that of *utopia*. His conclusion, worth reproducing at length, is interesting within the context of the present discussion, for whilst Kellehear stops short of declaring that NDEs simply *are* mythological in the sense of providing legitimization of certain, crucial functions of the social order, it is clear from his observations of what utopias *do* that NDEs viewed as transcendent, utopian societies can be seen to perform very similar functions. Thus he writes:

> The transcendent society and its tales, act as narratives by which we may orient ourselves, our cultures, and our roles and ambitions within them. In these ways, utopias are to adults what fairy tales are to children. They draw on current feelings and problems about the world and inspire both audiences to higher things without ever becoming a dense legislature. This is a commonly observed role of utopian imagery. This inspirational role makes utopias responsible for introducing or renewing a new and better set of human values. In the case of the transcendent society where the values are simply learning, love, and service, the task may arguably be one of renewal and revision.
>
> (Kellehear 1996: 110–11)

There is much more that could be said about the applicability of Kellehear's work to the exploration of the view of NDE-as-myth and particularly to the question of why such myths should be so popular at present. He notes, for example, that the Transcendent Society disclosed in many NDErs' narratives presents us with a particularly postmodern utopia: largely as a result of its incorporation into itself of a number of characteristics more typical of the other types. Thus, for example, the Transcendent Society has elements of the perfect moral commonwealth in its portrayal of the need for individuals to shape and nurture their own values and ideals. Like cockayne conceptions of the ideal society, it presents a world perfected and idyllic but also restrained, as in arcadia. There are even millenarian elements too, such as the presence of religious figures (however they may be seen to deviate in character from traditional expectation), and in at least some accounts elements of a somewhat attenuated and soft eschatology. As a pastiche of these other models therefore, the Transcendent Society depicted in many NDE narratives might be expected to have a broad, popular appeal to many in the contemporary West. In addition, in its implied criticism of many of the dominant values of modernity such as competition and selfishness and its promotion of others such as spirituality and humanism, it has a postmodern appeal: it shares postmodernity's loss of faith in many of the grounding convictions of modernity, including those which have exploited and oppressed the human spirit in the name of greed and the obsession to acquire.

Even this short detour through some of the arguments for and against the view of the NDE as representing a modern (or post-modern) myth of death has revealed enormous scope for future studies. Yet another direction is suggested by Michael Grosso, who, drawing on insights derived from within analytical psychology, views the NDE essentially *as* such an archetype, dubbed by him as the 'archetype of death and enlightenment'. This archetype, he writes, is specifically called forth by the imminent end of life and serves to 'compensate for the ego's onesided view of death' by diminishing fear of it whilst expanding consciousness, pointing towards 'a universal, indestructible spiritual reality' creating an expansion of cognitive abilities and heralding 'a new mode of being, a new birth'. In this way, he asserts, death itself can be transformed and effectively rescued from the 'curse of meaninglessness' that it would otherwise possess (Bailey and Yates 1996: 129–43).

Clearly, viewing the NDE in this way rests largely upon a willingness to view it in terms of Jungian (and post-Jungian) theories of archetypes. For Grosso, however, this is indeed the case. Like encounters with archetypes, he writes, the NDE encounter has a numinous quality and may result in the acquisition of paranormal powers. Again in common with archetypes, he asserts,

NDEs occur autonomously and are activated when consciousness is at its weakest. Further, NDEs, like archetypes, contain the cross-cultural consistency that the collective unconsciousness bestows, combined with the cross-cultural variation which their location in time and space inevitably creates. Thus we are presented in the NDE with the pattern of consistency and variety that belongs to the essence of archetypes and the images to which they give rise. Indeed, the application of such a developed theory of archetypes even explains, for Grosso, the existence of negative NDEs: for archetypes too are capable of disclosing both a positive and a negative aspect. In this regard, he quotes Jung's comment to Evans-Wentz that 'Just as all archetypes have a positive, favourable, bright side that points upwards, so they also have one that points downwards, partly negative and unfavourable', before adding, himself, that 'The bright, favourable side of the NDE is well-known, but there have also been dark, chthonic encounters, perhaps under-reported' (Bailey and Yates 1996: 138).

Grosso's archetypal theory of NDEs possesses potentially great explanatory power once the initial hurdles of accepting that archetypes exist and that the NDE may be one of them are overcome. At the very least, however, it points to further directions which future research into the NDE may usefully take: extending psychology's participation in future studies beyond the context of neuroscience and hinting at further ways in which the NDE viewed as modern myth might be explored.

A challenge and invitation

With typical candour, Raymond Moody threw out a challenge and invitation at the beginning of *Life After Life* for disbelievers and sceptics to look around for themselves: 'to poke around a bit', before dismissing the evidence for NDEs out of hand (Moody 1975: 6). This challenge prompted many researchers – myself included – to look for evidence that something significant was occurring to many persons at or near the point of death. I should like to issue a similar challenge and invitation at the *end* of this book, but it is extended in particular to those within religions which have yet to participate within the NDE debate and to those operating within academic disciplines who have so far not seen fit to enter the fray. The above suggestions for future research avenues are meant to be suggestive, not prescriptive or exhaustive. Yet much useful insight into the NDE remains to be derived from the participation of theologians and those in other subject areas who have so much to give.

There is, of course, a problem here – sensible academic disciplines have long shown themselves to be wary of entering into contexts where parapsychological claims are at stake and are under investigation, as we have seen. Nonetheless, within the context of the NDE, the fact that so much is at stake may help such academic disciplines to overcome their wariness. The stakes are indeed high, for the NDE continues to offer, for many, the possibility of proving the existence of the human soul, the possibility of that soul's immortality, the possibility of learning what lies beyond the grave, the potential for adjudicating between competing religious truth-claims and last, but by no means least, the need to deal with a growing number of sometimes confused NDErs. It is my heartfelt hope that this study has demonstrated how disciplines such as theology and philosophy can respond to the NDE without sacrificing their hard-won intellectual and academic integrity. It is also offered as a way of breaking up the very real log jam caused by the outbreak of religious hostility within near-death studies. Theologians and students of religious history are keenly aware of the futility of conflict surrounding religion, and the extent to which loss invariably outweighs gain within such struggles. In attempting to build a bridge between religion and the NDE, it is also my keen hope that the current study may offer a way for theological and religious differences among the pioneering NDE researchers to be themselves bridged. Too much remains at stake for the pioneers of near-death studies to remain at loggerheads with each other. The next quarter-century of near-death research may yet bring answers and closure to questions that remain, at present, unanswered and tantalizingly open.

NOTES

INTRODUCTION

1 RERC account 3522.
2 RERC account 3766.
3 Personal communication, 2 December 1999.
4 For more information, see www.alisterhardytrust.org.uk.

1 A BRIEF HISTORY OF NDEs

1 A more detailed account of his background can be found in Immanuel Hunt (2000), *Conversation with Raymond Moody*, http:www.spiritual-endeavours.org/basic/r-m.htm

2 A DEAFENING SILENCE

1 For further details regarding the history and contours of the controversy, see Kendrick Frazier (ed.) *Science Confronts the Paranormal*, New York: Prometheus, 1986.
2 Personal communication, 2 December 1999.
3 A point which the authors acknowledge whilst pointing to the distinction between perceptions claimed by these persons and the special cases of perceptions gained during NDEs.
4 See Gordon Kaufman, *An Essay on Theological Method*, Missoula: Montana, 1975, p. 6.
5 On this, see chapter 3.

3 DEFINING THE LIGHT

1 An assertion that underpins the concept of the numinous as found, famously, in Rudolf Otto, The *Idea of the Holy*, New York: OUP, 1950.
2 Ayer's experience, although vivid, was apparently not enough to convince him that he would survive his death. It included an encounter with two 'ministers' responsible for the inspection of time and space who had 'failed to do their work properly'. As a result, time and space were 'slightly out of joint'. In his NDE, Ayer

attempted to communicate with them by 'walking up and down, waving my watch, in the hope of drawing their attention not to my watch itself but to the time which it measured'. This seems to have failed, however. Ayer ends by remarking that 'I became more and more desperate, until the experience suddenly came to an end.' For more on this, see Ian Wilson, *Life After Death: The Evidence*, London: Sidgwick and Jackson, 1997, pp. 179–81.

3 RERC account 2733.
4 RERC account 2817.
5 For a more detailed discussion of this criticism, see Jess Byron Hollenback, *Mysticism: Experience, Response, and Empowerment*, Pennsylvania: Pennsylvania State University Press, 1996, pp. 12–17.
6 As far as I am aware no such study has ever been attempted.

4 OF PLOTS AND MINDS

1 RERC account 3766.
2 RERC account 3722.
3 RERC account 2817.
4 RERC account 3766.

5 SECOND SIGHT

1 For more on this, see Michael Shermer, *Why People Believe Weird Things*, New York: W.H. Freeman, 1997, pp. 73–87.
2 Kenneth Ring has seen an earlier version of this chapter and has declared it, encouragingly, to be 'the only sustained and thoughtful discussion I've seen in print dealing with the work that I did (with the help of Sharon Cooper) on NDEs in the blind' (personal communication, 12 October 2000). It is to be very much hoped, however, that it will not be the last. See Mark Fox, 'Second Sight? Near-Death Experiences in the Blind', *The Christian Parapsychologist* 14, 2000, pp. 155–67.

6 THE RERC STUDY

1 For a detailed biography of Hardy (from which this account was taken) and a description of the history and activities of the RERC, see David Hay, *Religious Experience Today: Studying the Facts*, London: Mowbray, 1990, pp. 16–27 and Meg Maxwell and Verena Tschudin, *Seeing the Invisible: Modern Religious and Other Transcendent Experiences*, Harmondsworth: Penguin, 1990, pp. 4–10.
2 I am indebted to Diana Hasting for this observation which is based on conversations she had with the ex-director of the RERC, Edward Robinson, when she was his secretary.
3 See, for example, Celia Green and Charles McCreery, *Apparitions*, London: Hamilton, 1989, pp. 8–17.
4 Glenys Howarth and Allan Kellehear, 'Shared Near-Death and Related Illness Experiences', unpublished, La Trobe University, Australia.

7 BUILDING BRIDGES OR FIGHTING WARS?

1 The contention that the NDE may be offering us a 'new myth of death' is advanced but not explored by David Lorimer in *Whole in One: The Near-Death Experience and the Ethic of Interconnectedness*, Harmondsworth: Penguin, 1990, p. 97. See also Michael Grosso, *The Final Choice*, New Hampshire: Stillpoint, 1986.

BIBLIOGRAPHY

Atwater, P. (1994) *Beyond the Light: The Mysteries and Revelations of Near-Death Experiences*, New York: Avon.

Badham, P. (1997) 'Religious and Near-Death Experience in Relation to Belief in a Future Life', *Second Series Occasional Paper 13*, Oxford: Religious Experience Research Centre.

Badham, P. and Badham, L. (1982) *Immortality or Extinction* 2nd edn, London: SPCK.

Bagger, M. (1999) *Religious Experience, Justification, and History*, Cambridge: Cambridge University Press.

Bailey, L. and Yates, J. (eds) (1996) *The Near-Death Experience: A Reader*, London: Routledge.

Barrett, W. (1986) *Deathbed Visions: The Psychical Experiences of the Dying* 2nd edn, Northampton: Aquarian.

Beckford, J. (1978) 'Accounting for Conversion', *British Journal of Sociology*, 29: 249–62.

Beit-Hallahmi, B. and Argyle, M. (1997) *The Psychology of Religious Behaviour, Belief and Experience*, London: Routledge.

Berman, P. (1996) *The Journey Home: What Near-Death Experiences and Mysticism Tell Us About the Gift of Love*, New York: Simon and Schuster.

Blackmore, S. (1982) *Beyond the Body: An Investigation of Out-of-the-Body Experiences*, London: Heinemann.

Blackmore, S. (1993) *Dying to Live: Science and the Near-Death Experience*, London: Grafton.

Bloom, H. (1996) *Omens of Millennium: The Gnosis of Angels, Dreams, and Resurrection*, London: Fourth Estate.

Bulle, F. (1983) *God Wants You Rich and Other Enticing Doctrines*, Minnesota: Bethany House.

Campbell, J. (1972) *Myths To Live By*, New York: Viking.

Carr, D. (1982) 'Pathophysiology of Stress-Induced Limbic Lobe Disfunction: A Hypothesis Relevant to Near-Death Experiences', *Anabiosis*, 2: 75–89.

Carr, D. (1991) 'Discussion: Ricoeur on Narrative' in D. Wood (ed.) *On Paul Ricoeur: Narrative and Interpretation*, London: Routledge.

Corcoran, D. (1996) *When Ego Dies: A Compilation of Near-Death and Mystical Conversion Experiences*, Texas: Emerald Ink.

Cotton, I. (1995) *The Hallelujah Revolution*, London: Warner.

Couliano, I. P. (1991) *Out of this World: Otherworld Journeys from Gilgamesh to Albert Einstein*, London: Shambala.

Cressy, J. (1994) *The Near-Death Experience: Mysticism or Madness*, Massachusetts, The Christopher Publishing House.

Crookall, R. (1961) *The Study and Practice of Astral Projection*, London: Aquarian Press.

Cupitt, D. (1990) *Out of this World*, London: SCM.

Cupitt, D. (1998) *Mysticism After Modernity*, London: SCM.

Damascio, A. (1994) *Descartes' Error: Emotion, Reason and the Human Brain*, New York: Crosset/Putnam.

Davis, C. (1989) *The Evidential Force of Religious Experience*, Oxford: OUP.

Dennett, D. (1991) *Consciousness Explained*, Boston: Little Brown & Co.

Dossey, L. (1989) *Recovering the Soul: A Scientific and Spiritual Search*, New York: Bantam.

Ebon, M. (1977) *The Evidence For Life After Death*, New York: Signet.

Edwards, J. (1986) *A Treatise Concerning the Religious Affections*, Edinburgh: Banner of Truth.

Eliade, M. (1964) *Shamanism: Archaic Techniques of Ecstasy*, London: Routledge.

Ellwood, G. (2000) 'Religious Experience, Religious Worldviews, and Near-Death Studies', *Journal of Near-Death Studies*, 19: 5–22.

Evans-Wentz, W. (ed.) (1957) [1927] *The Tibetan Book of the Dead or the After-Death Experiences on the Bardo Plane, according to Lama Kazi Dawa-Sumdip's English Rendering* 1927, 3rd edn Oxford:OUP.

Fenwick, P. and Fenwick, E. (1995) *The Truth in the Light: An Investigation of Over 300 Near-Death Experiences*, London: Headline.

Forman, R. (ed.) (1990) *The Problem of Pure Consciousness: Mysticism and Philosophy*, Oxford: OUP.

Fox, M. (1996) 'What Should We Do About the New Age? Exploring the Role of Religious Education in the Examination of a Cultural Phenomenon', *British Journal of Religious Education*, 19: 24–32.

Fox, M. (2000a) 'Tales of the Unexpected? Parapsychology, Near-Death Experiences and Christian Belief', *The Christian Parapsychologist*, 14: 9–14.

Fox, M. (2000b) 'Life After "Life After Life": Twenty-Five Years of Near-Death Studies', *Journal of Beliefs and Values*, 21: 135–40.

Fox, M. (2000c) 'Paranormal' in A. Hastings (ed.) (2000) *The Oxford Companion to Modern Christian Thought*, Oxford: OUP.

Fox, O. (1962) *Astral Projection: A Record of Out-of-the-Body Experiences*, New York: Citadel.

Frazier, K. (ed.) (1991) *The Hundredth Monkey and Other Paradigms of the Paranormal*, New York: Prometheus.

Gaarder, J. (1995) *Sophie's World*, London: Phoenix House.

Green, C. (1968) *Out-of-the-Body Experiences*, Oxford: Institute of Psychophysical Research.

Green, C. and McCreery, C. (1989) *Apparitions*, London: Hamilton.

Gregory, R. (1987) *The Oxford Companion to the Mind*, Oxford: OUP.

Gregory, R.L. and Wallace, J.G. (1963) *Recovery From Early Blindness: A Case Study*, Cambridge: CUP.

Grey, M. (1985) *Return from Death: An Exploration of the Near-Death Experience*, London: Arkana.

Grinspoon, L and Bakalar, J. (1979) *Psychedelic Drugs Reconsidered*, New York: Basic Books.

Haldane, J. (1989) 'A Glimpse of Eternity? Near-Death Experiences and the Hope for Future Life', *The Modern Churchman*, 30: 10–16.

Hampe, J. (1979) *To Die is Gain: The Experience of One's Own Death*, London: DLT.

Hardy, B. (1968) 'Towards a Poetics of Fiction: An Approach Through Narrative', quoted in Hauerwas and Jones, op cit.

Hastings, A. (ed.) (2000) *The Oxford Companion to Modern Christian Thought*, Oxford: OUP.

Hauerwas, S. and Jones L. (eds) (1989) *Why Narrative? Readings in Narrative Theology*, Michigan: Eerdmans.

Hay, D. (1990) *Religious Experience Today: Studying the Facts*, London: Mowbray.

Heaney, J. (1984) *The Sacred and the Psychic: Parapsychology and Christian Theology*, New Jersey: Paulist Press.

Hick, J. (1985) *Death and Eternal Life* 2nd edn, London: Macmillan.

Hollenback, J. (1996) *Mysticism: Experience, Response and Empowerment*, Pennsylvania: Pennsylvania State University Press.

Hufford, D. (1982) *The Terror That Comes in the Night: An Experience-Centred Study of Supernatural Assault Traditions*, Pennsylvania: University of Pennsylvania Press.

Jakobsen, M. (1999) *Negative Spiritual Experiences: Encounters with Evil*, Oxford: Religious Experience Research Centre.

James, W. (1960) *The Varieties of Religious Experience*, London: Collins.

Jung, C. (1963) *Memories, Dreams, Reflections*, Glasgow: Collins.

Kaplan, H. and Sadock, B. (eds) (1980) *Comprehensive Textbook of Psychiatry* 4th edn, Baltimore: Williams and Williams.

Kastenbaum, R. (1984) *Is There Life After Death? The Latest Evidence Analysed*, London: Rider.

Katz, S. (ed.) (1978) *Mysticism and Philosophical Analysis*, London: Sheldon.

Kellehear, A. (1996) *Experiences Near Death: Between Medicine and Religion*, Oxford: OUP.

Kellehear, A., Stevenson, I., Pasricha, S. and Cook, E. (1994) 'The Absence of Tunnel Sensation in Near-Death Experiences from India', *Journal of Near-Death Studies*, 13: 109–13.

Kent, R. and Fotherby, V. (1997) *The Final Frontier: Incredible Stories of Near-Death Experiences*, London: HarperCollins.

Kubler-Ross, E. (1991) *On Life After Death*, California: Celestial Arts.

Kung, H. (1984) *Eternal Life?*, London: Collins.

Lindbeck, G. (1984) *The Nature of Doctrine*, London: SPCK.

Loftus, E. and Ketcham, K. (1991) *Witness for the Defence: The Accused, the Eyewitness and the Expert Who Puts Memory on Trial*, New York: St Martins.

Lorimer, D. (1990) *Whole in One: The Near-Death Experience and the Ethic of Interconnectedness*, Penguin: Harmondsworth.

McClenon, J. (1994) *Wondrous Events: Foundations of Religious Belief*, Philadelphia: University of Philadelphia Press.

Maxwell, M. and Tschudin, V. (1990) *Seeing the Invisible: Modern Religious and Other Transcendent Experiences*, Harmondsworth: Penguin.

Monroe, R. (1971) *Journeys out of the Body*, New York: Anchor.

Moody, R. (1975) *Life After Life*, Atlanta: Mockingbird.

Moody, R. (1977) *Reflections on Life After Life*, Atlanta: Mockingbird.

Moody, R. (1999) *The Last Laugh: A New Philosophy of Near-Death Experiences, Apparitions, and the Paranormal*, Charlottesville: Hampton Roads.

Moody, R. and Perry, P. (1988) *The Light Beyond: The Transforming Power of Near-Death Experiences*, London: Macmillan.

Moody, R. and Perry, P. (1990) *Life Before Life: Regression into Past Lives*, London: Macmillan.

Moody, R. and Perry, P. (1993) *Reunions: Visionary Encounters With Departed Loved Ones*, London: Little, Brown & Company.

Morse, M. and Perry, P. (1991) *Closer to the Light: Learning from the Near-Death Experiences of Children*, London: Transworld.

Morse, M. and Perry, P. (1992) *Transformed by the Light: The Powerful Effect of Near-Death Experiences on People's Lives*, London: Piatkus.

Osis, K. and Haraldsson, E. (1997) *At The Hour of Death*, 3rd edn, Norwalk: Hastings House.

Pasricha, S. and Stevenson, I. (1986) 'Near-Death Experiences in India: A Preliminary Report', *Journal of Nervous and Mental Diseases*, 174: 165–70.

Penfield, W. (1955) 'The Role of the Temporal Cortex in Certain Psychical Phenomena', *J. Ment. Sci.*, 101: 45.

Penfield, W. and Perot, P. (1963) 'The Brain's Record of Visual and Auditory Experience: A Final Discussion', *Brain*, 86: 595–696.

BIBLIOGRAPHY

Persinger, M. (1989) 'Modern Neuroscience and Near-Death Experience: Expectancies and Implications. Comments on "A Neurobiological Model for Near-Death Experiences"', *Journal of Near-Death Studies*, 7: 233–9.

Rambo, L. (1993) *Understanding Religious Conversion*, New Haven: Yale University Press.

Rawlings, M. (1978) *Beyond Death's Door*, London: Sheldon.

Ring, K. (1980) *Life at Death: A Scientific Investigation of the Near-Death Experience*, New York: Coward, McCann and Geoghegan.

Ring, K. (1984) *Heading Toward Omega: In Search of the Meaning of the Near-Death Experience*, New York: William Morrow.

Ring, K. (2000) 'Religious Wars in the NDE Movement: Some Personal Reflections on Michael Sabom's *Light & Death*', *Journal of Near-Death Studies*, 18: 215–44.

Ring, K. and Cooper, S. (1997) 'Near-Death and Out-of-Body Experiences in the Blind: A Study of Apparent Eyeless Vision', *Journal of Near-Death Studies*, 16: 101–47.

Ring, K. and Cooper, S. (1999) *Mindsight: Near-Death and Out-of-Body Experiences in the Blind*, California: William James Center for Conscious Studies.

Ring, K. and Valarino, E. (1998) *Lessons from the Light: What We Can Learn from the Near-Death Experience*, Massachusetts, Persius.

Rinpoche, S. (1992) *The Tibetan Book of Living and Dying*, London: Rider.

Ritchie, G. and Sherrill, E. (1978) *Return from Tomorrow*, London: Kingsway.

Rodin, E. (1989) 'Comments on "A Neurobiological Model for Near-Death Experiences"', *Journal of Near-Death Studies*, 7: 255–9.

Rogo, D. (1989) *The Return from Silence: A Study of Near-Death Experiences*, Northampton: Aquarian.

Rose, S. (1980) *The Soul After Death: Contemporary 'After-Death' Experiences in the Light of the Orthodox Teaching on the Afterlife*, California: St Herman of Alaska Brotherhood.

Sabom, M. (1982) *Recollections of Death: A Medical Investigation*, London: Corgi.

Sabom, M. (1998) *Light and Death: One Doctor's Fascinating Account of Near-Death Experiences*, Michigan, Zondervan.

Sabom, M. (2000a) 'Response to Kennth Ring's "Religious Wars in the NDE Movement: Some Personal Reflections on Michael Sabom's *Light & Death*"', *Journal of Near-Death Studies*, 18: 245–72.

Sabom, M. (2000b) 'Response to Gracia Fay Ellwood's "Religious Experience, Religious Worldviews and Near-Death Studies"', *Journal of Near-Death Studies*, 19: 23–44.

Sacks, O. (1985) *The Man Who Mistook His Wife For a Hat*, London: Macmillan.

Sacks, O. (1995) *An Anthropologist on Mars*, New York: Alfred Knopf.

Siegel, R. (1977) 'Hallucinations', *Scientific American*, 237: 132–40.

Siegel, R. (1993) *Fire in the Brain: Clinical Tales of Hallucination*, London: Penguin.

Sutherland, C. (1992) *Reborn in the Light: Life After Near-Death Experiences*, New York: Bantam.

Sutherland, C. (1995) *Children of the Light: The Near-Death Experiences of Children*, New South Wales: Transworld.

Trigg, R. (1988) *Ideas of Human Nature: An Historical Introduction*, Oxford: Blackwell.

Valvo, A. (1971) *Sight Restoration After Long-Term Blindness: The Problems and Behaviour Patterns of Visual Rehabilitation*, New York: American Federation for the Blind.

Walsch, N.D. (1997) *Conversations with God*, London: Hodder.

Wiebe, P. (1997) *Visions of Jesus: Direct Encounters from the New Testament to Today*, Oxford: OUP.

Williams, D. (1956) 'The Structure of Emotions Reflected in Epileptic Experiences', *Brain*, 79: 29–67.

Wilson, C. (1985) *Afterlife*, London: Grafton.

Wilson, I. (1987) *The After Death Experience*, London: Sidgwick and Jackson.

Wilson, I. (1997) *Life After Death: The Evidence*, London: Sidgwick and Jackson.

Wood, D. (ed.) (1991) *On Paul Ricoeur: Narrative and Interpretation*, London: Routledge.

Zaleski, C. (1987) *Otherworld Journeys: Accounts of Near-Death Experiences in Medieval and Modern Times*, Oxford: OUP.

Zaleski, C. (1996) *The Life of the World to Come: Near-Death Experience and Christian Hope*, Oxford: OUP.

Zeig, J. (1987) *The Evolution of Psychotherapy*, New York: Bruher/Mazel.

INDEX